Biographical Memoirs

NATIONAL ACADEMY OF SCIENCES

NATIONAL ACADEMY OF SCIENCES
OF THE UNITED STATES OF AMERICA

Biographical Memoirs

VOLUME XLI

PUBLISHED FOR THE ACADEMY BY

COLUMBIA UNIVERSITY PRESS

NEW YORK AND LONDON 1970

COPYRIGHT © 1970 COLUMBIA UNIVERSITY PRESS

SBN: 231-03319-2

LIBRARY OF CONGRESS CATALOG CARD NUMBER: 5-26629

PRINTED IN THE UNITED STATES OF AMERICA

CONTENTS

Biographical Memoirs

VOLUME XLI

Arnold Cent Ball,

ARNOLD KENT BALLS

April 2, 1891–May 25, 1966

BY W. Z. HASSID

ARNOLD KENT BALLS was born in Toronto, Canada, on April 2, 1891. He was the son of Alfred Z. and Amelia C. (Arnold) Balls. When he was young his family emigrated from Canada, settled in Philadelphia, and became naturalized American citizens. Young Arnold Kent attended the Philadelphia Central High School, where he exhibited a high aptitude for science. He graduated with a gold medal for writing the best scientific essay. He then entered the University of Pennsylvania, from which he obtained his B.S. degree in chemistry in 1912.

After graduation he joined the U.S. Department of Agriculture, where he worked as an assistant chemist in analytical chemistry. Being imaginative and interested in fundamental science, Balls was not satisfied with daily routine work. Thus, he left his position in 1914 and entered Columbia University the following year, where he worked under the guidance of Professor William J. Gies. He presented a doctoral dissertation entitled "The Occurrence of Aluminum, and Its Absorption from Food, in Dogs," and received his Ph.D. degree in 1917. During that period he also served as instructor and was associated with Hans Zinsser, head of the Department of Bacteriology. When Zinsser was away on leave, Balls was left in charge of the bacteriological work in the department.

In 1917 he enlisted in the army as a private, and after two months was promoted to the rank of second lieutenant. From the beginning of his military service he worked in a scientific unit as a bacteriologist. Upon his discharge from the army in 1919, he entered private business as a research and consulting chemist in the yeast industry. In 1921 he obtained a position as associate chemist in the Department of Pharmacology at the University of Pennsylvania, where he remained until 1928.

In 1922 Dr. Balls married Elizabeth Charlotte Franke, a biochemist, who obtained her Ph.D. degree at Columbia University and later collaborated for three years with Professor Stanley Benedict.

Balls's work in the yeast industry and at Columbia University and the University of Pennsylvania brought him in close contact with the subject of enzymology, which at that time was still in the embryonic stage. Enzymes were considered to be fantastically specific catalytic agents that occurred in all living cells and had an important function in metabolic processes. However, none of the numerous investigations led to the knowledge that would enable anyone to classify an enzyme as belonging to a definite group of chemical substances. Endowed with an exceptionally keen native intelligence and intellectual curiosity, Balls became intrigued with the chemical nature of enzymes and the mechanism of their action. This subject became his lifework.

Enzymology had its beginning in Europe in the last century, and was vigorously pursued in the first quarter of this century in a number of laboratories, especially those of Buchner, Willstätter, and Waldschmidt-Leitz. Balls decided to go to Europe and devote himself to the study of this subject. In 1928 he and his family left for Germany, where he first spent a few months in the north learning to speak the German language. He then joined Professor Waldschmidt-Leitz, who had just moved his laboratory from Munich to Prague, Czechoslovakia. This laboratory was considered one of the most active centers of research in enzymology. After several months he went to Professor Pregl's laboratory in Graz for a brief period to learn microchemical methods applicable to his enzyme researches. When he returned to Prague, Balls was already proficient in the German language and soon became a very active collaborator of Waldschmidt-Leitz.

In 1930 he submitted another Ph.D. thesis entitled "Über das Wesen der Enzymwirkung: Mechanismus der Enzymatischen Peptidspalting." This thesis (*Habilitationsschrift*) gave him the title of *Privatdozent* with the privilege of lecturing students interested in enzyme chemistry, which he did very successfully in 1931.

Soon, in collaboration with Professor Waldschmidt-Leitz and other research workers in the laboratory, he published a series of papers dealing with the specificity and mode of action of peptidases on proteins.

While important resemblances between the proteases of animal and plant origin had already been recognized, the corresponding peptide-splitting enzyme systems appeared to be quite different. Balls and collaborators showed that the so-called erepsin (extracts of the animal intestinal tract and many animal tissues) is a mixture of two independently acting enzymes, a polypeptidase and a dipeptidase, and that the two enzymes are absolutely distinct in their behavior toward different substrates. He further found that peptides with more than three amino acids and polypeptide esters are readily hydrolyzed by peptidases, as shown in the accompanying formula (see p. 4).

About the same time he also obtained a specific α-amino acid amidase from the "ereptic enzymes." In addition, he was one of the first investigators to show that peroxidase is an important biological oxidizing agent in living cells.

$$_2HN \cdot CH \cdot CO - | NH \cdot CH \cdot CO - | NH \cdot CH_2 \cdot CO - | NH \cdot CH_2 \cdot CO - | NH \cdot CH \cdot COOH$$

| *a | *b | *c | *d |

C_4H_9 CH_3 CH_2

A OH B

Leucyl-   -alanyl   -glycyl   -glycyl   -tyrosine

This scheme shows the various ways in which a polypeptide may be hydrolyzed by peptidases. Thus leucine *a or tyrosine *d may be split off first, or a hydrolysis into di- and tripeptide may take place (*b and *c).

His researches provided the impetus for much of the intensive research in enzyme mechanisms. He was responsible to a large extent for bridging the gap between the primitive knowledge of enzymology and the modern sophisticated achievements of this most important area of biochemistry.

At the end of 1931 Dr. Balls returned to the United States, where he accepted a position in Washington, D.C., as Head Chemist in charge of the Enzyme Research Laboratory of the Bureau of Agricultural and Industrial Chemistry of the U.S. Department of Agriculture. He was invited to organize this laboratory because of the increasing realization that a fundamental understanding of the chemistry of enzymes and their mode of action was essential to future developments in the food industry. In 1943 Balls's Enzyme Research Laboratory was transferred to the Western Regional Research Laboratory in Albany, California. During his twenty years of service with the U.S. Department of Agriculture he conducted outstanding research for that department in both basic and applied aspects of food enzymes.

Balls and his associates developed methods of purifying and crystallizing enzymes. R. Willstätter found that papain was capable of hydrolyzing a synthetic peptide, but his observation was not generally accepted because it did not agree with the prevailing notions of protease action. This problem was clarified when Balls and Lineweaver succeeded in crystallizing the enzyme from fresh papaya latex. They showed that crystalline papain, like the crude enzyme preparation, was activated by H_2S, HCN, and other reducing agents and inactivated by iodoacetate, H_2O_2, and other oxidants. They also observed that hippurylamide and carboxy-L-isoglutamine were hydrolyzed by this enzyme. At present, papain is among the group of crystalline proteolytic enzymes which are intensively studied with respect to structure, mechanism of action, and the relation of structure to activity.

Chymopapain was later crystallized from papaya latex in collaboration with E. F. Jansen. They found this enzyme to be similar to papain in activation requirements and specificity, but, in contrast to papain, very stable to acid.

Balls's investigations of the effects of diisopropyl fluorophosphate and related compounds on the proteolytic and esterolytic enzymes was a major breakthrough in the identification of active centers. The diisopropyl fluorophosphate was found to undergo a stoichiometric reaction with a single serine at the active site of chymotrypsin, trypsin, and other related enzymes. The pioneering work was followed by intensive studies on "serine enzymes" in laboratories throughout the world. He later added a new major development in the area when he crystallized acetyl chymotrypsin and showed that the acetyl group is transferred to alcohols, indicating that chymotrypsin may act as an important transacetylating agent.

In 1946 Balls, Thompson, and Walden crystallized sweet potato β-amylase. They showed that this crystalline enzyme has a molecular weight of 152,000 and contains arginine, tyrosine, cystine and cysteine, and amide nitrogen (15.1 percent total N). The sulfur occurs mainly as masked SH groups. Three years later, in collaboration with S. Schwimmer, Balls crystal-

lized α-amylase from barley malt. The crystallization of α- and
β-amylase proved to be of value in fundamental studies of the
mechanism of starch degradation.

Throughout his long and productive scientific career, Balls's
prime interest was the understanding of the chemical nature of
enzymes and their mechanisms of action. He very successfully
applied the basic knowledge toward improvement and preservation of food products and other agricultural commodities.
Thus, the knowledge gained from his work on the action of
papain found wide practical application in the tenderizing of
meat. His work on the oxidation-reduction of the proteinases
of flour has provided useful information for the processing of
wheat and to the baking industry in general. The investigations
on the changes occurring in egg white contributed important
knowledge pertaining to the problem of egg preservation. Application of the information obtained from the basic research
of enzyme action by Balls and his coworkers resulted in more
than twenty industrial patents in the area of food technology.

In 1951 the U.S. Department of Agriculture adopted a policy that the research of the four regional laboratories should be
entirely devoted to work on agricultural products of the particular region in which the laboratory was located. Although
the many patents pertaining to agricultural food products were
a direct consequence of Dr. Balls's fundamental enzymological
researches, there was strong objection to the basic work with
which his laboratory was primarily concerned. As a result, Balls
resigned from the U.S. Department of Agriculture and accepted a position as Professor of Biochemistry at Purdue University in Lafayette, Indiana. There he taught biochemistry
and conducted research until his retirement in 1961, when he
became Professor Emeritus. He and his family then returned
to Berkeley.

The head of the Western Regional Laboratory provided

him with a laboratory and an office, where, with the support of a grant from the U.S. Public Health Service and the help of an assistant, Balls continued his researches. During this time, he was invited to return to Purdue University on a part-time basis to direct research of graduate students and to complete some unfinished projects. For three or four summers he returned to the Purdue campus for several months. In spite of his advanced age he spent several hours every day at the laboratory bench. After suffering a hemorrhage in one eye, Dr. Balls was unable to drive his car. Mrs. Balls then chauffeured him to and from the laboratory where he continued to work. His brain was fertile with ideas and unimpaired until the very end. During the last three years of his life he published eight papers on the mechanism of enzyme action of trypsin and chymotrypsin.

Dr. Balls belonged to a number of scientific societies. He was a member of the American Society of Biological Chemists (of which he was Secretary, 1941-1946, and Councilor-at-Large, 1946-1949); the American Chemical Society; the Society for Experimental Biology and Medicine; and the Institute of Food Technologists. He also served on the editorial board of the *Journal of Biological Chemistry* and the editorial committee of the *Annual Review of Biochemistry* (1950-1955).

Dr. Balls's contributions to biochemistry were widely recognized, as evidenced by the many awards he received. He was the recipient of the Superior Service Award in 1949 and the Distinguished Service Awared in 1953, both presented by the U.S. Department of Agriculture. In 1959 he was given the McCollum Award for outstanding biochemical research beyond the age of sixty. In 1962 he received the Nicolas Alpert Award for preeminence in and contributions to the field of food technology, and in the same year the Spencer Award for distinguished achievements in agricultural and food chemistry.

He was elected a member of the National Academy of Sciences in 1954. He was also a recipient of the Patriotic Service Award from the U.S. Army. Balls was among the first scientific investigators who followed American troops into occupied Germany during World War II to find out about the scientific activities which were going on in that country.

Balls was a man devoid of any prejudices. He valued people for their human and intellectual qualities, regardless of color, race, or religion. He and Mrs. Balls were exceedingly hospitable and generous people. They lavishly entertained guests in their spacious home for days or weeks. Often when a guest from Japan, China, or any other country arrived, they drove to the airport to meet him and brought him to their home where he would stay until the end of his visit.

To those who knew him, Balls was more than a prominent scientist. He was one of those rare personalities whose kindness and affection for his fellow men dominated his whole nature. His abiding faith in goodness and his cheerful outlook toward life were no doubt the qualities responsible for gaining him the affection of a large circle of friends. Dr. Balls was a man with a subtle sense of humor. He was adaptable and felt equally at ease with people of any stratum of society, regardless of whether the person was a waiter, truckdriver, or European nobleman.

True to his New England tradition, he believed in the unhurried, self-sufficient scholarship respected for its own sake, as contrasted with the constant pressure for rapid results and external recognition so prevalent in modern academic life. His scientific papers are models of conciseness and clarity. They show a flash of human feeling, excitement, a trace of self-effacement, and even a touch of humor.

With his tremendous capacity for work went a huge enjoyment of life. He loved good food, good wine, good company, and displayed a gay, exuberant character with his many friends. He was an enthusiastic fisherman. Frequently when he was living in Berkeley, he and his colleagues would spend the entire day salmon fishing on the San Francisco bay.

He was a person of winning charm and manners, and possessed tact with all societies. Beneath his amiable surface lay an inexhaustible energy. He had an intellectual curiosity which constantly drove him into many avenues of human learning. Although his specialty was enzymology, he was interested and well informed in history, comparative religion, literature, mythology, and political science.

He was a classicist, with a knowledge of Latin and Greek, and had a deep interest in history, especially ancient history, and the Greek philosophers. His knowledge in the fields of history and philosophy surprised even experts. He assiduously read Arnold Toynbee's ten volumes of the *Study of History* and *An Historian's Approach to Religion,* and liked to indulge in discussions of current events, interpreting them in the light of the past. He was not averse to setting his mind against that of others; and he was a skillful conversationalist, quick, logical, and incisive. But he had humor and kindliness. Very few people knew that he liked to read and write poetry.

In the memorial resolution for Professor Balls adopted by the Faculty of the School of Agriculture at Purdue University on November 2, 1966, the following quotations aptly characterize his personality:

"He was an aristocrat among men and he knew it. He played the true gentleman on the outside, but he truly lived the role on the inside. His concept of noblesse oblige imposed standards of behavior on him that most men would be taxed to meet. He was kind and considerate to everyone. He could neither be rude nor show indignation even to those who richly deserved it."

"All who knew Kent Balls well loved him, often with a

touch of awe, but with a deep and lasting sincerity. He was a fortunate man because he knew how his friends felt about him. His friends were fortunate because he knew and reciprocated their feelings with warmth."

His memory is treasured in the hearts of many friends.

He is survived by his widow, Elizabeth, and their only son, Dr. Kent F. Balls, a physician in Pennsylvania.

BIBLIOGRAPHY

KEY TO ABBREVIATIONS

Ann. Rev. Biochem. = Annual Review of Biochemistry
Ber. = Berichte der deutschen chemischen Gesellschaft
Cereal Chem. = Cereal Chemistry
Fed. Proc. = Federation Proceedings
Food Res. = Food Research
Food Technol. = Food Technology
Fruit Prod. J. = Fruit Products Journal
Ind. Eng. Chem. = Industrial and Engineering Chemistry
J. Am. Chem. Soc. = Journal of the American Chemical Society
J. Assoc. Offic. Agr. Chemists = Journal of the Association of Official
    Agricultural Chemists
J. Biol. Chem. = Journal of Biological Chemistry
J. Wash. Acad. Sci. = Journal of the Washington Academy of Sciences
Naturwiss. = Die Naturwissenschaften
Proc. Nat. Acad. Sci. = Proceedings of the National Academy of
    Sciences
Z. physiol. Chem.= Hoppe Seyler's Zeitschrift für physiologie Chemie

1915

With C. C. McDonnell. Electrolytic separation of zinc, copper, and
    iron from arsenic. Ind. Eng. Chem., 7:26-29.
A direct test of the degree of accuracy of the Schmidt-Hoagland
    method for the quantitative determination of aluminum. Ind.
    Eng. Chem., 7:195-202.

1918

With J. W. Korns. The mode of action *in vitro* of the preparation
    of hemolytic antibodies. Journal of Immunology, 3:575.
With J. D. Moral. The action of certain antiseptics, toxic salts,
    and alkaloids on the bacteria and protozoa of the intestines of the
    rabbit. Journal of Infectious Diseases, 23:382-91.

1922

With A. E. Hill. A sulfonated napthylarsenic acid. J. Am. Chem.
    Soc., 44:2051-54.

1925

With J. B. Brown. Studies in yeast metabolism. I. J. Biol. Chem.,
    62:789-821.

With J. B. Brown. Studies in yeast metabolism. II. Carbon dioxide and alcohol. J. Biol. Chem., 62:823-56.

1927

Pseudomorphine. J. Biol. Chem., 71:537-42.
The separation and estimation of morphine, pseudomorphine and related substances. J. Biol. Chem., 71:543.

1928

With W. A. Wolff. The determination of morphine. J. Biol. Chem., 80:379-402.
With W. A. Wolff. The optical activity of pseudomorphine. J. Biol. Chem., 80:403-11.

1929

With E. Waldschmidt-Leitz. Concerning animal dipeptidases. American Journal of Physiology, 90:272.
With J. Waldschmidt-Groser. Über Dipeptidase und Polypeptidasen aus Darm-Schleimhaut. Ber., 62:956-62.

1930

With E. Waldschmidt-Leitz. Zur Kenntnis der Amino-Polypeptidase aus Darm-Schleimhaut. Ber., 63:1203-11.
With E. Waldschmidt-Leitz and A. Purr. Über den naturlischen Aktivator der Katheptichen Enzyme. Naturwiss., 18:644.

1931

With E. Waldschmidt-Leitz. Zur Frage nach den Ursacher Sterischer Auslese durch Enzyme. Ber., 64:45-48.
With F. Köhler. Über den Mechanismus der enzymatischen Dipeptid-Spaltung. Ber., 64:34-45.
With F. Köhler. Über die Wirkungsweise der Peptidasen. Ber., 64:294-301.
With F. Köhler. Über eine neue proteolytische Wirkung von Darmschleimhaut-Auszugen. Ber., 64:383-87.
With F. Köhler. Über Aktivitat und Phosphorgehalt von Aminopolypeptidase. Naturwiss., 19:737.

1932

With F. Köhler. Über Aminopolypeptidase. Z. physiol. Chem., 205:157-70.

The quantitative determination of enzyme action. J. Assoc. Offic. Agr. Chemists, 15:131-36.

With W. S. Hale. The activator of catalase. J. Am. Chem. Soc., 54:2133-34.

With W. S. Hale. The estimation of catalase in agricultural products. J. Assoc. Offic. Agr. Chemists, 15:483-90.

1933

With F. Köhler. Aminopolypeptidase. II. Z. physiol. Chem., 219:128-37.

With W. S. Hale. A note on the determination of hydrogen peroxide. J. Assoc. Offic. Agr. Chemists, 16:395-97.

With W. S. Hale. The determination of peroxidase in agricultural products. J. Assoc. Offic. Agr. Chemists, 16:445-53.

Report on enzymes. J. Assoc. Offic. Agr. Chemists, 16:479-80.

1934

With T. L. Swenson. Proteolysis in stored eggs. Ind. Eng. Chem., 26:570-72.

With T. L. Swenson. Formation of thin white. United States Egg and Poultry Magazine, 40:20.

With T. L. Swenson. The anti-trypsin of egg-white. J. Biol. Chem., 106:409-19.

The importance of enzyme analysis in agricultural chemistry. J. Assoc. Offic. Agr. Chem., 17:531-34.

With W. S. Hale. On peroxidase. J. Biol. Chem., 107:767-82.

With W. S. Hale. Darkening of apples. Proceedings of the 9th International Congress on Pure and Applied Chemistry, p. 126.

1935

With W. S. Hale. Proteolysis in flours. J. Assoc. Offic. Agr. Chemists, 18:135-40.

With T. L. Swenson and L. S. Stuart. Assay of papain. J. Assoc. Offic. Agr. Chemists, 18:140-46.

With W. S. Hale. Peroxidase in the darkening of apples. Ind. Eng. Chem., 27:335-37.

With W. S. Hale.   Fruit darkening can be prevented by a new process.   Yearbook of U.S. Department of Agriculture, 1935, pp. 217-18.

1936

With W. S. Hale.   Proteolytic enzymes of flour.   Cereal Chem., 13: 54-60.

With W. S. Hale.   Report on enzymes.   J. Assoc. Offic. Agr. Chemists, 19:372-73.

With T. L. Swenson.   Dried egg white.   Food Res., 1:319-24.

With W. S. Hale.   Further studies on the activity of proteinase in flour.   Cereal Chem., 13:656-64.

1937

With H. Lineweaver and R. R. Thompson.   Crystalline papain. Science, 86:379.

With S. R. Hoover.   The milk-clotting action of papain.   J. Biol. Chem., 121:737-45.

With M. B. Matlack and I. W. Tucker.   The hydrolysis of glycerides by crude pancrease lipase.   J. Biol. Chem., 122:125-37.

1938

With H. Lineweaver.   Action of enzymes at low temperatures. Food Res., 3:57-67.

With L. Martin and H. H. McKinney.   The protein content of mosaic tobacco.   Science, 87:329-30.

With I. W. Tucker.   Activity of lipase at low temperatures.   Ind. Eng. Chem., 30:415-16.

With M. B. Matlack.   Mode of action of pancreatic lipase.   J. Biol. Chem., 123:679-86.

With W. S. Hale.   The preparation and properties of wheat proteinase.   Cereal Chem., 15:622-28.

With L. F. Martin.   Amylase activity of mosaic tobacco.   Enzymologia, 5:233-38.

Some modern aspects of enzyme catalysis.   J. Wash. Acad. Sci., 28: 425-33.

Enzyme action in food products and at low temperatures.   Ice and Cold Storage, 41:143. (Excerpt)

With M. B. Matlack. The enzymic hydrolysis of benzyl stearate and benzyl butyrate. J. Biol. Chem., 125:539-43.

Recent observations on the enzymic hydrolysis of fats and other esters. Journal of Bacteriology, 36:12-13. (Excerpt)

1939

With H. Lineweaver. Nature of a group in papain essential to its activity. Nature, 144:513.

With H. Lineweaver. Isolation and properties of crystalline papain. J. Biol. Chem., 130:669-86.

With L. F. Martin and H. H. McKinney. Protein changes in mosaic-diseased tobacco. J. Biol. Chem., 130:687-701.

Enzymes in foods and food preservation. *Food and Life,* Yearbook of U.S. Department of Agriculture, 1939, pp. 350-54.

1940

With E. F. Jansen and B. Axelrod. A chemical study of the virus of infectious myxomatosis. Enzymologia, 8:267-72.

Proteolytic enzymes. Ann. Rev. Biochem., 9:43-64.

With W. S. Hale. A sulphur-bearing constituent of the petroleum ether extract of wheat flour. Cereal Chem., 17:243-45.

With S. R. Hoover. The behavior of ovomucin in the liquefaction of egg white. Ind. Eng. Chem., 32:594-96.

With W. S. Hale. The effect of ethylene on freshly harvested wheat. Cereal Chem., 17:490-94.

With R. R. Thompson and W. W. Jones. Crude papain. Ind. Eng. Chem., 32:1144-47.

With H. Lineweaver and S. Schwimmer. Drying of papaya latex-stability of papain. Ind. Eng. Chem., 32:1277-79.

With Francisca Arana. Recent observations on the curing of vanilla bean in Pureto Rico. Proceedings of the 8th American Scientific Congress, 7:187-91.

1941

With F. E. Arana. The curing of vanilla. Ind. Eng. Chem., 33:1073-75; Revista de Agricultura, Industria y Comercio, 34(20):167-72.

With R. R. Thompson and M. W. Kies. Bromelin: properties and commercial production. Ind. Eng. Chem., 33:950-53.

With E. F. Jansen.   Chymopapain: a new crystalline proteinase from papaya latex. J. Biol. Chem., 137:459-60.
With F. E. Arana.   The determination and significance of phenols in vanilla extract. J. Assoc. Offic. Agr. Chemists, 24:507-12.
With G. Y. Gottschall and M. W. Kies.   Autolysis in meat.   Proceedings of the American Society of Biological Chemists, p. ix.
With M. W. Kies.   The effect of freezing on the autolysis of meat. Proceedings of the American Institute of Refrigeration, pp. 106-11.
Protein-digesting enzymes of papaya and pineapple.   United States Department of Agriculture, Circular No. 631, 9 pp.

1942

Liebig and the chemistry of enzymes and fermentation.   In: *Liebig and After Liebig: A Century of Progress in Agricultural Chemistry*, pp. 30–39. Washington, D.C., American Association for the Advancement of Science.
With W. S. Hale and T. H. Harris.   A crystalline protein obtained from a lipoprotein of wheat flour.   Cereal Chem., 19:279-88.
With B. Axelrod and M. W. Kies.   Inhibition of carotene.   Fed. Proc., 1:99. (A)
A crystalline sulphur-protein from wheat.   J. Wash. Acad. Sci., 32: 132-37.
With W. S. Hale and T. H. Harris.   Further observations on a crystalline wheat protein.   Cereal Chem., 19:840-44.
The fate of enzymes in processed foods.   Fruit Prod. J., 22:36-39.

1943

With B. Axelrod and M. W. Kies.   Soy bean lipoxidase.   J. Biol. Chem., 149:491-504.
Control of enzymatic action in foods.   Proceedings of the Institute of Food Technologists, pp. 165-69.
With I. W. Tucker.   The extraction of diastase and recovery of protein from wheat.   Fruit Prod. J., 23:15-16, 21.
Desmo enzymes.   Vortex, 4:10.
With W. S. Hale, W. G. Rose, I. W. Tucker, B. Axelrod, S. Schwimmer, J. J. Peruzzi, and M. K. Walden.   Separation of diastase and protein from wheat through the action of sulphites.

United States Department of Agriculture, Western Regional Research Laboratory, AIC-27, 37 pp.

1944

With T. H. Harris. Inhibitory effect of a protamine from wheat flour on the fermentation of wheat mashes. Cereal Chem., 21: 74-79.

With M. W. Kies. Concerning the mode of action of lipoxidase. J. Biol. Chem., 153:337.

With S. Schwimmer. Digestion of raw starch. J. Biol. Chem., 156: 203-10.

1946

With M. W. Kies. Proteases. In: *Enzymes and Their Role in Wheat Technology*, Vol. 1, ed. by J. A. Anderson, pp. 231-73. New York, Interscience Publishers, Inc.

With B. Axelrod and M. W. Kies. Activator for soy bean lipoxidase. Fed. Proc., 5:120. (A)

With R. R. Thompson and M. K. Walden. A crystalline protein with beta-amylase activity, prepared from sweet potatoes. J. Biol. Chem., 163:571-72.

1947

Enzyme actions and food quality. Food Technol., 1:245-51.

With E. F. Jansen and M. -D. F. Nutting. Apparent specific inhibition of plant acetylesterase by diisopropyl fluorophosphate. J. Biol. Chem., 170:417-18.

Obituary—Charles Albert Browne. J. Assoc. Offic. Agr. Chemists, 30(3):vi.

1948

What a foreman should know about enzyme action. Food Industries, 20:169.

With M. K. Walden and R. R. Thompson. A crystalline beta-amylase from sweet potatoes. J. Biol. Chem., 173:9-19.

With E. F. Jansen and M. -D. F. Nutting. Reversible inhibition of acetylesterase by diisopropyl fluorophosphate and tetraethyl pyrophosphate. J. Biol. Chem., 175:975-87.

With S. Schwimmer. Crystalline alpha-amylase from barley malt. J. Biol. Chem., 176:465-66.

1949

Enzyme problems in the citrus industry. Food Technol., 3:96-100.

With E. F. Jansen, M. -D. F. Nutting, and R. Jang. Inhibition of the proteinase and esterase activities of trypsin and chymotrypsin by diisopropyl fluorophosphate: crystallization of inhibited chymotrypsin. J. Biol. Chem., 179:189-99.

With E. F. Jansen and M. -D. F. Nutting. Mode of inhibition of chymotrypsin by diisopropyl fluorophosphate. I. Introduction of phosphorus. J. Biol. Chem., 179:201-4.

With E. F. Jansen, M. -D. F. Nutting, and R. Jang. Mode of inhibition of chymotrypsin by DFP. II. Elimination of fluorine and introduction of isopropyl. Fed. Proc., 8:210. (A)

With S. Schwimmer. Isolation and properties of crystalline alpha-amylase from germinated barley. J. Biol. Chem., 179:1063-74.

With S. Schwimmer. Starches and their derivatives as adsorbents for malt alpha-amylase. J. Biol. Chem., 180:883-94.

1950

With E. F. Jansen, M. -D. F. Nutting, and R. Jang. Mode of inhibition of chymotrypsin by DFP. II. Introduction of isopropyl and elimination of fluorine as hydrogen fluoride. J. Biol. Chem., 185:209-20.

With E. F. Jansen, M. -D. F. Nutting, and A. L. Curl. A crystalline, active oxidation product of α-chymotrypsin. Fed. Proc., 9: 186.

Enzymes and enzymology. In: Encyclopedia of Chemical Technology, Vol. 5, ed. by P. E. Kirk and D. F. Othmer, pp. 731-61. New York, Interscience Publishers, Inc.

With E. F. Jansen. The use and control of enzymes in food and feed products. Crops in Peace and War, Yearbook of U.S. Department of Agriculture, 1950-1951, pp. 76-81.

1951

With E. F. Jansen and A. L. Curl. A crystalline, active oxidation product of α-chymotrypsin. J. Biol. Chem., 189:671-82.

With E. F. Jansen and A. L. Curl. The reaction of α-chymotrypsin with analogues of diisopropyl fluorophosphate (DF). J. Biol. Chem., 190:557-61.

With S. Schwimmer. Probable maximum specific activity of macerans amylase. Fed. Proc., 10:245. (A)

1952

With E. F. Jansen. Proteolytic enzymes. Ann. Rev. Biochem., 21:1.

With E. F. Jansen. Stoichiometric inhibition of chymotrypsin. Advances in Enzymology, 13:321.

With E. F. Jansen and R. Jang. The inhibition of purified, human plasma cholinesterase with diisopropyl fluorophosphate. J. Biol. Chem., 196:247-53.

1955

With H. N. Wood. Enzymatic oxidation of α-chymotrypsin. J. Biol. Chem., 213:297-304.

With W. Cohen. The fate of antitrypsin in egg white during storage and incubation. Poultry Science, 34:296.

With F. L. Aldrich. Acetyl-chymotrypsin. Proc. Nat. Acad. Sci., 41:190-96.

1956

With H. L. Tookey. Plant phospholipase D. I. Studies on cottonseed and cabbage phospholipase D. J. Biol. Chem., 218:213-24.

With H. N. Wood. Acetyl-chymotrypsin and its reaction with ethanol. J. Biol. Chem., 219:245-56.

With H. L. Tookey. Plant phospholipase D. II. Inhibition of succinic oxidase by cottonseed phospholipase D. J. Biol. Chem., 220:15-23.

With C. E. McDonald. Transesterification reactions catalyzed by chymotrypsin. J. Biol. Chem., 221:993-1003.

1957

With C. E. McDonald. Analogues of acetyl-chymotrypsin. J. Biol. Chem., 227:727-36.

With A. S. Brecher. The catalysis of the non-chymotryptic hydrolysis of p-nitrophenyl acetate. J. Biol. Chem., 227:845-51.

With C. E. McDonald. On the esterolytic activities of papain and trypsin. J. Biol. Chem., 229:69-76.

1958

With C. E. McDonald and A. S. Brecher. Crystallization and some properties of trimethylacetyl chymotrypsin. Proceedings of the International Symposium on Enzyme Chemistry, Tokyo and Kyoto, 2:392-95.

With E. F. Jansen and R. Jang. Citrus aminopeptidase. Archives of Biochemistry and Biophysics, 76:461.

With F. L. Aldrich, Jr. The reversibility of inactivation of chymotrypsin. J. Biol. Chem., 233:1355-58.

1959

Enzymes affecting proteins. In: *Food Enzymes,* ed. by H. W. Schultz, pp. 85-96. Westport, Connecticut, The Avi Publishing Co., Inc.

1960

With A. S. Brecher. Precipitation of denatured chymotrypsin by sulfate and pyrophosphate. J. Biol. Chem., 235:2004-9.

Catheptic enzymes in muscle. Proceedings of the 12th Research Conference of the American Meat Institute Foundation, 1960, pp. 73-80.

1962

Early experiments in the quest of an active center in chymotrypsin. Journal of General Physiology, 45:47.

With C. A. Ryan. An inhibitor of chymotrypsin from *Solanum tuberosum.* Proc. Nat. Acad. Sci., 48:1839-44.

Catalysis and food technologists. Food Technol., 16:17.

With C. A. Ryan. Inhibitor of chymotrypsin isolated from potatoes. Science, 138:938-84. (A)

1963

With C. A. Ryan. The chymotryptic inhibitor of potatoes: A multisite inhibitor. Fed. Proc., 22:245.

With C. A. Ryan. Activities of directly and indirectly acetylated chymotrypsin. Proc. Nat. Acad. Sci., 50:448-53.

With C. A. Ryan. Concerning a crystalline chymotryptic inhibitor from potatoes and its binding capacity for the enzyme. J. Biol. Chem., 238:2976-82.

1964

With C. A. Ryan. Tryptic activation of acetylated chymotrypsinogen. Proc. Nat. Acad. Sci., 51:151-55.

With F. deEds and C. A. Ryan. Pharmacological observations on a chymotryptic inhibitor from potatoes. Proceedings of the Society for Experimental Biology and Medicine, 115:772-75.

1965

Concerning trypsinogen. Proc. Nat. Acad. Sci., 53:392-96.

U.S. PATENTS

(with co-inventors)

1,634,348—July 5, 1927. Preserving cane juice and preparing it for use in yeast production.

1,642,192—September 13, 1927. Propagating *Saccharomyces disjunctus* in a mash of crude West Indian cane molasses.

1,642,320—September 13, 1927. Food product from yeast.

1,643,947—September 20, 1927. Drying yeast in mixture with purified cellulose.

1,759,536—May 20, 1930. Yeast.

2,001,465—August 13, 1935. Process for inhibiting the discoloration of fruit and vegetables.

2,054,213—September 15, 1936. Process for the alteration of egg white.

2,062,387—December 1, 1936. Process for the alteration of egg white.

2,073,411—March 9, 1937. Process of producing thin egg white.

2,103,443—December 28, 1937. Method for the softening of dough.

2,274,120—February 24, 1942. Process for curing vanilla beans.

2,313,504—March 9, 1943. Sulphydryl compound.

2,313,875—March 16, 1944. Proteolytic enzyme process.

2,366,952—January 19, 1945. Proteinous material.

2,381,421—August 7, 1945. Method of treating cereal grains.

2,434,874—January 20, 1948. Separation of starch and protein in wheat grain products and extraction of disastase therefrom.

2,457,754—December 28, 1948. Process of extracting diastase.

2,496,261—February 7, 1950. Preparation of beta-amylase from sweet potatoes.

2,594,356—April 29, 1952. Isolation of alpha-amylase from malt extract.

2,676,906—April 27, 1954. Lipase concentrate.

2,680,090—June 1, 1954. Partial glycerides.

P. W. Bridgman

PERCY WILLIAMS BRIDGMAN

April 21, 1882–August 20, 1961

BY EDWIN C. KEMBLE AND FRANCIS BIRCH

PERCY WILLIAMS BRIDGMAN was a brilliant, intense, and dedicated scientist. His professional career involved him in three distinct, but closely related, kinds of activity. His early invention of a self-sealing and leak-proof packing opened up a virgin field for experimental exploration in the physics of very high pressures. In work of this kind he had no real competitor, but remained preeminent throughout a lifetime of vigorous and fruitful investigation. His second continuing interest grew out of the first. It did not take him long to discover in the technique of dimensional analysis an essential theoretical device needed in the planning of his experimental program. His success in eliminating what he regarded as metaphysical obscurities in that theory was the lure which eventually launched him on a career of philosophical analysis. In a period of perplexity and paradox in the field of physics, the basic lucidity of his operational point of view was of great value to students and fellow scientists all over the world. The third channel of his activity was that of classroom teaching. His classes were small, but for the young physicists who attended them they were an unforgettable experience. The penetration and tough-minded integrity of his thought, and his never-ceasing habit of probing the limits of scientific knowledge gave his students a heightened sense of the meaning of scientific understanding.

Bridgman's outstanding personal characteristics were the simplicity, directness, and rugged independence of his thinking and the single-minded tenacity with which he directed his life toward its central purposes. He refused to permit either self-indulgence, the demands of society, or the call of a faculty committee to divert his energy from his objectives as an experimenter, teacher, and apostle of clear-headed thinking.

Over Bridgman, the individualist, the scientific fashions of the day had but little influence. In a period when scientific thinking was dominated by the novel and paradoxical conceptions of relativity and the quantum, his laboratory was a place for the study of the mechanical and electrical properties of matter under the highest pressures his ingenuity could realize. He was a pioneer, but his field of exploration was one to which the new ideas had as yet little immediate application. To be sure, he welcomed the new conceptions which set the stage for his philosophical analysis, but he never joined the army of physicists who devoted themselves to the interpretation and exploitation of the quantum.

In his time a revolution in the relation of science to society produced a mushroom growth of large-scale scientific projects carried forward by teams of scientists and financed by government or industry. Bridgman, however, had no interest in the building of scientific empires. Throughout each academic year he worked steadily in his private laboratory and machine shop, taking little time off except for classes. In the summer he sought refuge with his family in the White Mountains. There, in an isolated study among the trees, were written both the papers reporting his experimental results and the essays on scientific logic and social criticism that made him famous. He preferred to work alone; his papers and books described his own experiments and recorded his own thoughts. Rarely did any of his papers bear the name of a collaborating author.

Percy Williams Bridgman was born in Cambridge, Massachusetts, on April 21, 1882. Both parents came of old New England stock. His father, Raymond Landon Bridgman, an author as well as a newspaperman assigned to statehouse affairs, was a profoundly religious and idealistic man—one of the first to advocate a world state. His mother, Mary Ann Maria Williams, was of "a more conventional, sprightly, and competitive" turn of mind.

While Percy was still a small child, the family removed to Auburndale in the town of Newton, a community with an exceptionally fine public school system in which the boy received his elementary and high school education.

In his school years Bridgman was a shy, proud youngster who loved to excel and was a keen competitor on the playground, in the classroom, and over the chess board. At home there were household and garden chores as well as card games and family music. Religion meant a great deal to the family; the Bible was read every morning, and attendence at the Congregational Church was taken as a matter of course. Though it was a matter of deep sorrow to his father that Percy did not feel that he could join the church, later Mr. Bridgman also expressed pride that his son had followed his conscience.

Entering Harvard College in 1900, Peter, as he came later to be known, chose a program of study strongly concentrated in mathematics, physics, and chemistry. The normal requirement for graduation at that time was the completion of a program of seventeen "full courses,"[1] but Bridgman managed to squeeze twenty-three such courses into his four years of undergraduate study. He was awarded an A.B. *summa cum laude* in 1904.

His entire academic and scientific career reflected an unflagging devotion to science formed early in life. He never left

[1] Harvard never did adopt the semester-hour unit of credit used in most American colleges.

Harvard, but stayed on in the Department of Physics, first as a graduate student (A.M. 1905, Ph.D. 1908) and then as a staff member. He was appointed Research Fellow in 1908, and thereafter Instructor in 1910, Assistant Professor in 1913, Professor in 1919, Hollis Professor of Mathematics and Natural Philosophy in 1926, and finally Higgins University Professor in 1950. His retirement and appointment as Professor Emeritus came in 1954 at the age of seventy-two, after forty-six years of university service.

In 1912 he was married to Olive Ware, of Hartford, Connecticut, daughter of Edmund Asa Ware, founder and first president of Atlanta University. Her gifts of mind and personality complemented his and made their home a harmonious one for a half century of married life together. Except for a brief period during World War I the Bridgmans resided in Cambridge with their two children, Jane and Robert. The family took full advantage of the opportunities for mountain climbing from their summer home at Randolph, New Hampshire. On these expeditions Peter frequently led the way at a pace that taxed the capacity of his companions and earned him a reputation in the local mountaineering circle.

When his daughter was married to the mathematician Bernard Osgood Keepman, in 1948, Bridgman composed the marriage service and secured the necessary authorization to perform the ceremony himself as a temporary justice of the peace.

Bridgman's basic talent as a penetrating analytical thinker was combined with a fertile mechanical imagination and exceptional manipulative dexterity in the ordinary mechanical arts. He took much pride in the opulence of the flower and vegetable gardens that provided his chief avocation during the summer. A skillful amateur carpenter and plumber, he scorned to call in professional assistance to solve household mechanical problems since he could take care of them more neatly himself. He was fond of music and made constant use of his piano as a means of relaxation.

Bridgman's early papers give no explanation of his interest in high pressures. Possibly he was influenced by Professor Theodore Richards of the Chemistry Department, who had measured the compressibility of elements to pressures of about 500 atmospheres; he may have been influenced by Professor Wallace Sabine, with whom he took a research course in "Heat and Light" for four years. Bridgman at first intended to investigate the effect of pressure upon the indices of refraction of liquids, but he was diverted from this plan by his success in developing new high-pressure techniques and never returned to the original problem. In his brief "Autobiographical remarks" filed with the National Academy of Sciences, under the heading "Discoveries which you regard as most important," Bridgman wrote: "Doubtless the most influential single discovery was that of a method of producing high hydrostatic pressure without leak. The discovery of the method had a strong element of accident."

His first three papers, published in successive issues of Volume 44 of the *Proceedings of the American Academy of Arts and Sciences* (1908-1909), laid the foundation for years of later work. The maximum pressure attained, 6500 kg/cm^2, was not much higher than was currently used by other investigators, and was produced inefficiently with a screw compressor turned with a six-foot wrench. Bridgman's first concern appears to have been the establishment of an adequate pressure scale rather than the production of drastically higher pressures. He developed the free piston gauge, or pressure balance, used by Amagat and introduced a more convenient secondary gauge based on the effect of pressure upon the electrical resistance of mercury. The new design of pressure seal, the key to so much subsequent achievement, appears in the discussion of the free piston gauge, with scarcely a suggestion of its importance; indeed he later explained that the self-sealing feature of his first high-pressure packing was incidental to the design of a closure for the pressure vessel so that it could be rapidly assembled or taken apart. The basic advantages of the scheme were realized only afterwards. In the third paper are given new measurements of the compressibility of steel, mercury, and glass, quantities required for various corrections. We recognize already the characteristic Bridgman style: the evident pleasure in the manipulations of shop and laboratory; the meticulous pursuit of the numerous corrections; the experiments with homely mixtures of mercury, molasses, glycerine, and marine glue. None of these early measurements proved definitive; the absolute gauge was soon improved, the mercury gauge was discarded in favor of a manganin wire gauge, the compressibilities were revised. But his rapid succession of publications quickly transformed the field of high-pressure research.

By 1910, a complete redesign of equipment had taken place. The screw compressor was replaced by a hydraulic ram and the new packing was systematically exploited. For the first time, pressures of the order of 20,000 kg/cm² and more are reported. Bridgman remarked: "The magnitude of the fluid pressure mentioned here requires brief comment, because without a word of explanation it may seem so large as to cast discredit on the accuracy of all the data." The techniques to be used for the next twenty years had been substantially perfected; they were described more fully in 1914 in a paper on "The Technique of High-Pressure Experimenting."

The essence of Bridgman's leak-proof packing is more easily shown by diagram than explained in words, and is now familiar to all high-pressure experimenters. In principle, its construction ensures that the sealing gasket, of rubber or soft metal, is always compressed to a higher pressure than the pressure to be confined; the high pressure itself is used to tighten the packing, instead of an external screw as in most conventional packings. The ultimate limitation becomes the strength of the metal parts.

Bridgman had the good fortune to begin his experiments at a time when metallurgical advances were providing steels of unprecedentedly high strength; his achievement of still higher pressures in the 1930s was made possible by the development of the cobalt-bonded tungsten carbides. The leak-proof packing would have been of little value with Amagat's steel, but the new alloys permitted spectacular increases of the useful pressure range. After a short period of experimentation with Krupp nickel steel, Bridgman settled on an electric-furnace chrome-vanadium steel (equivalent to the present AISI 6150) for most of his pressure vessels and connecting tubes. In small diameters, this steel can be heat-treated to give a yield point in tension of as much as 270,000 pounds per square inch (psi); it is not, however, a deep-hardening steel and in the sizes of Bridgman's pressure vessels, four or five inches in diameter, the interior remains relatively soft with a yield point of perhaps 150,000 psi, while at the outside, more rapidly quenched, the yield point might reach 220,000 psi. This condition is advantageous for pressure vessels; the elastic limit is reached first in the ductile material near the bore, which can be stretched appreciably without rupture; at the same time, the expansion of the inner part transmits the load to the strong outer parts, which are inefficiently stressed so long as the whole cylinder remains in the elastic range. Thus Bridgman found to his pleasure that pressures could be contained far in excess of predictions based on simple elastic criteria.

Bridgman's laboratory was first established in the basement of the Jefferson Physical Laboratory, built in 1884, and remained there until the construction of the Lyman Laboratory of Physics in 1931. The brick pillars of the old basement served as supports for galvanometers and other equipment, most of it homemade, small, and hand-operated. From the beginning, Bridgman made much of his own apparatus, and his papers contain many useful bits of shop lore which throw light on the amount of labor and persistence underlying his studies. One of the essential components of his pressure system was a pipe connecting the cylinder in which pressure was generated with the cylinder, usually maintained at a different temperature by a liquid bath, in which the material under investigation was compressed. He had to drill the pipe from solid alloy steel bars, as adequate tubing was not yet available. "The inside diameter . . . is 1/16 of an inch, and it is quite possible with a little practise to drill pieces at least 17 inches long. The drill should be cut on the end of a long piece of drill rod; it does not pay to try to braze a long shank onto a short drill. . . . The drill need not be expected to run more than 1/2 of an inch out of center on a piece 17 inches long. . . . It is easy, if all precautions are observed, to drill a hole . . . 17 inches long in from seven to eight hours."

The effort required to maintain these heavily stressed parts was severe. In his paper on "Mercury, Liquid and Solid, under Pressure," Bridgman records (p. 414) that between October 13 and December 3, 1910, "There were at least five . . . explosions; two lower cylinders being burst, two upper cylinders, and one connecting pipe." Each of these components represented several days of shop time and we find here an explanation of the rough appearance of much of Bridgman's equipment: it did not "pay" to invest superfluous labor in parts whose useful life might not exceed a few exposures to pressure. A similar consideration determined the choice of 12,000 kg/cm^2 as the maximum pressure for most of the work up to about 1935. This pressure could be reached repeatedly with little risk of rupture, but beyond this, even a small increase greatly diminished the life of the cylinder.

In 1911 Bridgman described a free-piston absolute gauge usable to 13,000 kg/cm², and with this he calibrated the manganin wire gauge originally proposed by Lisell, who had found a linear dependence of the electrical resistance of manganin upon pressure up to 4200 atmospheres. By comparison with his new absolute gauge, Bridgman showed that the linearity continues to at least 12,000 kg/cm². As a secondary gauge, the manganin coil proved invaluable, since, unlike the free piston gauge, it could be incorporated in a leak-free system requiring only an insulated electrical connection to an outside measuring device. It requires calibration, however, and whereas in principle the primary gauge can be used for this purpose, it is more convenient to make use of "fixed points" on the pressure scale, like the "fixed points" of a temperature scale commonly used in place of the primary gas thermometer.[2]

One may surmise that Bridgman thoroughly enjoyed the use of his muscles on the pumps and the complete personal control thus exercised over the functioning of his equipment. The manipulations took him from pumps to measuring apparatus—usually a set of electrical bridges or potentiometers requiring telescopic observation of galvanometer deflections—to notebook in which notations were made in his private shorthand, and back to pump for a new cycle. All of this was performed as fast as the various thermal and pressure lags would permit, sometimes on a fixed schedule of time and over periods

[2] The point most used by Bridgman and many later investigators is the melting pressure of mercury at 0°C, observable as a pressure of discontinuity either of electrical resistance or of volume when these quantities are measured as functions of pressure. The pressure value derived from his 1911 observations, 7640 kg/cm², was used as a standard for subsequent calibrations, entering directly into all his measurements of compressibility and other pressure coefficients in which the manganin gauge was used. Redeterminations in the last few years with much more elaborate apparatus suggest an error of possibly 1 percent in this value, Newhall, Abbot, and Dunn (1963) giving 7715.6 kg/cm².

of several hours. Much philosophical debate has taken place over the meaning of his term "operational," but his own original meaning must have been closely related to the manifold physical activities of his laboratory, with every adjustment and every measurement dictated by his own mind and controlled by his own muscles.

After the completion of the Lyman Laboratory of Physics midway in Bridgman's experimental career, he was "promoted" to more ample quarters in a suite of rooms in the new building. Here his office was adjacent to his experimental rooms and private machine shop. Mr. Leonard H. Abbot served him as experimental assistant and Mr. Charles Chase as his machinist, but Bridgman himself continued to work with his hands as well as his brain until retirement.

The new laboratory also provided room for his research students, who had previously to find cubbyholes in the maze of the Jefferson basement. There were rarely more than two or three of these at one time; the record shows fourteen doctoral theses on high-pressure topics in addition to several supervised by Bridgman on other subjects. He spent relatively little time on the direction of graduate students and was usually most pleased when least consulted, but was willing to put his mind on real difficulties, and rarely failed to make valuable suggestions when his advice was sought.

Most of Bridgman's measurements may be grouped in a few categories, in each of which successive increases of the pressure range and additions of new substances led to new investigations. The principal topics were compression (59 papers), melting (12), polymorphism (35), electrical resistivity (48), elastic constants (9), thermoelectricity (9), and mechanical properties such as fracture strength and plasticity (37). Besides these there were papers on viscosity (4), thermal conductivity (6), and miscellaneous matters of technique (11). Once a successful method of measurement was developed, Bridgman applied it rapidly to virtually every simple element or compound to which it was applicable. Characteristic titles are: "The compressibility of thirty metals as a function of pressure and temperature"; "Freezing parameters and compressions of twenty-one substances to 50,000 kg/cm²"; "The resistance of 72 elements, alloys and compounds to 100,000 kg/cm²." Whole shelves of chemicals were ransacked for some of these studies, and as new standards of purity were attained, many of the measurements were repeated. Bridgman noted the discrepancies which resulted on repetitions and sometimes indicated which measurements were in his opinion to be preferred, but on the whole spent little time in a search for perfect consistency.

This is not the place for a discussion of all the devices employed by Bridgman; later generations of experimenters will perhaps be most impressed by the simplicity of principle of his arrangements, nearly all depending upon pistons, springs, levers, falling weights, combined with direct-current electrical measurements of resistance and potential. Bridgman's special talent was for making these devices operate successfully in the limited spaces of his pressure vessels, and in coping with the innumerable corrections arising from dimensional and other changes under pressure. The vacuum tube played virtually no part in his instrumentation. The electrical parts of the measuring systems, like the pressure systems, were mostly home-made; the readings were made on meter-long slide wires with the aid of reading glasses, and the slide wires were subject to frequent checks for uniformity. The resolution and accuracy attainable with these instruments reached their culmination in the measurements of compression to 100,000 kg/cm², made on samples 1/8 inch long and 1/16 inch in diameter, compressed in a miniature tungsten carbide die which itself was subjected to 25,000 kg/cm² in an outer pressure system. These measurements are among the most amazing of Bridgman's many astonishing feats. Many of these determinations have since been repeated with remarkably concordant results by the completely independent technique of shock waves.

Bridgman's mastery of laboratory techniques was also applied to the preparation of samples. Reactive materials such as the alkali metals were encased in protective sheaths. A method of growing large single crystals of metals which has been widely used by later workers was described more or less in passing, and the purification of the solid phase by concentration of impurities in the melt, briefly noticed, foreshadowed the later process of zone refining.

Perhaps no aspect of Bridgman's work attracted more general interest than his studies of polymorphism under pressure; in one substance after another, unsuspected and unpredictable new forms were discovered. "Hot ice" was doubtless the most popular, and a railroad official is said to have inquired about the possibility of producing this on a large scale for refrigeration! The large number of new modifications observed within his pressure range led Bridgman to the conclusion, subsequently confirmed, that few of the minerals common at the earth's surface remain stable under the still higher pressures of the interior. His awareness of the importance of his studies for geology and geophysics was greatly stimulated by the interest shown in his work by geologists, especially his friend and neighbor, Reginald A. Daly, whose frequent visits to Bridgman's laboratory are reflected in several papers dealing with rocks and minerals. Bridgman realized, however, that geological problems opened up a whole vista of experiments with complex, unfamiliar materials and high temperatures which he was not prepared to undertake.

An account of his early feeling about this question, related by him, is revealing. After his first few publications on high-pressure research, Bridgman was approached by Arthur L. Day, the farsighted Director of the Geophysical Laboratory of the Carnegie Institution. Day offered him a free hand if he would come to the Geophysical Laboratory, but Bridgman preferred to remain in the Physics Department at Harvard. He felt that Day should not have made such an offer. "I told him that I was interested in pure physics, and he had no right to be," is what many years later he recalled his answer to have been. But Day might well have had the last word: virtually all of Bridgman's work has added to the understanding of the behavior of matter in the earth's depths.

His remaining at Harvard for the better pursuit of pure physics was on a modified schedule: on asking Mr. Eliot if Harvard had a place for a man who did no administrative work or undergraduate teaching so that he could devote more time to research, the answer was, "Yes, if he is good enough." Bridgman took the risk.

In 1932, in cooperation with Daly, Harlow Shapley, L. C. Graton, and others, Bridgman took an active part in initiating a program at Harvard for high-pressure studies devoted to geophysical problems, the first to be established in a university; with variations of emphasis, such studies are now pursued in many universities and industrial laboratories.

His activity on the Committee on Experimental Geology and Geophysics was one of the few diversions which he permitted himself in university affairs. To President Lowell he said, "I am not interested in your college, I want to do research," and got away with it. Committee life in the universities in the prewar days had not, of course, attained its present state of hypertrophy, but even then Bridgman was perhaps unique in his abstention. On the other hand he took an active part in the business of the American Academy of Arts and Sciences, with which he was closely linked in several ways. Nearly all of his investigations were published in its *Proceedings;* he received the Rumford Medal of the Academy in 1917; and from 1907 onward, his work was assisted by small grants from the Rumford Fund. He became a Fellow in 1912, a member of the Rumford Award Committee in 1919, serving to 1952, Vice President of Class I (Mathematics, Physics, Astronomy) from 1940 to 1944, a member of the Board of Editors of *Daedalus* from 1957 to 1961, and a member of several committees concerned with the general implications of science. Bridgman may have felt that he owed this service to the Academy in return for its consistent, if meager, support of his work. The American Academy grants, mainly from the Rumford Fund "for researches in light and heat," amounted to about $400 a year for a number of years, and, with similar aid from the Bache Fund of the National Academy, appear to have constituted most of his financial support up to about 1940. Since most of the grants were awarded for "Investigations of optical and thermal properties under high pressures," we infer that the original intention to study optical properties remained in Bridgman's mind, though it was never realized. Even with allowance for the greater purchasing power of the dollar before 1940, Bridgman's laboratory budget was remarkably small, and the return per dollar astonishingly large.

In both world wars, Bridgman applied his talents to wartime problems. In 1917 he moved to New London to take charge of a research group concerned with the detection of submarines by acoustical methods. A major difficulty was noise produced by a ship's own auxiliary motors which could not be shut down during listening intervals. Bridgman developed a sound-insulating system, which was subsequently widely applied, for mounting these auxiliaries. He also studied the possibility of using large areas of the ship's skin, coupled with receivers installed inside the ship, for the detection of underwater sound; this plan had the advantage of eliminating the need for dry-dock facilities, which were in short supply. The following details have been kindly supplied by Professor Louis B. Slichter: "A . . . design . . . for listening through the skin of the ship involved the use of large circular containers, usually called 'soup plates,' clamped against the skin of the ship with a gasket seal and filled with water. In this water cavity, sound receivers were placed. In May 1917 a multiple unit listening device of this type was installed on the troop ship *George Washington* for use on a trip to Brest. . . . The writer [Slichter] was placed in charge of the detachment of trained listeners who stood watches continuously at this detector [during the voyage]. . . . Apparently because of some mistake made in counting the many deck levels of this great ship, the installation was unfortunately made above the water line, far out of reach of submarine sounds. It seemed best not to emphasize this discouraging discovery, and so the listeners carried on their duties conscientiously in happy oblivion."

Another development, which came too late for World War I but was used extensively thereafter, was based directly upon his high-pressure techniques; this was a method for increasing the yield point of artillery gun barrels by a preliminary stretching with internal hydrostatic pressure, exactly the same procedure, though on an enlarged scale, which he had successfully applied to his pressure vessels. This process made it possible to produce guns from single forgings, instead of the series of shrunk-on tubes formerly required.

Bridgman was a rugged libertarian who anticipated World War II by a private declaration of his own closing his laboratory early in 1939 to visitors from totalitarian states. The following short statement (*Science,* February 24, 1939, p. 179) was handed to any such prospective visitors who presented themselves at his door:

"I have decided from now on not to show my apparatus or

discuss my experiments with citizens of any totalitarian state. A citizen of such a state is no longer a free individual, but he may be compelled to engage in any activity whatever to advance the purposes of that state. The purposes of the totalitarian states have shown themselves to be in irreconcilable conflict with the purposes of free states. In particular, the totalitarian states do not recognize that the free cultivation of scientific knowledge for its own sake is a worthy end of human endeavor, but have commandeered the scientific activities of their citizens to serve their own purposes. These states have thus annulled the grounds which formerly justified and made a pleasure of the free sharing of scientific knowledge between individuals of different countries. A self-respecting recognition of this altered situation demands that this practice be stopped. Cessation of scientific intercourse with the totalitarian states serves the double purpose of making more difficult the misuse of scientific information by these states, and of giving the individual opportunity to express his abhorrence of their practices.

"This statement is made entirely on my own initiative and has no connection with any policy of the university."

During World War II he undertook studies of plastic flow in steel related to the penetration of armor by projectiles; much of this work later appeared in his book *Studies in Large Plastic Flow and Fracture*. Measurements of the compressibility of uranium and plutonium were made at the request of the Los Alamos Laboratory.

A characteristic product of Bridgman's desire for intellectual efficiency was his reduction of thermodynamic formulas to tabular form. The ten fundamental thermodynamic functions have 720 first derivatives, among which there exist some eleven billion possible relations. By choosing three experimentally measurable first derivatives as fundamental, viz., compressibility, thermal expansion, and heat capacity, Bridgman was able to compress all of these possibilities to a table of 90 entries, as well as to provide a compact digest of the even more numerous second derivatives. Once and for all, these relationships were made readily available with a great economy of effort.

One of his early teaching assignments was the task of giving two advanced courses in electrodynamics suddenly thrust upon him in 1914 by the death of B. O. Peirce. Years later he commented on the obscurity of the underlying conceptual situation which he found in this area and the intellectual distress which it caused him. His efforts to meet the logical problems of electrodynamics provided the initial stimulus for his subsequent activity as a critic of the logical structure of physics.

His first publication dealing with the logical problems of physics was a 1916 paper on Tolman's newly proposed principle of similitude. In this article he showed—what Buckingham had surmised—that the valid conclusions drawn by Tolman from the rule of similitude can be independently derived by dimensional analysis and that, furthermore, the application of the Tolman rule to gravitational forces leads to an unacceptable result.

Returning to Harvard in the spring of 1920 from the antisubmarine project at New London, he turned his attention once more to the problems of dimensional reasoning, long a subject for sporadic controversy among physicists. Despite forward steps taken by Buckingham,[3] basic issues remained unsettled and Bridgman set to work to put the subject in order. His initial book-length publication, *Dimensional Analysis*, issued in 1922, was the result. It combined the first systematic and critical exposition of the principles involved with a rich variety of illustrative applications.

Basic to Bridgman's formulation of dimensional theory was his insistence that when, for example, we say that the speed of

[3] Edgar Buckingham, *Phys. Rev.*, 4 (1914):345, 357.

an automobile is 60 mi/hr, the assertion should not be interpreted as meaning that the speed in question is 60 times the ratio of one mile to one hour. "It is meaningless to talk of dividing a length by a time; what we actually do is to operate with numbers which are the measures of these quantities." For this reason he rejected the widely held view that the letter symbols for the different physical quantities in the equations of physics should be considered to represent corresponding physical quantities. It suffices to suppose that the symbols are placeholders for the numerical measure-values of the physical quantities. He recognized the practical convenience of the custom of treating the equations of physics as relations between numbers carrying dimensional unit labels, but considered that to call such labeled numbers "physical quantities" is to introduce an unwarranted and misleading verbalism.

A primary objective of the monograph *Dimensional Analysis* was accordingly to demonstrate that the dimensional properties of the equations of physics can be fully explained on the legitimate assumption that the letter symbols represent mere numbers. Hence the rule of dimensional homogeneity is not to be derived from a metaphysical interpretation of what the equations mean, but from the universal practice among physicists of writing their equations in a form that is *complete,* i.e., a form equally valid for all values of the primary units involved. Following the lead of Fourier, James Thomson, and Buckingham, Bridgman restricted his discussion of dimensional analysis to complete physical equations. The restriction was no handicap, for every physical equation can be put into complete form by the introduction of suitable dimensional constants; every physicist instinctively expresses himself in the language of such equations. Thus dimensional analysis is a technique for taking advantage of the language structure.

Perhaps the most significant of Bridgman's contributions to dimensional analysis was his recognition of the scientific so-

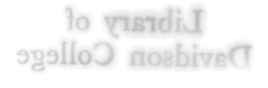

phistication required for the practice of the technique. The analyst must list all the physical quantities, including dimensional constants, relevant to the solution of the physical problem in hand. Any omission will falsify his result; the inclusion of any superfluous quantity will cheat him of full success. Making the decision requires a broad scientific background. The practitioner of the art must be familiar with the branch of science in which the problem falls and with the basic differential equations which rule that field, for the dimensional constants he must reckon with turn out to be those involved in the differential equations. This means that the specific problems to which dimensional analysis is applicable are those that in principle could be solved analytically with the help of appropriate differential equations.

The foregoing conclusion exposes the limitations of dimensional reasoning and at the same time removes the mystery of its power. Bridgman shows us that the technique owes most of its success in providing its practitioners with unearned information to the unconscious use which they have made of the normal background of the experienced professional scientist. The method is extremely useful, but it does not give the inquirer something for nothing after all.

Bridgman's success in thinking his way through the metaphysical confusions of dimensional analysis encouraged him to turn his attention to the larger task of eliminating similar confusions in the broader field of physics proper. Einstein's discovery that there is no such thing as absolute simultaneity between events at different places was proof that the basic concepts of time and space had been seriously misconceived. This revelation of shabby thinking at the core of physics seemed to Bridgman to call for a critical reexamination of the conceptual structure of physics as a whole. *The Logic of Modern Physics,* issued in 1927, is a report of his early conclusions.

This book was destined to have wide influence on the thinking of a generation of physicists struggling to make sense out of new and revolutionary facts in a time of change. Here his conception of operational analysis as a basic intellectual tool was clearly formulated. Its repercussions spread in time through the whole intellectual world and established the reputation of its author as a penetrating thinker of the first rank. The volume was written in a single half-year of sabbatical leave; Bridgman habitually rationed his time and would not allow himself a longer period of absence from his laboratory. Fortunately he had a natural facility in the use of words, for he rarely indulged in the luxury of rewriting to improve the phraseology of what he had once committed to paper.

The attitude with which he approached his task was one of pure empiricism. For him physics was the quantitative exploration and analysis of physical experience. The discoveries behind the revolution in physics then in progress seemed to prove the total folly of assuming that the possibilities of new experience can be limited by any known *a priori* principles. They showed, moreover, that the central intuitive concepts of physics had been seriously at fault because they had involved unwarranted presuppositions. In his view the time had come for every scientist to analyze afresh the relation between his conceptual apparatus and his actual experience. Only in this way can he hope to escape from the ruts and booby traps embedded in the language he inherits from the past. Specifically, Bridgman called for discontinuance of the practice of defining physical concepts in terms of their assumed properties without prior proof that something corresponding to those properties exists in nature. Since such proof can come only through laboratory activity, it was evident to him that the ultimate meaning of every physical concept is bound up with the physical and mental operations by which it is measured or tested. He took satisfaction in observing that Einstein's original breakthrough was achieved by testing the concept of the simultaneity of widely separated events by an analysis of the *operations* involved in the synchronization of clocks in different locations. In focusing attention on physical and mental operations and activities, Bridgman considered that he was maintaining the closest possible connection between the living reality of scientific experience and the physical theories designed to interpret that experience.

The Logic of Modern Physics includes a reexamination of a number of the key concepts of physics from his operational point of view. For many of his junior contemporaries the reading of its pages was a memorable and exhilarating experience. It swept away a fog of unverified assumptions and gave us a new conception of the possibilities of clear thinking. From it we learned that, when new techniques of measurement open up new domains of experience, the meanings of our concepts are altered. His emphasis on the multiplicity of operational meanings associated with specific scientific terms prepared us to meet new facts with flexible minds. Bridgman helped to free us from the compulsive need of the preceding generation of physicists to find mechanical explanations for all the phenomena of nature. He made no direct contribution to the development of quantum theory, but his point of view did much to alleviate the initial confusion over the paradoxical combination of wavelike and corpuscle-like properties of radiation and matter with which quantum theory is concerned. His thinking made it easier for us to accept the observed behavior of microscopic systems at its face value without trying to force it into a logical mold dictated by the language and categories of macroscopic experience and common sense. He saved our time and energy by pointing out the futility of efforts to find the answers to verbal questions that are in principle beyond the reach of experimental test.

In due course *The Logic of Modern Physics* was followed by other books and papers extending and deepening his critical examination of the concepts and theories of physics. His Princeton University lectures on *The Nature of Physical Theory* were published in 1936. *The Nature of Thermodynamics* followed in 1941 and *A Sophisticate's Primer of Relativity* appeared as a posthumous publication in 1962. In these studies he drew attention away from the apparent precision of the mathematical equations of physics and the seemingly rigorous logic of axiomatically constructed theories to the matrix of crude observations and approximate verbal explanations from which the symbols and equations derive their significance. His relentless probing exposed a surprising penumbra of uncertainty regarding the interpretation of the symbols in thermodynamics, for example, in different physical situations and regarding the limits of applicability of its concepts. He clarified the status of theoretical physics by putting the spotlight on what is unclear and by calling attention to the essential part which language plays in the making of theories.

From the beginning it was evident that the value of an operational analysis of concepts, assertions, and questions is not restricted to physics or the physical sciences. It can be used to help the thinker in any field to distinguish between facts firmly rooted in the ground of experience and pseudo facts which have no such basis. The lesson that it is not what we say that counts, but what we do, is of universal application. In Bridgman's view language which does not meet the operation test is basically spurious and meaningless. Thus, because there is no conceivable way to measure absolute position, it means nothing to ask whether a star is at rest or not. It seemed equally clear to Bridgman that "many of the problems with which the human intellect has tortured itself [are] only pseudo problems" because they can be formulated only in terms of questions that are essentially meaningless. Many of the traditional disputes in the areas of philosophy, religion, and ethics were assigned to this category. Consider, for example, the question of the freedom of the will: "You maintain that you are free to take either the right- or left-hand fork in the road. I defy you to set up a single objective criterion by which you can prove after you have made the turn that you might have made the other. The problem has no meaning in the sphere of objective activity; it relates only to my personal subjective feelings while making the decision."

He recognized that "there is a sense in which no serious question is entirely without meaning, because doubtless the questioner had in mind some intention in asking the question." But if the meaning of a question cannot be pinned down by some imaginable test operation, the question is footless. We should waste no time over it.

Perhaps inevitably, Bridgman found himself under compulsion to apply his point of view to the wider problems of society. He was a single-minded man to whom confusions of meaning, muddle-headedness, self-delusions, and misrepresentations of all kinds were anathema. The test of operational thinking gave him a logical weapon with which to attack the incubus of tangled nonsense which prevents intelligent action in a society interested only casually in the search for truth. In three volumes, *The Intelligent Individual and Society* (1938), *Reflections of a Physicist* (1950), *The Way Things Are* (1959), he used his weapon ruthlessly, giving little quarter as he subjected the traditional absolutist conceptions of duty, responsibility, right, justice, and law to the test of operational meaning.

Through the years the need to find intelligent answers to his own problems and the problems of society grew upon him. In the opening passage of *The Intelligent Individual and Society*, he said: "As I grow older a note of intellectual dissatisfaction becomes an increasingly insistent overtone in my life. I am becoming more and more conscious that my life will not stand intelligent scrutiny, and at the same time my desire to lead an intelligently well ordered life grows to an almost physical intensity." Far from accepting the sharp distinction which the average person draws between moral and intellectual issues, he tended to treat intellectual integrity as the supreme ethical problem facing mankind. In one lyrical passage discussing the effect of the practice of intellectual honesty on the scientific worker, he said: "The ideal of intellectual honesty comes to make a strong emotional appeal; he [the scientist] finds something fine in the selflessness involved in rigorously carrying through a train of thought careless of the personal implications; he feels a traitor to something deep within him if he refuses to follow out logical implications because he sees that they are going to be unpleasant; and he exults that he belongs to a race which is capable of such emotions."

In a note under the title "A Challenge to Physicists," published in the war year 1942, he said: "From a long-range point of view the deepest issues of the present crisis are intellectual. The failure of this country up to the present has been primarily an intellectual failure—intellectual sloth, lack of imagination, and wishful thinking. The crisis of a totalitarian victory is, from the perspective of a thousand years, an intellectual crisis. The day when the human race may evolve into a race capable of the intellectual mastery of its fate will be immeasurably postponed by such a victory. . . . The race will not save itself until it achieves intellectual morale. Perhaps the two chief components of intellectual morale are intellectual integrity and a fierce conviction that man *can* become the master of his fate."

Bridgman's emphasis on the correspondence between the words we use in organizing our experience and the operations which he thought of as atoms of experience brought with it a strong individualistic tone congenial to his temperament. The experience with which each one of us must deal is his own. Operational analysis is basically an introspective process. Bridgman pointed out that the custom of impersonal reporting in scientific work obscures the fact that all the observations, judgments, and interpretations involved in scientific activity are made by individuals. Although public science is created through communication and checking operations, it is preceded by the private science of the individual. Only the individual can have experience and only the individual can think about it. In writing Bridgman's own practice was to make frequent use of first-person pronouns.

In applying his operational method to the problems of society, he began with the proposition that society in general, as well as the scientific community, is simply the sum of the individuals who make it up. On this basis he drew the conclusion that the most important features of society are those to be discovered by the analysis of the relations between each individual and those others who make up the society of which he is a part. There is never any question of Bridgman's integrity or candor. Always a rebel against social controls, even when he realized how necessary they are, he despised the artifices of rationalization by which the leaders of society have always compelled their fellows to keep in step. His minimum code for the regulation of an ideal Bridgmanian Utopia is one that society as we know it could never accept. On the other hand, one of the most deep-seated of the many ailments of the world today is, perhaps, just the lack of intellectual honesty for which Bridgman fought.

To sum up: Bridgman's influence was strongest among scientists, who found his point of view congenial. Much of what he had to say is commonly accepted among them today. His philosophic writing, to be sure, was always iconoclastic and stimulated a good deal of controversy, especially among those philosophers of science who managed to misread his intent. Operational analysis, he had to explain, was proposed as an aid to clear thinking and not as a solution for all the problems of philosophy. Again and again he gave expression to his dislike of the word "operationalism" with its implication of an associated dogma.

He was disappointed as he grew older with the reaction to his attempts to promote operational thinking in the field of the social sciences. Yet he remained a warm, considerate, and courageous person who drew the admiration and affection of all who knew him well.

In the spring and summer of 1961 he became crippled in both legs, with increasingly intense pain and great fatigue. By mid-July an expert diagnosis was at last procured: intractable cancer of major bones, which would inevitably prove fatal in a matter of months or a year. It was characteristic of the man that then he did not hesitate to take his own life. The decision to do so was for him a matter of principle—one which he had faced many years before. In a last note, left in his pocket on the day of his death, he said, "It isn't decent for Society to make a man do this thing himself. Probably this is the last day I will be able to do it myself."

Bridgman was a member of the National Academy of Sciences (1918), the American Philosophical Society, the American Academy of Arts and Sciences, the Washington Academy of Sciences, the American Association for the Advancement of Science, the American Physical Society (president, 1942), foreign member of the Royal Society (London), honorary fellow of the Physical Society (London), a corresponding member of the Academia Nacional de Ciencias, Mexico, and a foreign member of the Indian Academy of Science.

In addition to the 1946 Nobel Prize in physics, he was the

recipient of the Rumford Medal of the American Academy of Arts and Sciences (1917), the Cresson Medal of the Franklin Institute (1932), the Roozenboom Medal of the Netherlands Royal Academy (1933), the Comstock Prize of the National Academy of Sciences (1933), the Research Corporation of America Award (1937), and the Bingham Medal of the Society of Rheology (1951).

He held honorary doctor of science degrees from Brooklyn Polytechnic Institute (1934), Harvard University (1939), Stevens Institute of Technology (1941), Princeton University (1950), Yale University (1951), and the degree D. Honoris Causa, Paris (1950).

BIBLIOGRAPHY

KEY TO ABBREVIATIONS

Am. J. Sci. = American Journal of Science
Am. Scientist = American Scientist
J. Am. Chem. Soc. = Journal of the American Chemical Society
J. Appl. Phys. = Journal of Applied Physics
J. Chem. Phys. = Journal of Chemical Physics
J. Colloid Sci. = Journal of Colloid Science
J. Franklin Inst. = Journal of the Franklin Institute
J. Wash. Acad. Sci. = Journal of the Washington Academy of Sciences
Mech. Eng. = Mechanical Engineering
Phil. Mag. = Philosophical Magazine
Philosophy Sci. = Philosophy of Science
Phys. Rev. = Physical Review
Proc. Am. Acad. Arts Sci. = Proceedings of the American Academy of Arts and Sciences
Proc. Nat. Acad. Sci. = Proceedings of the National Academy of Sciences
Psychol. Rev. = Psychological Reviews
Rec. trav. chim. Pays-Bas = Recueil des travaux chimiques des Pays-Bas
Rev. Mod. Phys. = Reviews of Modern Physics
Sci. Monthly = Scientific Monthly
Z. Physik. Chem. = Zeitschrift fuer Physikalische Chemie

1906

The electrostatic field surrounding two special columnar elements. Proc. Am. Acad. Arts Sci., 41:617-26.

1908

On a certain development in Bessel's functions.   Phil. Mag., 16:947-48.

1909

The measurement of high hydrostatic pressure. I. A simple primary gauge. Proc. Am. Acad. Arts Sci., 44:201-17.
The measurement of high hydrostatic pressure. II. A secondary mercury resistance gauge. Proc. Am. Acad. Arts Sci., 44:221-51.
An experimental determination of certain compressibilities. Proc. Am. Acad. Arts Sci., 44:255-79.

1911

The action of mercury on steel at high pressures. Proc. Am. Acad. Arts Sci., 46:325-41.

The measurement of hydrostatic pressures up to 20,000 kilograms per square centimeter. Proc. Am. Acad. Arts Sci., 47:321-43.

Mercury, liquid and solid, under pressure. Proc. Am. Acad. Arts Sci., 47:347-438.

Water, in the liquid and five solid forms under pressure. Proc. Am. Acad. Arts Sci., 47:441-558.

1912

The collapse of thick cylinders under high hydrostatic pressure. Phys. Rev., 34:1-24.

Breaking tests under hydrostatic pressure and conditions of rupture. Phil. Mag., 24:63-80.

Thermodynamic properties of liquid water to 80° and 12,000 kgm. Proc. Am. Acad. Arts Sci., 48:309-62.

Verhalten des Wassers als Flüssigkeit und in fünf festen Formen unter Druck. Zeitschrift für anorganische und allgemeine Chemie, 77:377-455.

1913

Thermodynamic properties of twelve liquids between 20° and 80° and up to 12,000 kgm. per sq. cm. Proc. Am. Acad. Arts Sci., 49:3-114.

1914

The technique of high-pressure experimenting. Proc. Am. Acad. Arts Sci., 49:627-43.

Über Tammanns vier neue Eisarten. Z. Physik. Chem., 86:513-24.

Changes of phase under pressure. I. The phase diagram of eleven substances with especial reference to the melting curve. Phys. Rev., 3:126-41, 153-203.

High pressures and five kinds of ice. J. Franklin Inst., 177:315-32.

Two new modifications of phosphorus. J. Am. Chem. Soc., 36:1344-63.

Nochmals die Frage des unbeständigen Eises. Z. Physik Chem., 89:252-53.

The coagulation of albumen by pressure. Journal of Biological Chemistry, 19:511-12.

A complete collection of thermodynamic formulas. Phys. Rev., 3: 273-81.

1915

Change of phase under pressure. II. New melting curves with a general thermodynamic discussion of melting. Phys. Rev., 6:1-33, 94-112.

Polymorphic transformations of solids under pressure. Proc. Am. Acad. Arts Sci., 51:55-124.

The effect of pressure on polymorphic transitions of solids. Proc. Nat. Acad. Sci., 1:513-16.

1916

On the effect of general mechanical stress on the temperature of transition of two phases, with a discussion of plasticity. Phys. Rev., 8:215-23.

Further note on black phosphorus. J. Am. Chem. Soc., 38:609-12.

Polymorphic changes under pressure of the univalent nitrates. Proc. Am. Acad. Arts Sci., 51:581-625.

The velocity of polymorphic changes between solids. Proc. Am. Acad. Arts Sci., 52:57-88.

Polymorphism at high pressures. Proc. Am. Acad. Arts Sci., 52:91-187.

Tolman's principle of similitude. Phys. Rev., 8:423-31.

1917

The electrical resistance of metals under pressure. Proc. Am. Acad. Arts Sci., 52:573-646.

The resistance of metals under pressure. Proc. Nat. Acad. Sci., 3:10-12.

Note on the elastic constants of antimony and tellurium wires. Phys. Rev., 9:138-41.

Theoretical considerations in the nature of metallic resistance, with especial regard to the pressure effects. Phys. Rev., 9:269-89.

1918

Thermo-electromotive force, Peltier heat, and Thomson heat under pressure. Proc. Am. Acad. Arts Sci., 53:269-386.

The failure of cavities in crystals and rocks under pressure. Am. J. Sci., 45:243-68.

Stress-strain relations in crystalline cylinders. Am. J. Sci., 45:269-80.

On equilibrium under non-hydrostatic stress. Phys. Rev., 11:180-83.

1919

A critical thermodynamic discussion of the Volta, thermo-electric and thermionic effects. Phys. Rev., 14:306-47.

A comparison of certain electrical properties of ordinary and uranium lead. Proc. Nat. Acad. Sci., 5:351-53.

1920

An experiment in one-piece gun construction. Mining and Metallurgy, No. 158, Section 14, pp. 1-16.

Further measurements of the effect of pressure on resistance. Proc. Nat. Acad. Sci., 6:505-8.

1921

Electrical resistance under pressure, including certain liquid metals. Proc. Am. Acad. Arts Sci., 56:61-154.

The electrical resistance of metals. Phys. Rev., 17:161-94.

Measurements of the deviation from Ohm's law in metals at high current densities. Proc. Nat. Acad. Sci., 7:299-303.

The discontinuity of resistance preceding supraconductivity. J. Wash. Acad. Sci., 11:455-59.

1922

Dimensional Analysis. New Haven, Yale University Press. 112 pp.

The electron theory of metals in the light of new experimental data. Phys. Rev., 19:114-34.

The effect of tension on the electrical resistance of certain abnormal metals. Proc. Am. Acad. Arts Sci., 57:41-66.

The effect of pressure on the thermal conductivity of metals. Proc. Am. Acad. Arts Sci., 57:77-127.

The failure of Ohm's law in gold and silver at high current densities. Proc. Am. Acad. Arts Sci., 57:131-72.

The compressibility of metals at high pressures. Proc. Nat. Acad. Sci., 8:361-65.

1923

The effect of pressure on the electrical resistance of cobalt, aluminum, nickel, uranium, and caesium. Proc. Am. Acad. Arts Sci., 58:151-61.

The compressibility of thirty metals as a function of pressure and temperature. Proc. Am. Acad. Arts Sci., 58:165-242.

The compressibility of hydrogen to high pressures. Rec. trav. chim. Pays-Bas, 42:568-71.

The thermal conductivity of liquids. Proc. Nat. Acad. Sci., 9:341-45.

The volume changes of five gases under high pressures. Proc. Nat. Acad. Sci., 9:370-72.

The compressibility and pressure coefficient of resistance of rhodium and iridium. Proc. Am. Acad. Arts Sci., 59:109-15.

The effect of tension on the thermal and electrical conductivity of metals. Proc. Am. Acad. Arts Sci., 59:119-37.

The thermal conductivity of liquids under pressure. Proc. Am. Acad. Arts Sci., 59:141-69.

1924

A suggestion as to the approximate character of the principle of relativity. Science, 59:16-17.

The compressibility of five gases to high pressures. Proc. Am. Acad. Arts Sci., 59:173-211.

The thermal conductivity and compressibility of several rocks under high pressures. Am. J. Sci., 7:81-102.

Some properties of single metal crystals. Proc. Nat. Acad. Sci., 10:411-15.

The connections between the four transverse galvanomagnetic and thermomagnetic phenomena. Phys. Rev., 24:644-51.

1925

A Condensed Collection of Thermodynamic Formulas. Cambridge, Harvard University Press. 34 pp.

Properties of matter under high pressure. Mech. Eng., 47:161-69.

Certain aspects of high-pressure research. J. Franklin Inst., 200:147-60.

The compressibility of several artificial and natural glasses. Am. J. Sci., 10:359-67.

Certain physical properties of single crystals of tungsten, antimony, bismuth, tellurium, cadmium, zinc and tin. Proc. Am. Acad. Arts Sci., 60:305-83.

Various physical properties of rubidium and caesium and the resistance of potassium under pressures. Proc. Am. Acad. Arts Sci., 60:385-421.

The effect of tension on the transverse and longitudinal resistance of metals. Proc. Am. Acad. Arts Sci., 60:423-49.

The viscosity of liquids under pressure. Proc. Nat. Acad. Sci., 11: 603-6.

Thermal conductivity and thermo-electromotive forces of single metal crystals. Proc. Nat. Acad. Sci., 11:608-12.

Linear compressibility of fourteen natural crystals. Am. J. Sci. 10: 483-98.

1926

The five alkali metals under high pressure. Phys. Rev., 27:68-86.

The universal constant of thermionic emission. Phys. Rev., 27: 173-80.

The effect of pressure on the viscosity of forty-three pure liquids. Proc. Am. Acad. Arts Sci., 61:57-99.

Thermal conductivity and thermal e. m. f. of single crystals of several non-cubic metals. Proc. Am. Acad. Arts Sci., 61:101-34.

Dimensional analysis again. Phil. Mag., 2:1263-66.

1927

Rapport sur les phénomènes de conductibilité dans les métaux et leur explanation théorique. In: Conductibilité Électrique des Métaux et Problèmes Connexes (Report of the Fourth Solvay Congress, April 24-29, 1924), pp. 67-114. Paris, Gauthier-Villars.

Some mechanical properties of matter under high pressure. In: Proceedings of the Second International Congress of Applied Mechanics, pp. 53-61. Zurich, Orell Füssli.

The Logic of Modern Physics. New York, The Macmillan Company. xiv + 228 pp.

The breakdown of atoms at high pressures. Phys. Rev., 29:188-91.

The transverse thermo-electric effect in metal crystals. Proc. Nat. Acad. Sci., 13:46-50.

The viscosity of mercury under pressure. Proc. Am. Acad. Arts Sci., 62:187-206.

The compressibility and pressure coefficient of resistance of ten elements. Proc. Am. Acad. Arts Sci., 62:207-26.

1928

Electrical properties of single metal crystals. In: *Atti del Congresso Internazionali dei Fisici* (Como, 1927), pp. 239-48. Bologna, Nicola Zanichelli.

General considerations on the photo-electric effect. Phys. Rev., 31: 90-100.

Note on the principle of detailed balancing. Phys. Rev., 31:101-2.

Thermoelectric phenomena in crystals. Phys. Rev., 31:221-35.

The linear compressibility of thirteen natural crystals. Am. J. Sci., 15:287-96.

The photo-electric effect and thermionic emission: a correction and an extension. Phys. Rev., 31:862-66.

The pressure transition of the rubidium halides. Zeitschrift fuer Kristallographie, 67:363-76.

Resistance and thermo-electric phenomena in metal crystals. Proc. Nat. Acad. Sci., 14:943-46.

The effect of pressure on the resistance of three series of alloys. Proc. Am. Acad. Arts Sci., 63:329-45.

The compressibility and pressure coefficient of resistance of zirconium and hafnium. Proc. Am. Acad. Arts Sci., 63:347-50.

1929

Thermo-electric phenomena and electrical resistance in single metal crystals. Proc. Am. Acad. Arts Sci., 63:351-99.

The effect of pressure on the rigidity of steel and several varieties of glass. Proc. Am. Acad. Arts Sci., 63:401-20.

General survey of the effects of pressure on the properties of matter. Proceedings of the Physical Society (London), 41:341-60.

With J. B. Conant. Irreversible transformations of organic compounds under high pressures. Proc. Nat. Acad. Sci., 15:680-83.

Die Eigenschaften von Metallen unter hohen hydrostatischen Drucken. Metallwirtschaft, 8:229-33.

On the application of thermodynamics to the thermo-electric circuit. Proc. Nat. Acad. Sci., 15:765-68.

On the nature of the transverse thermomagnetic effect and the transverse thermo-electric effect in crystals. Proc. Nat. Acad. Sci., 15:768-73.

The elastic moduli of five alkali halides. Proc. Am. Acad. Arts Sci., 64:19-38.

The effect of pressure on the rigidity of several metals. Proc. Am. Acad. Arts Sci., 64:39-49.

The compressibility and pressure coefficient of resistance of several elements and single crystals. Proc. Am. Acad. Arts Sci., 64:51-73.

Thermische Zustands grössen bei hohen Drucken und Absorption von Gasen durch Flüssigkeiten unter Druck. Handbuch der Experimentalphysik, 8:245-400.

General considerations on the emission of electrons from conductors under intense fields. Phys. Rev., 34:1411-17.

1930

The minimum of resistance at high pressure. Proc. Am. Acad. Arts Sci., 64:75-90.

Permanent elements in the flux of present-day physics. Science, 71:19-23.

1931

The Physics of High Pressure. London, G. Bell and Sons, Ltd. vii + 398 pp.

The volume of eighteen liquids as a function of pressure and temperature. Proc. Am. Acad. Arts Sci., 66:185-233.

Compressibility and pressure coefficient of resistance, including single crystal magnesium. Proc. Am. Acad. Arts Sci., 66:255-71.

The P-V-T relations of NH_4C_1 and NH_4B_r, and in particular the effect of pressure on the volume anomalies. Phys. Rev., 38:182-91.

The recent change of attitude toward the law of cause and effect. Science, 73:539-47.

Recently discovered complexities in the properties of simple substance. Transactions of the American Institute of Mining,

Metallurgical and Petroleum Engineers, General Volume, pp. 17-37.

1932

Volume-temperature-pressure relations for several non-volatile liquids. Proc. Am. Acad. Arts Sci., 67:1-27.
Physical properties of single crystal magnesium. Proc. Am. Acad. Arts Sci., 67:29-41.
A new kind of e.m.f. and other effects thermodynamically connected with the four transverse effects. Phys. Rev., 39:702-15.
Comments on a note by E. H. Kennard on "Entropy, reversible processes and thermo-couples." Proc. Nat. Acad. Sci., 18:242-45.
Statistical mechanics and the second law of thermodynamics. Bulletin of the American Mathematical Society, 38:225-45; Science, 75:419-28.
A transition of silver oxide under pressure. Rev. trav. chim. Pays-Bas, 51:627-32.
The time scale: the concept of time. Sci. Monthly, 35:97-100.
The pressure coefficient of resistance of fifteen metals down to liquid oxygen temperatures. Proc. Am. Acad. Arts Sci., 67:305-44.
The compressibility of eighteen cubic compounds. Proc. Am. Acad. Arts Sci., 67:345-75.
The effect of homogeneous mechanical stress on the electrical resistance of crystals. Phys. Rev., 42:858-63.

1933

The pressure-volume-temperature relations of fifteen liquids. Proc. Am. Acad. Arts Sci., 68:1-25.
Compressibilities and pressure coefficients of resistance of elements, compounds, and alloys, many of them anomalous. Proc. Am. Acad. Arts Sci., 68:27-93.
The effect of pressure on the electrical resistance of single metal crystals at low temperatures. Proc. Am. Acad. Arts Sci., 68:95-123.
On the nature and the limitations of cosmical inquiries. Sci. Monthly, 37:385-97.

1934

The Thermodynamics of Electrical Phenomena in Metals. New York, The Macmillan Company. vi + 200 pp.

Energy. Gamma Alpha Record, 24:1-6.

A physicist's second reaction to Mengenlehre. Scripta Mathematica, 2:3-29.

Two new phenomena at very high pressure. Phys. Rev., 45:844-45.

The melting parameters of nitrogen and argon under pressure, and the nature of the melting curve. Phys. Rev., 46:930-33.

1935

With R. B. Dow. The compressibility of solutions of three amino acids. J. Chem. Phys., 3:35-41.

Theoretically interesting aspects of high-pressure phenomena. Rev. Mod. Phys., 7:1-33.

Electrical resistances and volume changes up to 20,000 kg/cm². Proc. Nat. Acad. Sci., 21:109-13.

On the effect of slight impurities on the elastic constants, particularly the compressibility of zinc. Phys. Rev., 47:393-97.

The melting curves and compressibilities of nitrogen and argon. Proc. Am. Acad. Arts Sci., 70:1-32.

Measurements of certain electrical resistances, compressibilities, and thermal expansion to 20,000 kg/cm². Proc. Am. Acad. Arts Sci., 70:71-101.

The pressure-volume-temperature relations of the liquid, and the phase diagram of heavy water. J. Chem. Phys., 3:597-605.

Effects of high shearing stress combined with high hydrostatic pressure. Phys. Rev., 48:825-47.

Polymorphism, principally of the elements, up to 50,000 kg/cm². Phys. Rev., 48:893-906.

Compressibilities and electrical resistance under pressure, with special reference to intermetallic compounds. Proc. Am. Acad. Arts Sci., 70:285-317.

1936

The Nature of Physical Theory. Princeton, Princeton University Press. 138 pp.

Shearing phenomena at high pressure of possible importance for geology. Journal of Geology, 44:653-69.

William Duane, 1872-1935. National Academy of Sciences, *Biographical Memoirs*, 18:23-41.

1937

Flow phenomena in heavily stressed metals. J. Appl. Phys., 8:328-36.

Polymorphic transitions of inorganic compounds to 50,000 kg/cm². Proc. Nat. Acad. Sci., 23:202-5.

Shearing phenomena at high pressures, particularly in inorganic compounds. Proc. Am. Acad. Arts Sci., 71:387-460.

Polymorphic transitions of 35 substances to 50,000 kg/cm². Proc. Am. Acad. Arts Sci., 72:45-136.

The phase diagram of water to 45,000 kg/cm². J. Chem. Phys., 5:964-66.

1938

The Intelligent Individual and Society. New York, The Macmillan Company. vi + 305 pp.

The resistance of nineteen metals to 30,000 kg/cm². Proc. Am. Acad. Arts Sci., 72:157-205.

Rough compressibilities of fourteen substances to 45,000 kg/cm². Proc. Am. Acad. Arts Sci., 72:207-25.

Polymorphic transitions up to 50,000 kg/cm² of several organic substances. Proc. Am. Acad. Arts Sci., 72:227-68.

The nature of metals as shown by their properties under pressure. American Institute of Mining, Metallurgical and Petroleum Engineers, Technical Publication, No. 922.

Operational analysis. Philosophy Sci., 5:114-31.

With E. S. Larsen. Shearing experiments on some selected minerals and mineral combinations. Am. J. Sci., 36:81-94.

Reflections on rupture. J. Appl. Phys., 9:517-28.

1939

The high pressure behavior of miscellaneous minerals. Am. J. Sci., 37:7-18.

"Manifesto" by a physicist. Science, 89:179.

Considerations on rupture under triaxial stress. Mech. Eng., 61: 107-11.

Society and the intelligent physicist. American Physics Teacher, 7:109-16.

1940

Science, public or private. Philosophy Sci., 7:36-48.

Absolute measurements in the pressure range up to 30,000 kg/cm². Phys. Rev., 57:235-37.

Compressions to 50,000 kg/cm². Phys. Rev., 57:237-39.

New high pressures reached with multiple apparatus. Phys. Rev., 57:342-43.

The measurement of hydrostatic pressure to 30,000 kg/cm². Proc. Am. Acad. Arts Sci., 74:1-10.

The linear compression of iron to 30,000 kg/cm². Proc. Am. Acad. Arts Sci., 74:11-20.

The compression of 46 substances to 50,000 kg/cm². Proc. Am. Acad. Arts Sci., 74:21-51.

The second law of thermodynamics and irreversible processes. Phys. Rev., 58:845.

1941

The Nature of Thermodynamics. Cambridge, Harvard University Press. xii + 229 pp.

Explorations toward the limit of utilizable pressures. J. Appl. Phys., 12:461-69.

Compressions and polymorphic transitions of seventeen elements to 100,000 kg/cm². Phys. Rev., 60:351-54.

Freezings and compressions to 50,000 kg/cm². J. Chem. Phys., 9: 794-97.

1942

Freezing parameters and compressions of twenty-one substances to 50,000 kg/cm². Proc. Am. Acad. Arts Sci., 74:399-424.

Pressure-volume relations for seventeen elements to 100,000 kg/ cm². Proc. Am. Acad. Arts Sci., 74:425-40.

A challenge to physicists. J. Appl. Phys., 13:209.

1943

Science, and its changing social environment. Science, 97:147-50.

Recent work in the field of high pressures. Am. Scientist, 31:1-35.

On torsion combined with compression. J. Appl. Phys., 14:273-83.

1944

Some irreversible effects of high mechanical stress. In: *Colloid Chemistry*, Vol. 5, ed. by Jerome Alexander, pp. 327-37. New York, D. Van Nostrand Co., Inc.

The stress distribution at the neck of a tension specimen. Transactions of the American Society for Metals, 32:553-72.

Flow and fracture. Metals Technology, 11:32-39.

1945

Discussion of "Flow and fracture." Metals Technology, Technical Publication Supplement, No. 1782.

Discussion of Boyd and Robinson, "The friction properties of various lubricants at high pressures." Transactions of the American Society of Mechanical Engineers, 67:51-59.

The compression of twenty-one halogen compounds and eleven other simple substances to 100,000 kg/cm^2. Proc. Am. Acad. Arts Sci., 76:1-7.

The compression of sixty-one solid substances to 25,000 kg/cm^2, determined by a new rapid method. Proc. Am. Acad. Arts Sci., 76:9-24.

The prospect for intelligence. Yale Review, 34:444-61.

Polymorphic transitions and geological phenomena. Am. J. Sci., 243A:90-97.

Some general principles of operational analysis. Psychol. Rev., 52:246-49.

Rejoinders and second thoughts. Psychol. Rev., 52:281-84.

Effects of high hydrostatic pressure on the plastic properties of metals. Rev. Mod. Phys., 17:3-14.

1946

Recent work in the field of high pressure. Rev. Mod. Phys., 18:1-93.

The tensile properties of several special steels and certain other materials under pressure. J. Appl. Phys., 17:201-12.

Studies of plastic flow of steel, especially in two-dimensional compression. J. Appl. Phys., 17:225-43.

On higher order transitions. Phys. Rev., 70:425-28.

The effect of hydrostatic pressure on plastic flow under shearing stress. J. Appl. Phys., 17:692-98.

1947

Dimensional analysis. In: *Encyclopaedia Britannica,* Vol. 7, pp. 387-87J. Chicago, Encyclopaedia Britannica, Inc.

An experimental contribution to the problem of diamond synthesis. J. Chem. Phys., 15:92-98.

The rheological properties of matter under high pressure. J. Colloid Sci., 2:7-16.

The effect of hydrostatic pressure on the fracture of brittle substances. J. Appl. Phys., 18:246-58.

The effect of high mechanical stress on certain solid explosives. J. Chem. Phys., 15:311-13.

Scientists and social responsibility. Sci. Monthly, 65:148-54.

Science and freedom: Reflections of a physicist. Isis, 37:128-31.

1948

The compression of 39 substances to 100,000 kg/cm². Proc Am. Acad. Arts Sci., 76:55-70.

Rough compressions of 177 substances to 40,000 kg/cm². Proc. Am. Acad. Arts Sci., 76:71-87.

Large plastic flow and the collapse of hollow cylinders. J. Appl. Phys., 19:302-5.

Fracture and hydrostatic pressure. In: *Fracturing of Metals,* pp. 246-61. Novelty, Ohio, American Society for Metals.

General survey of certain results in the field of high pressure physics. In: *Les Prix Nobel,* pp. 149-66. Stockholm, P. A. Norstedt & Soner; J. Wash. Acad. Sci., 38:145-56.

The linear compression of various single crystals to 30,000 kg/cm². Proc. Am. Acad. Arts Sci., 76:89-99.

1949

Viscosities to 30,000 kg/cm². Proc. Am. Acad. Arts Sci., 77:117-28.

Further rough compressions to 40,000 kg/cm², especially certain liquids. Proc. Am. Acad. Arts Sci., 77:129-46.

Linear compressions to 30,000 kg/cm², including relatively incompressible substances. Proc. Am. Acad. Arts Sci., 77:187-234.

On scientific method. The Teaching Scientist, 6:23-24.

Science, materialism and the human spirit. In: *Mid-Century: The Social Implications of Scientific Progress,* ed. by John Ely Burchard, pp. 196-251. Cambridge, Technology Press.

Some implications of recent points of view in physics. Revue Internationale de Philosophie, 3:479-501.

Einstein's theories and the operational point of view. In: *Albert Einstein: Philosopher-Scientist,* ed. by P. A. Schlipp, pp. 335-54. Evanston, Illinois, Library of Living Philosophers.

Effect of hydrostatic pressure on plasticity and strength. Research (London), 2:550-55.

Volume changes in the plastic stages of simple compression. J. Appl. Phys., 20:1241-51.

1950

Reflections of a Physicist. New York, Philosophical Library, Inc. xii + 392 pp.

Impertinent reflections on history of science. Philosophy Sci., 17: 63-73.

The principles of thermodynamics. In: *Thermodynamics in Physical Metallurgy,* pp. 1-15. Novelty, Ohio, American Society for Metals.

The thermodynamics of plastic deformation of generalized entropy. Rev. Mod. Phys., 22:56-63.

Physics above 20,000 kg/cm². Proceedings of the Royal Society of London, 203A:1-17.

The operational aspect of meaning. Synthese (Amsterdam), 8:251-59.

1951

The effect of pressure on the electrical resistance of certain semiconductors. Proc. Am. Acad. Arts Sci., 79:125-28.

The electric resistance to 30,000 kg/cm² of twenty-nine metals and intermetallic compounds. Proc. Am. Acad. Arts Sci., 79:149-79.

The effect of pressure on the melting of several methyl siloxanes. J. Chem. Phys., 19:203-7.

Some implications for geophysics of high-pressure phenomena. Bulletin of the Geological Society of America, 62:533-35.

Some results in the field of high-pressure physics. Endeavor, 10:63-

69; Smithsonian Institution Annual Report for 1951, pp. 199-211.

The nature of some of our physical concepts. British Journal for the Philosophy of Science, 1:257-72; 2:25-44, 142-60.

1952

The Nature of Some of Our Physical Concepts. New York, Philosophical Library, Inc. 64 pp.

Studies in Large Plastic Flow and Fracture, with Special Emphasis on the Effects of Hydrostatic Pressure. New York, McGraw-Hill Book Co., Inc. x + 362 pp.

The resistance of 72 elements, alloys, and compounds to 100,000 kg/cm². Proc. Am. Acad. Arts Sci., 81:165-251.

Acceptance of the Bingham Medal. J. Colloid Sci., 7:202-3.

1953

Further measurements of the effect of pressure on the electrical resistance of germanium. Proc. Am. Acad. Arts Sci., 82:71-82.

Miscellaneous measurements of the effect of pressure on electrical resistance. Proc. Am. Acad. Arts Sci., 82:83-100.

The effect of pressure on several properties of the alloys of bismuth-tin and of bismuth-cadmium. Proc. Am. Acad. Arts Sci., 82:101-56.

High-pressure instrumentation. Mech. Eng., 75:111-13.

With I. Simon. Effects of very high pressures on glass. J. Appl. Phys., 24:405-13.

The effect of pressure on the tensile properties of several metals and other materials. J. Appl. Phys., 24:560-70.

The use of electrical resistance in high pressure calibration. Review of Scientific Instruments, 24:400-1.

The discovery of science. Proceedings of the Institute of Radio Engineers, 41:580-81.

The effect of pressure on the bismuth-tin system. Bulletin des Sociétés Chemiques Belges, 62:26-33.

Reflections on thermodynamics. Proc. Am. Acad. Arts Sci., 82:301-9; Am. Scientist, 41:549-55.

1954

Certain effects of pressure on seven rare earth metals. Proc. Am. Acad. Arts Sci., 83:1-22.

The task before us. Proc. Am. Acad. Arts Sci., 83:95-112.

Science and common sense. Sci. Monthly, 79:32-39.

Effects of pressure on binary alloys. II. Thirteen alloy systems of low melting monotropic metals. Proc. Am Acad. Arts Sci., 83:149-90.

Remarks on the present state of operationalism. Sci. Monthly, 79: 224-26.

Certain aspects of plastic flow under high stress. In: *Studies in Mathematics and Mechanics Presented to Richard von Mises by Friends, Colleagues and Pupils,* pp. 227-31. New York, Academic Press, Inc.

1955

Effects of pressure on binary alloys. III. Five alloys of thallium, including thallium-bismuth. Proc. Am. Acad. Arts Sci., 84:1-42.

Effects of pressure on binary alloys. IV. Six alloys of bismuth. Proc. Am. Acad. Arts Sci., 84:43-109.

Miscellaneous effects of pressure on miscellaneous substances. Proc. Am. Acad. Arts Sci., 84:112-29.

Synthetic diamonds. Scientific American, 193:42-46.

1956

Science and broad points of view. Proc. Nat. Acad. Sci., 42:315-25.

High pressure polymorphism of iron. J. Appl. Phys., 27:659.

Probability, logic and ESP. Science, 123:15-17.

1957

Effects of pressure on binary alloys. V. Fifteen alloys of metals of moderately high melting point. Proc. Am. Acad. Arts Sci., 84: 131-77.

Effects of pressure on binary alloys. VI. Systems for the most part of dilute alloys of high melting metals. Proc. Am. Acad. Arts Sci., 84:179-216.

Error, quantum theory, and the observer. In: *Life, Language, Law: Essays in Honor of Arthur F. Bentley,* ed. by R. W. Taylor, pp. 125-31. Yellow Springs, Ohio, Antioch Press.

Some of the broader implications of science. Physics Today, 10:17-24.

Theodore Lyman, 1874-1954. National Academy of Sciences, *Biographical Memoirs,* 30:237-56.

1958

Quo vadis. Daedalus, 87:85-93.
The microscopic and the observer. In: *La Méthode dans les Sciences Modernes*, ed. by François Le Lionnais, pp. 117-22. Paris, Editions Science et Industrie.
Remarks on Niels Bohr's talk. Daedalus, 87:175-77.

1959

The Way Things Are. Cambridge, Harvard University Press. 333 pp.
Compression and the α-β phase transition of plutonium. J. Appl. Phys., 30:214-17.
How much rigor is possible in physics? In: *The Axiomatic Method, with Special Reference to Geometry and Physics*, ed. by L. Henkin *et al.*, pp. 225-37. Amsterdam, North-Holland Publishing Company.
P. W. Bridgman's "The Logic of Modern Physics" after thirty years. Daedalus, 88:518-26.

1960

Sir Francis Simon. Science, 131:1647-54.
Critique of critical tables. Proc. Nat. Acad. Sci., 46:1394-400.

1961

Significance of the Mach principle. American Journal of Physics, 29:32-36.

1962

A Sophisticate's Primer of Relativity. Middletown, Connecticut, Wesleyan University Press. 191 pp.

1963

General outlook on the field of high-pressure research. In: *Solids under Pressure*, ed. by W. Paul and D. M. Warschauer, pp. 1-13. New York, McGraw-Hill Book Co., Inc.

1964

Collected Experimental Papers. Cambridge, Harvard University Press. 7 vols.

DIRK BROUWER

September 1, 1902–January 31, 1966

BY G. M. CLEMENCE

IRK BROUWER, who contributed more to dynamical astronomy than any other astronomer of his time, died on
January 31, 1966, after a week in hospital; his death was occasioned by an acute disorder of the heart. He is survived by his
widow and an only son, James.

Brouwer was born in Rotterdam, the Netherlands, on
September 1, 1902, the son of a civil service employee. As a student in the University of Leiden he studied mathematics and
astronomy, coming under the influence of Willem de Sitter,
who in his own day was the dean of that branch of astronomy
in which Brouwer was to do most of his work. Receiving the
Ph.D. degree in 1927 under de Sitter, Brouwer came to the
United States as a fellow of the International Education Board,
spending a year at the University of California in Berkeley and
at Yale University, where he was to remain the rest of his life.

His initial appointment at Yale was in 1928 as research assistant to Ernest W. Brown, who was then the greatest living
authority on the motion of the moon. After rising through the
usual junior ranks, in 1941 he was appointed professor, chairman of the Department of Astronomy, and director of the Observatory, and in 1944 Munson Professor of Natural Philosophy
and Astronomy, posts which he held until his death.

Also in 1941, when the American Astronomical Society acquired ownership of the *Astronomical Journal*, Brouwer was appointed editor, and later senior editor, another post he held until his death.

He was elected to the National Academy of Sciences in 1951, and was awarded the Gold Medal of the Royal Astronomical Society in 1955. Among his other honors were: George Darwin Lecturer, Fellow of the American Academy of Arts and Sciences, Correspondent of the Royal Netherlands Academy, Honorary Doctor of the University of La Plata, and Corresponding Member of the Academy of Sciences of Buenos Aires. He was also awarded the Bruce Medal of the Astronomical Society of the Pacific, the decision being taken the month before his death, and the actual award being made posthumously.

Brouwer was the author (jointly with the writer) of a successful book, *Methods of Celestial Mechanics* (1961), which has also been published in a Russian translation.

He was active in the International Astronomical Union, serving six years as President of the Commission on Asteroids and Comets, six years as President of the Commission on Celestial Mechanics, as chairman of a working group on photographic astrometry, and as a member of a working group on the system of astronomical constants.

The subject of dynamical astronomy (or celestial mechanics) traditionally comprises the study of the motions of planets and satellites. In any particular case the aim is to develop mathematical expressions that will yield the coordinates of the body in question as functions of the time, such that substitution of any value of the time, past or future, will yield the whereabouts of the body. Obviously this aim is not attainable unless knowledge of the beginning and end of the solar system is available; hence in practice it is attempted to solve the problem for the span of years during which a body has been observed, and to project the work as far into the future as is practicable, which in ordinary cases is some centuries.

The study of motions within a cluster of stars, or within a galaxy, is also included in dynamical astronomy, but this subject has become prominent only since 1950; Brouwer declined to interest himself in it, saying that there was plenty for him to do in the fields that he knew something about.

An indispensable adjunct of classical dynamical astronomy is astrometry, which includes the determination of accurate positions and motions of some tens of thousands of stars, to which in turn the positions of planets and satellites may be referred. Brouwer was early introduced to astrometry by Frank Schlesinger, his predecessor as director of the Yale Observatory, who devised and practiced new techniques in the field, and Brouwer never ceased to do all he could on the theoretical side for the advancement of the subject. Following Schlesinger's death, he also gave active support to the continuation of Schlesinger's astrometric program, until his own death.

Brouwer's most important contributions to dynamical astronomy proper are as follows.

He and W. J. Eckert devised a new scheme for the differential correction of orbits of planets and satellites, in which the differential coefficients are derived from the latest approximation to the orbit in the simplest possible way, with a minimum of calculation. The method is now used almost exclusively throughout the world.

He showed that, in the numerical integration of orbits, the errors in five of the six parameters increase proportionally to the square root of the number of steps of integration, whereas the error of the sixth (the position in the orbit) increases with the three-halves power of the number of steps.

He devised a plan for eliminating the systematic errors of star catalogues of position by means of selected minor planets.

He developed a new form of planetary theory, in which the use of rectangular coordinates is made to yield analytic expressions of the utmost elegance and simplicity.

He established a definite connection between Encke's comet and the Taurid group of meteors.

With W. J. Eckert and the writer he calculated precise values of the coordinates of the five outer planets for more than four hundred years. This work, the first extensive application of high-speed calculating machines to the subject, is still the standard of comparison for all similar work done since.

He established that the fluctuations in the rate of rotation of the earth are of a statistical character that would be produced by random disturbances in the interior of the earth, and in 1950 he proposed the name *ephemeris time,* which has been adopted throughout the world for the astronomical measure of time that is free from such fluctuations.

He solved the problem of the effect of the oblateness of the earth on the motions of artificial satellites. This solution, of great practical value as well as theoretical interest, is completely general, and immediately applicable to any satellite.

He solved the problem of the existence of the Kirkwood gaps in the ring of minor planets, which had baffled astronomers for half a century.

In mentioning his most important contributions I limit myself arbitrarily to ten. In fact there are many others that are hardly less important than these.

Although administrative and financial affairs did not interest him as a rule, he could be active enough when he thought the occasion required it. The most notable case in point was the construction after almost a decade of persistent effort of a twin-astrographic telescope, with the aid of the Ford Foundation, at the Yale-Columbia Southern Observatory, for the purpose of completing the extragalactic survey that had been undertaken for the northern sky by the Lick Observatory. He lived to see the first year of active operation of the new instrument, undertaken with the aid of the National Science Foundation.

The launching in 1957 of the first artificial satellite soon led to an upsurge of interest in dynamical astronomy, to an extent unprecedented in the history of the subject. In the immediately preceding decades the number of active workers in the field had been about six in the United States, with perhaps a slightly greater number in the rest of the world. Now within a single year scores of students were seized with the desire to study dynamical astronomy, and the demand for teachers of the subject far exceeded the supply. In part the demand was generated by government laboratories having responsibility for tracking space-vehicles, but more important seems to have been the general public interest in space activities. The Yale Department of Astronomy had many more prospective graduate students applying for admission than it could accommodate.

Brouwer conceived the idea of creating a summer institute in dynamical astronomy, afterwards popularly known as SIDA, consisting of an intensive six-week course of lectures, four or five daily, which would be open to college teachers and to employees of industry and government. With the aid of the National Science Foundation six such institutes were held before his death, and they were widely acclaimed.

With a view to the more distant future, Brouwer envisioned an Institute of Celestial Mechanics at Yale, which would consist of a small resident faculty, visiting lecturers, and graduate students. With the aid of the Office of Naval Research and the Air Force Office of Scientific Research the Institute was created in 1962 and is still flourishing.

These two educational activities demonstrate that Brouwer's power of innovation was by no means limited to his own research.

One of his more notable personal attributes was absolute

integrity. His word was always his bond, in small matters as well as great ones. Several times I knew him to decline to be released from obligations that must have been onerous, even when the circumstances in which they were made had been substantially altered.

He was also exceedingly persevering. An example was his study of the English language, which he continued unremittingly to the very end of his life, although his English was better than that of most native Americans. For more than twenty years he asked me to criticize nearly everything he published for grammar, rhetoric, and style; and when we were together he often requested me to justify the form of something I had said or written.

He disciplined himself to speak without notes, and most of his lectures were models of clarity and logical development. Usually he had a book or two with him but would refer to them only at rare intervals. He had an engaging custom, while at the blackboard, of giving emphasis to his remarks by jabbing vigorously with the chalk; when it broke, which was often, he habitually caught the flying piece in mid-air without obvious exertion; it seemed to fall into his hand.

He claimed to have no appreciation of the fine arts, and indeed to be unable to distinguish two musical pitches unless they were nearly half an octave apart. But he would sit cheerfully through musical performances or visit art galleries when the amenities seemed to require it, and he was always ready with a graceful comment afterwards.

He was nearly always cheerful, even-tempered, energetic, and active, very seldom ill, never moving slowly, but always anxious to get to the pending item of business. His principal exercise consisted of walking, mowing the lawn, and shoveling snow, all of which he did vigorously. He had nothing I would call a hobby, although he enjoyed watching an occasional game of baseball or soccer, and he could usually report the relative standings in major-league baseball at a moment's notice. He was also compassionate; among his most disagreeable duties were flunking a student and rejecting a manuscript, which he always did as gently as possible, often at considerable cost of his own time. With dishonesty, evasion, or malfeasance he had no patience; I saw his wrath break out on two occasions, and I am sure the miscreants never forgot it.

BIBLIOGRAPHY

KEY TO ABBREVIATIONS

Am. Astron. Soc. Publ. = American Astronomical Society Publications
Am. Phil. Soc. Year Book = American Philosophical Society Year Book
Astron. J. = Astronomical Journal
Astron. Nachr. = Astronomische Nachrichten
Astron. Pap. Am. Ephemeris Naut. Almanac = United States Naval
    Observatory. Astronomical Papers prepared for the use of the American
    Ephemeris and Nautical Almanac
Beob. -Zirk. Astron. Nachr. = Beobachtungs-Zirkular der Astronomischen
    Nachrichten
Bull. Astron. = Bulletin Astronomique
Bull. Astron. Inst. Neth. = Bulletin of the Astronomical Institutes of
    the Netherlands
Carnegie Inst. Wash. Year Book = Carnegie Institution of Washington
    Year Book
Monthly Notices Roy. Astron. Soc. = Monthly Notices of the Royal
    Astronomical Society
Res. Rev. = Research Reviews
Trans. Intern. Astron. Union = Transactions of the International
    Astronomical Union
Trans. Yale Univ. Astron. Obs. = Transactions of the Yale University
    Astronomical Observatory
Yale Sci. Mag. = Yale Scientific Magazine

1924

A new determination of the mass of Titan by Hill's method. Bull.
    Astron. Inst. Neth., 2:119-20.
On the constitution of the earth. Bull. Astron. Inst. Neth., 2:161-63.
Over de samenstalling der aarde. Koninklijke Akademie van Wet-
    enschappen Afdeeling natuurkunde Verslagen van de gewone
    vergaderingen, 33(7):617-18.

1927

The variable star of the Cephei type H.D. 154365; $16^h59^m.9$, $-26°$
    $27'$ (1900). Bull. Astron. Inst. Neth., 4:99-101.
Discussion of observations of Jupiter's satellites made at Johannes-
    burg in the years 1908-1926. Annals of the Observatory at Lei-
    den, 16(pt. 1):7-99.

1929

With E. W. Brown. Compilation and discussion of 413 occultations observed in 1927. Astron. J., 39:97-109.

1930

The correction to the central line of a solar eclipse with application to the eclipse of April 28, 1930. Astron. J., 40:27-30.
With E. W. Brown. Preliminary value of the error of the moon's mean longitude for 1929. Astron. J., 40:91.
Discussion of the annual term in the residuals in the moon's longitude. Astron. J., 40:161-68.
With E. W. Brown. Compilation and discussion of 746 occultations observed in 1928. Astron. J., 40:185-200.

1931

With E. W. Brown. Analysis of records made on the Loomis Chronograph by three Shortt clocks and a crystal oscillator. Monthly Notices Roy. Astron. Soc., 91:575-91.
With E. W. Brown. Compilation and discussion of 722 occultations observed in 1929. Astron. J., 41:53-69.
Interesting examples of the limb effect and errors in star positions in occultations. Astron. J., 41:69-70.

1932

With E. W. Brown. Compilation and discussion of 663 occultations observed in 1930. Astron. J., 41:185-96.
Occultations of Pleiades stars by the moon, observed at Yale Observatory on February 15, 1932. Astron. J., 42:17-19.
With E. W. Brown. Tables for the development of the disturbing function with schedules for harmonic analysis. Trans. Yale Univ. Astron. Obs., 6(pt. 5):69-157.
Occultation of Pleiades stars on December 10-11, 1932. Popular Astronomy, 40:612-13.

1933

With E. W. Brown. Change from 6″ to 5″ in the reduction of the occultations observed in 1933. Astron. J., 42:125.
With E. W. Brown. Occultations of the year 1924 collected and reduced by the Bond Club. Astron. J., 42:145-48.

With E. W. Brown. Compilation and discussion of 859 occultations observed in 1931. Astron. J., 42:181-93.

On the reduction to apparent place of occultation stars. Astron J., 43:25-29.

Theory and tables of the motion of (588) Achilles. Trans. Yale Univ. Astron. Obs., 6(pt. 7):177-88.

With E. W. Brown. Revision of the residuals from occultations of the years 1923-1926 with additions. Astron. J., 43:49-55.

1934

With E. W. Brown. Compilation and discussion of 1199 occultations observed in 1932. Astron. J., 43:137-52.

1935

The minor planets. Telescope, 2:12-18, 26.

On the determination of systematic corrections to star positions from observations of minor planets. Astron. J., 44:57-63.

With E. W. Brown. Compilation and discussion of 1194 occultations observed in 1933. Astron. J., 44:129-46.

1936

With F. E. Nisoli. Occultations of Pleiades stars by the moon, observed at Yale Observatory on February 10-11, 1935. Astron. J., 44:95-96.

Occultations—how and why. Amateur Astronomy, 2:2, 11-12.

Ephemeris of (287) Nephthys. Opposition 1936, September 6. Astron. Nachr., 259:361-62.

Report for Commission des Ephémérides. Trans. Intern. Astron. Union, 5:31.

With E. W. Brown. Compilation and discussion of 1483 occultations observed in 1934. Astron. J., 45:153-60.

1937

With E. W. Brown. Theory of the eighth satellite of Jupiter. Trans. Yale Univ. Astron. Obs., 6(pt. 2):189-211.

With E. W. Brown. Preliminary value for the deviation of the moon's mean longitude for the year 1935. Astron. J., 46:60.

With W. J. Eckert. The use of rectangular coordinates in the differential correction of orbits. Astron. J., 46:125-32.

On the accumulation of errors in numerical integration. Astron J., 46:149-53.

With E. W. Brown. Compilation and discussion of 1405 occultations observed in 1935. Astron. J., 46:181-88.

1938

New theories of Uranus and Neptune. Astron. Nachr., 265:143.

Editor and completer: On the system of astronomical constants, by W. de Sitter. Bull. Astron. Inst. Neth., 8:213-31.

Ernest William Brown. Science, 88:316-18.

1939

Change from 3″ to 1.5″ in the reduction of occultations observed in 1939. Astron. J., 47:184; Beob.-Zirk. Astron. Nachr., 21:3.

Obiturary notice of Ernest William Brown. Monthly Notices Roy. Astron. Soc., 99:300-7.

The occultation campaign. Outline of a revised program. Astron. J., 47:191-92.

Remarks on the theories of Uranus and Neptune. Am. Astron. Soc. Publ., 9:217-18.

Compilation and discussion of occultations observed in 1936. Astron. J., 48:116-18.

Report for Commission des Ephémérides. Trans. Intern. Astron. Union, 6:22-23.

Correction in the compilation and discussion of occultations observed in 1936. Astron. J., 48:160.

1940

Comparison of Newcomb's Tables of Neptune with an orbit obtained by numerical integrations, and discussion of the perturbations by Pluto. Am. Astron. Soc. Publ., 10:7-8.

The problem of Neptune's motion. Sky, 4(6):3-5.

Compilation and discussion of occultations observed in 1937. Astron. J., 49:17-19.

With Frank Schlesinger. Ernest William Brown, 1866-1938. National Academy of Sciences, *Biographical Memoirs,* 21:243-73.

1941

Occultations of the moon. Beob.-Zirk. Astron. Nachr., 23:8-9.

Forty years of photographic astrometry. Sky, 5(4):3-5, 8.

Yale looks at the sky. Yale Sci. Mag., 15(11):3-5.

The reference system with a view to planetary dynamics. Annals of the New York Academy of Sciences, 42(2):133-49.

Program for the determination of systematic corrections to fundamental catalogues from observations of minor planets. Carnegie Inst. Wash. Year Book, 40:31-33.

1942

Variation orbits of the restricted problem of three bodies. Am. Astron. Soc. Publ., 10:159. (A)

Compilation and discussion of occultations observed in 1938. Astron. J., 49:137-38.

Compilation and discussion of occultations observed in 1939. Astron. J., 50:4-5.

With Ann S. Young. Revision of the occultation results for the years 1933 to 1935. Astron. J., 50:43-45.

Summary of the parallaxes of forty-eight stars. Astron. J., 50:70-71.

Some problems in the development of new general theories of Uranus and Neptune. Am. Astron. Soc. Publ., 10:247.

Program for the determination of systematic corrections to fundamental catalogues from observations of minor planets. Carnegie Inst. Wash. Year Book, 41:25.

1943

Report of Grant Number 625. Determination by photography of the positions and proper motions of approximately 106,000 stars between declinations $+20°$ and $-30°$. Am. Phil. Soc. Year Book 1942, 98-101.

With Hans G. Hertz. Compilation and discussion of occultations observed in 1940. Astron. J., 50:105-6.

With F. W. Keator. McMillen's spherographical system of celestial navigation. Aero Digest, 42(4):116-18, 139-40, 266-68.

Frank Schlesinger, 1871-1943. Scientific Monthly, 57:375-77.

Program for the determination of systematic corrections to fundamental catalogues from observations of minor planets. Carnegie Inst. Wash. Year Book, 42:23.

1944

With Hans G. Hertz. Compilation and discussion of occultations observed in 1941. Astron. J., 51:30-31.

With F. Keator and D. McMillen. *Spherographical Navigation.* New York, The Macmillan Company. xxiii + 200 pp.

Integration of the equations of general planetary theory in rectangular coordinates. Astron. J., 51:37-43.

With Louise F. Jenkins. Measurements of the binary system 2398 on parallax plates taken at the Yerkes Observatory. Astron. J., 51:54-57.

Program for the determination of systematic corrections to fundamental catalogues from observations of minor planets. Carnegie Inst. Wash. Year Book, 43:19.

1945

Compilation and discussion of occultations observed in 1942. Astron. J., 41:144-45.

Frank Schlesinger, 1871-1943. National Academy of Sciences, *Biographical Memoirs,* 24:103-44.

1946

The motion of a particle with negligible mass under the gravitational attraction of a spheroid. Astron. J., 51:223-31.

Trojan planets. In: *Encyclopaedia Britannica,* Vol. 22, pp. 490-91. Chicago, Encyclopaedia Britannica, Inc.

Celestial mechanics. In: *Encyclopaedia Britannica,* Vol. 5, pp. 91-93. Chicago, Encyclopaedia Britannica, Inc.

A survey of the dynamics of close binary systems. Astron. J., 52:57-63.

With G. M. Clemence. Numerical development of the disturbing function by correction of an approximate development. Astron. J., 52:64-67.

In memoriam: Dr. Jan Woltjer, Jr. Hemel en Dampkring, 44:169.

1947

With C. B. Watts. A comparison of occultations and meridian observations of the moon. Astron. J., 52:169-76.

Jan Woltjer, Jr. Monthly Notices Roy. Astron. Soc., 107:59-60.

Secular variations of the elements of Encke's comet. Astron. J., 52: 190-98.

1948

Celestial mechanics. Res. Rev., pp. 19-22.

Search for minor planets that have not been observed in recent years owing to interruption of observations caused by the war. Am. Phil. Soc. Year Book 1947, pp. 114-15.

1949

The work of Commission 20 of the International Astronomical Union. The Griffith Observer, 13:29-30, 38.

One hundred years: 1849-1949. Astron. J., 55:1-2.

1950

Current problems of Pluto. Sky and Telescope, 9:103-5.

With A. J. J. van Woerkom. The secular variations of the orbital elements of the principal planets. Astron. Pap. Am. Ephemeris Naut. Almanac, 13:85-107.

Report for Commission du Mouvement et de la Figure de la Lune. Trans. Intern. Astron. Union, 7:170.

Report of Commission des Positions et des Mouvements des Petits Planètes, des Comètes et des Satellites. Trans. Intern. Astron. Union, 7:217-29.

With J. Schilt. Proper motions in the southern selected areas: Yale-Columbia Southern Station. Trans. Intern. Astron. Union, 7: 334-35.

Families of minor planets and related distributional problems. Astron. J., 55:162-63.

Contributions to Colloque International sur les Constantes Fondamentales de l'Astronomie. I. A new determination of the solar parallax from the parallactic inequality in the moon's longitude. II. Comments on the masses of the inner planets. III. Notes on investigations in progress. Bull. Astron., 15:165-80.

With G. M. Clemence. The motions of the five outer planets. Yale Sci. Mag., 35:13-14, 38, 40, 42, 44, 52; Res. Rev., pp. 6-13. (See 1951.)

1951

With G. M. Clemence. The motions of the five outer planets. Sky and Telescope, 10:83-86.

Secular variations of the orbital elements of minor planets. Astron. J., 56:9-32.

Comparison of numerical integration of the motions of Uranus and Neptune with Newcomb's tables. Astron. J., 56:35.

With Joseph Ashbrook. The minor planet 619 Triberga and the mass of the moon. Astron. J., 56:57-58.

The accurate measurement of time. Physics Today, 4(8):6-15.

With W. J. Eckert and G. M. Clemence. Coordinates of the five outer planets 1653-2060. Astron. Pap. Am. Ephemeris Naut. Almanac, 12:1-327.

1952

A new discussion of the changes in the earth's rate of rotation. Proceedings of the National Academy of Sciences, 38:1-12.

With A. J. J. van Woerkom. The H-R diagram, derived from the new General Catalogue of trigonometric parallaxes. Astron. J., 57:2-3. (A)

A study of the changes in the rate of rotation of the earth. Astron. J., 57:125-46.

1953

The polar motion and changes in the earth's orbit. In: *Climatic Change,* ed. by Harlow Shapley, pp. 159-64. Cambridge, Harvard University Press.

1954

How long is a second? Yale Sci. Mag., 28:18-20, 42.

Precise measurement of time. Astronomical League Bulletin, 4:1-2.

With J. J. Nassau. Soviet Astronomy. Science, 120:442-43.

Report of Sub-Commission de la Observation Photographique et Visual d'Etoiles jusqu'à la 9-me Grandeur. Trans. Intern. Astron. Union, 8:128-29.

Report of Commission du Mouvement et de la Figure de la Lune. Trans. Intern. Astron. Union, 8:218.

Report of Commission des Positions et des Mouvements des Petites

Planètes, des Comètes et des Satellites. Trans. Intern. Astron. Union, 8:275-89.

With J. J. Nassau. The dedication of the new Poulkovo Observatory. Sky and Telescope, 14:4-6.

The Yale photographic zone programme. Trans. Intern. Astron. Union, 8:778-81.

1955

With G. M. Clemence. The accuracy of the coordinates of the five outer planets and the invariable plane. Astron. J., 60:116-26.

The masses of the outer planets; accuracy of the numerical integration orbits; classical planetary theory in rectangular coordinates; generalized planetary theory. (Acceptance speech upon receiving the Gold Medal of the Royal Astronomical Society.) Observatory, 75:96-100.

The objective grating in photographic astrometry with wide-angle cameras. Publications of the Eleventh Astrometric Conference of the U.S.S.R., pp. 70-73.

Current research on planetary theory. Yale Sci. Mag., 39(5):13-16.

1956

The motions of the outer planets. Monthly Notices Roy. Astron. Soc., 113:221-35.

Current trends in minor planets research. Vistas in Astronomy, 2:943-48.

1957

Report on Sub-Commission des Catalogues Photographiques d'Etoiles jusqu'à la 9-me Grandeur. Trans. Intern. Astron. Union, 9:115-18.

Report on Commission des Positions et des Mouvements des Petites Planètes, des Comètes et des Satellites. Trans. Intern. Astron. Union, 9:284-93.

1958

Celestial mechanics. Astron. J., 63:401-2.

Outlines of general theories of the Hill-Brown and Delaunay types for orbits of artificial satellites. Astron. J., 63:433-43.

1959

The rotation of the earth and atomic time standards. Astron. J., 64:81-124.

Fluctuations and secular changes in the earth's rotation. Astron. J., 64:97-99.

With E. Lilley. The solar parallax and the hydrogen line. Astron. J., 64:338-39. (A)

Solution of the Problem of Artificial Satellite Theory without Drag. (Air Research Development Command, United States Air Force Project: Space Track, Air Force Cambridge Research Center; Contract No. TN-59-638.) New Haven, Yale University Observatory. 46 pp.

Solution of the problem of artificial satellite theory without drag. Astron. J., 64:378-97; a correction, *ibid.*, 65:108.

Comments on general theories of planetary orbits. Proceedings of Symposia in Applied Mathematics, 9:152-66.

1960

Report of Commission de la Mécanique Celeste. Trans. Intern. Astron. Union, 10:109-13.

Report of Sub-Commission des Catalogues Photographiques d'Etoiles jusqu'à la 9-me Grandeur. Trans. Intern. Astron. Union, 10: 114-16.

A method of constructing a revised General Catalogue. Astron. J., 65:186-89.

The use of a very wide-angle camera for catalogue work. Astron. J., 65:228-29.

Report on the First Inter-American Conference on Astronomy at La Plata and Cordoba, October 30 to November 3, 1959. Astron. J., 65:235-38.

With G. Hori. Theoretical evaluation of atmospheric drag effects in the motion of an artificial satellite. Astron. J., 65:342. (A)

1961

With G. Hori. Theoretical evaluation of atmospheric drag effects in the motion of an artificial satellite. II. Astron. J., 66:39. (A)

With G. Hori. Theoretical evaluation of atmospheric drag effects in the motion of an artificial satellite. Astron. J., 66:193-225.

With G. Hori.   Appendix to the theoretical evaluation of atmospheric drag effects in the motion of an artificial satellite.   Astron. J., 66:264-65.

With G. M. Clemence.   Orbits and masses of planets and satellites. In: *The Solar System,* Vol. 3, *Planets and Satellites,* ed. by Kuiper and Middlehust, pp. 31-94. Chicago, University of Chicago Press.

Research on the Theories of the Motion of Artificial Satellites. (Air Force Command Control Development Division—Yale University; Contract No. AF-19(604)-4137.) New Haven, Yale University Observatory. 11 pp.

The use of canonical variables in celestial mechanics.   Proceedings of the International Meeting on Problems of Astronomy and Celestial Mechanics, pp. 67-74.

With G. Clemence.   *Methods of Celestial Mechanics.* New York, Academic Press, Inc. xii + 598 pp.

1962

Analytical study of resonance caused by solar radiation pressure. *Dynamics of Satellites,* pp. 34-39.

Progress and problems in analytical celestial mechanics.   In: *Space Age Astronomy,* ed. by Armin J. Deutsch and Wolfgang B. Klemperer, pp. 347-52. New York, Academic Press, Inc.

With G. Hori.   The motion of the moon in space.   In: *Physics and Astronomy of the Moon,* ed. by Z. Kopal, pp. 1-26. New York, Academic Press, Inc.

An assessment of the present accuracy of the value of the astronomical unit.   Journal of the Institute of Navigation (London), 9(3): 306-10.

Report of Commission de la Mécanique Celeste.   Trans. Intern. Astron. Union, 11A:9-14.

Report of Sub-Commission des Catalogues Photographiques d'Etoiles jusqu'à la 9-me Grandeur.   Trans. Intern. Astron. Union, 11A:23-28.

1963

Review of celestial mechanics.   Annual Review of Astronomy and Astrophysics, 1:219-34.

The problem of the Kirkwood gaps in the asteroid belt. Astron. J., 68:152-59.

Canonical treatment of dissipative forces. In: *The Use of Artificial Satellites for Geodesy*, pp. 6-7. Amsterdam, North-Holland Publishing Company.

1965

With B. S. Yaplee, S. H. Knowles, A. Shapiro, K. J. Craig. The mean distance to the moon as determined by radar. Bull. Astron., 25:81-93.

Relations among some important astronomical constants. Bull. Astron., 25:241-68.

1966

With William H. Jefferys. Concerning Brouwer's paper on the Kirkwood gaps. Astron. J., 71:543.

Rollin T. Chamberlin

ROLLIN THOMAS CHAMBERLIN

October 20, 1881–March 6, 1948

BY F. J. PETTIJOHN

ROLLIN THOMAS CHAMBERLIN, the only son of Thomas Chrowder Chamberlin and Alma Isabel (Wilson) Chamberlin, was born on October 20, 1881, at Beloit, Wisconsin. His father, Professor of Geology at Beloit College, became the President of the University of Wisconsin (1887-1892), and was later called by William Rainey Harper to the new University of Chicago to establish and head the University's Department of Geology. Rollin Chamberlin's early years were, therefore, spent in Wisconsin. At the age of eleven he came to Chicago where he was destined to remain until his retirement and death.

Rollin Chamberlin spent virtually all his professional life at the University of Chicago, as a student, both undergraduate (S.B. 1903) and graduate (Ph.D. 1907), and as a member of the faculty of the Department of Geology. No other person had as long an association with the department.

After receiving his doctor's degree from Chicago, he was employed by the U.S. Geological Survey (1907-1908) to investigate dust explosions in coal mines. During this work he came up with the idea of using rock dust to reduce the explosion hazards. He returned to Chicago as Research Associate in 1909, was absent a year (1911-1912) studying the iron ores of

Brazil, was appointed instructor at Chicago in 1912, and was subsequently promoted to Assistant Professor in 1914, to Associate Professor in 1918, and to Professor in 1923. In 1923 he became managing editor of the *Journal of Geology* and its editor in 1929. Rollin continued as teacher and editor until 1947, the year he retired from active duty. He died March 6, 1948, at the age of sixty-six, from a coronary thrombosis, his third in the last six years of his life. He was survived by his wife, Dorothy (nee Dorothy Ingalls Smith), whom he married on November 11, 1922, at the age of forty-one, and his daughters, Frances and her twin sisters, Isabel and Louise.

Such are the bare facts of Rollin Chamberlin's career. Into what kind of a world was he born and in what way did his life reflect the times in which he lived?

THE BACKGROUND

The second half of the nineteenth century and the first decade of the twentieth were a period of ferment and excitement in geology. This was the time of the establishment of the U.S. Geological Survey and the Geological Society of America; it was the age of opening up the mining districts of the West and the iron ores of the Lake Superior region, of the unraveling of the glacial history of the continent, of the unearthing of the dinosaurs. The main lines of geologic history and its major concepts took form during this period of explosive development, which produced such leaders as G. K. Gilbert, C. R. Van Hise, A. C. Lawson, and T. C. Chamberlin in America and H. C. Sorby, J. J. Sederholm, H. Rosenbusch, and A. Heim in Europe. Petrography came into being with the study of thin sections in polarized light. Glacial geology, Precambrian geology, and the study of ore deposits became disciplines in their own right.

After an initial decade of activity, the first half of the

twentieth century was, in contrast, a period mainly of consolidation, of backing and filling, with no expansive developments other than in petroleum geology and exploration geophysics. Mining districts grew old and were worked out; old ideas were warmed over and lost their freshness; the hypothesis of continental drift was not yet respectable. The established schools lived largely on their past capital and basked in their former glory.

With the conclusion of World War II, a new era erupted, characterized by a tremendous expansion in the fringe areas and in other earth sciences—in geochemistry and geophysics, in meteorology and oceanography. The effect of these developments was to infuse new life, new techniques, new ideas into a discipline grown old. Radiogenic isotopes provide a new clock, stable isotopes a thermometer, the airborne magnetometer and scintillometer new exploratory tools, other remote sensing devices a new look at the oceans and the atmosphere, while paleomagnetism awakened new interest in continental drift. Experimental petrology and x-ray crystallography came of age. The results were overwhelming. Some schools moved with the times; others resisted. Chicago was one of the first to accept change, to promote it; the school became a model for change in other places. The influence of Barth, Bowen, Libby, and Urey at Chicago is felt to this day.

The Department of Geology at Chicago, established in 1892, was, at its inception, extraordinary, fully representative of the youth and vigor of the times. T. C. Chamberlin was its intellectual leader. It became, overnight, the leading department in the mid-continent and challenged the older schools of the East—Harvard, Yale, Johns Hopkins. The *Journal of Geology*, founded at the same time by T. C. Chamberlin, became the leading independent geological journal in America. The three-volume Chicago textbook of Chamberlin and Salisbury published in 1906 became the teacher's bible—after which virtually every textbook written during the next fifty years was patterned. Only the illustrations were changed. The department maintained its leadership without substantial change in thought or curriculum for several decades after T. C. Chamberlin's retirement. Only with the arrival of Bowen in 1937 was there evidence of the beginnings of a basic reorientation. It is in light of this background that we must look at R. T. Chamberlin's life and professional career. It spans the geological "Middle Ages" between the ebullient days of the nineteenth century and those of the present renaissance. Since all of Rollin Chamberlin's life and work was spent at Chicago, his career is inextricably bound up with the history of the department and is a mirror of the times in which he lived.

EDUCATION: FROM CHEMIST TO GEOLOGIST

Rollin Chamberlin's formal education began in 1889 at the First Ward Grammar School in Madison, Wisconsin. He attended this school until 1892 when his father left Wisconsin to go to Chicago. In Chicago, Chamberlin attended the Kenwood Grammar School, 1892-1895, and the Hyde Park High School from which he graduated in 1899. Rollin's interests in high school seemed largely to run to science, particularly physics and chemistry. His interest in the latter led to his setting up a chemistry laboratory in the basement of the family home in Chicago. The experiments performed were varied in character, leading among other things to the invention of a smokeless gunpowder—a line of experimentation that was terminated as a result of the complaint of the neighbors about the noise.

Following high school, Chamberlin spent one semester in 1899-1900 at the University of Geneva in Switzerland and one, in 1900, at the University of Zurich. Upon return to the United States he attended the University of Chicago, 1900-1903, and received departmental honors in chemistry. He continued his studies at Chicago, as a graduate student in geology, and received his Ph.D. (*summa cum laude*) in 1907. His doctoral dissertation reflected his interest in chemistry and dealt with the composition of gases occluded in rocks. Thus ended Rollin Chamberlin's formal education.

Until his senior year in the University, Chamberlin had planned to become a chemist, having had for some years a great enthusiasm for the subject. Chemistry, plus languages, had been his chief concern at the Swiss universities in 1899 and 1900. But his stay in the Alps kindled a lifelong interest in mountaineering and the out-of-doors. Field excursions and travel to faraway places appealed to Rollin and, as these fitted better in the career of a geologist, his interest shifted from chemistry to geology. For a time he was interested in both, as his doctoral thesis shows, but the issue was soon settled. Rollin accompanied his father as an assistant on the University of Chicago expedition to China—an expedition conceived by Mr. John D. Rockefeller. This round-the-world trip was a turning point in the younger Chamberlin's career. It tipped the scales in favor of geology and gave him a taste for travel and adventure from which he never recovered. The magnificent mountain ranges he traversed sparked an interest in crustal deformation and structure—a subject to which Rollin Chamberlin was to make his own contributions in due time.

GEOLOGIST

Chamberlin's main interest was in the problems of diastrophism, mountain building in particular. One of his earliest papers dealt with Appalachian folds (*J. Geol.*, 18:228), a study based on a traverse along the track of the Pennsylvania Railroad between Tyrone and Harrisburg, Pennsylvania. Along the traverse, nearly one hundred miles in length and made on foot, Chamberlin recorded many measurements of the dips of beds, his position being determined by railroad mile posts and telegraph poles (38 to the mile). From these data he prepared a cross-section with folded structures restored, calculated the apparent shortening of the earth's crust (his estimate later being confirmed by E. Cloos, *Bull. Geol. Soc. Am.*, 58:843), and calculated the depth of folding. A similar 135-mile traverse across the Colorado Rockies some years later made possible comparison of the two mountain systems. The Appalachians were considered to be a shallow, "thin-skinned" deformation; the folding in the Rockies was thought to involve a greater thickness of the earth's crust.

Chamberlin's interest in diastrophism extended to the larger problems. He was a supporter of the concept of the world-wide periodicity of diastrophism as the ultimate basis of correlation —a view strongly put forth by T. C. Chamberlin. He was interested also in the role of plutonism in the evolution of mountain chains. One of his papers dealing with this subject was whimsically titled "Whittling Down the Batholiths" (*Bull. Geol. Soc. Am.*, 38:109).

Chamberlin's interest in folds and overthrust faulting led to a period of pressure-box or structure model experimentation. Chamberlin's work with "pressure-box" models was considerable. Fashioned along the lines pioneered by Bailey Willis and earlier workers, his experiments had the same failings— wrong materials and improper scaling. It is of interest that three of Chamberlin's best-known students worked on model studies. F. P. Shepard, who got his doctor's degree at Chicago in 1923, was originally a structural geologist interested in the Rocky Mountain Trench. He was co-author with Chamberlin of a paper on some model experiments. T. A. Link, Ph.D. 1927, wrote a thesis based solely on experimentation. Shepard later became known as America's first marine geologist and

Link became one of Canada's leading petroleum geologists. Best known for his concern with model studies was M. King Hubbert, who, though he performed no experiments, placed the whole subject on a firmer footing by carrying over the theories of model scaling from engineering to geology. Hubbert, though nominally a student of Chamberlin's, can hardly be said to have done his work under Chamberlin's direction or supervision but, undoubtedly, his personal contact with the model studies of Chamberlin and his students while himself a graduate student at Chicago directed his attention to the problem of model studies. Hubbert provided the theoretical basis for model studies, though Hans Cloos and others had earlier achieved significant results by intuitive scaling.

Chamberlin's doctoral thesis on the gases occluded in rocks was a milestone in chemical geology—one which perhaps did not receive the attention due it at the time. The most recent work on the geochemical history of the earth and the acquisition of its atmosphere and the oceans by degassing of the mantle bears out the importance of Chamberlin's early work (see Rubey, *Bull. Geol. Soc. Am.,* 62:1111; *Geol. Soc. Am. Spec. Paper* 62:631).

So, also, it was with Chamberlin's work on glacial motion. His instrumental studies of ice movement and his demonstration of shear within the ice foreshadowed the sophisticated studies of what is now a science in its own right: glaciology. The methods initiated by Chamberlin have been refined and added to. The important point is the approach followed, namely instrumentation and measurements, which has now become the accepted pattern of study.

Chamberlin did not himself pursue the field of structural petrology of Hans Cloos nor the field of petrofabrics of B. Sander, though one of his students (J. T. Stark) did investigate the internal structures of a granite stock.

As far as this writer is aware, Rollin Chamberlin's name appears on no published geological map, that is, a map made from primary field observations. Chamberlin left field mapping to others, although his first assignment at the University of Chicago was to teach the summer field course, then given in the St. Croix region of Wisconsin and Minnesota. Chamberlin's contributions to tectonic theory were based mainly on exploration and field reconnaissance and on philosophical considerations. In some cases he relied on "pressure-box" experiments from which he reasoned by analogy to supplement data taken from the literature. On other topics, however, Chamberlin's publications were based on data collected firsthand. His work on the geology of the beds containing human bones at Vero, Florida, on the motion of glaciers, on the coral reefs of Samoa, and on the iron ores of Brazil falls into this category.

An objective examination of Rollin Chamberlin's earlier publications shows that many were records of work done to verify or test ideas earlier put forth by T. C. Chamberlin. Rollin Chamberlin's study of glacial motion was made to test ideas developed by the elder Chamberlin as a result of his studies of glaciers in north Greenland. The studies on the depth of folding in the Appalachians and Rockies were applications of a concept presented in the Chamberlin and Salisbury three-volume *Geology* (II:125). Even the study of gases occluded in rocks was an outgrowth of the planetesimal concept of earth formation and generation of the atmosphere and hydrosphere as formulated by T. C. Chamberlin. Rollin Chamberlin held rigidly to the notion of the permanence of the continents and ocean basins and he gave short treatment to the concept of drifting continents—as did most American geologists a few decades ago. He accepted the world-wide periodicity of diastrophism as the ultimate bases of correlation—a notion challenged in recent years.

In Chamberlin's later years he became involved in the

research program of the Yellowstone-Bighorn Research Association, of which he, Walter Bucher of Columbia, and especially W. T. Thom, Jr. of Princeton, were the moving spirits. For a period of years, from about 1932 to his retirement, Chamberlin and his students, Victor Church, E. C. H. Lammers, Vincent Nelson, and Leland Horberg among others, worked diligently on the geology and structure of the Wyoming-Montana region. Out of this work emerged an analysis and synthesis of the structural history of the region. These years were, in many ways, the most productive of Chamberlin's career. His work was more original, less hampered or restricted by his earlier indoctrination and training. Out of it came concepts of crustal deformation involving rigid block and incompetent sediments—principles of interest outside the geographic area from which they were formulated.

EDITOR

For nearly a quarter of a century Rollin Chamberlin was editor of the *Journal of Geology,* a journal founded and edited by his father and published by the University of Chicago. Rollin Chamberlin gave a considerable part of his life to the *Journal* and by his service to that publication rendered a great service to geologists and the science of geology. His association with the *Journal* exceeds in length even that of his father. Rollin Chamberlin was made a member of the editorial staff in 1912; he became managing editor in 1923 and editor in 1929. He remained in this capacity until his retirement on June 30, 1947. Readers and authors alike owe Rollin Chamberlin a great debt for this thirty-five years of painstaking and, at times, tedious labor. Many readers, perhaps, are unaware of the patient and unending effort contributed gratuitously by an editor in assisting authors in the preparation of their manuscripts for publication.

Rollin Chamberlin's service to the *Journal* did not consist solely of the discharge of his editorial duties. He was also the author of many articles and reviews. His first contribution, "The Glacial Features of the St. Croix Dalles Region," appeared in Volume 13 in 1905. His last paper, "The Moon's Lack of Folded Ranges," came out in Volume 53, 1945. In all, Chamberlin wrote some thirty-six articles and countless reviews for the *Journal*.

MOUNTAINEER

Rollin Chamberlin had an abiding love of mountains. He was an inveterate mountaineer. He combined his love of climbing and exploration with his professional interest in the origin and structure of mountains. It was his stay in Switzerland, as a student in 1899-1900, that kindled his interest in high places. He made his first ascent, the Titlis, alone in 1900. For the next forty years he traveled far and wide and, whenever the opportunity arose, spent his time in climbing the highest peaks. He made his last climb, Storm Point, in the Tetons in 1940.

Some of his mountaineering adventures found their way into print. He describes, for example, his explorations in the Cariboo Mountains of British Columbia where, with Allen Carpé of the American Alpine Club, he made first ascents of nine peaks in this range (*Geog. Soc. Phila.*, 25:59 and 27:121). His ascent of Orizaba, North America's second highest peak (elev. 18,696 feet), a climb made with A. P. Coleman and H. F. Reid, is reported in the *Journal* of the American Alpine Club (I:2, 160-66). In all, Chamberlin had sixty-three notable ascents to his credit, including the Matterhorn and all the other more famous peaks in the Alps (twenty-three in all), various peaks in Alaska, the Pyrenees, the Tetons, the Sierras, the Cascades, and the Canadian and Colorado Rockies. One of his last climbs was the Grand Teton in 1938, on which excursion he was accompanied by his oldest daughter, Frances. The latter was infected with her father's enthusiasm for the mountains and has a notable number of climbs to her own credit. Chamberlin joined the American Alpine Club in 1921, was a contributor to its journal, and presented the club with the gigantic ice-axe used by Professor Salisbury during the Peary Relief Expedition of 1895.

WORLD TRAVELER

Rollin Chamberlin traveled extensively at a time when world travel was far less common and far less easy than it now is. His first trip abroad was to Switzerland for a year of study when he was but eighteen. In 1909 he was a member of the Oriental Educational Investigation Commission to China—an assignment which involved a trans-Pacific journey with stops at Hawaii and Japan. The party assembled in Shanghai in February of 1909 and for nearly five months thereafter traveled by rail, river boat, sedan chairs, and Peking carts studying fifteen of the eighteen provinces of China with short excursions into Mongolia and Manchuria. The Chinese venture ended, the party returned by way of the Trans-Siberian railroad and Europe, across which they zigzagged from the North Cape to the Balkans. A partial account of this journey appeared in the *National Geographic Magazine* (XXII:1094-1119) and in the *University of Chicago Magazine* (March 1910:150-55).

In 1911 and 1912 Chamberlin was in Brazil studying the iron ores of that country. Upon completion of this task he visited Chile and other South American countries. In 1914 he visited Australia. In 1920 he participated in the Carnegie Institution Marine Biological Expedition to Samoa where he made a study of the coral reefs surrounding Tutuila. Interest in glacial motion took him to Alaska, Switzerland, and British Columbia. Other travel included attendance at the International Geological Congresses in Mexico in 1906, Canada in 1913, and South

Africa in 1929. In the course of time Chamberlin visited all the continents, Antarctica alone excepted.

Chamberlin's travels gave him a perspective few had and were perhaps the underlying reason for his interest in such subjects as continental structure, paleoclimatology, and mountain building. They certainly gave him a world-wide view held by few of his contemporaries. They also provided him with case histories and examples which he used effectively in discussion of controversial problems and which made him a formidable opponent.

His travels, as well as his writings, brought him into contact with the world's leading figures in geology. Many of these distinguished geologists were afterwards guests in Rollin Chamberlin's home in Chicago. Some of us were privileged to be included on such occasions.

THE MAN

The intellectual legacy left by Thomas Chrowder Chamberlin and Rollin D. Salisbury was husbanded and perpetuated in the Department of Geology after the death of these pre-eminent geologists. The senior faculty, and many of the junior staff also, were products of the early department, so it is small wonder that the general outlook and program inherited should be retained with little change for several decades. It is not surprising, therefore, that Rollin Thomas Chamberlin, named for the two principals, and wholly educated in the department when it was at its prime, should reflect in his professional outlook and orientation the tradition and philosophy inherited from the elder Chamberlin and Salisbury.

The relationship between father and son was very close indeed. As Rollin Chamberlin himself wrote in the memoir on his father: "They had many things in common and their companionship was most congenial. From early childhood the father talked to his son as to a grown person and so spontaneously there developed a complete understanding between them" (National Academy of Sciences, *Biographical Memoirs,* 15:391).

It is all the more remarkable, therefore, that, though he was not an innovator, nor one to depart much from traditional thought patterns, Rollin Chamberlin established a place for himself as an individual and as a scientist of some stature. He had, indeed, severe handicaps to overcome—having so preeminent a father and remaining in the institution in which he was educated—yet to a considerable degree he overcame them. His work on the degassing of rocks and the field measurement and study of glacial motion, as well as some of his work on continental evolution, was highly original and foreshadowed developments of more recent times.

Perhaps Rollin made his mark as a teacher as much as a scholar and an editor. At Chicago, he taught the courses in structural geology and shared the teaching of the course entitled "Continental Evolution" (first designated Geology 15-16, later Geology 215-216), a course geared to the second two volumes of *Geology* by T. C. Chamberlin and R. D. Salisbury. This course, together with its prerequisite, "Geologic Processes" (first taught by R. D. Salisbury and later by J H. Bretz), was the backbone of the Chicago curriculum for nearly four decades. These courses were taken by every Chicago student and were, for them, a memorable experience.

At an earlier stage in his career, Chamberlin taught the introductory courses in geology based on the well-known text, *College Geology*—an abridged version of the larger three-volume work. *College Geology* was ultimately revised by Rollin Chamberlin (and P. MacClintock) and brought out as two smaller volumes.

Chamberlin's basic honesty, sympathetic outreach, and

generosity with his time encouraged students to work with him. He sponsored more doctoral theses, perhaps, than any other member of the department at Chicago. In the later years many theses grew out of his association with the Yellowstone-Bighorn Research Association and its field camp at Red Lodge, Montana.

Rollin established a place for himself and grew steadily in stature. His achievements were recognized outside of the University. He served as Vice President of the Geological Society of America in 1933 and Vice President and Chairman of Section E, Geology and Geography, of the American Association for the Advancement of Science in 1933. He was awarded an honorary Sc.D. degree from Beloit College in 1929, was elected to the National Academy of Sciences in 1940, and became a member of the American Philosophical Society in 1943.

Rollin Chamberlin was a rather nervous individual. He was a pipe smoker whose pipe was continually going out, and a visit with him in his office was a conversation broken by intervals of silence for relighting his pipe. His energy was in part expended in his active life outside of the office. Of lean and wiry build, he engaged in strenuous sports. He was something of a baseball player in his early days, a very good handball player, at one time champion of the University, a tennis player all through his later years, and an active mountain climber all his life until a heart ailment put an end to all athletic activities. He was a baseball "fan" and had an astonishing knowledge of teams, players, and famous plays.

Rollin had a good sense of humor. He enjoyed a joke on himself, as well as on others. He was basically a conservative—in the best sense of the word—very loyal to the University of Chicago, but unhappy with the Robert M. Hutchins regime, and quite outspoken when he felt a principle was involved.

His open-mindedness and honesty made him a warm personal friend of all who knew him and, when disagreements arose, won the respect even of those who disagreed with him. He contributed much to the department at Chicago.

ACKNOWLEDGMENTS

Though the author alone is responsible for this memoir and for the judgments reflected therein, he has received help from many persons and sources. In particular, some factual details have been checked or supplied by Mrs. R. T. Chamberlin and Frances Chamberlin (Mrs. David A. Carter), and by J H. Bretz. Much information is contained in Fisher's history of the Department of Geology at Chicago (privately published) and in memorials prepared by J Harlen Bretz (*Science,* 108 [1948]:50), N. L. Bowen (*Proc. Geol. Soc. Am.,* 1948:135), D. J. Fisher (*Am. Phil. Soc. Yearbook* 1948: 244), and J. H. T. (*Am. Alpine J.,* 1949:205-6). Conversations with others who knew Rollin Chamberlin have helped fill in details.

BIBLIOGRAPHY

KEY TO ABBREVIATIONS

Am. Alpine J. = American Alpine Journal
Am. J. Sci. = American Journal of Science
Bernice Bishop Museum Spec. Publ. = Bernice Bishop Museum Special Publication
Bull. Am. Assoc. Petrol. Geologists = Bulletin of the American Association of Petroleum Geologists
Bull. Geol. Soc. Am. = Bulletin of the Geological Society of America
Carnegie Inst. Wash. Publ. = Carnegie Institution of Washington Publication
J. Geol. = Journal of Geology
Proc. Geol. Soc. Am. = Proceedings of the Geological Society of America
Univ. Chicago Mag. = University of Chicago Magazine

1905

The glacial features of the St. Croix Dalles region. J. Geol., 13:238-56.

1908

The gases in rocks. Carnegie Inst. Wash. Publ., pp. 106-80.
With T. C. Chamberlin. Early terrestrial conditions which may have favored organic synthesis. Science, 28:897-911.

1909

Notes on explosive mine gases and dusts, with special reference to explosions in the Monongah, Darr and Naomi coal mines. United States Department of the Interior, Geological Survey, Bulletin No. 383, 64 pp.; United States Department of the Interior, Bureau of Mines, Bulletin No. 26.
The gases in rocks. J. Geol., 17:534-68.

1910

With T. C. Chamberlin. Certain valley configurations in low latitudes. J. Geol., 18:117-24.
The Appalachian folds of central Pennsylvania. J. Geol., 18:228-51.
Older drifts in the St. Croix region. J. Geol., 18:542-48.
Travel in the interior of China. Univ. Chicago Mag., 2:150-55.

1911

With T. C. Chamberlin. Certain phases of glacial erosion. J. Geol., 19:193-216.

Populous and beautiful Szechuan. National Geographic Magazine, 22:1094-1119.

1912

The physical setting of the Chilean borate deposits. J. Geol., 20:763-68.

1913

With T. C. Chamberlin. Map of North America during the Great Ice Age. Chicago, Rand, McNally & Company.

1914

Diastrophism and the formative processes. VII. Periodicity of Paleozoic orogenic movements. J. Geol., 22:315-45.

1915

With E. C. Harder. The geology of central Minas Geraes, Brazil. I. General geology; II. Principal mineral deposits. J. Geol., 23:341-78, 385-424.

1917

Interpretation of the formations containing human bones at Vero, Florida. J. Geol., 25:25-39.

Further studies at Vero, Florida. J. Geol., 25:667-83.

1918

With W. Z. Miller. Low-angle faulting. J. Geol., 26:1-44.

On the mechanics of the great overthrusts. Science, 47:470. (A)

With J. T. Richards. Preliminary report on experiments relating to continental deformation. Science, 47:492. (A)

1919

The building of the Colorado Rockies. J. Geol., 27:145-64, 225-51.

A peculiar belt of oblique faulting. J. Geol., 27:602-13.

1920

Some glacier studies in Alaska. Science, 51:521. (A)

The geological interpretation of the coral reefs of Tutuila, Samoa. Carnegie Institution of Washington Year Book, 19:194-95.

1921

Vulcanism and mountain-making. A supplementary note. J. Geol., 29:166-72.

Tutuila, Samoa, and the coral reef problem. Bull Geol. Soc. Am., 32:28-29. (A)

Diastrophism and the formative processes. XIV. Groundwork for the study of megadiastrophism; part 2, The intimations of shell deformation. J. Geol., 29:416-25.

The framework of the Pacific and its relations to the Americas. Proceedings of the First Pan-Pacific Science Conference, Honolulu. Bernice Bishop Museum Spec. Publ. No. 7, Pt. I, 7.

The structure of the Cordillera of North and South America. Bernice Bishop Museum Spec. Publ. No. 7, Pt. I, 17.

1923

On the crustal shortening of the Colorado Rockies. Am. J. Sci., 6:215-21.

With F. P. Shepard. Some experiments in folding. J. Geol., 31:490-512.

1924

The significance of the framework of the continents. J. Geol., 32:545-74.

The geological interpretation of the coral reefs of Tutuila, American Samoa. Carnegie Inst. Wash. Publ., 340:145-78.

1925

Note on the geology of the Cariboo and Northern Gold Ranges. Alpine Journal (London), 37:85-86.

The wedge theory of diastrophism. J. Geol., 33:755-92.

1926

The origin and early stages of the earth. In: *The Nature of the World and of Man*, ed. by H. H. Newman, pp. 31-55. Chicago, University of Chicago Press.

1927

Exploration of the Cariboo Mountains of British Columbia. Bulletin of the Geographical Society of Philadelphia, 25:59-76; a correction, *ibid.*, 26:121-22, 1928.

Earthquakes. Transactions of the Kentucky Academy of Sciences, 2:155-64.

Whittling down the batholiths. Bull. Geol. Soc. Am., 38:109. (A)

Rewritten and revised by R. T. Chamberlin and Paul MacClintock. *College Textbook of Geology*, Pt. 1, *Geologic Processes and Their Results*, by T. C. Chamberlin and R. D. Salisbury. New York, Henry Holt & Co. xi + 445 pp.; 2d ed., 1933.

With T. A. Link. The theory of laterally-spreading batholiths. J. Geol., 35:319-53.

Glacier motion as a type of rock deformation. Science, 66:461. (A)

1928

Instrumental work on the nature of glacier motion. J. Geol., 36:1-30.

The strain ellipsoid and Appalachian structures. J. Geol., 36:85-90.

Some of the objections to Wegener's theory. In: *Theory of Continental Drift: A Symposium*, pp. 83-87. Chicago, University of Chicago Press.

More Cariboo climbs. Univ. Chicago Mag., 20:307-13.

1930

Rewritten and revised by R. T. Chamberlin and Paul MacClintock. *College Textbook of Geology*, Pt. 2, *Historical Geology*, by T. C. Chamberlin and R. D. Salisbury. New York, Henry Holt & Co. ix + 497 pp.

The level of baselevel. J. Geol., 38:166-73.

The injustice of misleading citations. Bull Am. Assoc. Petrol. Geologists, 14:521-22.

The ascent of Orizaba. Am. Alpine J., 1:2, 160-66.

Isostasy from the geological point of view. Journal of the Washington Academy of Sciences, 20:454-58.

1931

Isostasy from the geological point of view. J. Geol., 39:1-23.

Memorial of Rollin D. Salisbury. Bull. Geol. Soc. Am., 42:126-38.

The zone of cavities and the zone of continuity. Bull. Geol. Soc. Am., 42:194-95.

Richard Alexander Fullerton Penrose, Jr. J. Geol., 39:756-60.

1932

In memoriam: J. Claude Jones. Bull. Am. Assoc. Petrol. Geologists, 16:623-24.

1933

Geologic problems of the Beartooth-Bighorn region. III. Bull. Geol. Soc. Am., 44:76-77. (A)

With W. T. Thom, Jr., W. H. Bucher, R. M. Field, Yellowstone-Beartooth-Bighorn region. In: *International Geological Congress, 16th, Washington, D.C., Guidebook 24* pp. 3-4, 28-38, 47-55. Washington, D.C., United States Geological Survey.

With W. T. Thom, Jr. and W. H. Bucher. Results of structural research in Beartooth-Bighorn region, Montana and Wyoming. Bull. Am. Assoc. Petrol. Geologists, 17:680-93.

1934

Thomas Chrowder Chamberlin, 1843-1928. National Academy of Sciences, *Biographical Memoirs,* 15:307-407.

Geologic problems of the Beartooth-Bighorn region. III. Problems of basement structure. Bull. Geol. Soc. Am., 45:183-88.

Geologic analysis of the gravity anomalies of the Black Hills-Bighorn-Beartooth region. Proc. Geol. Soc. Am., 1933, pp. 56-57. (A)

The motion of glaciers. Science, 80:526-27.

1935

Certain aspects of geologic classifications and correlations. Science, 81:183-90, 216-18.

Geologic analysis of the gravity anomalies for the Black Hills-Bighorn-Beartooth region. Bull. Geol. Soc. Am., 46:393-408.

More than two pre-Cambrian granites in the Canadian Shield. Science, 82:126-27.

1936

Glacier motion as typical rock deformation. J. Geol., 44:93-104.

1937

The origin and history of the earth. In: *The World and Man as Science Sees Them,* ed. by F. R. Moulton, pp. 48-98. Chicago, University of Chicago Press.

Shifting orogenic belts of the southern Canadian Shield. J. Geol., 45:663-81.

1938

On the concept of earth shells. Proc. Geol. Soc. Am., 1937, p. 307. (A)

Structure of the middle Rocky Mountains. Tulsa Geological Society Digest, 2:21-25.

1939

Diastrophic behavior around the Bighorn Basin. Bull. Geol. Soc. Am., 50:1903. (A)

1940

Glacier mechanics. Am. Alpine J., 4:40-53.

In memoriam: Arthur Philemon Coleman, 1852-1939. Am. Alpine J., 4:119-21.

Diastrophic behavior around the Bighorn Basin. J. Geol., 48:673-716.

1943

Frank Dawson Adams, 1859-1942. J. Geol., 51:211.

Gerard (Jakob) De Geer, 1858-1943. J. Geol., 51:498.

1944

Memorial to William Frank Eugene Gurley, 1854-1943. Proc. Geol. Soc. Am., 1943, pp. 135-40.

Pleistocene coast range orogenesis in southern California. J. Geol., 52:357-58.

1945

Basement control in Rocky Mountain deformation. Am. J. Sci., 243A:98-116.

The moon's lack of folded ranges.   J. Geol., 53:361-73.
Harry Fielding Reid, 1859-1944.   Am. Alpine J., 5:413-14.

1949

Geological evidence on the evolution of the earth's atmosphere.
In: *The Atmospheres of the Earth and Planets,* ed. by G. P.
Kuiper, pp. 250-59. Chicago, University of Chicago Press.

Joseph Erlanger

JOSEPH ERLANGER

January 5, 1874–December 5, 1965

BY HALLOWELL DAVIS

J OSEPH ERLANGER, Nobel Laureate with Herbert Gasser in 1944, will best be remembered for the epoch-making introduction into neurophysiology of the cathode ray oscilloscope and the exploration of the electrical activity of nerve fibers. But Joseph Erlanger was also one of the great founders of American physiology in the first quarter of the twentieth century. His stature was already established in cardiac and circulatory physiology before he turned his attention and talents to the electrophysiology of nerves. By then he had already founded the Departments of Physiology at the University of Wisconsin and at Washington University in St. Louis.

In his autobiographical reminiscences in the *Annual Review of Physiology* in 1964, he noted that his eminent career was "fraught with a series of fortunate circumstances and fortunate decisions," but with characteristic modesty he did not mention his rare technical skill as an experimenter, his great ability as a teacher, as organizer, and as a quiet but forceful leader of men, or his mastery of the almost forgotten art of frugality—of accomplishing so much with limited technical support and resources. He was truly one of the pioneers of biological science in America, and he displayed magnificently the spirit and the strength of a pioneer. Few, even among his many admirers, are aware how this spirit of self-reliance and independence expressed itself equally in the physiological laboratory, in his independent political and religious point of view, and in his love of nature in the mountains of California and Colorado.

BACKGROUND AND BOYHOOD

Joseph Erlanger's origin was humble, with no running start toward academic eminence. Both of his parents were immigrants and neither had more than an elementary education. His father, Herman, born in Buchau am Feder See, in Württemberg, landed in New York without means in 1848. He made his way to New Orleans and thence by boat to Panama and on muleback across the Isthmus, and he finally arrived by boat in San Francisco in 1849. After unsuccessful attempts at placer mining, he settled in San Francisco, and became a merchant of moderate means. He married Sarah Galinger, the sister of his business partner. Joseph, born in San Francisco on January 5, 1874, was the sixth of their seven children, and he was the only one to complete a college education.

Thus, Joseph was the son of Californian pioneers. His boyhood was spent in the new and growing city of San Francisco. He knew and loved the outdoors and he developed an early interest in nature, particularly in the mountains and forests and in animals and how they lived and grew. His curiosity led him to examine and dissect both insects and plants. Here were the roots of his ambition to study medicine and his lifelong devotion to medical science and also of his lifelong hobby of camping and tramping in the mountains. He, in his turn, became a pioneer, not in gold mining but in medical teaching and in physiological research.

EDUCATION AND EARLY SCIENTIFIC CAREER

Erlanger himself, in his reminiscences already cited, has given us an account of his education and early career and his associations with his colleagues. The direct, simple style, mincing no words even when speaking of misfortune and death, and thoroughly objective and modest with regard to himself, is characteristic of his writing and of his attitudes throughout his life. He tells of his early schooling at the San Francisco Boys' High School where he took the three-year "classical" course. Early he formed the ambition to study medicine. His older sister nicknamed him "Doc" because of his interest in animals and plants. In 1891 he was accepted, without examination, by the University of California at the completion of only two years of the high school course, on the basis of his scholastic standing with only a condition in Latin. In the University, he enrolled in the "College of Chemistry" as a preparation for medicine. He does not tell us how high he stood in his class. A little-known sidelight on young Joseph Erlanger is that, although he did not engage in organized sports, he did take boxing lessons from the famous champion, Jim Corbett! His family relate that he had a "terrible temper" but that early in life he learned to control it. In later years he watched boxing on TV regularly every Wednesday night. These revelations may surprise some of those who knew him as a very restrained, soft-spoken teacher and scientist.

Erlanger had planned to enter the Cooper Medical School in San Francisco, but at the suggestion of a friend, Herbert Moffitt, he applied to the newly organized Johns Hopkins Medical School. He became a member of the third class to be admitted to that institution, and he received his medical degree from it in 1899 as the second-ranking member of his class.

As a medical student he had, during a summer vacation, engaged in research under Lewellys Barker on the locus of the anterior horn cells in the spinal cord that innervate a particular muscle. The results were not published separately but were incorporated by Barker, with due credit, in his volume *The Nervous System and Its Constituent Neurons*. A second research, in association with a fellow student, Walter Hewlett, dealt with the digestion and absorption of food in dogs with shortened intestines.

After a year of internship under Sir William Osler at the Johns Hopkins Hospital, Erlanger, influenced no doubt by his laboratory experiences, made his choice for a career as teacher and investigator rather than as a practicing physician. He was granted a coveted fellowship in pathology in William H. Welch's department, but resigned it at the last moment when he was offered an assistantship in physiology by William H. Howell. He knew that physiology was more to his liking.

THE YOUNG PHYSIOLOGIST

Erlanger taught at the Hopkins Medical School until 1906. His first lectures, given in 1902, dealt with digestion and metabolism. In the student laboratories he used to good advantage his deftness of hand, his ingenuity, and an intuitive understanding of physical principles. One episode is legendary. During the preparation for a demonstration to the medical students of a delicate and newly-imported blood-pressure machine, the Mosso sphygmomanometer, the glass instrument was smashed beyond repair. (Erlanger writes simply, "I broke it.") However, he immediately improvised a larger and more rugged substitute which measured and recorded the pulsation of the upper arm instead of the first fingers of the two hands. It worked. Later Erlanger described the instrument and it was manufactured by a New York firm. The present writer remembers this instrument lovingly from his use of it as a medical student and, in his turn, as a laboratory instructor in physiology. Actually, the Erlanger model was superseded in general use by the German instrument of von Recklinghausen which, according to Erlanger, "used the same principle but was of superior construction."

In the laboratory Erlanger used his sphygmomanometer in a study, with Donald R. Hooker, of the relation of blood flow to orthostatic albuminuria. A major generalization, set forth in their 233-page monograph, was that the output of albumin depended primarily on the pulse pressure, not on the mean blood pressure. Another important study during this period concerned the transmission of excitation from the auricle to the ventricle of the dog's heart. Reliable conduction with an appropriate delay is required for an effective coordinated beat. Failure is known as "heart block." Opinion varied as to whether the conduction depended exclusively on the narrow specialized atrioventricular "bundle of His," as to whether re-generation following injury was possible, and as to whether other tissue might perform the function vicariously. Erlanger followed carefully a clinical case of Stokes-Adams syndrome (slow pulse and fainting spells) with complete heart block. The heart block was gradually relieved during successful antisyphilitic treatment. Erlanger reproduced the sequence in dogs, first in acute and later, after he moved to Madison, in chronic experiments by carefully graded injury to the bundle of His. The cardiac surgery and the use of graded pressure, applied by a special clamp of Erlanger's design, represent technical achievements of a high order. These and related experiments firmly established the complete and permanent dependence of auriculoventricular conduction on the bundle of His.

A still later phase of these cardiac studies served to establish the locus of the origin of the cardiac impulse in normal and abnormal conditions. Erlanger was not alone in this work but he made major experimental contributions and his point of view relating the problem to the phylogenetic and embryonic development of the heart served to clarify confusing observations. His Harvey Lecture of 1912 entitled "The Localization of Impulse Initiation and Conduction in the Heart" had a profound influence on the thinking of both physiologists and cardiologists.

During and for a time after World War I, problems of blood pressure and wound shock dominated cardiac physiology in the United States. Erlanger undertook studies of these problems and became interested in the arterial sounds of Korotkoff that occur during partial compression of the artery and are routinely employed in determining arterial pressure in man. Erlanger analyzed the production of these sounds in experiments on dogs in which the exposed femoral artery was compressed in a special air-tight chamber under visual observation and with correlated mechanical records and auditory detection of the sounds. The first sound to appear, as the compressing pressure falls slowly, is about 3 mm Hg below the systolic pressure, i.e., the pressure at which the blood first penetrates through the compressed artery. The transition from a sharp to a dull sound, not the cessation of all sound, correctly signals the diastolic pressure. Actually the cessation of sound is still often employed clinically to determine the diastolic pressure. Erlanger commented briefly in 1964, "For routine purposes it may be good enough, but actually it is lower than the diastolic pressure."

All of these studies of the heart and circulation established Erlanger as one of the leading physiologists in this country long before he began the researches in neurophysiology for which he was awarded the Nobel Prize.

THE UNIVERSITY OF WISCONSIN AND
WASHINGTON UNIVERSITY

The story of the first phase of Erlanger's career as an investigator has outrun the story of his life and his development as a teacher.

During his sixth year as a physiologist at the Hopkins Medical School (1906), Erlanger accepted the appointment as Professor of Physiology and Physiological Chemistry in the medical school that was being started in Madison by the University of Wisconsin. (His salary at Baltimore had been $1500 a year. At Madison it was increased to $3000.) At Madison, Erlanger became a pioneer in organizing and equipping a department and laboratories for his two subjects. The space available was the attic and second floor of the old Chemical Engineering building. Two years were devoted to establishing laboratories and to developing a complete set of lectures, in manuscript form, covering the entire field of medical physiology. These manuscripts, updated year by year, he used throughout his teaching career. His lectures were famed for their clarity and organization, and they were completely devoid of byplay or attempts at humor!

Erlanger remained at Madison for only four years. In 1910 he was persuaded to pioneer once more and became one of a group of new department heads at the reorganized School of Medicine of Washington University in St. Louis. That group, recruited by the Chancellor, David Houston, and the President of the Board of Trustees, Robert S. Brookings, included, in addition to Erlanger (physiology), Dock (medicine), Howland (pediatrics), Opie (pathology), Shaffer (biochemistry), and Terry (anatomy). Others were added during the next decade but these constituted the nucleus. New quarters at the present location of the school began to be used in 1914. In 1916 Erlanger brought from Madison to St. Louis Herbert S. Gasser, with whom he collaborated so successfully in the second phase of his scientific career. Erlanger not only organized the Department of Physiology, he elevated it to international prominence and ran it for thirty-five years until his retirement from teaching in 1946.

JOSEPH ERLANGER: THE MAN AND HIS FAMILY

Erlanger was a strong personality, independent in his social, political, and religious views. He wore high collars long after other men had forgotten all about them. When his university sent him a personal-history questionnaire, he wrote in the space for politics the word "Mugwump" to express his disapproval of what he considered an unwarranted prying into his private life. He was a member of the Humanist Society, and to the extent that he had a religious affiliation it was Humanism. His wife and children were Unitarians. He could be outspoken when pressed on social issues. Asked, in a friendly gathering, for his views concerning the problem of the Negro in America, he replied quietly but firmly that racial intolerance will continue for generations until the color line is erased by intermarriage between the races. These were strong words in St. Louis, spoken before the days of integration.

In spite of firm convictions and a strong but carefully controlled temper, Joseph Erlanger enjoyed a singularly warm and close-knit family life and he was considered "good fun" by those who came to know his sense of humor. He never himself told an off-color story, but he was no prude and could laugh with the rest and not spoil the fun. Although he did not usually smoke, he would take a cigarette after dinner to make his guests feel at ease. In fact his social courtesy was such that once, when during a hike in the mountains he was received in a hut by the old caretaker of an unworked mine, he drank three cups of a singularly repugnant brew of "tea" rather than offend the feelings of his host.

On June 21, 1906, Joseph was married to Aimée Hirstel of San Francisco. She was a perfect wife and helpmate, who shared his love for nature and the great outdoors. She, like Joseph, was frugal, which, with a family of three children—Margaret

(b. March 1, 1908), Ruth Josephine (b. February 1, 1910, m. R. H. Swinney), and Hermann (b. April 17, 1912, d. October 14, 1959)—was a great asset with only an academic salary and no family resources in the days of World War I and later during the great depression. Aimée handled all the money, but Joseph balanced the accounts. Joseph talked only when he had something to say, not for the sake of making conversation. Aimée relieved the social situation by her easy steady flow of conversation, even although she sometimes seemed to embarrass Joseph by her unabashed adulation. But Joseph was quick to make unobtrusive but definite corrections of any misstatements of fact. Joseph and Aimée spread the warmth of their family life to include the younger members of the department. Their friendliness and Aimée's endless and excellent helpful practical advice, particularly to newcomers, were never forgotten by the recipients.

Both Joseph and Aimée were strong walkers and ardent campers. Their honeymoon was a camping trip in the Sierra Nevada Mountains of California. It nearly ended in disaster on the third day when, thanks to an incompetent guide, their pack horses, food, and equipment were all lost in a swollen river. They hiked on foot thirty miles back to civilization, and arrived exhausted, both physically and financially, but still very much in love. In spite of this misadventure, they re-outfitted themselves and continued their pack-trip for three weeks, without a guide. Later for many years they returned to the mountains of Colorado, Wyoming, or Montana habitually for six-week summer vacations as soon as the children were old enough to accompany them. Joseph no longer trusted to guides. He provided himself with excellent survey maps, backed with muslin, but scorned to carry a compass; instead he used the sun and his watch. He used his maps chiefly to identify the mountains and rivers in the landscape seen from the mountains that they climbed. In his love for the mountains and his urge to live among them and to climb them, he showed the spirit of a pioneer.

Joseph's health was good. He was not large of stature but tough and wiry and with great endurance. He enjoyed his food and had no patience with food-and-diet fads. He always walked to work at the medical school, carrying a simple lunch in a brown paper bag. He never returned to the laboratory at night or worked on Sundays. Sunday was a family day, for playing ball or other games with his family and often other members of his department also, and with many hikes and picnics in the environs of St. Louis.

Erlanger was the last member of his department to buy an automobile. Finally, about 1922, he bought a Model T Ford with a trailer and after only six weeks of experience he drove his family in it, through Missouri mud and across Kansas, to Colorado. In 1924 he purchased a second-hand Franklin from Herbert Gasser and later, in 1929, in the same car they drove from St. Louis to Boston to attend the XIII International Congress of Physiology.

Erlanger greatly enjoyed tennis and handball, but he did not participate, even as a young man, in team games except for lacrosse at the Hopkins Medical School. He became enthusiastic and very adept at pitching horseshoes. This was a favorite sport and form of relaxation at the laboratory at lunch time or at the end of the day. Erlanger practically coerced (or shamed) his younger colleagues into pitching, whatever the weather, once even when the ground was covered with glare ice. His opponent announced, as they returned to the laboratory that noon, "The Chief slid a ringer today."

Erlanger's great hobby was the outdoors, particularly walking and hiking. His research should also be considered a hobby. Next came music. He and Aimée attended the symphony concerts regularly until her health failed in later years. Joseph played a wooden flute and for some years participated in an informal orchestra, recruited chiefly among the medical faculty. He read the daily news regularly and the *Saturday Review* and the *New Yorker* avidly and also much biography and history. Like many careful readers, he marked freely the key passages in his books and magazines.

After retirement from teaching in 1946, Erlanger continued to go regularly to his laboratory and the library until Aimée's health and physical vigor began to fail. Then for several years, until her death, he turned completely to caring for her, with complete and unstinting devotion. He outlived her by several years, clear of mind and in good health until the time of his death in 1965.

ERLANGER THE TEACHER

Erlanger was an influential and effective teacher, both for medical students and for his graduate students. His lectures were models of clarity and logical devopment. The students dreaded his merciless Saturday morning oral quizzes, but they learned much from them. He taught meticulous attention to detail in the laboratory. His surgical skill was unusual. Even when operating on the heart of a dog in the World War I era, he wore a frock coat instead of a laboratory gown, and it is said that he never once soiled it with a drop of blood. He insisted on clear, direct, logical exposition in his own and his students' papers and theses. In only one form of communication did he have a weakness: his handwriting was atrocious. One time he even had to call on Miss Stubinger, his faithful secretary for thirty-five years, to decipher some of his numerous and devastating annotations on the draft of a graduate student's thesis.

Erlanger practiced and taught respect and kindness and good care for laboratory animals. Once an antivivisectionist, who had heard of his cardiac operations on surviving dogs, sneaked in and opened the cages to allow the animals to escape from their supposed life of torture. The animals all ran out, but Erlanger's care and treatment of them had been so good that every one of them returned home to the laboratory at night-fall. On another occasion he strongly reprimanded a graduate student for performing arterial ligations on surviving frogs without proper consultation with him as laboratory director concerning the necessity and propriety of such drastic procedure. He taught respect for the life of a frog as well as cats and dogs.

Erlanger had only three graduate students who achieved the Ph.D. degree. They were Francis O. Schmitt, Edgar A. Blair, and Albert S. Harris, but many of his junior department members and visiting fellows have achieved eminence. Among them are Herbert Gasser, George Bishop, A. M. Monnier, Georges Coppée, Pierre Rijlandt, Joseph Hinsey, Helen Graham, Peter Heinbecker, Arthur Gilson, H. L. White, Gordon Schoepfle, Crighton Bramwell, and Geoffry Bourne. Particularly in the second phase of his experimental career, the neurophysiological era, did his influence spread widely in the Washington University Medical School and its hospitals. He established an eminence in neurology and neurophysiology that still persists as the Erlanger tradition today.

ERLANGER AND AMERICAN PHYSIOLOGY

Erlanger was elected to the American Physiological Society in 1901, only one year after embracing physiology as his career. He was elected to its Council in 1910, and with the exception of a single year, 1924, remained on the Council in one capacity or another until 1929. He was Treasurer from 1913 to 1923, and as such he helped to shape the financial policies of the Society during and following the transfer of the *American Journal of Physiology* to the Society in 1922. He accomplished the incorporation of the Society as a Missouri corporation in 1923.

He served as President in 1926-1927 and 1928 and through the XIII International Congress of Physiology at Boston in 1929. He displayed conservative leadership in the business and organizational work of the Society and he carried a large share of responsibility.

In a less formal way, Joseph Erlanger and Alexander Forbes, as the two senior electrophysiologists of their generation, exerted a profound influence on the development of neurophysiology in America. This was accomplished through the formation, during the late 1920s, of a group of neurophysiologists, orginally twelve in number, interested in the fundamental nature of the nerve impulse, the electrical excitation of tissue, and so on. This group met regularly for lunch or dinner and a discussion during each annual meeting of the American Physiological Society. They called themselves "The Axonologists." No one is quite sure when the group was organized on an informal but continuing basis, but once it had been enlarged from the original twelve and its meetings opened to all, its numbers and its influence grew rapidly. Erlanger and Forbes were the spiritual leaders, and the ideas, the methods, the techniques, and the latest results of their laboratories and others were discussed and exchanged. The cathode-ray oscilloscope was soon recognized as the only adequate means of recording the nerve action potential. A forum was provided for lively debates concerning the nature of synaptic action, whether electrical or chemical. Only after "The Axonologists" had dissolved, when the group's increased membership made impossible the former lively spontaneous discussions, did the members realize how important it had been in stimulating and shaping the development of neuro-electrophysiology.

OTHER SOCIETIES AND HONORS

Joseph Erlanger was elected to the National Academy of Sciences in 1922. He served as section vice chairman of the

American Association for the Advancement of Science. As already mentioned, he shared a Nobel Prize with Herbert Gasser in 1944. Other memberships and activities are listed below. He received honorary degrees from the universities of California, Wisconsin, Pennsylvania, and Michigan, from The Johns Hopkins University, Washington University (St. Louis), and the University of Brussels.

ERLANGER AND THE CATHODE RAY OSCILLOSCOPE:
A NOBEL LAUREATE

The second phase of Erlanger's physiological research—his most famous piece of scientific pioneering—began soon after World War I. Erlanger had long been interested in the cardiac impulse, the wave of excitation which like a nerve impulse sweeps down the bundle of His, and in the excitation of cardiac tissue by electric shocks. The electrical action current associated with the impulse could be studied with fair precision by means of the Einthoven string galvanometer, but the currents were too weak and too rapid in their time course for really adequate recording and analysis, nor could the instruments portray the form of the electric shocks used as stimuli. Alexander Forbes at Harvard met the problem of weakness of the action currents by developing the condenser-coupled amplifier as an outgrowth of his wartime experience with the radio compass. He combined his amplifier with a string galvanometer, but even so the problem of the lag and the overshoot of the recording instrument due to its inertia still remained. By 1921 Gasser and Newcomer had also developed an amplifier and, with it and a string galvanometer, had studied the action potentials of the phrenic nerve. Gasser at this time learned of the cathode ray tube, or "Braun tube," made by the Western Electric Company, which made use of an inertialess stream of electrons. Such tubes in modern form are now familiar in daily life as the TV tube and are the basis of most high-speed electronic measurements, but when the Western Electric Company in 1921 refused to sell a cathode ray tube, presumably because of possible patent infringements, Erlanger and Gasser undertook to build one of their own! A distillation flask was the tube. Erlanger wrote of it thus: "One pair of deflection plates was mounted inside and a pair of solenoid coils outside. A mechanical revolving potentiometer provided the sweep circuit."

George H. Bishop, who joined Erlanger and Gasser in 1923, spoke as follows of the next steps, at the Joseph Erlanger Memorial Service in 1966.

"These two men were not particularly sophisticated in either electronics or physics, and their troubles were various and cumulative. Noise in the amplifier, noise in the environment, vibration from trucks and sparks from the trolley line called for shielding and insulation, switches had to be devised which would operate in fractions of a thousandth of a second, without chatter, etc. Finally, no camera would photograph the dim trace obtainable at the speed required to record the nerve impulse. The first records were obtained by holding a photographic film against the end of the tube and repeating the stimuli until an accumulation of superposed traces induced a bleary line on a somewhat fogged background. I can only compare their progress to the trek of the pioneers in oxcarts across the plains and mountains of the West. They were pioneers of electrophysiology, and they encountered every conceivable obstacle but the Indians. Far more time was spent upon reconstruction of apparatus than on the recording of nerve, when one good record occasionally made a successful day.

"I have gone back and read again those early papers. The problems now look so simple, the results so elementary, the difficulties met so trivial, that one has to think in terms of an era when electronics was at as elementary a stage as was the physiology of nerve, and as was the sophistication of the workers learning how to deal with both.

"This was the first application of the cathode ray device to biology, and one of the first at least of its applications to any specific problem. The present generation of electrophysiologists stand on the shoulders of Gasser and Erlanger."

The first major discovery made with the new instrument was the different velocities of conduction in nerve fibers of different diameter. This in turn led to the study of other properties of fibers of different sizes, with and without a myelin sheath. These distinctions and the resulting classification of nerve fibers are among the fundamentals of modern neuro-physiology.

Erlanger and Gasser transported their bulky homemade equipment to Boston in 1929 and at the XIII International Congress of Physiology gave the first public demonstration of the action potentials of the slow "C" fibers.

The next quest was to relate the different classes of fiber to different functions or sense modalities, such as motor *vs.* sensory and touch *vs.* temperature *vs.* pain. This problem proved far more difficult, and actually it now seems that only the broadest correlations of function with structure and conduction velocity, such as somatic *vs.* autonomic, are possible. Nature puts together its neuronal building blocks in complicated ways; perhaps, as Bishop has suggested, the groupings of nerve fibers are more significantly related to the successive phylogenetic projections and elaborations of central functioning than to specific sensory and motor modalities.

The point is that Erlanger and Gasser's great achievement lay not so much in the particular discoveries that they made as in blazing the trail and showing the way. They were duly and properly honored for this by the award to them jointly of the Nobel Prize for Physiology and Medicine in 1944.

Erlanger and Gasser have told their story, not only at the time of receiving the Nobel award in Stockholm, but in a series of lectures they delivered at the University of Pennsylvania and published as a book entitled *Electrical Signs of Nervous Activity*. In it each of them tells his own part of the story, divided naturally according to their individual interests. Characteristically, they did not always share the same interpretation of their own observations. Equally, they respected one another's views and each held to his own in friendly disagreement. In the preface of the book they report how and where they planned the lectures. It was on a holiday in Colorado in 934, and "as we sat upon a ledge high up in the Rocky Mountains . . . viewing the panorama of lofty peaks spread out before us, our conversation turned to problems of nerve physiology."

CHRONOLOGY

1874	Born January 5, San Francisco
1891	Admitted to University of California after two years of high school
1895	B.S., University of California
1899	M.D., Johns Hopkins Medical School
1899-1900	Resident Medical Officer, Johns Hopkins Hospital
1900-1903	Assistant and Instructor in Physiology, Johns Hopkins Medical School
1903-1904	Associate in Physiology
1904-1906	Associate Professor in Physiology
1906	Married June 21 to Aimée Hirstel, San Francisco
1906-1910	Professor and Head of Departments of Physiology and Physical Chemistry, University of Wisconsin
1910-1946	Professor and Head of Department of Physiology, Washington University (St. Louis)
1912	Harvey Lecture (New York): "The Localization of Impulse Initiation and Conduction in the Heart"
1922	First publication of use of cathode ray oscilloscope
1926-1929	President of American Physiological Society
1928	Harvey Lecture (New York): "Analysis of the Action Potential in Nerve"
1929	Demonstration of nerve impulses in "C" fibers at XIII International Congress of Physiology (Boston)
1930	Hitchcock Lecturer, University of California
1936	Eldridge Reeves Johnson Lectures (Philadelphia): "Electrical Signs of Nervous Activity" (with H. S. Gasser)
1944	Awarded Nobel Prize in Physiology and Medicine (with H. S. Gasser)
1946	Emeritus Professor of Physiology, Washington University School of Medicine
1947	Presentation of Nobel Prize, December 10, in Stockholm
1965	Died December 5 in St. Louis

HONORS AND DISTINCTIONS

HONORARY DEGREES

1932	LL.D., University of California
1936	Sc.D., University of Wisconsin
1936	Sc.D., University of Pennsylvania
1937	Sc.D., University of Michigan
1946	Sc.D., Washington University
1947	LL.D., The Johns Hopkins University
1948	Hon. D., Free University of Brussels

MEMBERSHIPS

National Academy of Sciences
American Philosophical Society
American Physiological Society
    1901   Member
    1910-1912 Councilor
    1913-1923 Treasurer
    1926-1929 President
American Medical Association
American Association for Advancement of Science
Society of Experimental Biology and Medicine
Association of American Physicians
Deutsche Acad. Naturforscher (Halle)
Societé Philomatique (Paris)
Alpha Omega Alpha
Sigma Xi

BIBLIOGRAPHY

KEY TO ABBREVIATIONS

Am. Heart J. = American Heart Journal
Am. J. Physiol. = American Journal of Physiology
Arch. Internal Med. =Archives of Internal Medicine
Bull. St. Louis Med. Soc. = Bulletin of the St. Louis Medical Society
J. Am. Med. Assoc. = Journal of the American Medical Association
J. Exp. Med. = Journal of Experimental Medicine
J. Neurophysiol. = Journal of Neurophysiology
Johns Hopkins Hosp. Bull. = Johns Hopkins Hospital Bulletin
Johns Hopkins Hosp. Rept. = Johns Hopkins Hospital Reports
Proc. Soc. Exp. Biol. Med. = Proceedings of the Society for Experimental
    Biology and Medicine
Wisconsin Med. J. = Wisconsin Medical Journal
Zentr. Physiol. = Zentralblatt für Physiologie

1901

With A. W. Hewlett. A study of the metabolism in dogs with
    shortened small intestines. Am. J. Physiol., 6:1-30.

1904

A new instrument for determining the minimum and maximum
    blood-pressures in man. Johns Hopkins Hosp. Rept., 12:53-
    100.
With D. R. Hooker. An experimental study of blood-pressure and
    of pulse-pressure in man. Johns Hopkins Hosp. Rept., 12:145-
    378.

1905

Vorläufige Mitteilung über die Physiologie des Herzblocks in Säu-
    getieren. Zentr. Physiol., 19:9-12.
With A. D. Hirschfelder. Eine vorläufige Mitteilung über weitere
    Studien in bezug auf den Herzblock in Säugetieren. Zentr.
    Physiol., 19:270-74.
On the union of a spinal nerve with the vagus nerve. Am. J.
    Physiol., 13:372-95.
A report of some observations on heart-block in mammals. Johns
    Hopkins Hosp. Bull., 16:202-5.

Cardiograms obtained from a case of operative defect in the chest wall. Johns Hopkins Hosp. Bull., 16:394-97.

On the physiology of heart-block in mammals, with especial reference to the causation of Stokes-Adams disease. J. Exp. Med., 7:676-724. (See 1906)

With A. D. Hirschfelder. Further studies on the physiology of heart-block in mammals. Am. J. Physiol., 15:153-206.

1906

On the physiology of heart-block in mammals, with especial reference to the causation of Stokes-Adams disease. J. Exp. Med., 8:8-58.

Further studies on the physiology of heart-block. The effects of extra systoles upon the dog's heart and upon strips of terrapin's ventricle in the various stages of block. Am. J. Physiol., 16:160-87.

Recent contributions to the physiology of the circulation. J. Am. Med. Assoc., 47:1343-51.

1907

With J. R. Blackman. A study of relative rhythmicity and conductivity in various regions of the auricles of the mammalian heart. Am. J. Physiol., 19:125-74.

1908

Irregularities of the heart resulting from disturbed conductivity. American Journal of Medical Sciences, 135:797-811.

1909

Über den Grad der Vaguswirkung auf die Kammern des Hundsherzens. Archiv für die gesamte Physiologie, 127:77-98.

Can functional union be re-established between the mammalian auricle and ventricles after destruction of a segment of the auriculo-ventricular bundle. Am. J. Physiol., 24:375-83.

1910

Observations on auricular strips of the cat's heart. Am. J. Physiol., 27:87-118.

With J. R. Blackman. Further studies in the physiology of heart-block in mammals. Chronic auriculo-ventricular heart-block in the dog. Heart, 1:177-230.

The role of the practicing physician in the defense of medical research. Wisconsin Med. J., 8:543-48.

Chronic auriculo-ventricular heart-block in the dog. Wisconsin Med. J., 8:624-31.

Animal Experimentation in Relation to Practical Medical Knowledge of the Circulation. Defense of Research Pamphlet No. 13. Chicago, American Medical Association. 40 pp.

1912

Observations on the physiology of Purkinje tissue. Am. J. Physiol., 30:395-419.

With E. G. Festerling. Respiratory waves of blood pressure, with an investigation of a method for making continuous blood pressure records in man. J. Exp. Med., 15:370-87.

Sinus stimulation as a factor in the resuscitation of the heart. J. Exp. Med., 16:452-69.

A criticism of the Uskoff sphygotonograph. Arch. Internal Med., 9:22-31.

1913

The localization of impulse initiation and conduction in the heart. Arch. Internal Med., 11:334-64; Harvey Lectures, 8:44-85.

1914

With R. Gesell. Device for interrupting a continuous blast of air, designed especially for artificial respiration. Am. J. Physiol., 33:33-34.

With W. E. Garrey. Faradic stimuli: a physical and physiological study. Am. J. Physiol., 35:377-473.

With W. B. Cannon, G. W. Crile, Y. Henderson, and S. T. Meltzer. Report of the Committee on Resuscitation from Mine Gases. United States Department of the Interior, Bureau of Mines, Technical Report, No. 77, pp. 1-33.

1915

An analysis of Dr. Kilgore's paper: "The large personal factor in blood pressure determinations by the oscillatory method." Arch. Internal Med., 16:917-26.

Studies in blood pressure estimations by indirect methods. I. The mechanism of the oscillatory criteria. Am. J. Physiol., 39:401-46.

1916

Studies in blood pressure estimations by indirect methods. II. The mechanism of the compression sounds of Korotkoff. Am. J. Physiol., 40:82-125.

A note on the contractility of the musculature of the auriculo-ventricular valves. Am. J. Physiol., 40:150-51.

Movements of the artery within the compression chamber during indirect estimations of blood pressure. Am. J. Physiol., 42:588-89.

1917

With R. Gesell, H. S. Gasser, and B. Elliott. An experimental study of surgical shock: preliminary report. J. Am. Med. Assoc., 69:2089-92.

With R. Woodyatt. Intravenous glucose injections in shock. J. Am. Med. Assoc., 69:1410-14.

1918

With R. Gesell, H. Gasser, and B. Elliott. Some reactions in the development of shock by diverse methods. Am. J. Physiol., 45:546-47.

The pre-anacrotic phenomenon and its relation to the arterial compression sounds of Korotkoff. Am. J. Physiol., 45:565-66.

With H. S. Gasser. The treatment of standardized shock. Comptes Rendus des Séances de la Société de Biologie et de ses Filiales, 81:898-909.

1919

With R. Gesell and H. S. Gasser. Studies in secondary traumatic shock. I. The circulation in shock after abdominal injuries. Am. J. Physiol., 49:90-116.

With H. S. Gasser. Studies in secondary traumatic shock. II. Shock due to mechanical limitation of blood flow. Am. J. Physiol., 49:151-73.

With H. S. Gasser. Studies in secondary traumatic shock. III. Circulation failure due to adrenalin. Am. J. Physiol., 49:345-76.

With H. S. Gasser and W. Meek. Studies in secondary traumatic shock. IV. The blood volume changes and the effect of gum acacia on their development. Am. J. Physiol., 50:31-53.

With H. S. Gasser. Studies in secondary traumatic shock. V. Restoration of the plasma volume and of the alkali reserve. Am. J. Physiol., 50:104-18.

With H. S. Gasser. Studies in secondary traumatic shock. VI. Statistical study of the treatment of measured trauma with solutions of gum acacia and crystalloids. Am. J. Physiol., 50:119-47.

With H. S. Gasser. Studies on secondary traumatic shock. VII. Note on the action of hypertonic gum acacia and glucose after hemorrhage. Am. J. Physiol., 50:149-56.

With H. S. Gasser. Hypertonic gum acacia and glucose in the treatment of secondary shock. Annals of Surgery, 69:389-421.

1920

With H. L. White. The effect on the composition of the blood of maintaining an increased blood volume by the intravenous injection of a hypertonic solution of gum acacia and glucose in normal, asphyxiated and shocked dogs. Am. J. Physiol., 54:1-29.

With C. M. Jackson, G. Lusk, W. S. Thayer, and V. C. Vaughan. An investigation of conditions in the departments of the preclinical sciences. J. Am. Med. Assoc., 74:1117-22.

1921

Studies in blood pressure estimation by indirect methods. III. The movements in the artery under compression during blood pressure determinations. Am. J. Physiol., 55:84.

Blood volume and its regulation. Physiological Reviews, 1:177-207.

1922

The past and the future of the medical sciences in the United States. Science, 55:135-45.

With H. S. Gasser. The cathode ray oscillograph as a means of recording nerve action currents and induction shocks. Am. J. Physiol., 59:473-75.

With H. S. Gasser. A study of the action currents of nerve with the cathode ray oscillograph. Am. J. Physiol., 62:496-524.

1924

With H. S. Gasser. The compound nature of the action current of nerve as disclosed by the cathode ray oscillograph. Am. J. Physiol., 70:624-66.

1925

With H. S. Gasser. The nature of conduction of an impulse in the relatively refractory period. Am. J. Physiol., 72:613-35.

1926

Department of Physiology, Washington University School of Medicine, St. Louis, Missouri. In: *Methods and Problems of Medical Education*, 5th Ser., pp. 43-50. New York, Rockefeller Foundation.

With G. H. Bishop and H. S. Gasser. Experimental analysis of the simple action potential wave in nerve by the cathode ray oscillograph. Am. J. Physiol., 78:537-73.

With G. H. Bishop and H. S. Gasser. The action potential waves transmitted between the sciatic nerve and its spinal roots. Am. J. Physiol., 78:574-91.

With G. H. Bishop and H. S. Gasser. Distortion of action potentials as recorded from the nerve surface. Am. J. Physiol., 78:592-609.

With G. H. Bishop. The effects of polarization upon the activity of vertebrate nerve. Am. J. Physiol., 78:630-57.

With W. J. Meek. An adjustable sphygmoscope for the recording sphygmomanometer. Journal of Laboratory and Clinical Medicine, 12:172-82.

1927

With H. S. Gasser. The role played by the sizes of the constituent fibers of a nerve trunk in determining the form of its action potential wave. Am. J. Physiol., 80:522-47.

With H. S. Gasser and G. H. Bishop. The absolutely refractory phase of the alpha, beta and gamma fibers in the sciatic nerve of the frog. Am. J. Physiol., 81:473-74.

The interpretation of the action potential in cutaneous and muscle nerves. Am. J. Physiol., 82:644-55.

1928

Analysis of the action potential in nerve. Harvey Lectures, 22: 90-113.

With F. O. Schmitt. Directional differences in the conduction of the impulse through heart muscle and their possible relation to extra-systolic and fibrillary contractions. Am. J. Physiol., 87: 326-47.

1929

With H. S. Gasser. The role of fiber size in the establishment of a nerve block by pressure or cocaine. Am. J. Physiol., 88:581-91.

1930

With H. S. Gasser. The action potential in fibers of slow conduction in spinal roots and somatic nerves. Am. J. Physiol., 92:43-82.

With H. S. Gasser. The ending of the axon action potential and its relation to other events in nerve activity. Am. J. Physiol., 94:247-77.

1931

With E. A. Blair. The irritability changes in nerve in response to subthreshold induction shocks, and related phenomena including the relatively refractory phase. Am. J. Physiol., 99:108-28.

With E. A. Blair. The irritability changes in nerve in response to subthreshold constant currents, and related phenomena. Am. J. Physiol., 99:129-55.

1932

With E. A. Blair. Responses of axons to brief shocks. Proc. Soc. Exp. Biol. Med., 29:926-27.

With E. A. Blair. On the effects of polarization of nerve fibers by extrinsic action potentials. Am. J. Physiol., 101:559-64.

1933

With E. A. Blair. A comparison of the characteristics of axons through their individual electrical responses. Am. J. Physiol., 106:524-64.

With E. A. Blair. The configuration of axon and "simple" nerve action potentials. Am. J. Physiol., 106:565-70.

William Beaumont's experiments and their present day value. Bull. St. Louis Med. Soc., 28:180-91.

1934

With E. A. Blair. Manifestations of segmentation in myelinated axons. Am. J. Physiol., 110:287-311.

1935

With E. A. Blair. On the process of excitation by brief shocks in axons. Am. J. Physiol., 114:309-16.

With E. A. Blair. On excitation and depression in axons at the cathode of the constant current. Am. J. Physiol., 114:317-27.

With E. A. Blair. Observations on repetitive responses in axons. Am. J. Physiol., 114:328-61.

1936

With E. A. Blair. Temporal summation in peripheral nerve fibers. Am. J. Physiol., 117:355-65.

1937

With H. S. Gasser. Eldridge Reeves Johnson Foundation for Medical Physics. *Electrical Signs of Nervous Activity*. Philadelphia, University of Pennsylvania Press. x + 221 pp.

1938

With E. A. Blair. Comparative observations on motor and sensory fibers with special reference to repetitiousness. Am. J. Physiol., 121:431-53.

With E. A. Blair. The action of isotonic, salt-free solutions on conduction in medullated nerve fibers. Am. J. Physiol., 124:341-59.

1939

With E. A. Blair. Propagation and extension of excitatory effects of the nerve action potential across nonresponding internodes. Am. J. Physiol., 126:97-108.

The initiation of impulses in axons. J. Neurophysiol., 2:370-79.

1940

With E. A. Blair. Facilitation and difficilitation effected by nerve impulses in peripheral fibers. J. Neurophysiol., 3:107-27.

The relation of longitudinal tension of an artery to the preanacrotic (breaker) phenomenon. Am. Heart J., 19:398-400.

With E. A. Blair. Interaction of medullated fibers of a nerve tested with electric shocks. Am. J. Physiol., 131:483-93.

1941

Remarks on some evidences of a subconducted process in medullated nerve fibers. Schweizerische Medizinische Wochenschrift, 22:394-95.

With G. M. Schoepfle. The action of temperature on the excitability, spike height and configuration, and the refractory period observed in the responses of single medullated nerve fibers. Am. J. Physiol., 134:694-704.

With E. A. Blair and G. M. Schoepfle. A study of the spontaneous oscillations in the excitability of nerve fibers with special reference to the action of strychnine. Am. J. Physiol., 134:705-18.

1942

With A. G. Krems and G. M. Schoepfle. Nerve concussion. Proc. Soc. Exp. Biol. Med., 49:73-75.

1943

Letter to the editor regarding "Histologic demonstration of accessory muscular connections between auricle and ventricle in the case of short P-R interval and prolonged QRS complex," by Wood, Wolferth, and Geckeler. Am. Heart J., 26:419-20.

1944

Obituary. Albert Ernest Taussig.   Transactions of the Association
of American Physicians, 58:35-36.

1945

Obituary. William Henry Howell.   Science, 101:575-76.
A reassessment of Beaumont the investigator.   Bull. St. Louis Med.
Soc., 40:147-50.

1946

With G. M. Schoepfle.   A study of nerve degeneration and regen-
eration. Am. J. Physiol., 147:550-81.

1949

With G. M. Schoepfle.   Relation between spike height and polariz-
ing current in single medullated nerve fibers.   Am. J. Physiol.,
159:217-32.
Some observations on the responses of single nerve fibers.   In: *Les
Prix Nobel en 1947,* pp. 173-95. Stockholm, Imprimerie Royale.

1950

William Henry Howell, 1860-1945.   National Academy of Sciences,
Biographical Memoirs, 26:153-80.

1951

With G. M. Schoepfle.   Observations on the local response in
single medullated nerve fibers.   Am. J. Physiol., 167:134-46.

1964

Prefatory Chapter: A physiologist reminisces.   Annual Review of
Physiology, 26:1-14.

M. Gomberg

MOSES GOMBERG

February 8, 1866–February 12, 1947

BY JOHN C. BAILAR, JR.

M OSES GOMBERG, one of the world's truly great organic chemists, was born in Elizabetgrad, Russia, on February 8, 1866, and died in Ann Arbor, Michigan, on February 12, 1947—four days after his eighty-first birthday. Aside from the fact that his parents were George and Marie Resnikoff Gomberg, and that he had a younger sister, Sonia, almost nothing is known of his family. In his mature life, he rarely, if ever, spoke of his boyhood, and even his closest friends did not know what sort of life he led before coming to America. It is known only that he attended the Nicolau Gymnasium in Elizabetgrad from 1878 to 1884. In the latter year, his father was accused of political conspiracy and, in order to avoid arrest and imprisonment, he fled from Russia to the United States, sacrificing all of his property in Russia. The son, although only eighteen years of age, was also under suspicion, and he either accompanied his father to America, or followed soon afterwards. There is no record of their flight from oppression, and we do not know whether they were allowed to depart peaceably and in comfort, or had to flee in secret. We do not even know whether Mrs. Gomberg came to America, but she probably did, for Sonia came, and lived for many years with her brother after he settled in Ann Arbor. Whether there were other brothers or sisters, and, if so, what happened to them, no one seems to know.

The Gombergs settled in Chicago, where they earned their living at whatever work they could find. Since they spoke no English, this work was usually common labor. Apparently the young Gomberg worked as a laborer in the stockyards—a job which must have been most repugnant to a person of such sensitive nature. Years later, when Upton Sinclair wrote his book *The Jungle,* describing the almost unbelievably horrible conditions that existed in the stockyards, Professor Gomberg told one of his friends that he could attest from personal experience that the description was not overdrawn.[1]

In addition to earning a living, the young man learned to speak English and prepared himself to enter college. He was determined to continue his education at any cost. Whether he attended high school in Chicago or studied independently, we do not know, but the record shows that he was admitted to the University of Michigan in 1886. (This is evidently the earliest written record of the events of his life.) It is reported that he chose the University of Michigan over the university in his "home" state of Illinois because he had to work his way through college and he had learned that student janitors at Michigan were paid better than those at Illinois.[2]

When he enrolled at the University of Michigan, he wanted to take the beginning course in physics, and he presented himself to Professor H. S. Carhart, who was then head of the Physics Department. Professor Carhart explained to the young man that he could not take the course because he had not had training in trigonometry. The youngster went away crestfallen, but three days later he returned, again requesting that he be

[1] Letter from Dr. E. C. Sullivan to Professor W. B. Pillsbury, January 14, 1960.

[2] Reported by Professor G. F. Smith, based on a conversation with Professor Gomberg.

allowed to enroll in the physics course. Again, Professor Car-hart told him that he could not take the course because he had not studied trigonometry. "But I have studied trigonometry," the young man answered. In order to show him how little he knew of the subject, Professor Carhart began to question him about his knowledge of trigonometry. Much to his amazement, he discovered that the young man was able to answer all of his questions and that he had a thorough knowledge of trigonometry. He had mastered the entire subject in three days.[3]

Young Gomberg received the Bachelor of Science degree from the University in 1890 and, with the help of an assistant-ship, he was able to continue in graduate work. He received the Master's degree in 1892 and the Ph.D. in 1894. His thesis work was done under the direction of Professor A. B. Prescott, and concerned the reactions of caffeine. In those days, chemistry was primarily concerned with analysis, and although Professor Prescott was principally an organic chemist, he was also widely known for his work in analytical chemistry, and was frequently called upon by commercial firms for help in analytical prob-lems. It was doubtless through Professor Prescott that Dr. Gom-berg was able to earn money in his spare time by analyzing materials for numerous clients. The samples which came to him were of wide variety and included minerals, drugs, foods, oils, and fats. The experience which he gained from this work, as well as his training under Professor Prescott, impressed upon him the importance of careful analysis. It was a lesson which he always remembered, and which he impressed strongly upon his own students.

Some of the analytical work which Dr. Gomberg did during this period was necessitated by patent infringement suits, and the young man soon found himself involved as an expert wit-ness, in which capacity he not only had to report the results of

[3] A. H. White, *Ind. Eng. Chem.*, 23 (1931):116.

his analysis but often had to match wits with opposing lawyers. Although he enjoyed this work, he looked upon it only as a means to earn money for further study and, since it took time from his research, he abandoned it as soon as it was economically feasible to do so.

Dr. Gomberg was appointed to an instructorship at Michigan in 1893, and continued as a member of the faculty there until his seventieth birthday in 1936. This remarkable tenure of forty-three years was interrupted only by a leave for foreign study in 1896 and 1897, a leave to do defense research during World War I, and a summer term during which he taught at the University of California. He was so devoted to his teaching and to his research that, aside from these three periods, he traveled little and seldom left Ann Arbor.

During his first leave of absence from Michigan, Dr. Gomberg spent two terms in Baeyer's laboratory in Munich, and one term with Victor Meyer in Heidelberg. The research which he did in Munich was concerned with the preparation of isonitramino- and nitroso-iso-butyric acid. The paper based on this work attests Gomberg's diligence and skill, for it reports a large number of experiments, and far more results than might have been expected from a man working for such a short period of time. The single term with Meyer, however, was even more fruitful, for it was the work he did there that laid the foundation for his discovery of free radicals.

Dr. Gomberg went to Meyer's laboratory bent on attempting the preparation of tetraphenylmethane, a synthesis which had been attempted, without success, by several noted chemists, including Victor Meyer himself. These repeated failures had convinced Meyer and others that tetraphenylmethane was inherently unstable for steric reasons, and that it could not be prepared. He tried to dissuade his young visitor from attempting the synthesis, but Gomberg was determined and went ahead with his plan. He had devised a new method of synthesis, involving the preparation of triphenylmethylhydrazobenzene, its oxidation to the azo compound, and the thermal decomposition of this material to the hydrocarbon shown in equation 1.

The first steps of the synthesis proceeded in a satisfactory manner, but when the azo compound was heated to 110-120°, a gummy, sticky residue was formed. Gomberg worked with this for several days, and was eventually able to isolate about three tenths of a gram of crystalline material from it. He believed this to be the desired tetraphenylmethane, but in order to be sure he had to fully characterize it. To appreciate the elegance of this characterization, one must remember that, in 1897, micro techniques had not been developed. The usual size of sample taken for elemental analysis was two tenths of a gram, which, in this case, would have taken nearly all of the available material. Before attempting the analysis, Gomberg tested the solubility of his compound in several solvents, took its melting point, and determined its molecular weight by the lowering of the freezing point of naphthalene in which he had dissolved the material. After the completion of these tests, he recovered and purified his compound, and analyzed it for carbon and hydrogen. The analysis showed 93.32 percent carbon and 6.36 percent hydrogen, which agreed remarkably well with the calculated values for tetraphenylmethane (93.75 percent and 6.25 percent). He felt, however, that tests performed on such small samples, and without checks, were inconclusive, so a year later, after he had returned to Michigan, he repeated the work and published another paper. The two tenths of a gram of substance which he obtained in the second run was nitrated to the tetranitro compound, which he obtained in practically quantitative yield. He determined the solubility of this material in several solvents, took its melting point, reduced a portion of it to the rosaniline dye, studied its reactivity (or rather, its lack of reactivity) with sodium ethylate and with metallic potassium to show that it contained no active hydrogen atoms, and analyzed the material for nitrogen. Still later, he had a student prepare the material on a much larger scale, and repeated his earlier measurements just to be sure that he was right.

His success with the preparation of tetraphenylmethane led Dr. Gomberg to attempt to prepare the next fully phenylated hydrocarbon, hexaphenylethane.

He planned to prepare this material by the treatment of triphenylmethyl chloride with metallic sodium (equation 2)

and was disappointed to find that the expected reaction did not occur. When he used "molecular" silver, however, reaction occurred readily, and from the solution he obtained a white, crystalline substance which he supposed was hexaphenylethane. However, analysis for carbon and hydrogen showed that the percentages of both elements were lower than the calculated values (calculated for carbon, 93.83, for hydrogen, 6.17; found for carbon, 87.93, for hydrogen, 6.04). He repeated the preparation and the analysis under a variety of conditions, but the results were always essentially the same. This led Gomberg to the conclusion that the compound contained oxygen, which he at first suspected came from silver oxide that might have been present as a contaminant in the silver; but especially prepared silver, which he knew to be free of silver oxide, gave the same result. Substitution of zinc and mercury for the silver yielded the same compound. He was finally forced to conclude that the oxygen must have come from the air. He then devised methods of performing the experiment in the complete absence of air, using apparatus with ground-glass joints. Such equipment is available now, even to elementary students, but in those days it was rare, and its use was almost revolutionary. Gomberg was unwilling to use either cork or rubber stoppers, for he feared that some oxygen might diffuse through them. When he treated triphenylchloromethane with metals in this new apparatus, the crystals which he had observed to form in the earlier experiments did not precipitate. By careful evaporation of the solution in the absence of air, he obtained a material which gave a satisfactory analysis for the hydrocarbon (calculated for carbon, 93.74, for hydrogen, 6.26; found for carbon, 93.28, for hydrogen, 6.22).

Not long before performing this critical experiment, Dr. Gomberg had read a paper by Carl Engler, who postulated that atmospheric oxidation always gives a peroxide as the initial product.[4] This peroxide may decompose to a normal oxide, but, according to Engler, the peroxide must be formed first. This hypothesis suggested to Gomberg that his oxygen-containing product was triphenylmethyl peroxide—a conclusion which subsequent study has confirmed.

The new, oxygen-free compound behaved as a highly unsaturated hydrocarbon. In benzene solution, it not only reacted with oxygen of the air but combined avidly with the halogens. Gomberg wrote: "The experimental evidence . . . forces me to the conclusion that we have to deal here with a free radical,

---

[4] Reported to the author by Professor Gomberg.

triphenylmethyl, $(C_6H_5)_3C$. On this assumption alone do the results described above become intelligible and receive an adequate explanation." Such a conclusion was quite at variance with the theories of organic chemistry which were then current, and Gomberg's compound attracted the attention of a large number of chemists—among them several of the best-known chemists of the day. Many questioned the existence of triphenylmethyl, for, although the chemical reactivity of "hexaphenylethane" indicated a highly unsaturated character, molecular weight determinations did not indicate a significant degree of dissociation. Moreover, Ullmann and Borsum prepared a compound (1902) which had the same elemental composition and which they supposed to be hexaphenylethane. This material was later shown to be the isomeric para-trityltriphenylmethane (equation 3).

(3)

The unwillingness of Ullmann and Borsum to accept the existence of trivalent carbon led other chemists to suggest that hexaphenylethane is unstable and decomposes in the presence of oxygen or halogens. Still others suggested quinoid formulas. Gomberg continued to maintain that none of these suggestions were supported by the experimental evidence. Studies of the molecular weights of a variety of hexaarylethanes eventually showed his view to be the correct one, for, although hexaphenylethane is only slightly dissociated in benzene solution, other hexaarylethanes are dissociated to much greater degrees, and hexa-para-biphenyl ethane is completely dissociated (equation 4). Even in the solid state it exists in the free radical form.

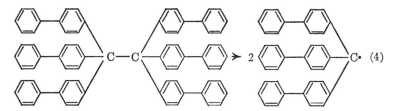

It is now well known, of course, that the formation of free radicals is not solely a property of triarylmethyls, but that a great number of organic compounds exist as free radicals, at least as reaction intermediates. It is generally accepted that organic reactions proceed by one of two types of mechanism—they are either "free radical" or "ionic." In many cases, "free radical intermediates" are of long enough life that they can be studied readily by modern techniques.

Dr. Gomberg's interest in compounds containing several aryl groups found an outlet also, in his early synthesis of pentaphenylethane, the first synthesis of unsymmetrical tetraphenylethane, and the synthesis of biaryls by the diazo reaction. The last of these syntheses is now commonly known as the Gomberg reaction.

Although Professor Gomberg is best known for his discovery of trivalent carbon, he made many other contributions to organic chemistry. Among these was his work on the quinoid structure of aromatic compounds. This work began with his explanation of Schmidlin's discovery that solutions of triphenylmethyl contain two forms of the substance. Gomberg assumed that one of these forms was quinoidal. Quinoid structures had been proposed for other compounds, chiefly to account for color in substances which might be expected to be colorless, and there was a good deal of debate on the entire matter. Gomberg had found that triphenylchloromethane forms highly colored complexes with some metallic salts, and Kehrmann suggested that these were quinoidal; e.g.,

Gomberg reasoned that if this was correct, the chlorine atom in p, p′, p′′-tribromotriphenylchloromethane should be able to shift to a para position under suitable conditions; thus, the chlorine atom and a bromine atom would occupy identical positions (equation 5). This point of view was vigorously at-

$$(5)$$

tacked by Baeyer, but Gomberg proved his point by allowing a solution of compound (I) in liquid sulfur dioxide to stand for several days, and then evaporating the solvent. The product was found to be a mixture of compounds (I) and (III), the latter, in some cases, being present to the extent of 85 percent. Other compounds of this class showed similar behavior.

Gomberg's last series of investigations concerned the reducing action of mixtures of magnesium and magnesium iodide. This system, in a mixture of benzene and ether, reduces many unsaturated systems, somewhat resembling metallic sodium in that respect. Gomberg accounted for these results by assuming that a free radical, •MgI, was present in the reducing system. For example, aromatic ketones are reduced to pinacols

(equation 6). Similarily, aldehydes, acids, and esters are reduced to benzoins.

Although Professor Gomberg is known almost exclusively
for his "academic" research, he also made notable contributions
to applied chemistry. He is credited with the development of
the first antifreeze compound used in automobiles, and with
the development of new solvents for automobile lacquers. The
manufacture of ethylenechlorohydrin, which was used in the
synthesis of mustard gas during World War I, followed a
method which he devised. As a major in the Ordnance Department, he served as an adviser in the manufacture of smokeless
powder and high explosives.

When Professor E. D. Campbell died in 1925, Dr. Gomberg
was invited to become Chairman of the Chemistry Department
at the University. He did not wish to do so, but agreed to
accept the position temporarily while a search was made for
someone else. This search proved fruitless; none of the men
who were suggested and who were acceptable to the department wished to assume the post. After two years, even Professor
Gomberg was persuaded that there was no profit in looking
further, so he accepted the position on a permanent basis. He
served until his retirement on his seventieth birthday.

Professor Gomberg was deeply committed to science and to
chemical research, but he was also extremely interesting as an

individual—brilliant, yet modest; shy, yet friendly; famous, yet humble. Since I was one of the last of his students, I knew him only in his later years, and for earlier descriptions of him I have had to rely upon students and colleagues who were acquainted with him before my time.

It may not be amiss to say a little about Professor Gomberg's appearance. He was of average size, perhaps five feet eight inches, and average build—not thin and not stocky. Dr. Lee Cone Holt, describing him as he was long before I knew him, spoke of his black hair, his close-clipped black mustache, and the glasses which he wore on a black ribbon that hung over his right ear.[5] By the time I made his acquaintance, his hair was gray and thinning and the mustache had long since been shaved off, but he still wore the pince-nez on a ribbon. I remember particularly well his hands, for it did not seem to me that a man with short, almost stubby, fingers could have the fine experimental technique that I had been told about. However, I soon learned that he had remarkable manipulative skill. He dressed neatly and in a conservative manner. In the Chemistry Building, he always wore a short lab coat of white or ecru color. His first act, when he came to his office, was to remove his street coat and don his laboratory jacket. He wore it even to his lectures. One could always tell whether the Professor was in the building by looking in his office to see whether his lab coat was hanging there. If it was, he was not in the building; if it was not there, he must be close by.

The picture of Professor Gomberg which accompanies this memoir must have been taken when he was about seventy years old, but it shows a man who looks much younger. There are few wrinkles in his face, his eyes are bright and twinkling, and he has the alert expression of a young man. He enjoyed his

[5] Lee Cone Holt, C. S. Schoepfle, F. W. Sullivan, Jr., A. H. White, and F. W. Willard, *Ind. Eng. Chem., News Ed.*, 14 (1936):65.

youthful appearance, as is illustrated by his telling a story on himself. It records an event which happened about the time he retired. One day, as he was driving across Ann Arbor, he came to a stop sign, but since it would have necessitated shifting gears to come to a stop, he merely slowed down and then went across the intersection. A policeman stopped him and gave him quite a lecture on his error in this matter, ending his talk with the statement, "The next time, I want you to come to a complete stop." The Professor, in what must have been wide-eyed innocence, asked, "Is there any other kind of stop?" The story would never have been told except that Professor Gomberg was highly pleased with the policeman's answer, "Don't give me none of your lip, young feller."

Professor Gomberg spoke with a slight accent—not enough to cause any trouble in understanding, but just enough to give his speech a charming individuality.

In collecting material for this biographical sketch, I have written to and talked with many persons who knew Professor Gomberg well over a period of many years. They have all commented on his modesty, politeness, kindness, and generosity—admirable traits, and all very true. It is because of his modesty and his unwillingness to talk about himself that so little is known of his childhood. In his lectures, if he spoke of his own research, it was referred to only as "work done in this laboratory." He received many honors, but he never mentioned them. Among these honors were membership in the National Academy of Sciences (1914), honorary membership in the Netherlands Chemical Society, the Nichols Medal (1914), the Willard Gibbs Medal (1925), the Chandler Medal (1927), the presidency of the American Chemical Society (1931), honorary Doctor of Science degrees from the University of Chicago (1929) and the Polytechnic Institute of Brooklyn (1932), and the degree of Doctor of Laws from his alma mater in 1937.

There is an interesting anecdote that illustrates his modesty and kindness. Professor Gomberg let it be known that he felt that it would be inappropriate for him to endorse applications for membership in the American Chemical Society during the time he was President of the society. He feared that his endorsement might indicate to some that he was using his presidency to push his friends ahead. One of the graduate students in the Chemistry Department at Michigan who wished to join the society evidently had not heard of Professor Gomberg's feeling on the matter, so he asked the Professor for his endorsement. When the Professor hesitated, the student asked, "You *are* a member of the society, aren't you?" to which the Professor responded, "Yes, I am a member," and signed. He could not bring himself to embarrass the boy by explaining that he was president of the society. Yet, this modesty was not built on an inferiority complex. Dr. Bertrand Summers, a long-time friend, has written: "Most of the men whom you consult will probably mention the fact that he seemed rather shy and reticent. My own memory of those years when I knew him best was not so much these pleasing attributes that impressed me as it was the idea that there was considerable strength in his personality."[6]

One of his early colleagues, Dr. Eugene C. Sullivan, wrote: "He was dignified, quiet, and modest, although even in his early days rather conscious of his powers."[7]

Although Professor Gomberg was extremely kind and gentle, he could become angry if sufficiently provoked. During World War I, the United States found it difficult to obtain important synthetic drugs such as veronal, novocaine, and salvarsan, and there was much talk of synthesizing them here in the United States. A chemistry student at Michigan became

[6] Letter from Dr. Summers, March 30, 1960.
[7] Letter from Dr. E. C. Sullivan to Professor W. B. Pillsbury, January 14, 1960.

interested in the preparation of salvarsan, and discussed his plan with Professor Gomberg. Although the Professor felt that the synthesis was too difficult for an inexperienced chemist, he did not discourage the boy, for it was quite foreign to his nature to discourage anyone who wanted to do something worthwhile. In his enthusiasm, the young man mentioned his plan to a reporter on one of the Detroit papers, and said that he had discussed it with Professor Gomberg. The reporter added his own misdemeanor to that of the student, and wrote that Professor Gomberg and one of his students had synthesized salvarsan. When this came to the Professor's attention, he was terribly upset. As soon as he could locate the offending student, he took him to his office, and chastised him verbally with such anger and ferocity that everyone in that part of the building heard what he said.[8]

The Professor was so extremely courteous that it was almost impossible to go through a door behind him. He always stood aside to wait for whoever was with him to precede him through the door. Many persons who have written to me about Professor Gomberg have commented on this. Of course, we noted it when we were students, and we sometimes tried to arrange things so that he would have to precede us, but always to no avail. Professor Halford tells me that on one rare occasion he was able to rig the situation so that there was no alternative, and the Professor had to go through the door first. He knew that he had been tricked into this situation, and he accepted his defeat gracefully. Both he and Halford laughed about it.[9]

Professor Gomberg's kindness and generosity are illustrated by his solicitude for his sister, and this also introduces a sad note into the story. During the early days in Ann Arbor, they lived very humbly, almost like Russian peasants, but by the

8 Reported by Professor H. H. Willard.
9 Reported by Professor J. O. Halford.

time I knew them, they had a modest, but delightful, home near the campus. They used to entertain his graduate students at dinner once or twice a year, and we all remember Miss Gomberg as a pretty, very gracious woman. About the time Dr. Gomberg retired, his sister's health began to fail, and he spent the years of his retirement taking care of her. Many of his friends felt that she needed his help less than she felt she did, and that he was more solicitous of her health than was necessary. In any event, his concern for her kept him close to home. He once told me, with sadness but with no bitterness, that he had planned to spend those years in research and in travel, but because of her illness such activities were impossible. After his retirement, he seldom came to the Chemistry Building, although he had an office there, and he felt that travel away from Ann Arbor was completely out of the question.

Dr. Summers has written that, in 1944, he and Dr. Sullivan called on the Professor, and he adds, "I thought Dr. Gomberg had aged perceptibly. He wanted to prolong our visit and he even walked with us part of the way back to the university. I think he was a lonely man after his energetic life's work."[10] The Gombergs' friends often speculated on what dire consequences would ensue if Sonia should outlive her brother. This concern, too, proved to be unjustified, for she did live for several years after his death, in relative comfort.

Professor Gomberg was deeply interested in his students, both professionally and personally—even in their love affairs. He counseled them not to marry until they had finished their training, but not to wait too long after that. When he learned that his assistant, D. D. Van Slyke, had become engaged, he shook his head sadly and said, "It is too bad. He was *such* a good assistant." When Lee Cone Holt joined the Professor's group, he was asked to promise that he would leave the girls

[10] Letter from Dr. Bertrand Summers, March 30, 1960.

alone. He kept this promise reasonably well, and when he finished the work for his degree, the Professor told him, "You have kept your promise well. Now, don't wait too long."[11] When Werner Bachman told the Professor that he was engaged and planned to marry soon, the Professor replied with astonishment, "But, Werner, I had other plans for you." It developed that these other plans involved a post-doctorate fellowship for Werner in Karrer's laboratory in Zurich. Fortunately, both the marriage and the other plans were soon arranged.

The laboratory in which we worked joined the Professor's private laboratory, and he usually came in to see us five or six times every day. He commonly came to the building about half-past eight in the morning, donned his laboratory jacket, and came directly into our laboratory. Usually, he found us all at work, but one morning I was the only one of the three students who was there. After he had talked with me about my research for a moment, he asked, "Where are the other boys?" I explained that one of them was teaching a class and the other one had not yet arrived at the Chemistry Building. A cloud passed over his face and he said, "But you should all be here every morning at eight o'clock." Of course, I told the others, as he knew I would, and thereafter we were always there before he arrived.

He advised us that we should not work in the laboratory in the evenings, but spend that time in the library. He was a prodigious reader, and he expected us to be so, too. He told us that when he decided to be a chemist he read the *Berichte* from cover to cover, starting with Volume 1, Number 1. I think that when I worked with him thirty years later he was still reading the *Berichte* from cover to cover, and he seemed to remember everything that he read. Sometimes, when discussing our research with us, he would suggest that we look up a

11 See footnote 5.

certain article. He could always give us the name of the author and almost the exact year in which the article had been published. When Bachman was preparing to go to Switzerland, the Professor had him read the *Helvetica* in its entirety, beginning with Volume 1, so he'd know who the Swiss chemists were and what they had done. When I won an appointment at the University of Illinois, he instructed me to read all of the papers that the organic chemists at Illinois had published. I had only a little over a month for this rather ambitious project, and I hardly made a start on it. Nor did we follow his advice about spending our evenings in the library, for we knew that he would greet us in the laboratory in the morning, as he always did, with "Well, what have you done here since I saw you last?" He rather discouraged us from working in the Chemistry Building on Sundays and asked that, if we did so, we pull down the blinds so that we wouldn't offend any passers-by who might object to our laboring on the Sabbath. This pattern must have been different in earlier days, for Lee Cone Holt records that the entire research group, including the Professor, sometimes worked all night and often took their lunches to the laboratory on Saturdays and Sundays, so they could work through the entire day without interruption.

During my tenure at Michigan, Professor Gomberg had a weekly seminar with his little group of three or four students. When the name of some well-known organic chemist came into the discussion, he frequently told us anecdotes about the man or gave us some interesting bit about his life or his character. How he learned all these things, I never understood, for he seldom left Ann Arbor, and he didn't have many guests. In any event, these interludes were important, for in later years, when we read articles by the men whom he had described to us, we knew the authors not just as names but as live human beings, not unlike other people. It made chemistry come alive for us.

I remember particularly well the Professor's story of the origin of the long scientific polemic between Arthur Michael at Harvard and John Ulrich Nef at Chicago. When these men were young, they were students together in Germany. There was also a young American woman, Miss Abbott, who was doing graduate work in botany in the same university. Both men fell in love with her and both wanted to marry her. Nef won. This embittered Michael and, thereafter, he lost no opportunity to criticize Nef's scientific theories. It is interesting to note in passing that Michael remained a bachelor throughout his life.

On another occasion, Professor Gomberg told us of an organic chemist who was well known then, but who shall remain anonymous here. This man had taught at one of the prominent midwestern universities, but he incurred the displeasure of the president of the university by frequenting certain places that a professor should not patronize. When the president remonstrated with him, the chemist protested that he did not go to these places for the usual purpose, but that he was interested in sociology, and he wanted to talk with the girls about their profession and the lives they led. The president replied that he was bringing discredit to the university and that he must stop his sociological studies. The chemist promised that he would do so, but he did not keep his resolution and was soon forced to resign from the university. Upon his solemn promise that he would do no more sociological studies, he obtained a professorship at an eastern school of somewhat lower prestige. Unfortunately, his desire for sociology had too great a hold on him, and he was again dismissed. No university would then give him a professorship, and he was out of work for some time. He finally obtained a position with one of the government bureaus in Washington, where there was less concern about his evening activities. Professor Gomberg added that he did not know whether the learned chemist had continued his work in sociology or not. He was amused by this story in a detached sort of way, and he enjoyed telling it to us. If he was trying to interest us in this man's published papers, he could not have found a more effective way.

The Professor knew a lot about us and what went on in the laboratory, too, though we thought we were keeping some things from him. One of the students in the laboratory secreted some small booklets of pornographic literature in his desk, and invited students from other laboratories to come in to read them. If the Professor entered the laboratory, the booklets were quickly slipped into a pocket or dropped into an open drawer. This went on for some days, and the Professor seemed to be completely unaware of this desecration of the laboratory. However, a year or so later, when the owner of the booklets had completed the work for his degree and left the university, Professor Gomberg commented to one of the other staff members, "I was very disappointed in that boy. He kept dirty pictures in his desk, and he thought I didn't know."[12]

His students always held the Professor in great respect, and they did their best to make a good impression on him and to hide their mistakes from him. On one occasion, a student was analyzing an organic compound by the Carius method, in which the sample and an excess of concentrated nitric acid are sealed in a strong glass tube. The whole is then heated to a high enough temperature to bring about the complete oxidation of the organic material. Not infrequently, the pressure within the tube builds up to the point where the tube explodes. In order to avoid any danger, should this happen, it is customary to place the glass tube inside a steel pipe so that flying pieces of glass will be caught. On this occasion, the student who was performing the analysis had his hand over the end of the steel pipe when the glass tube exploded. The palm of his hand was

[12] Reported by Professor J. O. Halford.

peppered with small pieces of flying glass. He knew that the Professor would ask how he had injured his hand and, since he was ashamed to tell the true story of his carelessness, he went to great lengths to make up what seemed to be a credible tale. He told the Professor that he had fallen from his bicycle and that his hand had been rather badly scuffed on the gravel pathway. Whether the Professor believed this story, I do not know, but I rather doubt it.[13]

Professor Gomberg worked very hard in the preparation and delivery of his lectures, and he often left the lecture room perspiring profusely and completely exhausted. Yet, some way, he occasionally slipped in bits of humor that seemed to be completely spontaneous and were doubly enjoyed by the class because they were so unexpected. On one occasion, he was telling the students in his class in organic chemistry about various chemical journals and what might be found in them. Among others, he mentioned the *Bulletin de la Société Chimique de France* and commented, "The name of this journal is abbreviated B-u-l-l, and frequently that's all you find there." On another occasion, in discussing an experiment that the class was to do, he noted that the laboratory manual said that the reaction mixture should be allowed to stand overnight. He explained that this meant that it should stand for several hours, adding slyly, "There is no virtue in darkness." On still another occasion, when he was lecturing about mercaptans, he passed a vial of material around the class and commented that it had such a strong odor that one could smell it even through the glass. The students readily confirmed this, but he told one of his colleagues later, "I didn't tell them that the bottle had a tiny pinhole in it."[14]

Fred Wiselogle served as the Professor's lecture assistant

[13] Reported by Professor H. H. Willard.
[14] *Ibid.*

during his graduate days, and has sent me the following story. It illustrates well the Professor's patience and his unwillingness to say anything about himself.

"During the First World War, Professor Gomberg, working with Jimmy Norris, developed a procedure for mustard gas—an experience that he told with great relish to the organic chemistry class. Furthermore, he impressed on his class the tremendous difference in the toxicity of mustard gas and of the intermediate β, β'-dihydroxydiethylsulfide, by dipping a stirring rod in a bottle of the liquid and running it across his tongue. He then proceeded to hold up a similar bottle of mustard gas and point out the horrible consequences of contact with the skin. As his assistant, it was my responsibility to have the bottles on the lecture table for the lecture—although prior to this I had no idea what he proposed to do with them. Much to my horror, the next day Gomberg came to work with an acute burn on his lip. You can imagine my feeling, since I could only assume that inadvertently he had picked up the wrong bottle or somehow I was responsible for the sore. Professor Gomberg never criticized me nor appeared to give any thought to the burn, and it was only several weeks later that I learned from others that he recalled the stopper of the mustard gas bottle popping out while he was holding it and ascribed the lip burn to a transfer of the spilled mustard gas from his finger to his lips."[15]

The Professor did not enjoy writing, and it was hard for him, but he worked at every paper until it was a model of diction and clarity. When we prepared our Ph.D. theses, he had us read them aloud to him, for he felt that one couldn't get the real meaning of a paper without reading it aloud. Of course, he interrupted us frequently to question and criticize, or to suggest additional experiments. These sessions sometimes

[15] Letter from F. Y. Wiselogle, August 6, 1965.

lasted for two or three hours, and they were very tiring and frustrating. After each such session, we retired to our own laboratory to rewrite and then to read aloud again to him. In some cases, this was done several times before he was satisfied with the writing. It is reported that one student never did get his thesis in such shape that the Professor could accept it; finally, Dr. Gomberg wrote most of the thesis himself. One fairly large section of my thesis was rewritten four times, until at last he seemed to be satisfied. But, as I was leaving the room, he asked, "Is it really important to include this section in your thesis?" The question amazed me, but after a little reflection I had to agree that the section was not important to the thesis, and we decided to omit it. I was angry that he had let me do so much work all to no avail, but I have never forgotten the lesson. Say what needs to be said, and no more.

When it came to making compounds, Dr. Gomberg was amazingly adept. He had remarkably good laboratory technique, and he gave us countless suggestions about the tricks of the trade. I fear that I didn't master them as well as I should have. I remember especially one occasion when I had a compound that refused to crystallize. I had worked for a week on it and had tried all the tricks that I knew, even to leaving the dish open on the desk while I swept the floor, in the hope that a seed crystal in the dust might fall into the mixture, but even this did not work. I was very discouraged, and when he came to the laboratory and asked about my progress, I told him that I felt that I would never get crystals from this material. He took the dish in his hand, looked at it carefully, and said, "This looks very promising. Give me some benzene." When I handed him the bottle of benzene, he poured a few drops of the liquid into the syrup in the dish and stirred it slowly. "Now, some ligroin." He added a few drops of this liquid and stirred some more. Suddenly, crystals appeared. I questioned him eagerly. "How did you do that? How did you know what solvents to use?" He smiled, but his only answer was, "You learn with experience." No doubt this is true, but he had more than experience —he had chemical intuition and keen perception.

Professor Gomberg told us repeatedly, "It is not serious if someone finds your interpretation of an experiment to be wrong, but it is disgraceful if there are errors in your experiments." So he did every experiment over and over until he was sure the results were correct. This habit was most annoying to those of us who were more easily convinced, but time has proved the wisdom of his method.

At the Organic Symposium in Ann Arbor in 1941, Professor Gomberg was the guest of honor at the banquet. When he was called upon to speak, he reminisced about his life and work in Ann Arbor. Many of those in the audience had known him for many years, but they had never heard him open his heart as he did that evening. He talked for more than two hours while the audience sat enthralled by his story and by his warm, friendly personality. Unfortunately, no one took notes. Later, when I began to collect material for this memoir, several persons recalled hearing that talk, and the spell that it cast over them. But, alas, none could remember what the Professor said! Like a fine symphony or the masterpiece of a great artist, this talk lifted the spirits of those who heard it, but none could later describe it. They knew only that it was a wonderful talk and that it recounted the events and the philosophy of an amazingly interesting and productive life.

And so it is. The beginning of the story is quite unknown, and the talk that summed it up is lost. All that can be recorded are the facts which are of public record and the anecdotes that tell something of the spirit of this remarkable man.

ACKNOWLEDGMENTS

Very little has been written about Professor Gomberg's life and work. In addition to the works mentioned in footnotes 3 and 5, there are evidently only two articles—an anonymous obituary, *Chem. Eng. News,* 25 (1947):548, and a somewhat longer obituary by Professor C. S. Schoepfle and Professor W. E. Bachmann, *J. Am. Chem. Soc.,* 69 (1947):2921. The remainder of the material in this article has been obtained by correspondence and conversations with Professor Gomberg's friends. References are given to several of these sources. In addition, I am greatly indebted to Professor L. C. Anderson, Professor B. A. Soule, Professor W. B. Pillsbury, Professor E. H. Kraus, Professor F. F. Blicke, and Mrs. H. S. Bull.

BIBLIOGRAPHY

KEY TO ABBREVIATIONS

Am. Chem. J. = American Chemical Journal
Ann. Chem. = Justis Liebigs Annalen der Chemie
Ber. = Berichte der deutschen chemischen Gesellschaft
Chem. Rev. = Chemical Reviews
Ind. Eng. Chem. News Ed. = Industrial and Engineering Chemistry, News Edition
J. Am. Chem. Soc. = Journal of the American Chemical Society
J. Ind. Eng. Chem. = Journal of Industrial and Engineering Chemistry

1892

Trimethylxanthine and some of its derivatives. Am. Chem. J., 14:611.

1893

A chemical study of the resinous contents and their distribution in trees of the long-leaf pine, before and after tapping for turpentine. Bulletin, United States Department of Agriculture, Division of Forestry, 8:34.

1895

On the action of some inorganic cyanides upon chlorocaffeine. Am. Chem. J., 17:403.

1896

On the action of Wagner's reagent upon caffeine and a new method for the estimation of caffeine. J. Am. Chem. Soc., 18:331.
Perhalides of caffeine. J. Am. Chem. Soc., 18:347.
A new form of potash bulb. J. Am. Chem. Soc., 18:941.

1897

Tetraphenylmethan. Ber., 30:2043.

1898

Ueber Isonitramin und Nitrosoisobuttersäure. Ann. Chem., 300:59.
On tetraphenylmethane. J. Am. Chem. Soc., 20:773.

With A. Campbell. Hydrazo- and azo derivatives of triphenylmethane. J. Am. Chem. Soc., 20:780.

A periodide of triphenylbromomethane.   J. Am. Chem. Soc., 20:790.

1899

With A. Van Zwaluwenburg.   Does *Taraxacum officinalis* contain
an alkaloid?   American Pharmaceutical Association Proceedings, 47:305.

1900

Diazocaffeine.   Am. Chem. J., 23:51.

Ueber die Darstellung des Triphenylchlormethans.   Ber., 33:3144;
J. Am. Chem. Soc., 22:752.

Triphenylmethyl, ein Fall von dreiwerthigem Kohlenstoff.   Ber.,
33:3150; J. Am. Chem. Soc., 22:757.

1901

On triphenylchloromethane.   J. Am. Chem. Soc., 23:109.

With O. W. Voedisch.   On tritolylchlormethane.   J. Am. Chem.
Soc., 23:177.

On trivalent carbon.   Am. Chem. J., 25:317.

On trivalent carbon.   J. Am. Chem. Soc., 23:496.

Ueber das Triphenylmethyl. III.   Ber., 34:2726.

1902

Ueber das Triphenylmethyl. IV.   Ber., 35:1822; J. Am. Chem. Soc.,
24:597.

Ueber Triphenylmethyl. V. Ein Beitrag zur Kenntniss der Car-
boniumsalze.   Ber., 35:2397.

Triphenylmethyl. VI. Condensation zum Hexaphenyläthan.   Ber.,
35:3914.

1903

Triphenylmethyl. VII. Condensation Mittels Salzsäure zum Hexaphenyläthan.   Ber., 36:376.

The action of zinc on triphenylchloromethane.   Am. Chem. J.,
29:364.

With H. W. Berger.   Ueber Tetraphenylmethan.   Ber., 36:1088.

With G. T. Davis.   Ueber Triphenylmethylacetat.   Ber., 36:3924;
J. Am. Chem. Soc., 25:1269.

Ueber die Existenzfähigkeit einer Klass von Körpern, die dem Triphenylmethyl analog sind. Ber., 36:3927; J. Am. Chem. Soc., 25:1274.

1904

Ueber Triphenylmethyl. VIII. Ber., 37:1626.

With L. H. Cone. Ueber Triphenylmethyl. IX. Ber., 37:2033.

With L. H. Cone. Ueber Triphenylmethyl. X. Ber., 37:3538.

With N. E. Tousley. Some tri-p-tolylmethane derivatives. J. Am. Chem. Soc., 26:1516.

1905

With L. H. Cone. Ueber Triphenylmethyl. XI. Ber., 38:1333.

With L. H. Cone. Ueber Triphenylmethyl. XII. Ber., 38:2447.

1906

With L. H. Cone. Ueber Triphenylmethyl. XIII. Ber., 39:1461.

With L. H. Cone. Ueber Triphenylmethyl. XIV. Ber., 39:2957.

With L. H. Cone. Ueber Triphenylmethyl. XV. Ber., 39:3274.

1907

Ueber Triphenylmethyl. XVI. Tautomerie in der Triphenyl-methan-Reihe. Ber., 40:1847.

1909

Ueber Triphenylmethyl. XVII. Tautomerie in der Triphenyl-methan-Reihe. Ber., 42:406.

With L. H. Cone. Ueber Triphenylmethyl. XVIII. Zur Kenntniss der Chinocarboniumsalze. Ann. Chem., 370:142; a correction, *ibid.*, 371:388.

1910

With L. H. Cone. Ueber Triphenylmethyl. XIX. Zur Kenntniss der Chinocarboniumsalze. Ann. Chem., 376:183.

1911

With D. D. Van Slyke. On triphenylmethyl. XX. J. Am. Chem. Soc., 33:531.

With C. J. West. The action of halogen acids upon the oxyaryl-xanthenols. J. Am. Chem. Soc., 33:1211.

1912

With C. J. West. On triphenylmethyl. XXI. Quinocarbonium salts of the hydroxyxanthenols. J. Am. Chem. Soc., 34:1529.

1913

Triphenylmethyl. XXII. Ethers or oxides in the triphenylmethane series. J. Am. Chem. Soc., 35:200.

Ueber Triphenylmethyl-oxyd. Ber., 46:225.

With R. L. Jickling. Thiophene analogs of triphenylmethyl. J. Am. Chem. Soc., 35:446.

On triphenyl. XXIII. Tautomerism of the hydroxytriphenylcarbinols. J. Am. Chem. Soc., 35:1035.

1914

The existence of free radicals. J. Am. Chem. Soc., 36:1144.

1915

With C. S. Schoepfle. Triphenylmethyl. XXIV. The additive compounds of triphenylmethyl and some saturated hydrocarbons. J. Am. Chem. Soc., 37:2569.

With R. L. Jickling. Triphenylmethyl. XXV. Preparation of p-hydroxy-triphenylcarbinol and attempts to isolate the corresponding triarylmethyl. J. Am. Chem. Soc., 37:2575.

1916

With N. E. Van Stone. Triphenylmethyl. XXVI. Tautomerism of triarylcarbinols. J. Am. Chem. Soc., 38:1577.

1917

With C. S. Schoepfle. The molecular weights of the triarylmethyls. Proceedings of the National Academy of Sciences, 3:457.

With C. S. Schoepfle. Triphenylmethyl. XXVII. The molecular weights of the triarylphenylmethyls. J. Am. Chem. Soc., 39:1652.

With L. C. Johnson. Triphenylmethyl. XXVIII. Tautomerism of the triarylcarbinols. J. Am. Chem. Soc., 39:1674.

With Oliver Kamm. Tetraphenylmethane. J. Am. Chem. Soc., 39:2009.

With J. D. Todd. 4,4′-Dimethyl-benzophenone and its condensation with phenol. J. Am. Chem. Soc., 39:2392.

1919

Ethylene chlorohydrin and β,β-dichloroethylsulfide. J. Am. Chem. Soc., 41:1414.

With C. S. Schoepfle. Triphenylmethyl. XXIX. A study of the properties of diphenyl-α-naphthylmethyl. J. Am. Chem. Soc., 41:1655.

1920

With F. W. Sullivan, Jr. Tautomerism in the triaryl carbinol series: di-phenyl-4-hydroxy-1-naphthyl carbinol and diphenyl-2-hydroxy-1-naphthyl carbinol. J. Am. Chem. Soc., 42:1864.

With N. A. Lange. Tautomerism in the triaryl-carbinols: mono-para-hydroxy-diphenyl-α-naphthyl carbinol. J. Am. Chem. Soc., 42:1879.

With C. C. Buchler. The preparation of benzyl esters and other benzyl derivatives from benzyl chloride. J. Am. Chem. Soc., 42:2059.

1921

With C. C. Buchler. Benzyl ethers of carbohydrates. J. Am. Chem. Soc., 43:1904.

With Wesley Minnis. Phenyl-thio-xanthyl. J. Am. Chem. Soc., 43:1940.

With E. C. Britton. 2,2′-Sulfonido-triphenylmethyl. J. Am. Chem. Soc., 43:1945.

1922

With F. W. Sullivan, Jr. Triphenylmethyl. XXX. Diphenyl-beta-naphthylmethyl and the color of free radicals. J. Am. Chem. Soc., 44:1810.

With D. L. Tabern. The composition of erythrosin. J. Ind. Eng. Chem., 14:1115.

1923

With D. Nishida. Triphenylmethyl. XXXI. Tautomerism of ortho-hydroxy-triphenyl carbinol: ortho-hydroxy and alkyloxy-triphenylmethyl. J. Am. Chem. Soc., 45:190.

With C. C. Buchler. Triphenylmethyl. XXXII. Para-benzyloxy and para-methoxy-triphenylmethyl. J. Am. Chem. Soc., 45:207.

The reaction between silver perchlorate and iodine. Chlorine tetra-oxide. J. Am. Chem. Soc., 45:398.

With F. F. Blicke. Triphenylmethyl. XXXIII. Quinoidation in the triaryls. J. Am. Chem. Soc., 45:1765.

1924

Organic radicals. Chem. Rev., 1:91.

With W. E. Bachmann. The synthesis of biaryl compounds by means of the diazo reaction. J. Am. Chem. Soc., 46:2339.

1925

With H. R. Snow. The condensation of carbon tetrachloride and phenol: aurin. J. Am. Chem. Soc., 47:198.

With L. C. Anderson. 3^1, 3^2, 3^3-Trimethyl-aurin (ortho-cresaurin) and 3^1, 3^2, 3^3-trimethyl-N^1, N^2, N^3-triphenyl-para-rosaniline (triphenyl-ros-ortho-toluidine). J. Am. Chem. Soc., 47:2022.

With G. C. Forrester. Triphenylmethyl. XXXIV. 2,5-, 2,4- and 3,4-Dimethoxy-triphenylmethyls. J. Am. Chem. Soc., 47:2373.

With W. J. McGill. Tautomerism of ortho-hydroxy-triaryl carbinols which contain naphthyl groups. J. Am. Chem. Soc., 47:2392.

Elements with anomalous valences. Chem. Rev., 2:301.

1926

With D. L. Tabern. Triphenylmethyl. XXXV. Halogen-substituted acridyls. The reactivity of the halogen in them. J. Am. Chem. Soc., 48:1345.

With J. C. Pernert. Methylbiphenyls. J. Am. Chem. Soc., 48: 1372.

1927

With W. E. Bachmann. The reducing action of a mixture of magnesium iodide (or bromide) and magnesium on aromatic ketones. Probable formation of magnesium subiodide (or subbromide). J. Am. Chem. Soc., 49:236; a correction, *ibid.*, 49: 2666.

With W. E. Bachmann. The reduction of benzil by the binary

system, magnesium + magnesium iodide (or bromide). J. Am. Chem. Soc., 49:2584.

1928

Radicals in chemistry, past and present. J. Ind. Eng. Chem., 20:159.

With L. C. Anderson. Tautomerism of hydroxytriarylcarbinols. J. Am. Chem. Soc., 50:203.

With W. E. Bachmann. p-Bromodiphenyl. Organic Syntheses, 8: 42.

With W. E. Bachmann. The reaction between the binary system, magnesium + magnesium iodide, and aromatic acids and acid derivatives. J. Am. Chem. Soc., 50:2762.

1929

With J. C. Bailar, Jr. Halogen-substituted aromatic pinacols and the formation of ketyl radicals, $R_2(IMgO)C$-. J. Am. Chem. Soc., 51:2229.

With F. J. Van Natta. Reduction of aromatic 1,2-diketones by the binary system magnesium iodide (or bromide) + magnesium. J. Am. Chem. Soc., 51:2238.

With J. C. Bailar, Jr. and F. J. Van Natta. The reducing effect of the binary system (MgX_2 + Mg) upon organic compounds in anhydrous solvents. Recueil des travaux chimiques de Pays-Bas, 48:847.

1930

With W. E. Bachmann. The action of the system Mg + $MgBr_2$ upon triphenylcarbinol, triphenylbromomethane and upon triphenylmethyl. J. Am. Chem. Soc., 52:2455.

With R. G. Clarkson. Spirans with four aromatic radicals on the spiro carbon atom. J. Am. Chem. Soc., 52:2881.

With W. E. Bachmann. The reaction between the binary system magnesium + magnesium iodide and aromatic aldehydes. J. Am. Chem. Soc., 52:4967.

The R. V. Shankland. The reducing action of compounds containing the group > CHOMgI. J. Am. Chem. Soc., 52:4973.

1931

Some reflections concerning valence variation and atomic structure. Science, 74:553.

1932

A survey of the chemistry of free radicals. Journal of Chemical Education, 9:439.

Chemical achievements of a decade and the relation between theoretical and applied chemistry. Ind. Eng. Chem. News Ed., 10:167.

1934

With H. R. Gamrath. Concerning the $(ClO_4)_x$ radical. Transactions of the Faraday Society, 30:24.

1935

With W. E. Gordon. Halochromic salts from some triarylmethylthioglycolic acids. J. Am. Chem. Soc., 57:119.

1936

The American Chemical Society and the science of chemistry. Ind. Eng. Chem. News Ed., 14:342.

Edwin Hubble

EDWIN POWELL HUBBLE

November 20, 1889–September 28, 1953

BY N. U. MAYALL

E DWIN HUBBLE, by his inspired use of the largest telescope of his time, the 100-inch reflector of the Mount Wilson Observatory, revolutionized our knowledge of the size, structure, and properties of the universe. He thus became the outstanding leader in the observational approach to cosmology, as contrasted with the previous work that involved much philosophical speculation. Although he regarded himself primarily as an observational astronomer assembling and analyzing empirical data, Hubble, from the very beginning of his astronomical career, took the widest possible view of the relationship of his investigations to the general field of cosmology. Indeed, Edwin Hubble advanced the astronomical horizon on the universe by steps relatively as large in his time as those taken by Galileo in his studies of the solar system, and by the Herschels in their investigations of our own Milky Way stellar system.

PERSONAL HISTORY

In a conversation with the author Bernard Jaffe, Hubble is reported to have said that the best biographical memoir of a scientist would be written if each man set down, as well as he could, the way he came to do the work he did. In this way his work would be separated completely from the man's own personal history, which Hubble thought need not enter the picture. Jaffe is reported to have replied that the personal side also had value, possibly in reflecting the effect of the man's times and environment in determining what he went about doing.

Since Hubble firmly kept his personal history in the background, there is little about it in the literature of astronomy. Through the generosity of Mrs. Hubble, however, the present writer was given access to her journals, which form an important part of the collection of biographical materials in the Huntington Library, San Marino, California. These journals contain a wealth of information, enough for a biography of much greater scope than this memoir. From the many events and experiences described so perceptively and understandingly in the journals, a selection has been made of some that seem especially revealing of Hubble's character and philosophy. In many cases the wording follows closely that of the journal entries, particularly when they quote Hubble's remarks. The verbatim record should be accurate, since Hubble himself read, corrected, and made suggestions, such as, for example, "The next time at camp there should be more about fish."

The Hubble family for many generations produced pioneering and patriotic individuals. Hubble's ancestors were from the British Isles; Richard Hubble, an officer in the Royalist army, came to the United States in the seventeenth century. About him Hubble remarked, "I was always glad that he waited until after the king was beheaded . . . whenever there was trouble in England someone of the family left in a hurry." Richard settled in Connecticut, prospered, and left five thousand dollars to each of his eleven children, "a good deal of money in the seventeenth century," Hubble commented. Justus Hubble, one of Edwin's forefathers, fought in the Revolutionary War and later settled in Virginia. At the time of the Civil War the family was divided in its loyalty. Edwin's paternal grandfather joined the Union army, while other members of the family fought for the Confederates. Edwin's mother was Virginia Lee James, from Virginia City, Nevada, and his father was John Powell Hubble, from Missouri, where Edwin himself was born in Marshfield on November 20, 1889, during a visit of the parents to his grandparents. Hubble, however, said later that he would rather have been born in Kentucky, where his relatives had been living and where his ancestors had established themselves. There were seven children in the family, three brothers and four sisters; Edwin was the fifth child and the second son.

Among the many pleasant childhood memories Hubble recalled were long country wanderings spent in watching birds and animals, swimming, and ice skating. He was expected to obey at once, without questioning. He was spanked when small, and had "good lickings" when older. In later years he approved of this discipline, saying, "It did me a lot of good." He liked and read many books, such as novels by Jules Verne and H. Rider Haggard, especially *King Solomon's Mines*. His father was connected with an insurance company; he had his office in Chicago and settled his family in suburban Wheaton, where many years later Grote Reber carried out his pioneering research in radio astronomy. Young Edwin corresponded with his grandfather, who once wrote to his twelve-year-old grandson to ask some questions about Mars. The reply so pleased the grandfather that he had it printed in a Springfield newspaper.

Like many other youngsters, Edwin earned his first money by delivering morning papers in Wheaton. At Wheaton High School he participated actively in athletics, with football as his favorite game, although he also entered many track events. In a later year Mrs. Hubble once was surprised by her husband's exact estimate of her height of 5 feet 4 inches. Hubble's explanation was, "I was a high jumper, my dear." On his high school commencement day in 1906, the principal said, "Edwin Hubble, I have watched you for four years and I have never seen you study for ten minutes." He then paused for what was an awful moment for Edwin, and continued, "Here is a scholarship to the University of Chicago."

By a mistake, this high school scholarship was also awarded to another student, thus the money had to be halved, and Edwin had to supply the rest. He paid his expenses by tutoring, by summer work, and, in his junior year, by a scholarship in physics and by working as a laboratory assistant to Robert Millikan. When Edwin left home his mother asked him to give up football. Instead he played basketball, and in 1909 was on the team that won the championship of the West. He also took up college boxing and was so successful that promoters urged him to turn professional and train to fight the heavyweight champion, Jack Johnson. He received a college letter in athletics for his participation in track, boxing, and basketball.

During summer vacations he worked as a surveyor and civil engineer in the woods around the Great Lakes, in the regions where railroads were competing for rights-of-way to iron mines. At that time the border towns were very rough; one evening when walking through the railroad yards, Edwin was held up by two ruffians. He laughed at them, walked on past, but was stabbed in the back below his shoulder. He turned and knocked one man out, while the other ran away. Another time, two girls stopped him to ask help in getting a drunken lumberjack from a bridge. Edwin's friendly words changed the drunken man's challenging mood to one of affection, so he was able to get the lumberjack home, where the man's wife thought Edwin was responsible for her husband's state. At the end of one summer he and another worker were the last to leave, but by a change of schedule they were left waiting in vain at the railroad station, without provisions. They walked out of the woods in three days, without food, although Edwin said, "We could have killed a porcupine or small game, but there was no need, and anyway, there was plenty of water." The experience gained from his work as a surveyor later served him well during World War II at Aberdeen, where he laid out the firing and bombing ranges for ballistic research.

In 1910 Hubble received his B.S. degree from the University of Chicago, and in the same year was awarded a Rhodes Scholarship, under which he read Roman and English Law at Queen's College, Oxford. In athletics he was an Oxford Blue, taking part in track and boxing and rowing stroke in the Queen's boat. Some years later he was made an Honourary Fellow of Queen's College. He returned to the United States in 1913, passed the bar examination September 2, and practiced law halfheartedly for a year thereafter in Louisville, Kentucky. He reported that at this time he "chucked the law for astronomy, and I knew that even if I were second-rate or third-rate, it was astronomy that mattered." Thus in 1914 he returned to the University of Chicago for postgraduate work leading to his doctoral degree in astronomy. He found congenial men among the faculty—Millikan, Gale, Michelson, Breasted, and Moulton. Hubble's undergraduate experiences were helpful to him when he was asked to serve as head of Snell Hall, which had the reputation of housing the toughest campus elements. "They never gave any trouble," Hubble recalled, "partly perhaps because I had been a C man and because I boxed." He had, in fact, appeared in an exhibition bout with the French champion, Carpentier.

During his graduate student days at Yerkes Observatory he once strolled down to a lakeside pier, where a professor and his wife also were walking. She fell in and Edwin dived in to help her out. She struggled and grabbed him, but Hubble related that "I didn't like to knock her out, so as the water was not too deep, I set her on my shoulders, which just brought her head above the surface while I walked underwater until it became shallow and I could put her down on the shore. I thought it odd," he added reflectively, "that her husband showed no warmth in his thanks, nor did he seem particularly glad to see her."

While finishing work for his doctorate early in 1917, Hubble was invited by Hale to join the staff of the Mount Wilson Observatory, Pasadena, California. Although this was one of the greatest of astronomical opportunities, it came in April of that fateful year. After sitting up all night to finish his Ph.D. thesis, and taking the oral examination the next morning, Hubble enlisted in the infantry and telegraphed Hale, "Regret cannot accept your invitation. Am off to the war."

Hubble was commissioned a captain in the 343d Infantry, 86th Division, and later became a major. His first assignment was to take discards (many of whom were AWOL's), called "replacements," to camp. An armed guard brought two men to the station in handcuffs. Edwin said, "I have enough to do without looking after you. Take the handcuffs off these men." In return the grateful men offered to inspect food supplies for bulged tins (of spoiled food), since they were experts after so much KP. The result was that there were no food-poisoning cases on the long, slow train trip. The train arrived with no deserters, no sick men, and no men unaccounted for.

The official history of the 86th Division relates the following story. One of the commanding general's standing orders was that, when he met an officer, the latter should stop work, stand at attention, salute, give his name and rank, and account for the activities of the moment. One morning Edwin was riding a bicycle on the drill field and saw the general. He dismounted, saluted, and said, "Good Morning, General, nice day, sir." The general snapped, "Major, can it be that you do not know what my orders stipulate on the procedure to be taken by an officer whom I meet?" The major looked the general squarely in the eyes, saluted, hopped on the bike, and said, "Sir, Major Hubble, 86th Infantry, getting on his bicycle and riding away." On another occasion at a dinner of civilians in Rockford, his hostess challenged him to inspect her kitchen for cleanliness, because he had said army standards were very high. He reluctantly agreed, so with guests and hostess looking on, he took out a white handkerchief and wiped the inside of a stove leg, the joint between blade and handle of a knife, and the electric light cord, all of which produced black marks. "This," he said, "is a test for army kitchens," and afterwards doubted if his hostess ever forgave him.

Hubble was sent to France where he served as a field and line officer. Early in November 1918 he was injured by a bursting shell, from which he suffered a concussion and some damage to his right elbow. After the armistice he was called to serve as a judge advocate on courts-martial because of his Oxford law degree, and later he became administrative head of the American officers assigned to the universities of Oxford, Cambridge, and Wales.

He returned to the United States in the summer of 1919, was mustered out in San Francisco, and went immediately to Pasadena, California. Although he deplored the evils of war, he nevertheless admitted enjoying army life. He liked the plain hard living under campaign conditions, the simple rations, the discipline and adventure, and the living and working together with fighting men. He took no war insurance, no pensions, no wound remuneration, or allowance of any kind. He kept only his tin hat, the crossed rifles of the 343d Infantry, the gold maple leaves of a major, and a German trench dagger "to cut the pages of French books."

On February 26, 1924, Edwin Hubble and Grace Burke

were married in Pasadena, California. Mrs. Hubble recalls that the first description of her future husband was given to her by W. H. Wright, at that time Astronomer in the Lick Observatory. "He is a hard worker," he said, "he wants to find out about the universe; that shows how young he is."

Hubble worked at the Mount Wilson Observatory until the summer of 1942, when he left to do war work at the Aberdeen Proving Ground. He has described his assignment in the following manner: "Some time after Pearl Harbor, while I was trying to get back into the Infantry, I was called in by Army Ordnance and told, in effect, to stop that nonsense, that I had been ear-marked long before for a job in Ordnance. . . . My name, they told me, was top of the list because ballistics had a curious affinity with astronomy, and, moreover, as a line officer in the last war I might appreciate the significance of some of the problems as viewed from positions in front of the guns as well as behind the guns. . . . I rushed to a dictionary. Ballistics, it seemed, is the science of hurling missiles against an enemy. This seemed a trifle thin so I turned to the encyclopaedia; there I found a long article, but it puzzled me. Ballistics was either underdeveloped or highly classified. So I went to Aberdeen, partly to find out. . . . I found out. . . . Ballistics was both underdeveloped and highly classified." At the Ballistics Research Laboratory, Aberdeen Proving Ground, Hubble was Chief of Exterior Ballistics and Director of the Supersonic Wind Tunnel. In a letter to Mrs. Hubble, September 2, 1942, Hubble wrote: "I am more and more impressed with the place. It is not the home of genius but it knows the answers to many problems and how to get the answers for others. And best of all, it fights for high standards—when a conclusion is reached and a statement formulated, you treat it with respect or get into trouble." For his valuable service to his country during the war he was awarded the Medal of Merit in 1946.

After World War II Hubble returned to his position at the Mount Wilson Observatory where his research, so brilliantly carried out between two world wars, had provided strong evidence of the need for a telescope larger than the 100-inch reflector. He had assisted greatly in the design of the 200-inch Hale telescope, and had served on the Mount Wilson Observatory Advisory Committee for building the Mount Palomar Observatory. "With the 200-inch," he said in a BBC broadcast in London, "we may grasp what now we can scarcely brush with our fingertips." As Chief of Research, he planned in advance a broad program for this great instrument. "What do you expect to find with the 200-inch?" he was asked, and he replied, "We hope to find something we hadn't expected."

Hubble was also active in his community. He was elected to the Board of Trustees of the Huntington Library, as successor to George Ellery Hale, and he served on this Board from 1938 until his death. He organized the Los Angeles Committee on Foreign Relations and served as a member and its chairman.

He was elected to the National Academy of Sciences in 1927.

Hubble had considerable foresight not only in matters pertaining to astronomy but also in political and international affairs. He recognized very early that the European policy of appeasement in the 1930s was doomed to failure, and that this country would again be drawn into war. When Germany committed her first acts of aggression, he said, "This is a world war and we are in it." In the months preceding the U.S. entry into the war, he made many speeches throughout the country, and he advocated immediate participation by the United States as an ally of Great Britain. In October 1941 Hubble was introduced to two visiting Englishmen as "Pro-British," to which he replied, "Hell, I'm for civilization."

Hubble was an accomplished and eloquent speaker, well able to hold the attention of his audience. An interesting example of this ability occurred in Pasadena after a very damaging earthquake in March 1933. The guests at the Huntington Hotel had panicked and were agitatedly canceling their reservations and trying to leave as soon as possible. The hotel manager, a friend of Hubble, called him to come over in order to try to calm the guests. Hubble suggested getting a man from the Cal Tech Seismology Laboratory, but the manager insisted that he wanted Hubble because he "could give them confidence." Hubble agreed and told his audience they were fortunate to have experienced an earthquake without suffering any damage. He described the geological history of southern California, the locations of the major faults, and explained that damage occurred in poorly planned and constructed buildings. He told his audience that they need have no fear about the hotel falling down, because he and the manager had inspected it that morning. What he did not tell them was that his own house and the hotel were built on an earthquake fault, later named the "Huntington-Hubble" fault by a geologist at Cal Tech. Hubble's talk at the hotel saved the season.

Hubble had a deep interest in science and philosophy, and he gave his library to the Mount Wilson Observatory. He had collected many books covering his three principal interests: Nicolas de Cusa (1401-1464), Giordano Bruno (1548-1600), and selections from Chinese science and philosophy.

Hubble was a very skillful dry-fly fisherman and did much fishing in this country in the Rockies, in England on the River Test at Longstock, and at Bossington House near Stockbridge. In July 1949, while fishing in the Rockies, he suffered an attack of coronary thrombosis. In May 1953 Hubble went to England, where he gave the George Darwin Lecture, the Cormac Lecture of the Royal Society of Scotland, and a lecture before the Royal Institution of Great Britain. In Paris he attended a meeting of the Institut de France, of which he was a member. He came back to Bossington House, the residence of his friend Sir Richard Fairey. Upon his return home, he continued his researches at the Mount Wilson and Palomar Observatories, where he was active until the time of his death, from a cerebral thrombosis, on September 28, 1953.

RÉSUMÉ OF RESEARCH

In order truly to appreciate the remarkable contributions to the field of extragalactic research made by Edwin Hubble, it is necessary to review briefly the state of this knowledge in the early part of the twentieth century. About 1900 only speculation as to the nature of the thousands of faint nebulous objects was available. Nebular research in the eighteenth and nineteenth centuries was restricted primarily to the cataloguing of these faint objects. With the application of photography, spectrographs, and telescopes of increasingly larger size to the study of the nebulae, several different types of objects were differentiated. A large number of these made up the group called "extragalactic nebulae" by Hubble, who never accepted the term "galaxy" to describe them. These small, usually symmetrical objects, found everywhere in the sky, except in the plane of the Milky Way, were beyond the limit of detailed study with small or moderate-sized telescopes in operation during the first two decades of the twentieth century.

Toward the end of 1923, Hubble, using the 100-inch reflecting telescope on Mount Wilson, was able to resolve several of the largest spiral nebulae into stars. In particular, among the brighter resolved stars Hubble was able to identify some having characteristics identical to a type of variable stars called Cepheids. These objects had been recognized and carefully studied in our own galaxy and in the Magellanic Clouds, and their intrinsic brightnesses, or luminosities, were known with order-of-magnitude accuracy. Thus, by measuring the apparent brightnesses of these Cepheids in a few of the largest extra-galactic nebulae, and by knowing the luminosities of these variables, Hubble determined the first reliable extragalactic distances, which were of the order of a million light-years— far greater than any previously measured. He then extended this research to determinations of secondary distance criteria, such as estimates of luminosities of the brightest nonvariable stars in spiral nebulae, and finally of the total luminosities of the nebulae themselves, which provided a distance indicator so bright as to be useful for distances hundreds of times greater than those measurable by Cepheids. With these observationally developed methods of distance measurement, he was able to sound the depths of space to distances out to 500 million light-years.

Hubble combined his results on extragalactic distances with the radial velocities from the pioneering spectroscopic work of V. M. Slipher on bright nebulae, and with those from the work on fainter ones by his colleague Milton Humason, to develop a relationship between distance and velocity of recession for these extragalactic nebulae. The straight line relationship between these observational quantities, now known as Hubble's law of red-shifts, had immediate and far-reaching influence on all subsequent cosmological theories, particularly those given by Einstein's theory of relativity.

Hubble's observational approach to the study of extra-galactic nebulae is set forth in his classical book *The Realm of the Nebulae,* based on his Silliman Lectures given at Yale in 1935. This monograph, first published in 1936, met with immediate acclaim from both scientific and lay readers. Sir James Jeans's review of Hubble's book, the first review he had consented to write in ten years, states: "The author sets to work to record, in simple language and with much charm, the story of the recent enlargement of the visible universe. . . . It is a chapter of scientific history which has stirred the imagination not only of professional astronomers but also of the public at large. . . . Such is the arresting feast of 'plums' which Dr. Hubble might have served up in sensational setting had he elected to play the sensation-monger. He has preferred, and we will all thank him, to give a straight-forward record of patient and often laborious work, carried through with a skill, persistence and flair which often reminds us of Faraday. He sees the whole exploration as 'a case history of scientific research in a rather simple form,' and this determines the style of his record."

In the preface to a 1958 reprint of this book, Allan R. Sandage wrote: "*The Realm of the Nebulae* is important because it is still a source of inspiration in the scientific methods in this field. . . . Of course many of the details of the subject have changed since 1936 . . . but these are changes in numerical detail and not in fundamental philosophy or direction of attack. Hubble's original approach to observational cosmology remains."

In addition to his renowned study of the red-shifts of nebulae, Hubble undertook a detailed and comprehensive study of the nebulae as individuals, and he set up in 1926 a classification system generally used as the standard to the present time. A revision of this system based on manuscript notes left by Hubble has recently been included by Allan Sandage in his discussion of the magnificent collection of photographs reproduced in *The Hubble Atlas of Galaxies* (Carnegie Institution of Washington, Publication No. 618, 1961).

SCIENTIFIC WORK

In addition to being an active observer in astronomical research, Hubble also was a keen student of the history of science. He collected many books on this subject, because he held the opinion that, whenever possible, one should go to the original source materials; books written by the men themselves were of greater interest and significance than books written about them. In deference to his opinion, this account of his multifarious contributions to astronomy will consider chronologically his most outstanding papers, with copious use of his own words because they are so well chosen.

1920: "Photographic Investigations of Faint Nebulae." "Extremely little is known of the nature of nebulae, and no significant classification has yet been suggested; not even a precise definition has been formulated. The essential features are that they are situated outside our solar system, that they present sensible surfaces, and that they should be unresolved into separate stars. . . . Some at least of the great diffuse nebulosities . . . lie within our stellar system; while others, the great spirals, with their enormous radial velocities and insensible proper motions apparently lie outside our system." Thus Hubble summarized the state of knowledge of nebulae in the year 1920. This paper, based on his doctoral dissertation, deals with a statistical study of the "numerous small faint nebulae, vague markings on the photographic plate, whose very forms are indistinct." Hubble studied several clusters of these small, faint nebulae that he had discovered by photographing fields with the 24-inch reflector of the Yerkes Observatory. Until this time only 76 nebulae were known in clusters; Hubble added 512 more in seven well-defined clusters. These objects he classified according to form, brightness, and size, and he measured their positions accurately.

Hubble went on to estimate the minimum sizes of these objects by reasoning that "the spirals form a continuous series from the great nebula of Andromeda to the limit of resolution, the small ones being much more numerous. Considering them to be scattered at random as regards distance and size, some conception may be formed of their dimensions from the data at hand. The average radial velocity of those so far observed is about 400 km/sec, while the proper motion is negligible. Putting the annual proper motion at 0″.05 the lower limit of the average distance is found to be 7500 light years. If they are within our sidereal system, then, as they are most numerous in the direction of its minimum axis, the dimensions of our system must be much greater than commonly supposed." Hubble continued with an estimate of the velocity of escape from a spiral, which he found to be comparable to that of the galaxy. Thus he concluded, "Considering the problematic nature of the data, the agreement is such as to lend some color to the hypothesis that the spirals are stellar systems at distances to be measured often in millions of light years."

1922: "A General Study of Diffuse Galactic Nebulae." This paper contains a wealth of information concerning the galactic nebulae, obtained by Hubble with the Mount Wilson telescopes. In it Hubble laid the cornerstone upon which rest many contemporary theories of the nature of galactic nebulae. By first setting up an unambiguous classification system of nebulae "based upon the fundamental differences between galactic and non-galactic nebulae," and by subdividing the galactic nebulae into planetary and diffuse (in turn subdivided into luminous and dark), Hubble paved the way to a piercing analysis of both the distribution of galactic nebulae and the origin of their luminosity. The following excerpt is quoted not only for its basic importance in the study of galactic nebulae but also because it is a typical example of the mastery of scientific thought, ease, and clarity of style characteristic of all of Hubble's writings.

"Association of Galactic Nebulosity with Stars—This intimate relation between spectral type of nebula and of involved stars raises a presumption that one is a consequence of the other. It seems more reasonable to place the active agency in the relatively dense and exceedingly hot stars than in the nebulosity, and this leads to the suggestion that nebulosity is made luminous by radiation of some sort from stars in certain physical states. The necessary conditions are confined to certain ranges in stellar spectral type and hence are possibly phenomena of effective temperature. The nebulous material itself must be in a physical state sensitive to the stellar radiation, and close enough for the density of radiation to be effective. The abrupt transition from emission to 'continuous' nebulosity between spectral type B0 and B1 suggests a critical point in the spectral sequence or possibly effective temperature below which stellar radiation is incapable of exciting nebulous material to emission luminosity. From thence down the spectral sequence the luminosity gives a continuous spectrum and probably partakes more and more of the nature of reflected light." More than forty years later, this conclusion still stands, except that the large amount of subsequent work indicates the division into emission and reflection nebulae is not so sharp.

1922: "The Source of Luminosity in Galactic Nebulae." Hubble continued his study of galactic nebulae in this paper, and he presented the observational evidence necessary to support his theory of the source of luminosity of galactic nebulae described in the above quotation. To test his theory he obtained for 82 nebulae data on angular extent of the nebulosity as a function of the apparent brightness of the stars associated with them. For nebulae showing continuous spectra, Hubble reported the general conclusion from this investigation: "Within the errors of observation, the data can be represented on the hypothesis that diffuse nebulae derive their luminosity from involved or neighboring stars and that they re-emit at each point exactly the amount of light radiation which they receive from the stars. Where stars of sufficient brightness are lacking in the neighborhood, or, if present, are not properly situated to illuminate the nebula as seen from the earth, the clouds of material present themselves as dark nebulosity." The second section of this paper is devoted to a study of planetary nebulae, for which he shows that the luminosities of planetaries do not follow the relation found for galactic nebulae.

1925: "NGC 6822, a Renote Stellar System." With this paper Hubble returned to the field of extragalactic nebulae. In this "faint irregular cluster of stars with several small nebulae involved," Hubble was able to identify eleven variables as Cepheids. By using the period-luminosity relation, he found a distance of 214,000 parsecs for this object. From star counts and measurements of surface brightnesses he determined the absolute luminosity and the mean density of the system, and compared it with the Magellanic Clouds. The importance of this study for the extragalactic distance scale is clearly stressed by Hubble himself in his conclusion:

"The present investigation identifies NGC 6822 as an isolated system of stars and nebulae of the same type as the Magellanic Clouds, although somewhat smaller and much more distant. A consistent structure is thus reared on the foundation of the Cepheid criterion, in which the dimensions, luminosities and densities, both of the system as a whole and of its separate members, are of orders of magnitude which are thoroughly familiar. The distance is the only quantity of a new order.

"The principle of the uniformity of nature thus seems to rule undisturbed in this remote region of space. This principle is the fundamental assumption in all extrapolations beyond the limits of known and observable data, and speculations which follow its guide are legitimate until they become self-contradictory. It is therefore a matter of considerable importance that familiar relations are found to be consistent when applied to the first system definitely assigned to the regions outside the galactic system.

"Of especial importance is the conclusion that the Cepheid

criterion functions normally to this great distance. Cepheid variables have recently been found in the two largest of the spiral nebulae, and the period-luminosity relation places them at distances even more remote than NGC 6822. This criterion seems to offer the means of exploring extra-galactic space; NGC 6822 furnishes a critical test of its value for so ambitious an undertaking and the results are definitely in its favor."

1926: "A Spiral Nebula as a Stellar System: Messier 33." Hubble continued his study of the nearest nongalactic nebulae by using "the highest resolving power available—the full aperture of the 100-inch reflector working under exceptionally fine conditions of mirror surface and seeing." His results, as presented in this paper and the following one, were epoch-making. A study of the plates clearly established the stellar appearance of the images of the condensations: "They are as small and as sharp as those of ordinary stars of the same magnitude. The two most successful plates, each of 30 minutes exposure . . . show images with angular diameters smaller than any previously obtained on any astronomical photograph." On the collection of photographs available to him, Hubble was able to identify forty-five variables and two novae. Thirty-five of the variables were shown to be typical Cepheids; using the period-luminosity relation, Hubble found a distance about 8.1 times that of the small Magellanic Cloud. Hubble emphasized that "hitherto, wherever Cepheids have been found in isolated systems, the criterion has led to distances entirely consistent with other characteristics that could be observed. . . . Here also, the period-luminosity relation functioned normally and the order of resulting distances was confirmed by several independent criteria. A presumption is thus raised in favor of the general validity of the Cepheid criterion, which only strong and cumulative evidence to the contrary will destroy."

1926: "Extra-Galactic Nebulae." In Part I of this paper

Hubble set forth his classification of nebulae, with detailed discussion of his classification of extragalactic nebulae. He emphasized that "the basis of the classification is descriptive and entirely independent of any theory." The photographs of typical elliptical, irregular, normal, and barred spirals appearing in this paper are perhaps the most familiar set of photographs in present-day astronomy books. This classification system, later revised by Hubble, and completed by Sandage after Hubble's death, is the standard system used today.

Part II of this paper contains a statistical study of some 400 extragalactic nebulae. Hubble reported that "the various types are homogeneously distributed over the sky, their spectra are similar, and the radial velocities are of the same general order. These facts, together with the equality of the mean magnitudes and the uniform frequency distribution of magnitudes, are consistent with the hypothesis that the distances and absolute luminosities as well are of the same order for the different types. This is an assumption of considerable importance, but unfortunately it cannot yet be subjected to positive and definite tests."

Hubble next proceeded to give detailed analyses of the relations between luminosities and diameters of spiral and elliptical nebulae. He reported that "among the nebulae of each separate type are found linear correlations between total magnitudes and logarithms of diameters. . . . The residuals without regard to sign average 0.87 mag., and there appears to be no systematic effect due either to type or luminosity. The scatter, however, is much greater for the spirals, especially in the later types, than for the elliptical nebulae. The limiting cases are explained by peculiar structural features. The nebulae which fall well above the line usually have bright stellar nuclei, and those which fall lowest are spirals seen edge-on in which belts of absorption are conspicuous."

In those extragalactic systems in which individual stars had been resolved, Hubble used them as distance criteria to make estimates of the total absolute magnitudes of the parent nebulae, because from the Cepheid criterion "the number of nebulae of known distance is too small to serve as a basis for estimates of the range in absolute magnitude among the nebulae in general. Further information, however, can be derived from a comparison of total apparent magnitudes with apparent magnitudes of the brightest stars involved, on the reasonable assumption, supported by such evidence as is available, that the brightest stars in isolated systems are of about the same intrinsic luminosity." Finally, using what observational evidence was available, he determined the mean density of nebulae in space, and applied this result in the theory of general relativity to get the radius of curvature of the finite universe —"600 times the distance at which normal nebulae can be detected with the 100-inch reflector." This calculation represented the boldest probe of the universe yet made, and it greatly stimulated theoretical work in cosmology.

1929: "A Spiral Nebula as a Stellar System, Messier 31." This paper, 55 pages long, contains a detailed discussion of the Andromeda nebula, the first giant spiral nebula for which Hubble was able to get a reliable distance, by use of the period-luminosity relation for Cepheids. "The present discussion," Hubble wrote, "is based on the study of about 350 photographs taken with the 60- and 100-inch reflectors, distributed over an interval of about eighteen years. Two-thirds of the total number were obtained by the writer during the five years 1923-1928." The same procedure used by Hubble in his 1926 paper on M33 was adopted in his study of M31, with the result that forty Cepheids were identified and used to construct the period-luminosity relation for this great stellar system. "The distance of M31 has been derived by comparing Figure 2 [the period-luminosity relation for M31] with corresponding diagrams

for Cepheids in M33 and in the Small Magellanic Cloud. . . .
The distance of M31 is about 0.1 mag., or 5 percent, greater
than that of M33, and 8.5 times the distance of the Small Cloud.
Using Shapley's value for the Cloud (m − M = 17.55) we
find for M31 . . . Distance = 900,000 light years. . . . The
accuracy of the relative distances is very satisfactory. . . . The
accuracy of the distances in parsecs or light-years, however,
depends largely upon the accuracy of the zero-point of the
period-luminosity curve. Accumulating evidence indicates that
Shapley's value is certainly of the right general order of magnitude, but there still remains the possibility of a considerable
correction when more data on galactic Cepheids become available."

The extensive amount of observational data assembled by
Hubble enabled him to make a detailed study of the characteristics of the 85 novae observed photographically in the
Andromeda nebula. He reported that "their mean light-curve
is of the same general character as that for galactic novae," and
that the distribution of novae in M31 "follows the distribution
of luminosity in the nebula."

Hubble was unable to resolve the nuclear region of M31
with the 100-inch reflector, but he summarized what evidence
he was able to obtain regarding this particularly interesting
portion of the nebula: "The observational data bearing on
the composition of the nuclear region are: (1) the lack of
absorption, (2) the infrequency of very bright giants, (3) the
appearance of novae, and (4) the characteristic dwarf-solar-
type spectrum with broad, fuzzy lines. A superficial interpretation of these data suggests a star cloud in which bright giants
are rare, in contrast with the outer arms of the spiral, where
giants are abundant. The Cepheids would then follow the distribution of the giants, while the novae would follow that of
the faint stars, or possibly that of the stars in general."

Finally, Hubble estimated the mass, luminosity, and density distribution in M31, and concluded that "the galactic system is five or six times the diameter of the spiral." This disparity in size nearly vanished when, within a year, Trumpler demonstrated the existence of interstellar absorption of light in the galaxy—a phenomenon that gave too large a measure of distance.

1930: "Distribution of Luminosity in Elliptical Nebulae." This paper is concerned with "a preliminary attempt to determine the actual luminosity distribution in the images of a selected list of elliptical nebulae. The results emphasize the dynamical pattern on which they are constructed." Hubble photographed 15 of these nebulae at the Newtonian focus of the 100-inch reflector. From these plates he then derived the distribution of luminosity within the nebulae, i.e., the spatial light density, and compared the results with the distribution in density of the Emden isothermal gaseous sphere. From the comparison he concluded: "The nuclei of the nebulae appear to be relatively more concentrated, and in the outer regions the luminosity falls off faster than the density, as would be expected in the case of finite rotating bodies such as the nebulae." At the time, no elliptical nebula had been resolved into stars, and this result was available for consideration by rival theories of ellipticals as gaseous or stellar systems. Hubble did not venture an interpretation in this respect in the present paper. He was content to offer the new data with the hope "that they may furnish an observational basis for the dynamical study of elliptical nebulae."

1931: "The Velocity-Distance Relation among Extra-Galactic Nebulae" (with Milton L. Humason). In Part I, "Distances of Nebulae," Hubble and Humason listed the 10 nebulae in which types of stars were identified, which enabled them to determine the individual distances of the nebulae from the criterion of brightest-star absolute magnitude. They stated:

"The range in the magnitudes of the brightest stars is about 1.8, with an average residual of 0.4 around the mean value −6.1. . . . These facts lend color to the assumption of a fairly uniform upper limit to the luminosity of stars in the great isolated systems, which may be used as a criterion of distance where stars can be seen but no types identified." Thus they derived a formula for the distance of a nebula, "as indicated by the brightest stars involved," as

$$\log D = 0.2 \, m_s + 2.2,$$

where D = distance in parsecs and m_s = photographic magnitude of the brightest star. For the restricted types of objects studied, they found the mean absolute total magnitude, or luminosity, of these 10 extragalactic nebulae to be −14.9.

The measurement of total apparent magnitudes of nebulous objects is, however, a very difficult technical problem of photographic photometry. In this paper, therefore, the authors described in detail the method developed and adopted at Mount Wilson. Based upon extra-focal exposures, this method gave results of improved accuracy mainly for distances of clusters of nebulae, because "the luminosity criterion is purely statistical and is reliable only when large numbers of nebulae are available. One direct application concerns the great clusters of nebulae. The mean or most frequent apparent magnitude of the many members is a good indicator of the distance of the cluster, and hence clusters offer the greatest distances that can definitely be assigned to individual objects. If observations of very remote objects are desired, the brightest members of very faint clusters may be selected."

In Part II, "The Velocity-Distance Relation," the writers compiled data on 26 new velocities of nebulae belonging to 8 clusters or groups, together with 14 new velocities for isolated objects. These highly significant results were summarized as follows: "The relation [between radial velocity and distance] is a linear increase in the velocity amounting to about +500 km/sec per million parsecs of distance." The cosmological consequences and implications of this simple statement have had enormous influence on astronomical and philosophical thought.

The authors pointed out, nevertheless, that "the interpretation of red-shifts as actual velocities does not command the same confidence, and the term 'velocity' will be used for the present in the sense of 'apparent' velocity, without prejudice as to its ultimate significance."

1932: "Nebulous Objects in Messier 31 Provisionally Identified as Globular Clusters." Hubble continued his detailed studies of the nearer spiral systems, and in this paper he reported the discovery of 140 "nebulous objects" in and around the Andromeda nebula. These objects he described as "nebulous stars—small, highly concentrated, round and perfectly symmetrical. . . . The observed characteristics of the objects appear to admit of but one interpretation. On the basis of structure, luminosity, diameters and colors, the objects are provisionally identified as globular star clusters. Their absolute magnitudes are systematically fainter by one or two magnitudes than the absolute magnitudes of the globular clusters in the galactic system derived from Shapley's distances." Hubble lived to learn the reason for this discrepancy: the Cepheid distance criterion as formulated by Shapley gave distances too small by a factor of two, as reported in 1952 by Baade.

1932: "The Surface Brightness of Threshold Images." The problem of the measurement of apparent total magnitudes of nebulae is difficult photographically, because it involves the comparison of surfaces (nebulae) with point sources (stars). Since Hubble's greatest distance criteria were based on such measurements, and since he himself was engaged in extensive

counts of faint nebulae, he was naturally concerned to develop
as accurate a method as possible for detemining nebular magnitudes. This paper discusses one practical aspect of the problem: "The photographic photometry of threshold images involves an effect depending on the areas. It is well known that
the photometry of surfaces differs from that of point-source
images, but the manner in which one merges into the other
is seldom discussed in the literature. The question bears on the
estimates of limiting magnitudes of nebulae recorded under
given exposure conditions."

The results of Hubble's studies of both nebular and stellar
images produced under threshold conditions with the 100- and
60-inch reflectors resulted in "a relation between surface brightness and size of image, according to which the surface brightness
diminishes as the size increases, at first rapidly and then more and
more slowly. . . . For very small images the total magnitudes
are independent of the size; for very large images the surface
brightness is independent of the size. The observed relation is
a smooth transition between these limiting conditions." With
this relationship he was able to obtain more accurate magnitudes
of nebulae from those of stars used as standards.

1934: "Red-Shifts in the Spectra of Nebulae." In this beautifully written paper, the Halley Lecture of the Royal Astronomical Society delivered in London on May 8, 1934, Hubble discussed "some of the more recent explorations in the realm of
the nebulae which bear more or less directly on the structure
of the universe." Here he invoked the "Principle of the Uniformity of Nature, which supposes that any other equal portion
of the universe, chosen at random, will exhibit the same general characteristics. As a working hypothesis, serviceable until
it leads to contradictions, we may venture the assumption that
the realm of the nebulae *is* the universe—that the Observable
Region is a fair sample, and that the nature of the universe may

be inferred from the observable characteristics of the sample." After a condensed description of observational techniques for determining the velocity-distance relation, Hubble considered briefly its significance: "The significance of this strange characteristic of our sample of the universe depends upon the interpretation of red-shifts. The phenomena may be described in several equivalent ways—the light from distant nebulae is redder than normal, the light waves are longer, the vibrations are slower, the light quanta have lost energy. Many ways of producing such effects are known, but of them all, only one will produce large red-shifts without introducing other effects which should be conspicuous but actually are not found. This one known permissible explanation interprets red-shifts as due to actual motion away from the observer. . . . We may say with confidence that red-shifts are due either to actual motion or to some hitherto unrecognized principle of physics. Theoretical investigators almost universally accept the red-shifts as indicating motion of recession of the nebulae, and they are fully justified in their position until evidence to the contrary is forthcoming."

1934: "The Distribution of Extra-galactic Nebulae." In an introduction to this long paper containing an immense amount of new material, Hubble referred to his work on distance estimates of the nebulae as giving a "hasty sketch of some of the general features of the Observable Region as a unit. The next step," he said, "was to follow the reconnaissance with a survey —to repeat carefully the explorations with an eye to accuracy and completeness. The program, with its emphasis on methods, will be a tedious series of successive approximations, but the procedure is necessary, since extrapolations beyond the frontiers will be significant only in proportion to the accuracy with which the trend of correlations has been established out to the frontier itself." These words were prophetic, for the remainder of Hubble's research reflected his belief expressed in these thoughts. This paper, 69 pages in length, incorporates counts of about 80,000 nebulae identified on photographs taken with the Mount Wilson 60- and 100-inch reflectors. In this work, generally recognized as a classic, Hubble obtained on a firm quantitative basis, for the first time, information on the large-scale occurrence of obscuring matter along the plane of the galaxy, on the numbers of the nebulae to successively fainter magnitude limits, on the tendency of nebulae to cluster, and on the average density of matter in extragalactic space. The impact of these new data on cosmology and galactic structure investigations can hardly be overestimated. There are innumerable references to this work in many subsequent papers by theorists and observers.

1935: "Two Methods of Investigating the Nature of Nebular Red-Shift" (with Richard C. Tolman). Although Hubble had no official connection with the California Institute of Technology until he served on the Advisory Committee for the construction of the large Palomar telescopes, he had many friends and colleagues on its faculty. In particular, he enjoyed many scientifically productive associations with H. P. Robertson and R. C. Tolman, and this paper is an example of the cooperative spirit that existed between Hubble and these theoreticians at Cal Tech.

In Part I of the paper, their empirical approach to the analysis of the nebular red-shift was stated as follows: "Until further evidence is available, both the present writers wish to express an open mind with respect to the ultimately most satisfactory explanation of the nebular red-shift and, in the presentation of purely observational findings, to continue to use the phrase 'apparent' velocity of recession." Surely this seems a warning for some not to "rush in where angels fear to tread."

On the basis of (a) an expanding cosmological model using relativistic mechanics and (b) the case in which "the red-shift is due to some cause other than recession," the authors derived a theoretical relation between locations in space and photographic magnitudes of nebulae, for tests of the nature of the red-shift. The derived formula contained the distance to a nebula as an unobservable quantity. It was eliminated by connecting "either nebular dimensions with observed luminosities, or nebular counts with observed luminosities."

Part II of the paper presented the existing status of the observational work pertinent to the problem. The authors concluded: "In the case of the relation between nebular dimensions and luminosities, the observations are such as to confirm our general ideas as to the extra-galactic character of the objects in question, but are not yet sufficient to permit a decision between recessional or other causes for the red shift."

They next considered in some detail the uncertainties in the counts of galaxies, such as the difficulties in determining the number of nebular images per plate, in measuring the limiting magnitudes, in evaluating the fractional red-shift, and in determining the spectral energy correction term K. They concluded finally that "the observations now available show a rate of increase in counts with distance which seem rather large compared with what would be expected for a homogeneous distribution of nebulae on the basis of either a recessional or a non-recessional theory."

1936: "Effects of Red Shifts on the Distribution of Nebulae." In this paper Hubble added two additional groups of nebular counts to the three groups already discussed in his 1935 paper with Tolman. After a detailed analysis of the observational data, and a comparison with the theoretical models computed with Tolman, Hubble found that "the observations may be fitted into either of two quite different types of universes. If the red-shifts are velocity shifts, the model is closed, small and dense. It is rapidly expanding, but over a long period the rate of expansion has been steadily diminishing. Existing instruments range through a large fraction of the entire volume and, perhaps, through a considerable fraction of past time since the expansion began.

"On the other hand, if red-shifts are not primarily due to velocity shifts, the Observable Region loses much of its significance. The velocity-distance relation is linear; the distribution of nebulae is uniform; there is no evidence of expansion, no trace of curvature, no restriction to the time scale. The sample, it seems, is too small to indicate the particular type of universe we inhabit.

"Thus the surveys to about the practical limits of existing instruments present as alternatives a curiously small-scale universe, or a hitherto unrecognized principle of nature. A definitive choice, based upon observational criteria that are well above the threshold of uncertainty may not be possible until results with the 200-inch reflector become available."

1936: "The Luminosity Function of Nebulae." "Consider all the nebulae *in a given volume of space,*" Hubble wrote in *The Realm of the Nebulae* (p. 59). "The relative numbers of giants and dwarfs and normal objects—more precisely, the frequency-distribution of absolute magnitudes (candle powers) among these nebulae—form the 'luminosity-function.' It was assumed that the luminosity-function remains constant throughout the regions covered by the surveys—that the function is independent of distance or direction—that the giants do not tend to congregate in one region and the dwarfs in another region. The assumption has not been fully established by direct observations, but it seems reasonable and it is consistent with all information available at the present time."

In this paper Hubble attempted to estimate the luminosity function for the nebulae, and he did so by two separate methods: (1) the luminosity function of resolved nebulae as indicated by their brightest stars, and (2) the luminosity function as indicated by residuals in velocity-magnitude relations. The first of these methods utilizes the criterion of the brightest star in a nebula, "which is arbitrarily defined as the mean of the three or four brightest objects which are judged to be individual, non-variable stars situated in a nebula." Hubble pointed out the observational pitfalls in identifying these stars, and added: "Regardless of their true nature, the objects selected as brightest stars . . . form a homogeneous group in which the absolute magnitudes do not vary systematically with apparent magnitudes (or distances)." Therefore, the difference in the apparent magnitude of the brightest star within the nebula and the magnitude of the nebula itself should give an indication of the intrinsic luminosity of the nebula; and the compilation of a large number of such differences for many nebulae should give a reasonable evaluation of the luminosity function of the nebulae. Hubble listed about 125 nebulae in which stars were identified "with some confidence." From these he determined the frequency distribution of the differences between apparent magnitudes of nebulae and of their brightest stars. His general conclusion was that the luminosity function of nebulae approximates a normal error-curve.

The second method used by Hubble in determining the nebular luminosity function employed the velocity-distance relation. He pointed out that this relation furnishes individual distances of unresolved field nebulae, and that the percentage errors actually diminish as distances increase. Following a new evaluation of the velocity-magnitude relation, Hubble derived the residuals from the relation for 109 field nebulae. Of these objects, 29 are resolved nebulae included in the first method, and Hubble found that the luminosity function derived from their residuals agrees closely with that determined in the first method from the brightest stars in resolved nebulae alone.

1939: "The Motion of the Galactic System among the Nebulae." In this paper Hubble analyzed the residual radial motions of the nebulae, after removing the systematic red-shifts. His analysis of these residual motions of many nebulae well distributed over the sky assumed that the peculiar motions tend to cancel out, since they are presumably distributed at random in all directions; thus there was left only the reflection of the motion of the galactic system. Hubble concluded: "A relatively small velocity and a high inclination to the plane of the Milky Way seem to be definitely indicated, although precise numerical values cannot be derived from the data now available."

1943: "The Direction of Rotation in Spiral Nebulae." Hubble's survey of the nearby nebulae led him to the recognition of four spirals in which the direction of rotation could be determined unambiguously from the silhouetting of absorption lanes against the bright nuclear regions. For fifteen other spirals for which spectrographic rotation had been observed, spiral arms could be traced, and the dissymmetry of obscuration offered a general criterion of tilt. He found that the consistent application of this general criterion indicated all these nebulae appear to be rotating in the same direction; the sense of this direction could be found from the four spirals for which the tilt could be determined without ambiguity. By this process he found that in all these nebulae the arms are trailing—the outer parts lag behind as the inner regions rotate faster.

1949: "First Photographs with the 200-inch Hale Telescope." Here Hubble reported that the photographs taken while testing the 200-inch telescope recorded stars and nebulae fully 1.5 magnitudes fainter than the extreme limit of the 100-inch reflector on Mount Wilson, and that at high galactic latitudes the 200-inch telescope records many more nebulae than stars, as he had predicted about fifteen years earlier. This paper also contains a reproduction of the first photograph taken with the

Hale Telescope on January 26, 1949, about 10:00 P.M. (after waiting more than a week for a break in the weather). The object was NGC 2261, a well-known galactic nebula, now generally known as Hubble's Variable Nebula because of the remarkable changes in its brightness that he discovered.

1951: "Explorations in Space: The Cosmological Program for the Palomar Telescope." Few astronomers have equaled Hubble's impressive eloquence in popular lectures. This paper, presented as the Penrose Memorial Lecture to the American Philosophical Society, is a prime example of such talks. It contains a résumé of extragalactic research already done, and then concentrates on the program for Palomar: "The cosmological program for the Palomar telescope has been formulated to get new answers to the observational problems, free from systematic errors and with the accidental errors sufficiently small to be unimportant. Specifically, the problems are, first, to find the mean density of matter in space, and the rate of increase of red-shifts in our immediate vicinity—say within 50 million light-years of our own system—and second, to determine whether or not there are any appreciable systematic changes with distance or direction in either of the two data."

1954: "The Law of Red-Shifts." This paper, the George Darwin Lecture delivered by Hubble on May 8, 1953, in London, was edited by Sandage, and published after Hubble's death. In it, he discussed the emergence of the law of red-shifts, first in its discovery phase, which ended with a crude formulation in 1928-1929, then its rapid extension and improved formulation out to the limit of the 100-inch reflector in 1929-1936, and finally the recent attempts to reach the limit of the 200-inch reflector with the definite formulation of the law. He discussed in some detail the current efforts at this definitive formulation with the 200-inch reflector, including the problems of magnitude standards, measurement of nebular magnitudes, and effects of red-shifts on apparent magnitudes. He concluded by reporting the latest evaluation of the red-shift magnitude relation, stating that the correlation is linear within the uncertainties of the data, and that the residuals are surprisingly small.

It seems fitting to conclude this memoir with Hubble's own words, to indicate how he viewed the continuation of extragalactic research in a field he had made so much his own:

"As for the future, it is possible to penetrate still deeper into space—to follow the red-shifts still farther back in time—but we are already in the region of diminishing returns; instruments will be increasingly expensive, and progress increasingly slow. The most promising programmes for the immediate future accept the Observable Region as presently defined, hope for only modest extensions in space, but concentrate on increased precision and reliability in the recorded description. The reconnaissance is being followed by an accurate survey; the explorations are pushed towards the next decimal place instead of the next cipher. This procedure promises to reduce the array of possible worlds as surely as did the early inspections of the new territory. And later, perhaps in a happier generation, when the cost of a battleship can safely be diverted from insurance of survival to the consolations of philosophy, the march outward may be resumed.

"For I can end as I began. From our home on the Earth, we look out into the distances and strive to imagine the sort of world into which we are born. Today we have reached far out into space. Our immediate neighborhood we know rather intimately. But with increasing distance our knowledge fades, and fades rapidly, until at the last dim horizon we search among ghostly errors of observations for landmarks that are scarcely more substantial. The search will continue. The urge is older than history. It is not satisfied and it will not be suppressed."

BIBLIOGRAPHY

KEY TO ABBREVIATIONS

Am. Astron. Soc. Publ. = American Astronomical Society Publications
Astrophys. J. = Astrophysical Journal
Carnegie Inst. Wash. News Serv. Bull. = Carnegie Institution of Washington News Service Bulletin
Contrib. Mt. Wilson Obs. = Contributions from the Mount Wilson Observatory
Leaflet Astron. Soc. Pacific = Leaflet of the Astronomical Society of the Pacific
Monthly Notices Roy. Astron. Soc. = Monthly Notices of the Royal Astronomical Society
Mt. Wilson Obs. Commun. = Mount Wilson Observatory Communications
Mt. Wilson Palomar Obs. Reprint = Mount Wilson and Palomar Observatories Reprint
Popular Astron. = Popular Astronomy
Proc. Nat. Acad. Sci. = Proceedings of the National Academy of Sciences
Publ. Astron. Soc. Pacific = Publications of the Astronomical Society of the Pacific
Sci. Monthly = Scientific Monthly
Smithsonian Inst. Ann. Rept. = Smithsonian Institution, Annual Report

1916

Twelve faint stars with sensible proper-motions. Astronomical Journal, 29:168-69.
The variable nebula N.G.C. 2261. Astrophys. J., 44:190-97.
Changes in the form of the nebula N.G.C. 2261. Proc. Nat. Acad. Sci., 2:230-31.

1917

Recent changes in the variable nebula N.G.C. 2261. Astrophys. J., 45:351-53.

1920

The spectrum of N.G.C. 1499. Publ. Astron. Soc. Pacific, 32:155-56.
The planetary nebula I.C. 2003. Publ. Astron. Soc. Pacific, 32:161.
Twelve new variable stars. Publ. Astron. Soc. Pacific, 32:161-62.

Photographic investigations of faint nebulae. (Ph.D. Dissertation.)
Publications of the Yerkes Observatory, 4:69-85.
With Frederick H. Seares. The color of the nebulous stars. As-
trophys. J., 52:8-22; Contrib. Mt. Wilson Obs., 9:273-88.

1921

Twelve new planetary nebulae. Publ. Astron. Soc. Pacific, 33:
174-76.

1922

A general study of diffuse galactic nebulae. Astrophys. J., 56:
162-99; Contrib. Mt. Wilson Obs., 11:217-54.
The source of luminosity in galactic nebulae. Astrophys. J., 56:
400-38; Contrib. Mt. Wilson Obs., 11:397-436.
With Knut Lundmark. Nova Z Centauri (1895) and N.G.C. 5253.
Publ. Astron. Soc. Pacific, 34:292-93.

1923

Density distribution in the photographic images of elliptical
nebulae. Am. Astron. Soc. Publ., 5:63; Popular Astron., 31:
644. (A)
Messier 87 and Belanowsky's Nova. Publ. Astron. Soc. Pacific,
35:261-63.

1924

Cepheids in spiral nebulae. Am. Astron. Soc. Publ., 5:261-64. (A)

1925

N.G.C. 6822, a remote stellar system. Astrophys. J., 62:409-33;
Contrib. Mt. Wilson Obs., 14:1-26.
Cepheids in spiral nebulae. Observatory, 48:139-42; Popular As-
tron., 33: 252-55; Science, 61:278-79. (A)

1926

A spiral nebula as a stellar system: Messier 33. Astrophys. J.,
63:236-74; Contrib. Mt. Wilson Obs., 14:83-122.
Extra-galactic nebulae. Astrophys. J., 64:321-69; Contrib. Mt. Wilson Obs., 14:379-428.

Non-galactic nebulae. I. Classification and apparent dimensions; II. Absolute dimensions and distribution in space. Publ. Astron. Soc. Pacific, 38:258-60. (A)

1927

The classification of spiral nebulae. Observatory, 50:276-81.

Exploring depths of space. Carnegie Inst. Wash. News Serv. Bull., Vol. 1, No. 6.

With John Charles Duncan. The nebulous envelope around Nova Aquilae No. 3. Astrophys. J., 66:59-63; Contrib. Mt. Wilson Obs., 15:145-49.

1928

Novae or temporary stars. Leaflet Astron. Soc. Pacific, 1:55-58.

Novae in nebulae. Observatory, 51:108-9, 114.

1929

A spiral nebula as a stellar system, Messier 31. Astrophys. J., 69:103-57; Contrib. Mt. Wilson Obs., 17:99-154.

The structure of the universe—a clue. Carnegie Inst. Wash. News Serv. Bull., 6(8):49-51.

On the curvature of space. Carnegie Inst. Wash. News Serv. Bull., 6(13):67-68.

The exploration of space. Harper's Monthly Magazine, 158:732-38.

A relation between distance and radial velocity among extra-galactic nebulae. Proc. Nat. Acad. Sci., 15:168-73; Mt. Wilson Obs. Commun., No. 105.

Preliminary estimate of the coma cluster of nebulae. Publ. Astron. Soc. Pacific, 41:247-48. (A)

1930

Distribution of luminosity in elliptical nebulae. Astrophys. J., 71:231-76; Contrib. Mt. Wilson Obs., 18:131-76.

Velocity-distance relation among extra-galactic nebulae. Science, 72:407. (A)

With John C. Duncan. The nebulous envelope around Nova Aquilae 1918. Popular Astron., 38:598-99; Am. Astron. Soc. Publ., 6:365. (A)

1931

The distribution of nebulae. Publ. Astron. Soc. Pacific, 43:282-84. (A)

With Milton L. Humason. The velocity-distance relation among extra-galactic nebulae. Astrophys. J., 74:43-80; Contrib. Mt. Wilson Obs., 19:137-68.

1932

Nebulous objects in Messier 31 provisionally identified as globular clusters. Astrophys. J., 76:44-69; Contrib. Mt. Wilson Obs., 20: 81-106.

The surface brightness of threshold images. Astrophys. J., 76: 106-16; Contrib. Mt. Wilson Obs., 20:107-18.

The distribution of extra-galactic nebulae. Science, 75:24-25.

1934

The distribution of extra-galactic nebulae. Astrophys. J., 79:8-76; Contrib. Mt. Wilson Obs., 21:139-208.

Red-Shifts in the Spectra of Nebulae. (Halley Lecture, 1934.) Oxford, The Clarendon Press. 17 pp.

The award of the Bruce Gold Medal to Professor Alfred Fowler. Publ. Astron. Soc. Pacific, 46:87-93.

The realm of the nebulae. Sci. Monthly, 39:193-202.

With Milton L. Humason. The velocity-distance relation for isolated extragalactic nebulae. Proc. Nat. Acad. Sci., 20:264-68; Mt. Wilson Obs. Commun., No. 116.

1935

Angular rotations of spiral nebulae. Astrophys. J., 81:334-35; Contrib. Mt. Wilson Obs., 22:191-92.

With Richard C. Tolman. Two methods of investigating the nature of nebular red-shift. Astrophys. J., 82:302-37; Contrib. Mt. Wilson Obs., 22:391-426.

1936

The luminosity function of nebulae. I. The luminosity of resolved nebulae as indicated by their brightest stars. Astrophys. J., 84:158-79; Contrib. Mt. Wilson Obs., 23:279-300.

The luminosity function of nebulae. II. The luminosity function as indicated by residuals in velocity-magnitude relations. Astrophys. J., 84:270-95; Contrib. Mt. Wilson Obs., 23:301-26.

Effects of red shifts on the distribution of nebulae. Astrophys. J., 84:517-54; Contrib. Mt. Wilson Obs., 23:445-82.

Ways of science. Occidental College Bulletin, n.s., Vol. 14, No. 1.

Effects of red shifts on the distribution of nebulae. Proc. Nat. Acad. Sci., 22:621-27; Mt. Wilson Obs. Commun., No. 120.

The Realm of the Nebulae. (Silliman Lectures.) New Haven, Yale University Press. xii + 210 pp.

With Glenn Moore. A super-nova in the Virgo Cluster. Publ. Astron. Soc. Pacific, 48:108-10.

1937

Red shifts and the distribution of nebulae. Monthly Notices Roy. Astron. Soc., 97:506-13.

Observational Approach to Cosmology. (Rhodes Memorial Lectures, 1936.) Oxford, The Clarendon Press. vi + 68 pp.

Our sample of the universe. Sci. Monthly, 45:481-93; Carnegie Institution of Washington Supplementary Publication, No. 33, pp. 1-13.

1938

Adventures in cosmology. Leaflet Astron. Soc. Pacific, 3:120-23.

The nature of the nebulae. Publ. Astron. Soc. Pacific, 50:97-110.

Das Reich de Nebel. Braunschweig, Friedrich Vieweg & Sohn. x + 192 pp.

Explorations in the realm of the nebulae. In: *Cooperation in Research,* pp. 91-102. Washington, D.C., Carnegie Institution of Washington.

1939

The nature of the nebulae. Smithsonian Inst. Ann. Rept., 1938, pp. 137-48.

Barred spirals. Am. Astron. Soc. Publ., 9:249-50. (A)

The motion of the galactic system among the nebulae. Journal of the Franklin Institute, 228:131-42.

Points of view: experiment and experience. Huntington Library Quarterly, 2(3):243-50.

With Walter Baade. The new stellar systems in Sculptor and Fornax. Publ. Astron. Soc. Pacific, 51:40-44; Mount Wilson Observatory Reprint, No. 160.

1940

Problems of nebular research. Sci. Monthly, 51:391-408.

1941

Supernovae. Publ. Astron. Soc. Pacific, 53:141-54.

The role of science in a liberal education. In: *The University and the Future of America,* pp. 137-55. Stanford, Stanford University Press.

With Nicholas U. Mayall. The direction of rotation of spiral nebulae. Science, 93:434. (A)

1942

The problem of the expanding universe. American Scientist, 30: 99-115; Science, 95:212-15. (A)

The problem of the expanding universe. In: *Science in Progress,* 3d Ser., ed. by E. O. Lawrence *et al.,* pp. 22-44. New Haven, Yale University Press.

1943

The problem of the expanding universe. Smithsonian Inst. Ann. Rept., 1942, pp. 119-32.

The direction of rotation in spiral nebulae. Astrophys. J., 97:112-18; Contrib. Mt. Wilson Obs., 27:225-32.

The problem of the expanding universe. Sci. Monthly, 56:15-30.

1945

The exploration of space. In: *The Scientists Speak,* ed. by Warren Weaver, pp. 37-40. New York, Boni & Baer.

1946

The exploration of space. Popular Astron., 54:183-86.

1947

The 200-inch telescope and some problems it may solve. Publ. Astron. Soc. Pacific, 59:153-67.

1948

The greatest of all telescopes.   Listener, Vol. 15, No. 1025.

1949

First photographs with the 200-inch Hale Telescope.   Publ. Astron. Soc. Pacific, 61:121-24.
Five historic photographs from Palomar.   Scientific American, 181 (5):32-39.

1950

The 200-inch telescope and some problems it may solve.   Smithsonian Inst. Ann. Rept., 1949, pp. 175-88.
Fotografías históricas del Cielo tomadas en el Observatorio Palomar.   Boletín de Ciencia y Technología, No. 2, pp. 23-31.

1951

Explorations in space: the cosmological program for the Palomar Telescope.   Proceedings of the American Philosophical Society, 95(5):461-70; Mt. Wilson Palomar Obs. Reprint, No. 55.

1953

With Allan Sandage.   The brightest variable stars in extragalactic nebulae. I. M31 and M33.   Astrophys. J., 118:353-61; Mt. Wilson Palomar Obs. Reprint, No. 107.

1954

The Nature of Science and Other Lectures. San Marino, California, The Huntington Library. 83 pp.
The law of red-shifts.   (The George Darwin Lecture.)   Monthly Notices Roy. Astron. Soc., 113:658-66; Mt. Wilson Palomar Obs. Reprint, No. 131.

1958

The Realm of the Nebulae. New York, Dover Publications, Inc. 207 pp.

ALBERT WALLACE HULL

April 19, 1880–January 22, 1966

BY C. G. SUITS AND J. M. LAFFERTY

THE DEATH OF Albert W. Hull on January 22, 1966, at the age of eighty-five ended the career of the world's most prolific inventor of electron tubes. Hull was one of the group of five people (the others being Whitney, Coolidge, Langmuir, and Dushman) whose lifelong contributions provided firm foundations for the growth and expansion of scientific research in the General Electric Company.

Hull's start in science was unusual. As an undergraduate at Yale he majored in Greek, and it was his acquaintanceship with this language that was to impart Greek roots to the names of early electron tube types. Thus Pliotron, Dynatron, Pliodynatron, Thyratron, and Magnetron are functionally correct adaptations of Greek roots to the terminology of the early electron tube art.

Some years ago Hull recalled how he, a farm boy, became first a Greek scholar and then a physicist. His remarks reflect the modesty and directness that were characteristic of him:

"I was brought up on a Connecticut farm. I remember on one occasion, when my father was ill, I milked twenty cows before breakfast. That was when I was twelve years old. However, that was an interesting experience rather than a hardship. I remember those years only as a happy and carefree life.

"I had no idea of going to college until a friend of mine went to Yale, and was able to pay his own expenses. That was a new idea, so I decided I would try it. I arrived in New Haven with a hundred dollars in my pocket, and enrolled in Yale College.

"A fortunate experience in high school led to the solution of the financial problem at Yale. During the next to last year, I had completed all but two of the subjects that were needed for entrance. So I had some extra time during the last year and did some extra reading in Greek. I think we read at sight nearly all of the *Odyssey*. Our teacher was a very unusual young man who was a graduate student at Yale, taking time off in order to earn some money. He was a real Greek scholar, and I caught by contagion his love for Greek, Greek poetry especially, and developed some facility in Greek.

"About four months after entering college, I came unprepared to a Greek class and being called on—as *always* happens—proceeded to try to read the assignment at sight. The professor didn't tell me to stop until I had read about a page beyond the end of our proper assignment. He then told me to sit down and said he would like to see me after class. I had visions of some discipline, but what he wanted to tell me was that he would like to have me do some tutoring in Greek.

"From that time on, my financial worries, if I ever had any, were ended. I tutored in Greek for the first two years, and in mathematics and physics and a little English during the last two. I majored in Greek, with a minor in social science, under William ("Billy") Sumner. Up to this time, I had not been interested in science or at least had not realized it. I took only one course in physics and one in chemistry during my whole college career.

"After graduation I taught French and German at the Albany Academy in Albany, New York, for one year. Dr. Warren, the headmaster, had come down to New Haven to get a teacher, and wanted someone who could manage the class in German. For the previous two years, he had had native German teachers and the students had forced them to resign before the end of the year. He picked me out, as someone who looked husky enough to manage the situation. I was twenty-five, having stayed out of school four years before entering college.

"In the Albany Academy I had no difficulty in managing the students, and I found that I could teach. But I certainly didn't want to teach anything in which I wasn't really an expert. I didn't wish to make modern languages my career, so I stopped for the first time in my life to think about what I was most interested in.

"I decided that, of all the things I had come in contact with in college, the subject I really liked best was physics—in spite of the fact that I had had only one course in it. I had had a very unusual teacher, Dr. Albert Kreider, and my course in physics stood out in my memory as something that I had liked and found very easy. I went back to Yale for graduate work in physics. It was the first correct decision I had ever made, and I have never regretted it.

"After finishing my postgraduate work, I taught for five years in the Worcester Polytechnic Institute. During those years I spent all the spare time I could snatch from sleep in research work. Dr. A. Wilmer Duff, the head of the department, was very generous in giving me encouragement and equipment. My wife often accompanied me to the laboratory in the evening, and sat and read while I made glassware apparatus. Generally we went home when the apparatus broke.

"I have always felt that I owed my introduction to the General Electric Company to my wife's intuition. After five years I was getting a bit discouraged about the future prospect of teaching. I couldn't see the way ahead. There was to be a meeting of the American Physical Society in New Haven, and my wife decided it was time for me to give another paper. I had been working for a long time on a photoelectric problem and had an immense amount of material, but my ideals were too high and I felt that I wasn't ready to present it. At her insistence, however, I did give the paper. At that meeting I met Langmuir and Coolidge of the General Electric Research Laboratory. They asked me to have lunch with them, and a couple of weeks later I received an invitation to talk at the colloquium of the General Electric Research Laboratory in Schenectady.

"The result of this introduction was an invitation to spend the summer of 1913 in the Research Laboratory at Schenectady. In the fall of that year, Dr. Willis R. Whitney, the director of the Laboratory, invited me to join the Laboratory staff. I was a little hesitant about accepting the offer, and told him that I didn't think I could do anything practical. His answer was wonderful: 'Don't worry about the practical part, that's my business. Just go ahead and do anything you want to.' He was as good as his word. His typical greeting, as he made his daily rounds of the Laboratory, was not 'Have you solved that problem?' but 'Are you having any fun?' Before the year was over I was so happy in this new work that there wasn't any question about the decision. This was the place where I wanted to be. It still is."

At the age of thirty-four, Hull had begun a research career in physics and electronics that was to continue for over half a century.

In 1914, during Hull's first year at the Research Laboratory, he invented the Dynatron, a vacuum tube having true negative resistance. While this tube never came into widespread use, it demonstrated the negative resistance concept, and his study of the dynatron action contributed to the development of other uses for secondary emission.

"I called this tube a *pliodynatron*," Hull wrote of a later invention, "because it combined with the dynatron the grid-control principle of Langmuir's newly invented *pliotron*. With the pliodynatron, I was able to radio-telephone to Ballston Spa, a distance of about 16 miles, using a crystal detector at the other end as a receiver. This was quite good at that time, for radio-telephony was new."

Early in his career, Hull developed a new powder method of X-ray crystal analysis, the details of which were published in December 1917. After the end of World War I, it was learned that this technique had been discovered independently by Peter Debye and P. Scherrer and published in Germany a few months earlier. Since the publications took place almost simultaneously, the method has been known subsequently as the Debye-Scherrer-Hull technique. Hull told of his decision to begin this work as follows:

"My work in electronics was interrupted for several years by a lecture by Sir William Bragg. Sir William was in this country early in 1915, and we invited him to speak at our colloquium. He told us about his new work on the study of crystal structure by means of X-rays. At the close of the lecture, I asked him if he had been able to find the structure of iron. He had told us about some structures, sodium chloride and copper and a few other materials that he had successfully analyzed. His answer to my question was typical of him. He might have said, 'No, but we think we'll have it very soon.'

"Instead of that he answered very simply, 'No, we've tried, but we haven't succeeded.'

"Well, that was a challenge—such a challenge as a young man needs—and I decided that I'd like to try to find the crystal structure of iron, reasoning that it might throw some light on the fact that iron is magnetic material. I made this decision in spite of the fact that I was almost totally unfamiliar with either X-rays or crystallography."

The technique Hull developed is probably the most powerful tool that has ever been discovered for crystal analysis, and it has had widespread use ever since. Hull determined the crystal structure of a number of metals and was awarded the Potts Medal from the Franklin Institute in 1923 for his crystal analysis work. To obtain a steady source of high D-C voltage for his X-ray work, he placed two capacitors across the high voltage output of a Kenotron rectifier with an inductive choke between them. This filter circuit was patented and later used in practically all radio receiver power supplied throughout the United States.

During World War I, Hull originated the use of Rochelle salt crystals to pick up noise from submarines. Rochelle salt had not previously been used as a piezoelectric element, and he developed a method of growing and cutting these crystals to obtain maximum sensitivity.

Hull is perhaps best known for his work in the field of electronic phenomena and devices. His contributions to basic electron tube types probably exceed those of any other scientist.

In 1920, Hull first conceived the idea of the smooth-bore Magnetron—a tube comprising a coaxial cylindrical anode and filament operated in an axial magnetic field. With F. R. Elder, he developed high-power magnetron oscillators and multistage, high-gain magnetron amplifiers. The multianode magnetron concept was developed by others, primarily by the British, for generating microwave power for radar. As a result of this, Hull's World War II work consisted largely in directing the development of these magnetrons for radar and radar countermeasures. In 1929, the Axitron, a magnetron controlled by the magnetic field resulting from current through the filament, was also invented by Hull.

"At the end of World War I," Hull wrote, "small electronic tubes were in considerable production, although still there were no high-power tubes, such as were needed for broadcasting. However, the chief obstacle to broadcasting was not the tubes but the patent situation. The radio patents were about equally divided between three different companies and there seemed to be no way in which any one of the three could proceed with a development. I conceived the idea of breaking this stalemate by the development of a magnetically controlled tube which would be free from these patents.

"Essentially the *magnetron* is a simple diode in which the electron current from a cylindrical cathode or filament to a coaxial cylindrical anode is controlled by a magnetic field parallel to the filament. Electrons leaving the wire when there is no magnetic field travel straight across to the cylinder in radial paths, but under the influence of the magnetic field the paths are bent. The amount of bending increases with the strength of the magnetic field until at a certain critical field they are bent all the way around and fail to strike the anode at all. The current then falls abruptly to zero. The magnetic field, therefore, affords the means of controlling the current from the cathode filament to the anode.

"After the fundamental studies of the magnetron were completed, I spent considerable time developing it as an audio-amplifier and as a generator of radio-frequency waves. While these efforts were successful, they did not prove to be the solution of the patent impasse. That problem was solved in a much better way by the formation of the Radio Corporation, and the magnetron wasn't necessary.

"It was in 1940 that Randall in England developed the first multi-cavity, pulsed magnetron, which was destined to play such an important part in radar, the uncanny 'seeing eye' that made it possible for the RAF to save England from the furious onslaught of Hitler's bombs and rockets, and which profoundly influenced the final outcome of the war. The Germans used conventional tubes in their radio-ranging or radar equipment, and hence were limited to relatively long wave lengths. Almost at the start, the British conceived the idea of using magnetrons, thereby obtaining much shorter waves and greater power. The very first model of Randall's magnetron exceeded the most optimistic expectations. It was immediately flown to New York and duplicated at the Bell Telephone Laboratories. Then followed a race against time and one of the finest examples in history of cooperative effort between countries, England and the United States, and between widely separated scientific groups in each country, working in a common cause. The American effort was coordinated under NDRC with the cooperation of several industrial laboratories, notably the Bell Telephone Laboratories and the Raytheon Company.

"The Radiation Laboratory, which was operated by Division 14 of NDRC at M.I.T., was devoted almost exclusively to the development of microwave radar, and undertook an extensive magnetron program. There the development of the ten-centimeter pulsed magnetron was carried to the astounding output of two million watts peak power."

The problem of noise in superheterodyne receivers prompted Hull to measure the shot-effect in temperature-limited diodes and space-charge limited triodes. This work was done in 1923 in collaboration with N. H. Williams, on leave from the University of Michigan, and laid the basis for the understanding and cure of the heterodyne noise problem. His invention of the screen-grid tube was a by-product of this work on the shot-effect. The necessity for obtaining an amplification of 100,000 at a megacycle prompted him to make a special tube in which there was no feedback; namely, a tube in which the grid and plate were completely screened from each other.

In studying the disintegrating effects on thermionic cathodes by gas ion bombardment Hull discovered in 1927 that the ions did no harm if their velocities were kept below a critical value, which he called the "disintegration voltage." For mercury, it is 22 ev. This discovery led directly to his invention of the Phano-tron and the Thyratron, which he considered to be his most important inventions. In connection with these devices, he later developed several efficient cathodes with a very long life ex-pectancy that were also applicable to gas discharge lamps. The Thyratron opened up the whole field of industrial electronics and power control.

At one period in Hull's work, he became immersed in the problems of high-power transmission lines. One of the great General Electric engineers in this field was C. W. Stone, and through a personal acquaintanceship he interested Hull in some of the basic problems of future high-power transmission lines. Hull and Stone spent long hours plotting and replotting various strategies in this field. The stability problems of alternating current transmission lines of great length were well known, and the alternative of D-C transmission links was under discussion.

Somewhat prior to this time, D. C. Prince and associates, who were then in the Company's General Engineering Labo-ratory, had demonstrated that it was possible to make a D-C to A-C inverter, employing high-power, high-vacuum triode tubes, of the type then used in radio broadcasting. This inverter, plus the mercury arc rectifier, provided the basic terminal com-ponents required for a D-C transmission line. However, the rectifier had fundamental problems of arc-back, and the efficiency of the high-power vacuum tubes, even at very high voltage, was not satisfactory. Hull developed the Thyratron inverter, employing circuitry similar to that used by Prince, and Hull and Stone then set up a D-C transmission line between Schenec-tady and Mechanicville, New York (about fifteen miles), which operated for a long period of years on a demonstration basis. This development was somewhat ahead of its time, and did not attain useful application during that period.

Hull also invented the vacuum lightning arrester. While this device worked initially, it became gassy on repeated operation. It was not until the recent development of gas-free electrode materials for vacuum switches that this difficulty was avoided. His pioneering work on this device, however, laid the foundation for the triggered vacuum gap.

Large glass-to-metal seals were in a very rudimentary state in the early 1930s, and presented a serious handicap in making large, high-power electron tubes. It was at this point that Hull's industrial research work took a wide detour into metallurgy and glass. He was prompted, with the help of E. E. Burger, to make an intensive investigation of the general problem of sealing glass to metal. Prior to his work, the only available solutions to this problem were the Dumet seal, suitable for low currents, and the Housekeeper seal. The latter could be used for high-power tubes, with, however, serious limitations owing to fragility. Hull first identified the alloy and glass requirements for glass-to-metal seals, and studied their expansion coefficients over the range of temperatures employed in making seals. This work resulted in a number of matched combinations of glass and metal capable of producing strain-free seals. The most notable of these was Fernico, an alloy that would permit a true match of expansion coefficients between metal and glass. In collaboration with Louis Navias, Hull developed sealing glasses for 42 percent nickel-iron and pure iron. This led to low-cost, cast-glass bushings with sealed metal inserts, the development of metal receiving tubes, and later the lighthouse tube.

During Hull's early work on mercury-arc tubes, he had visions of replacing the mercury with cesium vapor, an idea conceived by J. M. G. Mackay and E. E. Charlton. The low ionization potential of cesium would ensure a low arc drop, and by continuous condensation on the cathode surface the cesium would provide an efficient electron emitter with infinite life.

His early attempts to make a practical tube failed because all known sealing glasses were attacked by the chemically active cesium. Some twenty-five years later, with the availability of ceramic-metal seals, he succeeded in making a practical cesium-vapor rectifier, but this development came too late and could not compete with the semiconductor rectifier. While many ardent electron tube men were resentful of the inroads made in their field by semiconductor devices, Hull welcomed them and encouraged his young colleagues to pursue the new field, for he felt that it offered them the same opportunity that he had experienced in the early days of the electron tube.

Hull's industrial scientific work with General Electric has had tremendous scientific and practical consequences. Together with Dr. Coolidge's work on tungsten, and Dr. Langmuir's work on high vacuum electronic phenomena, his developments provided the foundation for the electronics business of General Electric.

It is difficult to summarize a great career like Albert Hull's, but in all of his many accomplishments, two outstanding characteristics seem to have provided the essence of his success. First and foremost was his great courage. In a group of people around a conference table, discussing research proposals and projects, one could depend upon him to point out the reasons why the idea had merit, might work, might even be better than anticipated, and by all means should be pushed forward. He was sometimes wrong, but his batting average was exceptionally high, and his courage and optimism opened doors that were closed to many people.

The second outstanding feature of Albert Hull's career was his willingness to enter a brand new field. He started in Greek, then entered the field of physics, first in X-ray diffraction, then later became fascinated by Langmuir's high vacuum electronics, which led to power electron devices, because of which he took a broader detour into metallurgy and glass science. At many points in his career he might have relaxed to become the continuing authority in his field. Instead, he was constantly challenged by new problems, and he had the courage to become a neophyte in a new field where, after a few years, the same native research abilities again brought him to the top as an expert and an authority.

"In my experience," Hull once remarked, "the initiation of projects or inventions comes from two different directions. One is a chance observation, such as that which led to the gas-filled tube. This is the most prolific source of invention. It should be noted that such observations in general are fruitful of results only when one is sufficiently familiar with the field and its problems to be aware of the significance of the observation.

"The other type of stimulus which may lead to invention is need of some kind, most often a need that is only incidental to the main problem under investigation. For example, the screen grid tube was the result of such a need for an amplifier free from feedback in order to measure the shot-effect. In general, when the need occurs in this form, the solution appears quite naturally."

Although Albert W. Hull officially retired in 1949, he continued as a consultant and could be found in the Laboratory almost every day—usually with the younger men—observing, advising, and inspiring. His fifty-seven-year span of technical publications is an accomplishment seldom witnessed.

In recognition of his work contained in 74 papers and 94 patents, Hull received honorary degrees from four colleges. He was president of the American Physical Society in 1942 and was a member of the National Academy of Sciences (to which he was elected in 1929) and an honorary member of the Brazilian Academy of Sciences. He received the Morris Liebmann prize from the Institute of Radio Engineers in 1930 for his research on electron tubes and the Institute's Medal of Honor in 1958. Less than two months before his death he was awarded the U.S. Army's Decoration for Distinguished Civilian Service for his contributions as a member of the Scientific Advisory Committee at the Ballistics Research Laboratories from 1940 to 1964.

While Hull was mostly widely known for his individual research contributions, as assistant director of the Research Laboratory from 1928 until his retirement in 1949 he did much to maintain the spirit of enthusiasm and friendly cooperation implanted by the Laboratory founder, Willis R. Whitney. Hull was not one to spend time on writing books, calling meetings, or participating in organized classroom study. He much preferred to forge ahead on research problems and encouraged others to do the same. He was not embarrassed by mistakes and thought there was much to be learned from experience, provided the same mistake did not reoccur. He always insisted that real research needed very little direction and that one of the greatest assets of the Laboratory was the freedom of individuals to do research without interference or guidance. It is of interest that those who enjoyed this freedom most were the ones who made the most valuable contributions to the electrical industry. Albert Hull's inspiring leadership and encouragement of the men who worked under him have resulted in an unusually high number of rugged individualists who have gone on to make prominent names for themselves.

BIBLIOGRAPHY

KEY TO ABBREVIATIONS

Am. J. Phys. = American Journal of Physics
Elec. Eng. = Electrical Engineering
Gen. Elec. Rev. = General Electric Review
J. Am. Inst. Elec. Engrs. = Journal of the American Institute of Electrical Engineers
J. Appl. Phys. = Journal of Applied Physics
Phys. Rev. = Physical Review
Proc. Inst. Radio Engrs. = Proceedings of the Institute of Radio Engineers
Proc. Nat. Acad. Sci. = Proceedings of the National Academy of Sciences
Rev. Sci. Instr. = Review of Scientific Instruments
Trans. Am. Inst. Elec. Engrs. = Transactions of the American Institute of Electrical Engineers

1909

The initial velocities of the electrons produced by ultra-violet light. American Journal of Science, 28:251-59; Physikalische Zeitschrift, 10:537-42.

1912

Experimental evidence concerning the structure of the atom. Journal of the Worcester Polytechnic Institute, 15:269-79.

1915

Roentgen ray spectra. American Journal of Roentgenology, 2:893-99.

1916

The maximum frequency of x-rays at constant voltages between 30,000 and 100,000. Phys. Rev., 7:156-58.
The reflection of slow moving electrons by copper. Phys. Rev., 7:1-17.
With M. Rice. The law of absorption of x-rays at high frequencies. Phys. Rev., 8:326-28.
The production of constant high potential with moderate power capacity. Gen. Elec. Rev., 19:173-81.
The x-ray spectrum of tungsten. Gen. Elec. Rev., 19:603-10.

With Marion Rice. The high frequency spectrum of tungsten. Proc. Nat. Acad. Sci., 2:265-70.

1917

The crystal structure of magnesium. Proc. Nat. Acad. Sci., 3:470-73.
A new method of x-ray crystal analysis. Phys. Rev., 10:661-96.

1918

The dynatron: a vacuum tube possessing negative resistance. Proc. Inst. Radio Engrs., 6:5-35.

1919

A new method of chemical analysis. Journal of the American Chemical Society, 41:1168-75.
The positions of atoms in metals. Proceedings of the American Institute of Electrical Engineers, 38:1171-92.

1920

Absorption and scattering of x-rays. Journal of Radiology, 1:3-15.
The arrangement of atoms in some common metals (9 new determinations). Science, 52:227-29.

1921

The crystal structure of calcium. Phys. Rev., 17:42-44.
With W. P. Davey. Graphical determination of hexagonal and tetragonal crystal structures from x-ray data. Phys. Rev., 17:549-70.
X-ray crystal analysis of thirteen common metals. Phys. Rev., 17:571-88.
The effect of a uniform magnetic field on the motion of electrons between coaxial cylinders. Phys. Rev., 18:31-57.
The magnetron. J. Am. Inst. Elec. Engrs., 42:715-23.

1922

The crystal structures of the common elements. Journal of the Franklin Institute, 193:189-216.
With E. F. Hennelly and F. R. Elder. The dynatron detector:

a new heterodyne receiver for continuous and modulated waves. Proc. Inst. Radio Engrs., 10:320-43.

Electrons and crystal structures. Albany Medical Annals, 43:239-44.

1923

A combined kenotron rectifier and pliotron receiver capable of operation by alternating current power. Proc. Inst. Radio Engrs., 11:89-96.

The axially controlled magnetron. J. Am. Inst. Elec. Engrs., 42:1013-18.

The measurement of magnetic fields of medium strength by means of a magnetron. Phys. Rev., 22:279-92.

Vacuum tube progress. Journal of the Western Society of Engineers, 28:558-72.

1925

With N. H. Williams. Determination of elementary charge E from measurements of shot-effect. Phys. Rev., 25:147-73.

The motion of electrons between coaxial cylinders under the influence of current along the axis. Phys. Rev., 25:645-70.

Review of literature on ultra-violet therapy. Gen. Elec. Rev., 28:790-97.

1926

With N. H. Williams. Characteristics of shielded grid pliotrons. Phys. Rev., 27:432-38.

Measurements of high frequency amplification with shielded grid pliotrons. Phys. Rev., 27:439-54.

1928

Gas-filled thermionic tubes. Trans. Am. Inst. Elec. Engrs., 47:753-63.

1929

With Irving Langmuir. Control of an arc discharge by means of a grid. Proc. Nat. Acad. Sci., 15:218-25.

Hot-cathode thyratrons. Gen. Elec. Rev., 32:213-23, 390-99.

1931

Mercury arc rectifier research. Trans. Am. Inst. Elec. Engrs., 50: 744-56.

With Herbert D. Brown. Solving the mystery of mercury arc rectifiers. Elec. Eng., 50:788-93.

The future of vacuum tubes in engineering. Yale Scientific Magazine, 5:13-15, 42-47.

1932

Qualifications of a research physicist. Science, 73:623-27.

Electronic devices as aids to research. Physics, 2:409-31.

New vacuum valves and their applications. Transactions of the American Institute of Mining and Metallurgical Engineers, 102: 17-32.

1933

Characteristics and functions of thyratrons. Physics, 4:66-75.

1934

Fundamental electrical properties of mercury vapor and monatomic gases. Elec. Eng., 53:1435-42.

With E. E. Burger. Glass-to-metal seals. Physics, 5:384-405.

1935

Putting physics to work. Rev. Sci. Instr., 6:377-80.

1936

With E. E. Burger. A simple strain-analyzer for glass seals. Rev. Sci. Instr., 7:98-100.

Changing direct current to alternating current by means of thyratrons. Proc. Nat. Acad. Sci., 22:389-93.

1938

A new type of thermionic cathode: the migration cathode. Phys. Rev., 53:936.

1939

The dispenser cathode. Phys. Rev., 56:86-93.

Sealed glass bushings for electrical apparatus. Gen. Elec. Rev., 42:525-28.

1941

With E. E. Burger and L. Navias. Glass-to-metal seals. II. J. Appl. Phys., 12:698-707.

1942

The phase of arcback. J. Appl. Phys., 13:171-78.
With Frank R. Elder. The cause of high voltage surges in rectifier circuits. J. Appl. Phys., 13:372-77.

1943

Dr. Willis Rodney Whitney, recipient of the John Fritz Medal. Scientific Monthly, 56:483-84.

1944

The outlook for the physicist and prospective physicist in industry. Am. J. Phys., 12:62-70.

1945

Research—creator of employment. Elec. Eng., 64:25-27.
Selection and training of students for industrial research. Science, 101:157-60.

1946

Stresses in cylindrical glass-metal seals with glass inside. J. Appl. Phys., 17:685-87.
Thirty years of x-ray research at the General Electric Research Laboratory. Am. J. Phys., 14:71-79.

1947

With V. Vacquier and R. F. Simons. A magnetic airborne detector employing magnetically controlled gyroscopic stabilization. Rev. Sci. Instr., 18:483-87.
Selection and training of men for industrial research. (Proceedings of the Conference on the Administration of Research, October 6-7, 1947.) State College of Pennsylvania, School of Engineering, Technical Bulletin, No. 29, pp. 97-108.

1950

Fundamental processes in gaseous tube rectifiers. Elec. Eng., 56: 695-700.

1951

With E. E. Burger and R. E. Turrentine. The cesium-vapor rectifier. Gen. Elec. Rev., 54:16-22.

1954

Saul Dushman, unofficial "Dean of Men" at the General Electric Research Laboratory. Science, 120:686-87.

1958

Dr. Irving Langmuir's contributions to physics. Nature, 181:148.
Dr. Willis R. Whitney. Nature, 181:1037.
X-ray crystallography. I. An account of early studies at Schenectady. Physics Today, 11(10):19.
W. R. Whitney, the man and his contribution to science. Science, 128:581-82.

1962

Cathode spot. Phys. Rev., 126:1603-10.
The bertele arc. Nature, 195:370-71.

1964

A basic theory of the mercury cathode spot. J. Appl. Phys., 35: 490.

1966

Time delay in triggered vacuum gap. Institute of Electrical and Electronics Engineers Transactions on Electron Devices, ED-13:529-30.

Adolph Knopf

ADOLPH KNOPF

December 2, 1882–November 23, 1966

BY CHESTER R. LONGWELL

A DOLPH KNOPF was born in San Francisco, California, December 2, 1882. Both parents were migrants from Germany. The father, a building contractor, acquired a ranch about twenty-five miles to the south, in open country along the San Andreas fault zone. In later years Adolph remembered the time spent on the ranch, during summers and holidays, as the most enjoyable part of his youthful experience. On his retirement from Yale University in 1951, he and his wife Eleanor made their home at a pleasant site in the hills of Woodside only a few miles from the location of the old ranch.

On reaching college age, Adolph entered the University of California at Berkeley. Boyhood interest in the open country no doubt played a part in the choice of geology as his major subject of study. Andrew C. Lawson had started his notable career as Professor of Geology at Berkeley in 1890, and largely under his tutelage Adolph began his mastery of petrology, ore deposits, and other aspects of Earth Science. His profound respect and personal liking for the old master continued until Lawson's death in 1952.

After completing undergraduate requirements in 1904, Adolph began graduate study at Berkeley and was awarded the M.S. degree in 1905, the date also of his first publication. In undergraduate years he and other students were introduced by Lawson to one of his favorite geologic haunts, a rugged part of the Sierra Nevada including the headwaters of Kern River. Adolph and a companion, Paul Thelen, spent considerable time in the upper Kern basin and prepared a report with the title "Sketch of the Geology of Mineral King, California." This first venture into print was based on field study and mapping of a sizable area in which plutonic igneous bodies are intrusive into sedimentary and metamorphic rocks, with related development of ore minerals. Similar geologic materials and problems were to claim the attention of the senior author in numerous subsequent field projects.

In 1906, with resident graduate study completed, Adolph accepted appointment as Geologic Aide with the United States Geological Survey. His first assignment for field work was in Alaska, at that time a territory with its geology largely unknown. The chief of his field party, Louis M. Prindle, was a small man physically but exceptionally capable and vigorous. In the long summer days near the Arctic Circle his party was awakened at 4 A.M. and continued work to a correspondingly late hour in the evening; long work days were to compensate for short field seasons. Mineral deposits were a prime objective of the field program, and in the course of five successive seasons Adolph saw and studied many kinds of ore deposits, at locations ranging from the Seward Peninsula to eastern parts of Alaska. He had particular interest in tin deposits of the Seward Peninsula, on which was based a report accepted at Berkeley as his doctoral dissertation in 1909. Together with Waldemar Schaller, a companion during one field season, he discovered in a Seward ore-complex two new borate minerals. To one of these they assigned the name *hulsite*, in honor of the Alaskan geologist Alfred Hulse Brooks; the other mineral was named *paigeite*, in recognition of their young friend Sidney Paige.

Adolph's merit was recognized by advancement in grade through assistant geologist to geologist within six years of his first appointment as aide. His record reflects energetic enthusiasm in his work. Summers were devoted to field projects, other months to preparation of reports. After the five seasons in Alaska he was assigned by the Geological Survey to study the mining district between Butte and Marysville, Montana, a distance of nearly 100 miles. In that field project he made acquaintance with the Boulder batholith, a major feature that occupied much time and thought in his later years. After the Marysville experience he attacked varied field problems in Nevada and in his native state, California. His record in completing projects is notable. For each of the fifteen years 1905 through 1919, his bibliography lists from one to six titles. Many of the papers concern varied aspects of minerals in ore deposits. One, however—a professional paper devoted to the Inyo Range and the southeastern part of the Sierra Nevada—presents a broad vista of major geologic problems that still command wide interest.

Through much of his full-time career with the Geological Survey, Adolph made his home in Washington, D.C. In 1908 he was married to Agnes Burchard Dillon; three daughters and a son were born to them. The wife died in November 1918, victim of a widespread influenza epidemic. About a year later Adolph accepted appointment to the faculty of Yale University; his teaching career there began in January 1920. In June of that year he was married to Eleanor Frances Bliss, daughter of General Tasker H. Bliss, herself a geologist with an established reputation. They made their home in New Haven until Adolph's retirement in 1951. He kept a part-time connection with the U.S. Geological Survey until 1945, and with Eleanor as field companion he spent many summer seasons of field study in western states.

At Yale his teaching program was varied, for a time including a course for advanced undergraduates with the title "Geology of the United States." Much of his attention, however, was given to graduate students whose interests were in petrology. He had exceptional ability in directing microscopic study of thin sections, with emphasis on the broad implications of rock compositions. Outside formal classroom hours he devoted much time to discussing special problems with individual students. As a master of the German language he was of course entrusted with examining students for the reading requirement in German. In the period 1933-1950 he was Director of Graduate Studies in his department, a function requiring close liaison with other faculty members as well as with students. His abilities in teaching and research were recognized by advancements in rank. Appointed in 1920 as Associate Professor, he became a Professor in 1923, was awarded the Silliman Professorship on retirement of the incumbent in 1937, and a year later was made a Sterling Professor, a title of special distinction in the Yale Faculty.

During his early years in New Haven he devoted considerable time to completing some Geological Survey projects started when he was based in Washington. A notable example is his contribution on the Mother Lode gold belt of California. F. L. Ransome, whose general report on that district appeared in 1900 as U.S.G.S. Folio 63, wished to have the treatment refined and updated. In 1915 he assigned Adolph to the task of restudying the complex belt, 120 miles long, with emphasis on the gold-bearing quartz veins. After the initial season, funds to continue the field work were not available until 1924. The report, published in 1929 as Professional Paper 157, is a classic in its field, portraying the kinds and relations of complex bedrock units transected by an intricate network of mineral veins and faults.

His strong interest in intrusive igneous bodies led to a study of the Spanish Peaks district in southeastern Colorado. Part of that remarkable area had been mapped on a small scale by R. C. Hills. Using Hills's results as a basis, in 1932 the Knopfs began a field study with emphasis on modes of emplacement of the varied igneous bodies, the variations in their compositions, and relative dates of emplacement. Publication of the results in 1936 marks the beginning of a lengthy sequence of studies devoted to plutonic igneous bodies. Adolph's early work in the mineral district between Butte and Marysville, Montana, inspired him with a desire to study the great Boulder batholith and related igneous masses. Following the experience at Spanish Peaks he and Eleanor spent many summer seasons, including that of 1966, with headquarters at Helena and major attention focused on the igneous geology. Products of the studies are available in several publications of great interest.

At Yale Adolph had a group of close acquaintances in the faculty, including not only scientists but members of departments in varied disciplines. Classicists with whom he associated persuaded him that the spelling *batholith* involves an unfortunate distortion of the Greek root. Following their judgment, in his later publications he used the form *bathylith*. He was happy to meet the chemist B. B. Boltwood, who in 1907 had demonstrated that lead is a product of slow disintegration of uranium and suggested that proportions between uranium and thorium and associated lead can be used to determine ages of the containing rocks. Among results from his first analyses Boltwood announced an age value of 2,200 million years for a mineral from Ceylon. At the time of this announcement, the estimate by Joly and Clarke of 100 million years for the age of the ocean was widely accepted as a first approximation to the age of the earth. In 1913 Arthur Holmes, reviewing results of Boltwood and others, proclaimed his strong indorsement of the higher age values. Barrell in 1917 accepted the time estimates based on evidence from radioactivity; and Adolph, shortly after his arrival in New Haven, announced his convictions in favor of the results from study of lead isotopes. In a paper entitled "The Age of the Earth," published in 1931, he championed the view that earth-history began more than 2,000 million years ago. With continued study of accumulating data, the figure he accepted for length of geologic time grew larger. In 1949, when he took part in a symposium "Time and Its Mysteries," he cited an age value of 2,200 million years for minerals in a pegmatite body in Canada that is intrusive into older rocks. Eight years later, in a paper entitled "Measuring Geologic Time," he agreed with Holmes that the earth was born at least 4,500 million years ago.

Inspection of the Knopf bibliography reveals exceptional growth of his interests in breadth and depth. Early papers are concerned largely with locations and descriptions of rock masses and mineral deposits. Later he became intrigued with the problem of balance in the earth's crust and compiled an exhaustive bibliography of isostasy, a contribution in a field advanced by Joseph Barrell, who preceded him at Yale. Studies of the Spanish Peaks complex and the Boulder batholith involve major problems of igneous activity in the earth's crust. Two papers on geosynclinal theory express his concern with problems of crustal deformation and mountain history. Such major concepts, with continuing attention to geologic dating, occupied much of his thinking in his later years.

After retirement from Yale and return to his native California, Adolph was welcomed into the School of Earth Sciences at Stanford University, first as Visting Professor, later with the title Consulting Professor. There through his final fifteen years he was an element of strength in the teaching staff, much appreciated by advanced students. Retired status brought no fundamental change in his program; he was in the field each summer, the remainder of the year at Stanford, engaged in his own research and informal teaching activities. Groups of geologists, taking advantage of his superior knowledge of geology in parts of Montana, used his services as guide and instructor in successive field seminars.

In 1959 he was recipient of the Penrose Medal awarded annually by the Geological Society of America, which he had served as President in 1944. Before retirement he was active also in other professional societies. Honorary societies to which he was elected include the National Academy of Sciences (1931) and the American Academy of Arts and Sciences.

In the two universities that he served so well the name of Adolph Knopf is now on permanent record in practical form. He arranged for generous endowment of a professorship at Yale, and with his wife he established at Stanford a liberal Graduate Fellowship in Petrology.

After a brief illness Adolph passed away November 23, 1966, nine days before his eighty-fourth birthday. Numerous close friends who survive him include many of his former students, who agree that his apparent shyness and reserve on first acquaintance did not for long conceal his warm, helpful personality. Those who knew him well will keep in mind his tall, well-built physique, his thoughtful features, and his astonishing memory which retained details of his wide experience and broad reading. These friends mourn his passing, but are happy to have been associated with this man of exceptional ability and fine character.

BIBLIOGRAPHY

KEY TO ABBREVIATIONS

Am. J. Sci. = American Journal of Science
Am. Mineralogist = American Mineralogist
Bull. Dept. Geol. Univ. Calif. = Bulletin of the Department of Geology,
    University of California
Bull. Geol. Soc. Am. = Bulletin of the Geological Society of America
Econ. Geol. = Economic Geology
J. Wash. Acad. Sci. = Journal of the Washington Academy of Sciences
Mining Sci. Press = Mining and Scientific Press
Sci. Monthly = Scientific Monthly
U.S. Geol. Surv. Bull. = United States Department of the Interior,
    Geological Survey, Bulletin
U.S. Geol. Surv. Mineral Resources of the U.S. = United States Depart-
    ment of the Interior, Geological Survey, Mineral Resources of the
    United States
U.S. Geol. Surv. Profess. Pap. = United States Department of the
    Interior, Geological Survey, Professional Paper

1905

With P. Thelen. Sketch of the geology of Mineral King, Cali-
    fornia. Bull. Dept. Geol. Univ. Calif., 4(12):227-62.

1906

Notes on the foothill copper belt of the Sierra Nevada. Bull.
    Dept. Geol. Univ. Calif., 4(17):411-23.
An alteration of Coast Range serpentine. Bull. Dept. Geol. Univ.
    Calif., 4(18):425-30.

1907

With Sidney Paige. Stratigraphic succession in the region north-
    east of Cook Inlet, Alaska. Bull. Geol. Soc. Am., 18:325-32.

1908

The Seward Peninsula tin deposits. U.S. Geol. Surv. Bull., No.
    345, pp. 251-67.
The mineral deposits of the Lost River and Brooks Mountain
    region. Seward Peninsula, Alaska. U.S. Geol. Surv. Bull., No.
    345, pp. 267-71.

Geology of the Seward Peninsula tin deposits, Alaska. U.S. Geol. Surv. Bull., No. 358, 71 pp.
With W. R. Schaller. Two new boron minerals of contact metamorphic origin. Am. J. Sci., 25:323-31; Zeitschrift fuer Kristallographie, 48:1-15.

1909

Some features of the Alaskan tin deposits (Seward Peninsula). Econ. Geol., 4:214-23; Mining World, 30:969-97.

1910

With F. H. Moffit. Mineral resources of the Nebesna-White River district, Alaska. U.S. Geol. Surv. Bull., No. 417, 64 pp.
Mining in southeastern Alaska. U.S. Geol. Surv. Bull., No. 442, pp. 133-43.
The occurrence of iron ore near Haines (southeastern Alaska). U.S. Geol. Surv. Bull., No. 442, pp. 144-46.
The probable Tertiary land connection between Asia and North America. Bulletin of the Department of Geology, University of California Publications, 5(28):413-20.
The copper-bearing amygdaloids of the White River region, Alaska. Econ. Geol., 5:247-56.

1911

Mining in southeastern Alaska. U.S. Geol. Surv. Bull., No. 480, pp. 94-102.
The Eagle River region, Alaska. U.S. Geol. Surv. Bull., No. 480, pp. 103-11.

1912

The Eagle River region, southeastern Alaska. U.S. Geol. Surv. Bull., No. 502, 61 pp.
The Sitka mining district, Alaska. U.S. Geol. Surv. Bull., No. 504, 32 pp.

1913

The tourmalinic silver-lead type of ore deposit. Econ. Geol., 8:105-19.

A magnetic sulfide ore body at Elkhorn, Montana. Econ. Geol., 8:323-36.

The fineness of gold in the Fairbanks district, Alaska. (Discussion.) Econ. Geol., 8:800-2.

Ore deposits of the Helena mining region, Montana. U.S. Geol. Surv. Bull., No. 527, 143 pp.

1914

Is the Boulder batholith a laccolith? (Discussion.) Econ. Geol., 9:396-402.

Mineral resources of the Inyo and White Mountains, California. U.S. Geol. Surv. Bull., No. 540, pp. 81-120.

The Darwin silver-lead mining district, California. U.S. Geol. Surv. Bull., No. 580, pp. 1-18.

A platinum-gold lode deposit in southern Nevada. Mining Sci. Press, 109-990. (A)

1915

Plumbojarosite and other basic lead-ferric sulphates from the Yellow Pine district, Nevada. J. Wash. Acad. Sci., 5:497-503.

A gold-platinum-palladium lode in southern Nevada. U.S. Geol. Surv. Bull., No. 620, pp. 1-18; Mining Sci. Press, 110:876-79, map (A); J. Wash. Acad. Sci., 5:370.

Some cinnabar deposits in western Nevada. U.S. Geol. Surv. Bull., No. 620, pp. 59-68.

Platinum-gold lode deposit in southern Nevada. Bull. Geol. Soc. Am., 26:85. (A)

1916

Tin ore in northern Lander County, Nevada. U.S. Geol. Surv. Bull., No. 640, pp. 126-38.

Wood tin in the Tertiary rhyolites of northern Nevada. Econ. Geol., 11:652-61.

The composition of the average igneous rock. Journal of Geology, 24: 620-22.

1917

Tin ore in northern Lander County, Nevada. J. Wash. Acad. Sci., 7:15. (A)

Tungsten deposits of northwestern Inyo County, California. U.S. Geol. Surv. Bull., No. 640, pp. 229-49; J. Wash. Acad. Sci., 7:357. (A)

An andalusite mass in the pre-Cambrian of the Inyo Range, California. J. Wash. Acad. Sci., 7:549-52.

1918

A geologic reconnaissance of the Inyo Range and the eastern slope of the southern Sierra Nevada, California; with a section on the stratigraphy of the Inyo Range, by Edwin Kirk. U.S. Geol. Surv. Profess. Pap., No. 110, 130 pp., maps.

Geology and ore deposits of the Yerington district, Nevada. U.S. Geol. Surv.Profess. Pap., No. 114, 68 pp.

The antimonial silver-lead veins of the Arabia district, Nevada. U.S. Geol. Surv. Bull., No. 660, pp. 249-55.

Strontianite deposits near Barstow, California. U.S. Geol. Surv. Bull., No. 660, pp. 257-70, map; J. Wash. Acad. Sci., 8:94-95. (A)

Tin. U.S. Geol. Surv. Mineral Resources of the U.S., 1916, Pt. 1, pp. 617-22; 1917, Pt. 1, pp. 63-72.

Occurrence of the silver halides in the oxidized zone of ore deposits. (Discussion.) Econ. Geol., 13:622-24.

1919

Present tendencies in geology; metalliferous deposits. Econ. Geol., 14:543-54; J. Wash. Acad. Sci., 9:543. (A)

Tin in 1918. U.S. Geol. Surv. Mineral Resources of the U.S., 1918, Pt. 1, pp. 23-31.

1921

The Divide silver district, Nevada. U.S. Geol. Surv. Bull., No. 715, pp. 147-70.

Ore deposits of Cedar Mountain, Mineral County, Nevada. U.S. Geol. Surv. Bull., No. 725, pp. 361-82.

1922

With B. L. Johnson. Tin in 1919. U.S. Geol. Surv. Mineral Resources of the U.S., 1919, Pt. 1, pp. 747-50.

The Candelaria silver district, Nevada. U.S. Geol. Surv. Bull., No. 735, pp. 1-22.

1924

Geology and ore deposits of the Rochester district, Nevada. U.S. Geol. Surv. Bull., No. 762, 78 pp.

1925

Discovery of andalusite in California. Engineering and Mining Journal, 120(20):778.

1926

Recent developments in the Aspen district, Colorado. U.S. Geol. Surv. Bull., No. 785, pp. 1-28.

1929

The Mother Lode system of California. U.S. Geol. Surv. Profess. Pap., No. 157, 88 pp.

1930

With C. A. Anderson. The Engels copper deposits, California. Econ. Geol., 25:14-35.

1931

Age of the earth; summary of principal results. Bulletin of the National Research Council, No. 80, pp. 3-9.
Age of the ocean. Bulletin of the National Research Council, No. 80, pp. 65-72.

1932

Geothermal gradient of the Mother Lode belt, California. J. Wash. Acad. Sci., 22:389-90.
With L. W. Westgate. Geology and ore deposits of the Pioche district, Nevada. U.S. Geol. Surv. Profess. Pap., No. 171, 79 pp.
With C. R. Longwell and R. F. Flint. *Physical Geology.* New York, John Wiley & Sons, Inc. 514 pp.; 2d rev. ed., 543 pp., 1939; 3d ed., xvii + 602 pp., 1948.

1933

Pyrosomatic deposits. In: *Ore Deposits of the Western States,* ed. by Committee on the Lindgren Volume, pp. 537-57. New York, American Institute of Mining and Metallurgical Engineers.

The age of the earth and the age of the ocean. Bulletin of the National Research Council, No. 80, pp. 59-72; Smithsonian Annual Report, 1932, pp. 193-206.

1934

With C. R. Longwell and R. F. Flint. *Outlines of Physical Geology.* New York, John Wiley & Sons, Inc. v + 356 pp.; 2d ed., ix + 381 pp., 1941.

1935

The Plumas County copper belt, California. In: *Copper Resources of the World,* pp. 241-45. Washington, D.C., 16th International Geological Congress.

1936

Igneous geology of the Spanish Peaks region, Colorado. Bull. Geol. Soc. Am., 47:1727-84. (See 1956.)

The world's gold resources. Sci. Monthly, 42:62-67.

1937

The origin of primary lead ores. Econ. Geol., 32:1061-64.

William Henry Collins (1878-1937). Am. J. Sci., 33:397-98.

1938

Partial fusion of granodiorite by intrusive basalt, Owens Valley, California. Am. J. Sci., 36:373-76.

Edward Salisbury Dana, 1849-1935. National Academy of Sciences, *Biographical Memoirs,* 18:349-65.

1939

With C. R. Longwell and R.F. Flint. *Physical Geology.* 2d ed. New York, John Wiley & Sons, Inc. 543 pp.

1940

Memorial of William E[benezer] Ford (1878-1939). Am. Mineralogist, 25:174-80.

1941

The geologic records of time. Sky, 5(9):12-14; *ibid.*, 5(10):7-9.
Petrology. In: *Geology, 1888-1938, Fiftieth Anniversary Volume,* pp. 333-63. Washington, D.C., Geological Society of America.

1942

Ore deposition in the pyrometasomatic deposits. In: *Ore Deposits as Related to Structural Features,* ed. by W. H. Newhouse, pp. 63-72. Princeton, Princeton University Press.
Ludwigite from Colorado Gulch, near Helena, Montana. Am. Mineralogist, 27:824-25.

1946

Strategic mineral supplies. Sci. Monthly, 62:5-14.

1948

The geosynclinal theory. Bull. Geol. Soc. Am., 59:649-69.
With C. R. Longwell and R. F. Flint. *Physical Geology.* 3d ed. New York, John Wiley & Sons, Inc. 602 pp.

1949

The geologic records of time. In: *Time and Its Mysteries,* pp. 33-59. New York, New York University Press.
Time in earth history. In: *Genetics, Paleontology, and Evolution,* ed. by G. L. Jepson, pp. 1-9. Princeton, Princeton University Press.

1950

The Marysville granodiorite stock, Montana. Am. Mineralogist, 35:834-44.

1952

Memorial of Charles Hyde Warren (1876-1950). Proceedings of the Geological Society of America, 1951, pp. 159-64.
Charles Schuchert, 1858-1942. National Academy of Sciences, *Biographical Memoirs,* 27:363-89.

1953

Clintonite as a contact-metamorphic product of the Boulder bathylith, Montana. Am. Mineralogist, 38:1113-17.

1955

Bathyliths in time. In: *Crust of the Earth,* ed. by A. Poldervaart, pp. 685-702. New York, Geological Society of America Special Paper No. 62.

1956

Argon-potassium determination of the age of the Boulder bathylith, Montana. Am. J. Sci., 254:744-45.

Igneous geology of the Spanish Peaks region, Colorado. In: *Guide-book to the Geology of the Raton Basin, Colorado,* pp. 56-57. Denver, Rocky Mountain Association of Geologists. (Condensation.)

1957

Measuring geologic time. Sci. Monthly, 85:225-36.

The Boulder bathylith of Montana. Am. J. Sci., 255:81-103.

With Donald E. Lee. Fassaite from near Helena, Montana. Am. Mineralogist, 42:73-77.

1960

Analysis of some recent geosynclinal theory. Am. J. Sci., 258A: 126-36. (Bradley Volume.)

Louis Valentine Pirsson, 1860-1919. National Academy of Sciences, *Biographical Memoirs,* 34:228-48.

1963

Geology of the northern part of the Boulder bathylith and adjacent area, Montana (with colored geologic map). United States Department of the Interior, Geological Survey, Miscellaneous Geological Investigations.

1964

Time required to emplace the Boulder bathylith, Montana—a first approximation. Am. J. Sci., 262:1207-11.

Ernest Lawrence

ERNEST ORLANDO LAWRENCE

August 1, 1901–August 27, 1958

BY LUIS W. ALVAREZ

IN HIS RELATIVELY short life of fifty-seven years, Ernest Orlando Lawrence accomplished more than one might believe possible in a life twice as long. The important ingredients of his success were native ingenuity and basic good judgment in science, great stamina, an enthusiastic and outgoing personality, and a sense of integrity that was overwhelming.

Many articles on the life and accomplishments of Ernest Lawrence have been published, and George Herbert Childs has written a book-length biography. This biographical memoir, however, has not made use of any sources other than the author's memory of Ernest Lawrence and things learned from Lawrence himself. A more balanced picture will emerge when Herbert Childs's biography is published; this sketch simply shows how Ernest Lawrence looked to one of his many friends.

Lawrence was born in Canton, South Dakota, where his father was superintendent of schools. When Lawrence was a boy, his constant companion was Merle Tuve, who went on to establish a reputation for scientific ingenuity and daring, much like that of his boyhood chum. Together, Lawrence and Tuve built and flew gliders, and they collaborated in the construction of a very early short-wave radio transmitting station. This experience can be seen reflected in their later work—Lawrence was the first man to accelerate particles to high energy by the application of short-wave radio techniques, and Tuve, with Breit, was the first to reflect short-wave radio pulses from the ionosphere, a technique that led directly to the development of radar. In the early thirties, Lawrence and Tuve were leaders of two energetic teams of nuclear physicists. Lawrence with his cyclotron, and Tuve with his electrostatic accelerator, carried the friendly rivalry of their boyhood days into the formative stages of American nuclear physics, and all nuclear physicists have benefited greatly from the results.

Lawrence began his college work at St. Olaf's in Northfield, Minnesota, and then went to the University of South Dakota for his B.S. degree. He worked his way through college by selling kitchenware to farmers' wives in the surrounding counties. Very few of the scientific colleagues who admired his effectiveness in selling new scientific projects to foundation presidents and government agencies knew that he had served an apprenticeship in practical salesmanship many years before. But it would be quite wrong to attribute his later successes in this field to any early training. It was always obvious that he convinced his listeners by an infectious enthusiasm, born of a sincere belief that his ideas were sound and should be supported in the best interests of science and the country.

Although Lawrence started his college career as a premedical student, he switched to physics under the guidance of the talented teacher one so often finds in the background of a famous scientist's career. In Lawrence's case, this role was played by Dean Lewis E. Akeley, who tutored him privately and sent him on to the University of Minnesota as a graduate student. On the wall of Lawrence's office, Dean Akeley's picture always had the place of honor in a gallery that included photographs of Lawrence's scientific heroes: Arthur Compton, Niels Bohr, and Ernest Rutherford.

At Minnesota, Lawrence came under the influence of Professor W. F. G. Swann, and when Swann moved to Chicago and then went on to Yale, Lawrence moved both times with him. Lawrence received his Ph.D. degree at Yale, in 1925, and remained there three years more, first as a National Research Fellow, and finally as an assistant professor. From this period of his formal training in physics, very little remained on the surface in his later years. To most of his colleagues, Lawrence appeared to have almost an aversion to mathematical thought. He had a most unusual intuitive approach to involved physical problems, and when explaining new ideas to him, one quickly learned not to befog the issue by writing down the differential equation that might appear to clarify the situation. Lawrence would say something to the effect that he didn't want to be bothered by the mathematical details, but "explain the *physics* of the problem to me." One could live close to him for years, and think of him as being almost mathematically illiterate, but then be brought up sharply to see how completely he retained his skill in the mathematics of classical electricity and magnetism. This was one of the few heritages he brought from his apprenticeship with W. F. G. Swann and the Physics Departments of the 1920s. Almost everything that Lawrence did—and more particularly, the way he did it—came from himself, not from his teachers.

In 1928 Lawrence left Yale for Berkeley, where, two years later at the age of twenty-nine, he became the youngest full professor on the Berkeley faculty. It is difficult for one starting on a scientific career today to appreciate the courage it took for him to leave the security of a rich and distinguished university and move into what was, by contrast, a small and only recently awakened physics department. In later life, when he needed to reassure himself that his judgment was good even though he disagreed with the opinions of most of his friends, he would recall the universally dire predictions of his eastern friends; they agreed that his future was bright if he stayed at Yale, but that he would quickly go to seed in the "unscientific climate of the West."

The predictions of a bright future for Ernest Lawrence were solidly based. His doctor's thesis was in photoelectricity. Later, he made the most precise determination, to that time, of the ionization potential of the mercury atom. In his characteristically candid manner, he often depreciated this highly regarded measurement. He had a preconceived "correct value" of the ionization potential in mind, and he would say in a contrite manner that he looked for possible errors of the correct sign and magnitude to make his preconception come true. Every scientist has fought this battle with himself, but few have used themselves as an example to impress their students with the necessity of absolute honesty in scientific inquiry. Lawrence's value for the ionization potential has stood the test of time, but he always shrugged it off by saying he was lucky; if he had looked hard for errors of the opposite sign, he would have found them, too. After this early experience with looseness in science, Lawrence formed the habit of critically examining any scientific result, regardless of its origin. He applied the same rigid standards of criticism to his own work, to that of his associates, and to the reports from other laboratories. Visitors sometimes formed an early impression that Lawrence was overly critical of the experimental results of others, but they soon found he encouraged his juniors to criticize his own work with equal vigor. He believed that a scientific community that did not encourage its members to criticize each other's findings in an open manner would quickly degenerate into an association of dilettantes. Scientific criticism was with him an impersonal reaction; he gave it or received it without any feelings of hostility. He did, however, reserve a bit of scorn for some members of the profession who, in his opinion, drew unwarranted conclusions from each "bump and wiggle" of a curve obtained with poor counting statistics.

Lawrence's name is so closely associated with the field of nuclear physics in the minds of most physicists today that it often comes as a surprise to them to find that he had a distinguished career in other branches of physics before he invented the cyclotron. After he moved to California, he continued his work in photoelectricity, and together with his students published a number of papers in this field. It is difficult for one not intimately familiar with a particular area of physics to appraise the value of another's work in that area. But one can gain some idea of the esteem in which the work was held by examining the literature of the period, and seeing how often the work was referred to by the experimenter's peers. Fortunately for this purpose, an authoritative treatise on photoelectricity was published shortly after Lawrence left the field to concentrate his efforts on the cyclotron. Hughes and DuBridge's *Photoelectric Phenomena* appeared in 1932, and it contains a biographical index of about 700 names. A quick examination of the "multi-lined entries" shows that only twelve of the 700 experimenters were referred to more often than Ernest Lawrence. His contributions were referred to in all eight of the chapters that dealt with non-solid-state photoelectricity, which is a measure of Lawrence's breadth of coverage of the field in the few years he devoted to it.

One of the references in Hughes and DuBridge's book is to Lawrence's investigation of possible time lags in the photoelectric effect. He published several papers in the field of ultrashort-time-interval measurement while he was at Yale, and in this work he was closely associated with Jesse Beams, who is now Professor of Physics at the University of Virginia. Beams was a pioneer in the use of the Kerr electrooptical effect as a light shutter capable of opening in times of the order of 10^{-9} second. He and his students investigated time lags in the Faraday (magnetic rotation) effect, and he has devoted a major portion of his distinguished scientific career to the study of short times, high accelerations, and other related phenomena. Lawrence and Beams showed that photoelectrons appeared within 2×10^{-9} second after light hit the photoelectric surface. Although these measurements were made more than thirty-five years ago, they are modern in every other sense of the word. Only in the last few years has the measurement of time intervals of 10^{-9} second come into routine use in the laboratory. This renaissance is a direct result of the expenditure of vast sums of money on the development of photomultiplier tubes, wideband amplifiers, high-speed oscilloscopes, and a host of auxiliary equipment, such as coaxial cables and shielded connectors— *none* of which were available to Beams and Lawrence.

In this period, Lawrence and Beams performed their well-known experiment of "chopping up a photon." The uncertainty principle states that the energy of a system cannot be determined more accurately than about $h/\Delta t$, where h is Planck's constant and Δt is the time available for the measurement. A narrow line in the optical spectrum is a system with a very small energy spread; each light quantum, or photon, has the same energy to within an uncertainty ΔE. Lawrence and Beams showed that, if they decreased the time available for the energy measurement (by turning the light on and off again in a small time Δt), the width of the spectral line increased as predicted by the uncertainty principle. It is not generally known that Lawrence played an important part in the evolution of the high-speed rotating top which Beams later developed so beautifully. But the bibliographies of Beams and Lawrence show that the first reference to the high-speed rotor is in an abstract by Lawrence, Beams, and Garman, dated 1928.

As a result of their scientific collaboration, Lawrence and Beams became very close personal friends. They took one summer away from their work, and toured Europe together. Lawrence often referred nostalgically to that period in his life, when he could travel and see the sights without the responsibilities of the speeches and receptions which marked his later tours in foreign lands.

Shortly before Lawrence left Yale, he had an experience that is known to only a few of his close associates, but which was most important in his development as a scientist. At that time, television was considered to be a rather impractical dream, because the basic element was the rotating scanning wheel. It was obvious to everyone that this mechanical device would limit the development of picture quality by restricting the number of "picture lines" to less than 100. Lawrence's experience with photoelectricity and the newly developing cathode-ray tube led him to believe that he could make an all-electronic television system without rotating wheels. He quickly put together a rudimentary electronic television system, and being quite sure that he was not only the first to have the idea, but also the first to "reduce it to practice," he contacted a friend at the Bell Telephone Laboratories. After hearing Lawrence say that he had an important new idea in the field of television, his friend invited him down to the Bell Laboratories to talk about it. The friend took him through what Lawrence later described as a "whole floor" full of electronic television apparatus, with excellent pictures on cathode-ray tubes that were beyond anything he had imagined might exist. After dreams of the financial reward his invention would bring him, it was a real shock for him to see how far ahead a good industrial laboratory could be in a field that was important to it. He resolved then and there to concentrate on the things that he knew most about, and not to dilute his effort by competing in the commercial area. He kept firmly to this resolve until the last decade of his life, when he had received all the honors that were available in the scientific world. He then turned some of his creative ability to the problem of color television, a field in which he contributed many new ideas. Paramount Pictures supported an extensive development of the "Lawrence tube," or "Chromatron." In the last few years of his life, Lawrence was issued dozens of patents on his inventions in the field of color television.

Since it has only recently been considered "respectable" for a scientist to hold patents, it is worth reviewing Ernest Lawrence's attitude toward patents and the financial rewards from inventions. The cyclotron and the other Lawrence inventions of the prewar era were patented in Lawrence's name, and assigned by him to the Research Corporation. No royalties were ever asked by the Research Corporation, and Lawrence encouraged and helped scientists throughout the world to build cyclotrons. Lawrence was legally the inventor of the Calutron isotope separator, but he assigned the patent to the government for the nominal one dollar. Some of his colleagues in the atomic bomb project were awarded large sums of money by the government for the infringement of their patents, but Lawrence never allowed his name to be used in any litigation, and therefore received no compensation for his wartime inventive efforts beyond his normal salary. Although he greatly enjoyed the luxuries that came with wealth, and encouraged others to follow his example of inventing for profit in peripheral areas, he felt that it was unwise to foster the patenting of scientific discoveries or developments for personal profit. One of his greatest accomplishments was the encouragement of scientific colleagues to work closely together in an atmosphere of complete freedom for exchanging ideas. (As an extreme example of the pre-Lawrence method, one can recall that Roentgen spent several weeks in a detailed study of the properties of X rays before he told the men in the adjacent research rooms of his discovery.) Lawrence was acutely aware of the change he had wrought in the methods of doing physics, and was worried that patent consciousness might turn back the pages of progress. As he expressed it, a man would be very careful how he talked over his new ideas if the person to whom he was talking might enlarge on them and subsequently make a fortune from a patent.

While at New Haven, Lawrence was a frequent visitor in the home of Dr. George Blumer, Dean of the Yale Medical School. It was soon obvious that he particularly enjoyed the company of the eldest of the four Blumer girls, sixteen-year-old Mary, or Molly as she is known to all her friends. They were engaged in 1931; he returned to New Haven the next year and brought her as his bride to live in Berkeley. Two years later Eric, the first of the six Lawrence children, was born; he was followed by Margaret, Mary, Robert, Barbara, and Susan. With Ernest and the children, Molly Lawrence created a home that was famous throughout the world of physics for its warmth and hospitality. In it, they entertained the steady parade of visitors to the Radiation Laboratory. In 1941, Molly's sister Elsie became the wife of Edwin McMillan, the present director of the Laboratory. Completing the family group in Berkeley were Ernest's parents, who settled there when the elder Dr. Lawrence retired from his distinguished career in education, and Ernest's brother, John, whose pioneering role in the medical aspects of radiation is mentioned later in this memoir. Surely one of Ernest Lawrence's greatest satisfactions must have come from the knowledge that his mother's life had been saved by radiation therapy, using the one-million-volt "Sloan-Lawrence" X-ray machine at the University of California Medical School. After Mrs. Lawrence had been told by many distinguished specialists that she had an inoperable tumor, she was treated, more or less in desperation, with the novel resonance transformer device which Lawrence and his co-workers, in the incredibly busy days of the early 1930s, had installed in the San Francisco Hospital. At the time of her son's death, she was still living in Berkeley, twenty-one years after Dr. Robert Stone treated her with the only million-volt X rays then available in the world.

In the period when Ernest Lawrence was moving from New Haven to Berkeley, physicists were excited by the news of the nuclear transformations being achieved in Lord Rutherford's Cavendish Laboratory, at Cambridge, England. It was generally recognized that an important segment of the future of physics lay in the study of nuclear reactions, but the tedious nature of Rutherford's technique (using the alpha particles from radium) repelled most prospective nuclear physicists. Simple calculations showed that one microampere of electrically accelerated light nuclei would be more valuable than the world's total supply of radium—if the nuclear particles had energies in the neighborhood of a million electron volts. As a result of such calculations, several teams of physicists set about to produce beams of "million-volt particles." Cockcroft and Walton at the Cavendish Laboratory used a cascade rectifier plus a simple acceleration tube, and although they never reached their initial goal of a million volts, they found that nuclear reactions took place copiously at a few hundred kilo electron volts.

Lawrence had spent enough time in the study of spark discharges with the Kerr electrooptical shutter to develop a very healthy respect for the spark-breakdown mechanism as a voltage limiter. He followed the early work of Van de Graaff, whose electrostatic generator made spectacular high-voltage sparks, and the work of Brasch and Lange, who attempted to harness lightning discharges to the acceleration of charged particles. Although he wanted to "get into the nuclear business," the avenues then available didn't appeal to him, because they all involved high voltages and spark breakdown.

In his early bachelor days at Berkeley, Lawrence spent many of his evenings in the library, reading widely, both profession-ally and for recreation. Although he had passed his French and German requirements for the doctor's degree by the slimmest of margins, and consequently had almost no facility with either language, he faithfully leafed through the back issues of the foreign periodicals, night after night. On one memorable oc-casion, while browsing through a journal seldom consulted by physicists, *Arkiv für Electroteknik,* he came across an article by R. Wideröe entitled "Über ein neues Prinzip zur Herstellung hoher Spannungen." Lawrence was excited by the easily under-stood title, and immediately looked at the illustrations. One showed the arrangement Wideröe had employed to accelerate potassium ions to 50,000 electron volts, using a double accelera-tion from ground to ground, through a "drift tube" attached to a radio-frequency source of 25,000 volts. Lawrence immediately sensed the importance of the idea, and decided to try the obvi-ous extension of the idea to many accelerations through drift tubes attached alternately to two radio-frequency "bus bars." Since he could do his own thinking faster than he could trans-late Wideröe's classic paper, Lawrence had the pleasure of in-dependently arriving at many of Wideröe's conclusions. It struck him almost immediately that one might "wind up" a linear accelerator into a spiral accelerator by putting it in a magnetic field. He was prepared to arrange the magnetic field to vary in some manner with the radius, in order that the time of revolution of an ion would remain constant as its orbit in-creased in radius. A simple calculation, on the spot, showed that no radial variation of the magnetic field was needed—ions in a constant magnetic field circulate with constant frequency, regardless of their energy.

One of my most cherished memories is of a Sunday afternoon in the Lawrence living room, about fifteen years ago. Young Eric came in to tell his father that his high school physics teacher had assigned him the responsibility of explaining the cyclotron to his class. His father produced a pad of paper and a pencil, and while I pretended to read a magazine, but listened with one ear, he explained the cyclotron to his eldest son. He told how when the particles were going slowly, they went around in little circles, and when they were going faster, the magnet couldn't bend them so easily, so they went in bigger circles, and had farther to go. The interesting thing was that the slow ions in the little circles took the same time to go around as the fast ions in the big circles, so one could push and pull on all of them at the same rate, and speed them all up. Eric thought about this for a short while, looked at his father with admiration, and said, "Gee, Daddy, that's neat!" I've always thought that the Nobel Committee must have had something of that feeling when they voted the Nobel Prize to Ernest Lawrence in 1939.

According to Lawrence, an ion with a charge-to-mass ratio of e/m will circulate in a magnetic field H, at an angular velocity ω, given by the equation

$$\omega = 2\pi f = (H/c)\ (e/m);$$

here f is the rotational frequency of the ion, in cycles per second, and c is the velocity of light. If an ion is to be accelerated as it circulates in a magnetic field, one must impose on it an alternating electric field of the same frequency. If there was any element of "luck" in Lawrence's career, it was the ready availability in the 1930s of electronic components appropriate to the frequency range of about 10 megacycles. This is the frequency one obtains by substituting into the cyclotron equation the e/m value for the hydrogen molecular ion (or the soon-to-be-discovered deuteron) together with the magnetic field strength that is most easily obtained with an iron-cored electromagnet. Had the calculated frequency turned out to be 4000 times as great (as it is for the electron), cyclotrons would probably not have appeared on the scene until World War II had fathered the necessary microwave oscillators. I originally wrote the last sentence without the qualifying word "probably," but inserted it after recalling the many other technical innovations created by Lawrence in his drive to make the cyclotron a reality. He and his co-workers, M. Stanley Livingston and David Sloan, found it necessary to develop and build their own vacuum pumps and high-power oscillator tubes, because none with the required capacity were commercially available at a price they could pay. They were soon using the largest high-vacuum pumps in the world, the highest-power radio oscillators ever seen, and the largest magnet then in operation. Had they needed high-power microwave oscillators, they would probably have invented and built them, just as Hansen and his co-workers did a decade later at Stanford.

Lawrence is best known for his application of the cyclotron equation to nuclear physics, but he also used the equation to help devise the most accurate method of measuring the specific charge, e/m, of the electron. The method was employed by Frank Dunnington, one of Lawrence's students, in what remained for many years the most precise measurement of this important fundamental constant.

The first demonstration of the cyclotron resonance principle was reported at the Berkeley meeting of the National Academy of Sciences, in the fall of 1930, by E. O. Lawrence and N. E. Edlefson. Their original apparatus is on permanent exhibit at the Lawrence Radiation Laboratory, together with the brass vacuum chamber of the first 4-inch-diameter cyclotron of Lawrence and Livingston, which accelerated hydrogen molecular ions to an energy of 80,000 electron volts. Lawrence and Livingston went on at once to build an 11-inch cyclotron, which they hoped would be the first accelerator to yield "artificial disintegration" of light nuclei. The device was giving protons with an energy of several hundred keV (which we now know would have been quite adequate for the job) in the spring of 1932, but Lawrence and Livingston pressed on to their goal of 1 million electron volts, which appeared to be well within reach. They had no counting equipment in their laboratory, but two friends from Yale, Donald Cooksey and Franz Kurie, were to bring counters to Berkeley in the summer of 1932, to help with the observations. When the visitors arrived, they made it possible for the Berkeley team to repeat the now famous work of Cockcroft and Walton, who had announced their discovery of the disintegration of lithium by protons in early 1932. This was the first of several important discoveries in nuclear physics that could almost as well have been made in Lawrence's laboratory. But, of course, many laboratories in the world, including all the accelerator laboratories, missed the same later discoveries. The first "miss" at Berkeley—the disintegration of lithium—involved the identical mistake Cockcroft and Walton had also made earlier; neither group had looked at the lower energies we now know were sufficient to have done the job. The successful Berkeley experiment was planned for the summer of 1932 when counting equipment would be available, and it was carried off on schedule. Cockcroft and Walton simply got their experiment done first.

But for those who became physicists after World War II and who may be unacquainted with the primitive world of the early accelerator laboratory, a few words will provide an understanding of how Lawrence and his co-workers missed artificial radioactivity, and after that, the discovery that neutrons can produce artificial radioactivity. We should keep in mind that the development of the cyclotron, which actually had been ridiculed by some physicists as impractical, was an extremely difficult technological task that only a man of Lawrence's daring would have undertaken. To make it work required the development of technologies and arts that were not then known. What seems to easy today was won only with sweat and long hours by Lawrence and his associates in the early thirties. In the beginning most of the time of the Berkeley group was concentrated on developing the cyclotron into the efficient tool that was subsequently used with such proficiency in many research areas.

The 27-inch cyclotron was built with incredible speed in an old wooden building near Le Conte Hall, the home of the Physics Department, and the birthplace of the smaller cyclotrons. The old wooden Radiation Laboratory, which was finally torn down in 1959, was the first of the modern nuclear physics laboratories—institutes in which experimentalists collaborated on joint projects, or worked on their own research projects, as they saw fit. The great enthusiasm for physics with which Ernest Lawrence charged the atmosphere of the Laboratory will always live in the memory of those who experienced it. The Laboratory operated around the clock, seven days a week, and those who worked a mere seventy hours a week were considered by their friends to be "not very interested in physics." The only time the Laboratory was really deserted was for two hours every Monday night, when Lawrence's beloved "Journal Club" was meeting. He initiated this weekly meeting when the cyclotron looked as though it might become useful in nuclear physics; he and his associates reported to each other the latest publications in nuclear physics, so they would know what to do when their new tools were ready. But soon the Journal Club became a forum in which the rapidly growing Laboratory staff discussed their own discoveries in radioactivity and allied fields.

The 27-inch cyclotron—later converted to a 37-inch pole diameter—was originally used in studies of artificial transmutations induced by high-energy protons. Immediately after the discovery of deuterium by Urey in 1932, Professor G. N. Lewis of the Chemistry Department supplied the Laboratory with a few drops of heavy water, and Lawrence, Lewis, and Livingston observed the first reactions induced by deuterons. The detecting device used in all these early experiments was a "thin ionization chamber" plus a linear amplifier. Such a chamber responds to fast atomic ions (protons and α particles) but not to the β rays from radioactive substances; to detect β rays, one needs a more sensitive device, for example, a Geiger counter. Lawrence and his collaborators made several attempts to manufacture Geiger counters in the Radiation Laboratory, but all their counters suffered from excessively high "background rates." Today, when Geiger counters are commercially available from dozens of companies, it is difficult to believe that Lawrence and his associates could have overlooked the fact that the high backgrounds were the result of a general high level of radioactivity in the whole laboratory—artificial radioactivity, to be more exact! But in those days, the rare experimentalists who could make good Geiger counters were looked upon as practitioners of witchcraft; their less fortunate friends might try for months without hitting the magic formula. So after several abortive attempts to make useful counters, the Berkeley group went back to the linear amplifier technique that others considered even more difficult, but which was nonetheless one that they had mastered. It was not until the announcement in 1934 of the discovery of artificial radioactivity by Curie and Joliot that Ernest Lawrence and his associates realized why they couldn't make a decent Geiger counter; their whole laboratory was radioactive!

The discovery of artificial radioactivity had been missed by all the accelerator teams then operating throughout the world, so the next few months saw the discovery of dozens of radioactive species by members of the accelerator fraternity. The fact that none of the "machine builders" had noticed the phenomenon of artificial radioactivity puts the oversight by the cyclotron group in proper perspective. Their oversight was symptomatic of the general unrealiability of all detection devices in those days, coupled with the great complexity of the accelerators themselves, rather than a deficiency in the men as scientists.

It is interesting to note that Irène Curie and Frédéric Joliot had the largest source of "trouble-free" polonium in the world. For a quarter of a century, doctors all over the world had taken pleasure in sending their old "radon needles" to Madame Curie, as a token of respect. From many thousands of these otherwise useless glass tubes, she had isolated more than a curie of polonium—by far the strongest sample of the element in the world. Her daughter and son-in-law put this precious sample to good use in their nuclear investigations in the early 1930s. They used their polonium to generate neutrons, but they didn't realize what they had done. Chadwick read their report and immediately recognized its significance; a few days later he had proved that the neutron existed. (So Lawrence was in good company when he let two big discoveries go unnoticed in his Laboratory.)

The Joliot-Curies used their unique source two years later in the discovery of artificial radioactivity. The fact that polonium does not emit β or γ rays made it possible for them to observe the "induced activity" during the time the α particles were bombarding their aluminum target. Accelerator physicists were denied this simple technique, because of the background radiation from their machines. But even with this advantage, the Joilot-Curies almost missed their great discovery; they al-

most dismissed the change in counting rate of their first artificially radioactive source as being due to the erratic behavior
of their Geiger counter! It was only after the builder of the
counter had insisted for several days that his handiwork was
reliable that the Joliot-Curies became convinced that the phenomenon of artificial radioactivity really did exist.

That Lawrence's group, and all the other accelerator teams,
did not anticipate the work of Fermi and his collaborators in
the field of neutron-induced radioactivity is a different story,
but again one which has an easy explanation in terms of its
setting in time. Calculations of "yields" of nuclear reactions
were made every day, and it was painfully obvious that one
had to bombard a target with more than a million fast particles
in order to observe one nuclear reaction. Everyone had thought
of the possibility of using the high-energy α particles from the
artificial disintegration of lithium as substitutes for the slower
α particles from the decay of polonium. But "that factor of a
million" always stood in the way, and it finally led to a firmly
held conviction that "secondary reactions can't be observed."
Certainly, Lawrence and others considered the use of neutrons
to produce artificial radioactivity, but the factor of a million
always made them turn their minds to other things. But Fermi,
who was far removed from the pressures of an accelerator laboratory, looked at the problem from first principles, and realized immediately that *every* neutron would make a nuclear
reaction. In other words, secondary reactions would be as prevalent as primary ones, if neutrons were involved. The story of
his success is well known and need not be repeated here. Lawrence often spoke of the day he first heard of Fermi's classic
experiments, and how he verified Fermi's discovery of the neutron-induced radioactivity of silver within a minute or two.
He merely took a fifty-cent piece from his pocket, placed it near
the cyclotron, and then watched it instantaneously discharge

an electroscope after the cyclotron had been turned off.

One normally does not dwell so long in a scientific obituary on those occasions when the subject failed to find what he was apparently equipped to find. But Ernest Lawrence would not want such interesting bits of history to be swept under a rug. He was so accustomed to his own success and to that of his laboratory colleagues that he enjoyed recounting his mistakes, without ever mentioning the mitigating factors just related. From 1931 until 1950, Lawrence's laboratory was the home of the highest-energy beams of particles in the world, and for several years in the mid-fifties the Bevatron was the highest-energy machine in operation. Such figures by themselves mean nothing, but they do indicate that in that period the Radiation Laboratory could do important experiments that were difficult, if not impossible, at other institutions. Ernest Lawrence was always conscious of the importance of beam intensity in addition to beam energy, and worked diligently to see that all his accelerators kept producing larger currents of accelerated ions. He often spoke with satisfaction of the proven value of his long campaign to increase beam current (often in the face of opposition from his younger colleagues, who wanted to "use what we have" rather than shut down for improvements).

By 1937 Lawrence had succeeded in pushing the cyclotron current up to 100 microamperes, at 8 million electron volts. Other accelerator builders of this period were content with 1 microampere at 1 million electron volts. Lawrence's young associates felt sure that the cyclotron had reached its peak in the "beam intensity department," but Lawrence soon found that the cyclotron was doing ten times as well as anyone had suspected. Lawrence was always the best cyclotron operator in this period; he could "get more beam" than anyone else. One day, he noticed that, as the magnetic field passed through the resonance value, the meters in the oscillator power supply showed a "loading" ten times as great as the 800 watts one would predict (100 microamperes times 8 million volts = 800 watts). Lawrence knew at once that this power must be going into an accelerated beam that wasn't reaching the detector. It was soon after this that Lawrence encouraged Martin Kamen to install two water-cooled probes to intersect the circulating beam that had formerly been lost. So now, in addition to the 100 microamperes of "external beam," another milliampere was always at work producing radioactive isotopes for Dr. John Lawrence's medical program.

One of the important reasons for Lawrence's concern with high intensity was his great interest in the medical and biological applications of the radiations from the cyclotron and from the radioactive substances it produced. A physicist can ordinarily compensate for a lower intensity by building more sensitive detectors. But in medicine, one must accept the human body as it is; if the radiation levels are too low, the body uses its healing mechanisms to minimize the effects that are under investigation.

Lawrence persuaded his brother John to come to Berkeley at first as a visitor to advise him on the potential hazards of the neutrons from the 27-inch cyclotron. Later, John Lawrence headed a strong research team that investigated many phases of the new radiation medicine and biology. Ernest Lawrence, who had abandoned a medical career for one in physics, now had the vicarious pleasure of a "second life" in medical physics. He gave the Laboratory medical program his strongest support, often in the face of keen disappointment on the part of some of the physicists who worked so hard to keep the cyclotron in operating condition and whose research efforts had to be curtailed. In 1938 and 1939, all physics at the cyclotron was suspended for a full day each week, so that terminal cancer patients could be treated with neutrons from the 37-inch cyclotron. The oil-stained cyclotron was cleverly disguised with a set of white panels, and the patients were led through a side door into what appeared to be an immaculate hospital room.

Lawrence was actively engaged in promoting the use of radioactive isotopes throughout the biological and chemical fields, both as tracers and as sources of radiation. He committed his Laboratory to furnishing the materials for experimental programs in many University of California departments, and he derived great satisfaction from the important discoveries made by his colleagues in other scientific disciplines. The collaboration between physicists and biologists naturally blossomed after the development of the nuclear reactor, when radioactive isotopes became widely available. But the real pioneer in this area was Ernest Lawrence, who shared the hardearned fruits of his labor with his University colleagues because he thought it was in the best interest of science.

Everyone recognized that Lawrence was responsible for the steady increase in the peak energy of the accelerated beams available in the Radiation Laboratory, and throughout the world. But Lawrence himself seemed to derive even more satisfaction from his steady drive toward higher beam intensities. He could point to the discovery of carbon-14, by Rubin and Kamen, as an immediate dividend of his obsession with higher intensities. ^{14}C could not have been discovered at any other laboratory in the world with the detection techniques then available. And although Lawrence never said so to anyone but his closest associates, he was convinced that his great concern for beam intensity was what had really made the whole Manhattan District program possible.

Physicists on both sides of the Atlantic had spent a great deal of effort in theoretical and experimental design studies for nuclear chain reactors, but these devices apparently had no relevance to the "war effort." It was not until the discovery of plutonium and its fissionable properties by Lawrence's co-workers at the Radiation Laboratory that the reactor program had a clearly defined role in the military program. And as was true in the case of ^{14}C, plutonium could not have been found anywhere but at Berkeley; its discovery required the enormous particle fluxes that came from Lawrence's long campaign to increase both the energy and the intensity of his ion beams.

As is well known, the Manhattan District's program was three-pronged; uranium-235 for bombs was made by two isotope separation processes and plutonium-239 was created in the chain reactors. Lawrence spent several of the war years perfecting the Calutron, or mass-spectrometer method of separating ^{235}U from ordinary uranium. It is probably true that no one but Ernest Lawrence could have made a success of the Calutron process; the ion currents required were millions of times as great as anyone had even dreamed of before. So Lawrence's concern with beam intensity was the key element in two of the three successful attempts to produce fissionable material in the war period.

In believing that his own pioneering work in two of the three major processes was the key to the acceptance of the Atomic Bomb Project by the government, Lawrence in no way depreciated the accomplishments of the reactor designers or of the gaseous diffusion experts. He simply felt, from a great deal of experience with high-level government officials, that the project could not have "been sold" unless there was one "sure way" to make fissionable material before the war was over. (The threat of postwar Congressional investigations into the waste of money on "boondoggles" hung over the scientific policy makers in those days.) The Calutron process was complicated and expensive relative to the gaseous diffusion process, but once a single unit had worked, there was no doubt that the application of large amounts of money could produce enough material for a bomb. Lawrence, who was personally involved in many of the key sessions that culminated in the establishment of the Manhattan District, always felt that this argument convinced the decision makers in Washington to authorize all three approaches to the production problem.

To return to the cyclotron development, we can note two milestones: the initial operation of the 60-inch cyclotron in 1939, and the authorization of the 184-inch cyclotron in 1940. The 60-inch cyclotron was installed in the new Crocker Radiation Laboratory; its historic contribution to the discovery of plutonium has already been mentioned. The Rockefeller Foundation gave the University of California 1.25 million dollars in 1940 to build the 184-inch cyclotron on the hill behind the Berkeley campus.

Before work could be started on the "giant cyclotron," as Lawrence referred to it in those days, international events conspired to change the character of the Laboratory. In the summer of 1940, Lawrence returned to Berkeley from a New York visit with his longtime friend, Dr. Alfred Loomis. Loomis had played a key role in the discussions with the Rockefeller Foundation officials, and Lawrence had great respect for his counsel. Loomis had been active in the establishment of the National Defense Research Committee, which was headed by Vannevar Bush, Karl Compton, and James Conant. Loomis introduced Lawrence to the members of the British Scientific Mission, who were visiting the country at the time. From his old friend, Sir John Cockcroft, Lawrence learned for the first time of the outstanding scientific contributions to the British war effort, many of them made by nuclear physicists. Before returning to Berkeley, he joined the NDRC Microwave Committee, under the chairmanship of Alfred Loomis. He assumed the responsibility for recruiting a group of young experimental nuclear physicists to help the British "fight the scientific war."

He persuaded Lee DuBridge to leave his own cyclotron at Rochester, New York, and head the embryonic Radiation Laboratory at Massachusetts Institute of Technology. (The name of the laboratory, together with its staff of nuclear physicists, was intended as a "cover" to mislead the curious into believing that its mission was in the field of nuclear fission. In those days, fission was not treated seriously as a war project, but the mere idea that planes could be detected by radio echoes was considered to be exceedingly secret information.) Lawrence recruited a fine staff of young physicists, many of them his former students. Most of them gave up their exciting careers in nuclear physics, more than a year before Pearl Harbor, for the simple reason that Ernest Lawrence came to see them and told them it was the most important thing they could do. From his own Laboratory he recruited McMillan, Salisbury, and Alvarez. The M.I.T. Radiation Laboratory came into being in November of 1940, and its contributions to radar are too well known to be recounted here. Lawrence visited the laboratory frequently in its first year and kept abreast of its activities in that period. But it was soon obvious that the laboratory could stand on its own feet, and Lawrence had other demands on his talents.

In the summer of 1941 Lawrence became involved in the antisubmarine warfare program; German submarines were then close to destroying the convoy system that was supplying Great Britain from the United States. Lawrence again acted as the chief recruiting agent for the new underwater sound laboratories, and persuaded McMillan to leave M.I.T. for San Diego. Shortly thereafter, he converted the 37-inch cyclotron into a mass spectrometer for separating small amounts of ^{235}U from ordinary uranium. This work convinced him that the electromagnetic separation technique could be expanded to become a large-scale process for producing ^{235}U. In his characteristic manner, he immediately committed his Laboratory and his reputation to the project. Although he had recently staffed two laboratories with many of his best students, he still could call on a number of his top-flight protégés to restaff the Berkeley Radiation Laboratory.

From the summer of 1941 until the summer of 1945, the Radiation Laboratory worked around the clock on the technical problems involved in the electromagnetic separation of ^{235}U. The 184-inch cyclotron magnet, assembled in a new laboratory high above the Berkeley campus, served as a working model for the hundreds of mass spectrometers soon to be constructed in Oak Ridge, Tennessee. Lawrence himself, and all his associates, worked twelve hours a day, seven days a week. It was a Herculean effort, and it was almost solely responsible for the ^{235}U that made up the Hiroshima bomb. The thermal diffusion process and the gaseous diffusion process contributed only in a minor way to the over-all separation of the isotopes for the first bomb; Lawrence's fantastic mass spectrometer plant at Oak Ridge bore the brunt of the effort. (Shortly after the war, Lawrence's plant was shut down, and the more efficient gaseous diffusion plant took over the peacetime production of ^{235}U.)

One of the greatest difficulties one encounters in writing of Ernest Lawrence's career is that so much must be omitted in order to keep the account within reasonable bounds. It is also a pity that Lawrence himself wrote nothing of the experiences he had in his five intensely busy war years, nor of the technical problems he met and solved in that period. Because of this, there exists an apparently comprehensive book on the electromagnetic separation of isotopes with but a single mention of his name. However, in the minds of those who worked with him during the war there is no question that his foresight, daring, leadership and technical ingenuity were the key ingredients in the success of the venture.

In early 1945, when the completed Oak Ridge plant was in

full production, Lawrence turned his thoughts toward the post-war period. He persuaded General Groves (for whom he had a great respect that was apparently reciprocated) to authorize the conversion of the Laboratory to its peacetime mission. Manhattan District funds were accordingly made available to complete the 184-inch cyclotron, and to build a proton linear accelerator and an electron synchrotron. The synchrotron had just been invented by McMillan, and Alvarez's radar experience had convinced him that a proton linear accelerator could be built.

In the fall of 1945 the prewar Berkeley team was reassembled, together with some talented newcomers whose abilities had first come to light in the wartime effort. One of the first major decisions Lawrence had to make concerned the 184-inch cyclotron. It had been planned as a "conventional cyclotron," but its performance under those circumstances would have been marginal at best. McMillan's theory of phase stability indicated that the 184-inch machine would perform more satisfactorily as a synchrocyclotron; its proton energy should rise to 350 MeV, from the earlier design figure of perhaps 70 MeV. But, on the other hand, no one had ever built a synchrocyclotron, and the problems foreseen were formidable. Lawrence and McMillan called for the immediate rebuilding of the old 37-inch cyclotron. It was soon operating as the world's first synchrocyclotron, and it showed that the new device was much simpler to build and operate than the originally proposed conventional cyclotron. As a result of these early model tests, the 184-inch synchrocyclotron was accelerating deuterons to 180 MeV, and helium nuclei to 360 MeV, in late 1946.

Since this is the story of Ernest Lawrence's career, very little will be said about the new laboratory activites that were primarily the responsibilities of his younger colleagues. In addition to the two accelerators built under the supervision of

McMillan and Alvarez, there were two important new chemical projects under Seaborg and Calvin. Seaborg returned to Berkeley from his successful wartime duties as director of the chemical phases of the Plutonium Project in Chicago. Calvin had played several important roles in the OSRD Chemistry Section, and was anxious to study photosynthesis with ^{14}C, which was soon to be in plentiful supply as a direct result of the huge neutron fluxes now available from nuclear reactors. In effect, all of us had "gone away as boys, and come back as men." We had all initiated large technical projects, and carried them to completion as directors of large teams of scientists and technicians. We were all prepared to reassume our subordinate roles, with Ernest Lawrence as our "leader" once again. But he made it clear by his actions, if not by his words, that we were to be free agents. We made all our own technical and personnel decisions, and for the first few years after the war, at least, we had unlimited financial backing. It was not until the "blank check" from the Manhattan District was replaced by more normal budgeting procedures that we felt any limitations on our ability to do whatever we thought should be done in our own areas of responsibility. Ernest Lawrence showed a keen interest in what we were doing, but in these early postwar years he never gave a sign that he thought his function was to give us advice of any kind. Wise parents let their children solve all the problems they can, but they stand by to help when the problems are too difficult. Ernest Lawrence was always a wise "scientific parent"; all of us who were fortunate enough to be his "scientific children" will remember with gratitude the help and understanding he gave us when we needed it, as well as the freedom he gave us to solve our own problems when it seemed that we could eventually succeed.

With the completion of the 184-inch cyclotron, Lawrence once again became an active research worker. He had not been directly involved in any particular experiment since his 1935 work on deuteron-induced radioactivities. As soon as the 184-inch cyclotron was operating, Lawrence became an active participant in experiments using the recently discovered high-energy neutrons produced by "deuteron stripping." He personally discovered the delayed neutron activity that he and his colleagues soon showed was due to nitrogen-17. It was a refreshing experience for many of his young colleagues, who had known him largely as a laboratory director and as a person with great skill in diagnosing troubles in complicated scientific tools, to see the complete devotion he now showed to personal involvement in basic scientific research. Soon after the ^{17}N mystery was unraveled, Lawrence became convinced that the 184-inch cyclotron could produce the newly discovered π mesons. Edward Teller had pointed out that, even though the cyclotron's energy seemed too low to produce pions, there was some hope that with the aid of the Fermi momentum of an incident α particle, and of a carbon target nucleus, the job could be done. Lawrence worked closely with Eugene Gardner in this period, designing experimental setups using nuclear emulsions as detectors, but their efforts were unsuccessful.

Shortly after these early experiments, C. M. J. Lattes arrived in Berkeley. He had been a member of the Bristol team that, under the leadership of C. F. Powell, had recently discovered the π meson. He quickly showed that the difficulties encountered by Gardner and Lawrence had been due to improper processing of the nuclear emulsions. Lattes immediately corrected the Berkeley development techniques, and a new set of exposures was made soon after his arrival, using the apparatus designed by Lawrence and Gardner. Lattes also brought a familiarity with the tracks of π mesons in emulsion that was available to only a few physicists in the world at that time, and he applied his keen eyesight to the tedious scanning of the ex-

posed plates. His diligence was rewarded with success, one evening, when he observed tracks of the first artificially produced
negative pion coming to rest in an exposed nuclear emulsion
plate. He and Gardner immediately called Lawrence, who was
entertaining visitors at an Oakland restaurant. Lawrence left the
dinner, and as soon as he looked through the microscope, he
experienced one of the greatest thrills of his life. Although he
had played a major role in the discovery by his activities both
in procuring the money for and designing the 184-inch cyclotron and, more particularly, in designing the apparatus used
in the experiment, he characteristically insisted that the historical paper should be signed "Gardner and Lattes."

For a period of several years after the war, Lawrence devoted all his waking hours to the pursuit of basic science at the
Radiation Laboratory. Lawrence was fortunate in having an
administrative staff that had learned to cope with the problems
of a much larger wartime organization, so he was relatively
free to concentrate on the scientific activities of the many sections of his Laboratory. He took a great personal interest in the
programs on photosynthesis, medical physics, and nuclear chemistry, but the intensity of his involvement in the physics program
was a source of amazement to his younger colleagues. It was a
rare week that he did not spend several hours each evening and
much of Saturday and Sunday in the cyclotron building, or
wandering through other laboratories, talking to everyone from
research assistants to visiting professors. Even though the Laboratory was now almost a hundred times as large in manpower
as it had been fifteen years earlier, everyone still had the feeling
that he was a "member of Ernest Lawrence's team"—not simply
an employee of the Radiation Laboratory. Even at present, almost twenty years after this exciting phase of the Laboratory's
history, technicians as well as senior staff members continue to
swap their favorite stories of "the time Professor Lawrence

looked over my shoulder at 3:00 A.M. and asked what I was doing."

In 1948 William Brobeck convinced the Laboratory staff that a proton synchrotron could be built in the multibillion-electron-volt range. Lawrence immediately assumed the responsibility of securing financial backing for the "Bevatron" from the Atomic Energy Commission and Congress. The Brookhaven National Laboratory had recently been established, and it was simultaneously asking for support for a similar accelerator. The AEC eventually authorized the 6.2-BeV Bevatron at Berkeley and the 3-BeV Cosmotron on Long Island. The Cosmotron came into operation before the Bevatron, for two reasons. Lawrence, with a conservatism that many of his associates had not observed before, decided to build a quarter-scale model of the Bevatron, to be sure that the untried principle of "external injection" into a synchrotron would work. The model, as designed by Brobeck, worked within nine months of the decision to build it, and the "go-ahead signal" for the Bevatron was immediately given by Lawrence. But soon after this decision had been made, the USSR exploded its first nuclear device, and Lawrence turned his attention once again to problems of national security.

Lawrence played a key role in the U.S. decision to embark on a program leading to the development of a thermonuclear bomb. Soon after President Truman made the decision to build the hydrogen bomb, Lawrence became concerned with the serious shortage of uranium reserves available to the United States. He felt that the country might soon be plagued with a neutron shortage, occasioned by the dwindling supply of ^{235}U. His solution to the problem was the construction of a high-energy, high-current deuteron linear accelerator that would produce neutrons by impact on heavy targets. Experiments at the 184-inch cyclotron had shown surprisingly high "neutron multiplicities" in such collisions. A 60-foot-diameter 60-foot-long test section of the accelerator was built at the Laboratory's newly acquired Livermore site, and it accelerated unprecedented currents of close to one ampere to several million electron volts. The project was abandoned when another solution to the neutron shortage problem proved successful; the AEC offered substantial cash payments for uranium finds in the continental United States. A flood of prospectors with Geiger counters promptly showed that there were enormous and previously unknown reserves of uranium in the Rocky Mountain states. (At the present date, the Canadian government is considering a program patterned after Lawrence's scheme of electronuclear neutron production, as an effective competitor to nuclear reactors. An advantage of the accelerator method is the lower power density in the neutron-producing target, per unit of neutron flux, than in nuclear reactors.)

In 1952 Lawrence expressed concern that all the U.S. nuclear weapons design effort was concentrated in a single government laboratory. He had great respect for the members of the Los Alamos Laboratory, and for their extraordinary accomplishments. Nonetheless, his extensive experience as a scientific consultant to many of the largest U.S. technical corporations gave him firsthand experience with the benefits of a healthy competition between independent development laboratories. He therefore urged the AEC and the Joint Congressional Committee on Atomic Energy to set up a second weapons laboratory. He offered the Livermore site as a suitable location, and pledged his personal oversight of the new project. The Laboratory was established in 1952, with Herbert York as director and Edward Teller as a senior member of the staff. Most of the key group leaders were young physicists, chemists, and engineers trained in the Berkeley Laboratory. Lawrence spent most of his remaining time and effort on the affairs of the Livermore Laboratory until his death in 1958. The young competitor in the field of nuclear weapons "stubbed its toe" several times in the early years, but later it made the substantial contributions to the design of nuclear weapons that Lawrence had forseen as its destiny. Without the steadying hand of Ernest Lawrence in the difficult early years, the Livermore Laboratory might easily have failed in its purpose, and the country as a whole would have been the loser. Lawrence's last protégés, the first three directors of the Livermore Laboratory, are a remarkable group of young men. Each of them, in turn, went from Livermore to a position of great responsibility in the Pentagon—the Director of Defense Research and Engineering. Herbert York left Washington to become Chancellor of the San Diego campus of the University of California, Harold Brown became Secretary of the Air Force at the age of thirty-eight, and John Foster is still "DDR and E."

Concurrently with the establishment of the Livermore Laboratory, Lawrence developed what he called his "hobby," in order to divert his mind from the enormous pressures to which it was subjected in these years. He became fascinated with the technical challenges of color television, and invented some very ingenious solutions to the difficult problems of that field. Unfortunately, the business problems involved in the financing of initially unprofitable color television tube production lines were more difficult than the technical problems Lawrence tackled and solved, largely by himself. For these reasons, the Lawrence "Chromatron" was never put into production in this country. But it is now being sold in Japan, and the Sony Company announced plans to introduce it into the U.S. market in 1967.

In the mid-fifties John Lawrence and Dr. Albert Snell, Ernest's personal physician, urged him to shed some of the great burdens he was carrying. On one occasion Ernest and Molly

Lawrence took a leisurely ocean voyage to India, and it seemed that the period of rest had greatly relieved the intestinal problems that were aggravated by the pressures under which he had worked for so long. But the problems were only temporarily ameliorated; surgical treatment was recommended, but it was unsuccessful. Ernest Lawrence died in a Palo Alto hospital on August 27, 1958, without recovering consciousness after major surgery.

Lawrence's untimely death at the end of his fifty-seventh year was a great shock to his wide circle of friends in science, government, and industry. He had led a life of enormous usefulness to science and his country; his influence was evident largely by his example and by the strength of his character. He had great admiration for his scientific colleagues who could influence national policies through high administrative office, or by writings, or in public speeches. But he felt that the proper way for him to be useful was to let policy makers know that he was available for consultation on his own personal opinions— never as a spokesman for a pressure group. Leaders in government and industry respected his distaste for the limelight, and sought his counsel. His long record of success in the difficult tasks he set for himself, and the accuracy of his prognostications in diverse fields, made his advice most compelling to those who sought it.

For those who had the good fortune to be close to him both personally and scientifically he will always seem a giant among men. At present, when government support for basic science appears to be on the wane, one hears more and more frequently the lament, "The real difficulty is that there isn't an Ernest Lawrence any more."

Lawrence's place in the history of science is secure. He will always be remembered as the inventor of the cyclotron, but more importantly, he should be remembered as the inventor of the modern way of doing science. Element 103 was named Lawrencium by his young associates who discovered it shortly after his death. Also following his death, his friends endowed the Lawrence Hall of Science, to which science teachers from all over the country will come on year-long fellowships to learn the most modern methods of teaching their subjects. The Lawrence Hall of Science will soon be in operation, just above the Laboratory that Ernest Lawrence founded and nurtured and loved for so long, and that is now appropriately known as the Lawrence Radiation Laboratory.

HONORS AND DISTINCTIONS

HONORARY DEGREES

Sc.D., University of South Dakota, 1936
Sc.D., Stevens Institute of Technology, 1937
Sc.D., Yale University, 1937
Sc.D., Princeton University, 1937
LL.D., University of Michigan, 1938
Sc.D., University of Chicago, 1941
Sc.D., Harvard University, 1941
Sc.D., Rutgers University, 1941
LL.D., University of Pennsylvania, 1942
Sc.D., McGill University, 1946
Sc.D., University of British Columbia, 1947
Sc.D., University of Southern California, 1949
Sc.D., University of San Francisco, 1949
LL.D., University of Glasgow, 1951

AWARDS AND MEDALS

Elliot Cresson Medal of Franklin Institute, 1937
Research Corporation Prize and Plaque, 1937
Comstock Prize of National Academy of Sciences, 1937
Hughes Medal of Royal Society (England), 1937
Nobel Prize in Physics, 1939
Duddell Medal of Royal Physical Society, 1940
William S. Dunn Award, American Legion, 1940
National Association of Manufacturers Award, 1940
Holley Medal, American Society of Mechanical Engineers, 1942
Copernican Citation, 1943
Wheeler Award, 1945
Medal for Merit, 1946
Medal of Trasenster, Association of Graduate Engineers, University of Liège, Belgium, 1947
Officer de la Légion d'Honneur, France, 1948
Phi Delta Epsilon Annual Service Award, 1948
William Proctor Prize of the Scientific Research Society of America, 1951

Faraday Medal, 1952
American Cancer Society Medal, 1954
Enrico Fermi Award, 1957
Sylvanus Thayer Award, 1958

MEMBER

American Representative at Solvay Congress, Brussels, 1933
National Academy of Sciences, 1934
American Philosophical Society, 1937
Phi Beta Kappa
Sigma Xi
Gamma Alpha
American Scandinavian Foundation, 1942
Board of Foreign Scholarships, Department of State (Fulbright
    Act—79th Congress), 1947
Newcomen Society, 1948-1951
Physical Society of Japan, 1954
Board of Trustees: Carnegie Institution of Washington, 1944
                     Rand Corporation, 1956
Board of Directors: Yosemite Park & Curry Company
                     Monsanto Chemical Company, 1957

FOREIGN MEMBER

Royal Swedish Academy of Sciences, 1952

HONORARY MEMBER

Bohemian Club (California), 1940
California Academy of Sciences, 1940
Academy of Science, USSR, 1943
Royal Irish Academy of Science, 1948

FELLOW

American Physical Society
American Association for the Advancement of Science
American Academy of Arts and Sciences

HONORARY FELLOW

Leland Stanford Junior University, 1941
National Institute of Sciences of India, 1941
The Institute of Medicine of Chicago, 1941
Royal Society of Edinburgh, 1946
The Physical Society, 1948
Indian Academy of Sciences, 1953

APPOINTMENTS

National Defense Research Committee, June 1940
National Academy of Sciences, National Research Council Reviewing Committee, April 1941
Office of Scientific Research and Development, 1941
Program Chief, S-1 Section of the Office of Scientific Research and Development (Uranium Section), November 1941–May 1942
S-1 Executive Committee of the Office of Scientific Research and Development, May 1942–March 30, 1946
Scientific Adviser and Project Leader, Manhattan District, May 1, 1943
Research Board for National Security, 1945-1946
Elector, The Hall of Fame of New York University, 1947
Adviser to the U.S. Delegation to the International Conference on the Peaceful Uses of Atomic Energy, Geneva, Switzerland, August 1955
Physical Science Administration Officer (Consultant), Brussels Universal International Exhibition of 1958, Department of State, 1956-1958
U.S. Delegation to the Conference of Experts to Study the Possibility of Detecting Violations of a Possible Agreement on Suspension of Nuclear Tests, Geneva, Switzerland, July 1958 (three-member committee appointed by President Eisenhower)

BIBLIOGRAPHY

KEY TO ABBREVIATIONS

J. Franklin Inst. = Journal of the Franklin Institute
Phil. Mag. = Philosophical Magazine
Phys. Rev. = Physical Review
Proc. Nat. Acad. Sci. = Proceedings of the National Academy of
    Sciences
Rev. Sci. Instr. = Review of Scientific Instruments

1924

The charging effect produced by the rotation of a prolate iron
    speroid in a uniform magnetic field. Phil. Mag., 47:842-47.

1925

The photo-electric effect in potassium vapour as a function of
    the frequency of the light. (Ph.D. Dissertation.) Phil. Mag.,
    50:345-59.

1926

The role of the Faraday cylinder in the measurement of electron
    currents. Proc. Nat. Acad. Sci., 12:29-31.
Transition probabilities: their relation to thermionic emission and
    the photo-electric effect. Phys. Rev., 27:555-61.
A principle of correspondence. Science, 64:142.
The ionization of atoms by electron impact. Phys. Rev., 28:947-
    61.

1927

With J. W. Beams. On the nature of light. Proc. Nat. Acad.
    Sci., 13:207-12.
Ultra-ionization potentials of mercury. J. Franklin Inst., 204:91-
    94.
With J. W. Beams. On the lag of the Kerr effect. Proc. Nat.
    Acad. Sci., 13:505-10.

1928

With J. W. Beams. On relaxation of electric fields in Kerr

cells and apparent lags of the Kerr effect. J. Franklin Inst., 206:169-79.

With J. W. Beams. Element of time in the photoelectric effect. Phys. Rev., 32:478-85.

1929

With N. E. Edlefsen. Photo-ionization of the vapors of caesium and rubidium. Phys. Rev., 34:233-42.

With N. E. Edlefsen. Photo-ionization of potassium vapor. Phys. Rev., 34:1056-60.

With L. B. Linford. Effect of intense electric fields on the photo-electric behavior of alkali films on tungsten. Phys. Rev., 34:1492.

With F. G. Dunnington. Early stages of electric spark discharges. Phys. Rev., 34:1624-25.

1930

With N. E. Edlefsen. Intense source of continuous ultraviolet light. Rev. Sci. Instr., 1:45-48.

With F. G. Dunnington. Broadening of spectrum lines during early stages of spark discharges. Phys. Rev., 35:134. (A)

With F. G. Dunnington. On the early stages of electric sparks. Phys. Rev., 35:396-407.

With L. B. Linford. Effect of intense electric fields on the photoelectric properties of metals. Phys. Rev., 36:482-97.

With M. A. Chaffee. On the direction of emission of photoelectrons from potassium vapor by ultraviolet light. Phys. Rev., 36:1099-1100.

With N. E. Edlefsen. On the production of high speed protons. Science, 72:376-77.

1931

With David H. Sloan. Production of high speed canal rays without the use of high voltages. Proc. Nat. Acad. Sci., 17:64-70.

With M. S. Livingston. Production of high speed protons without the use of high voltages. Phys. Rev., 38:834.

With D. H. Sloan. Production of heavy high speed ions without the use of high voltages. Phys. Rev., 38:2021-32.

1932

With M. S. Livingston. Production of high speed light ions without the use of high voltages. Phys. Rev., 40:19-35.

With M. S. Livingston and M. G. White. Disintegration of lithium by swiftly moving protons. Phys. Rev., 42:150-51.

1933

Disintegration of boron by swiftly moving protons. Phys. Rev., 43:304-5.

With M. S. Livingston. The disintegration of aluminum by swiftly moving protons. Phys. Rev., 43:369.

With G. N. Lewis and M. S. Livingston. The emission of alpha-particles from various targets bombarded by deutons of high speed. Phys. Rev., 44:55-56.

With G. N. Lewis and M. S. Livingston. The emission of protons from various targets bombarded by deutons of high speed. Phys. Rev., 44:56.

With M. S. Livingston and M. C. Henderson. Neutrons from deutons and the mass of the neutron. Phys. Rev., 44:781-82.

With M. S. Livingston and M. C. Henderson. Neutrons from beryllium bombarded by deutons. Phys. Rev., 44:782-83.

1934

With M. S. Livingston. The emission of protons and neutrons from various targets bombarded by three million volt deutons. Phys. Rev., 45:220.

With G. N. Lewis, M. S. Livingston, and M. C. Henderson. The disintegration of deutons by high speed protons and the instability of the deuton. Phys. Rev., 45:242-44.

With M. C. Henderson and M. S. Livingston. Artificial radioactivity produced by deuton bombardment. Phys. Rev., 45:428-29.

With G. N. Lewis, M. S. Livingston, and M. C. Henderson. On the hypothesis of the instability of the deuton. Phys. Rev., 45:497.

With M. S. Livingston. The multiple acceleration of ions to very high speeds. Phys. Rev., 45:608-12.

With M. C. Henderson and M. S. Livingston. The transmutation of fluorine by proton bombardment and the mass of fluorine 19. Phys. Rev., 46:38-42.

With M. Stanley Livingston and Malcolm C. Henderson. Radioactivity artificially induced by neutron bombardment. Proc. Nat. Acad. Sci., 20:470-75.

Radioactive sodium produced by deuton bombardment. Phys. Rev., 46:746.

1935

Transmutations of sodium by deutons. Phys. Rev., 47:17-27.

With E. McMillan and M. C. Henderson. Transmutations of nitrogen by deutons. Phys. Rev., 47:273-77.

With E. McMillan. Transmutations of aluminum by deutons. Phys. Rev., 47:343-48.

With E. McMillan and R. L. Thornton. A new type of excitation function for nuclear reactions. Science, 81:421-22.

With E. McMillan and R. L. Thornton. The transmutation functions for some cases of deuteron-induced radioactivity. Phys. Rev., 48:493-99.

Artificial radioactivity. Ohio Journal of Science, 35:388-405.

1936

With John H. Lawrence. The biological action of neutron rays. Proc. Nat. Acad. Sci., 22:124-33.

With J. M. Cork. The transmutation of platinum by deuterons. Phys. Rev., 49:788-92.

With John H. Lawrence and Paul C. Aebersold. Comparative effects of x-rays and neutrons on normal and tumor tissue. Proc. Nat. Acad. Sci., 22:543-57.

With Donald Cooksey. On the apparatus for the multiple acceleration of light ions to high speeds. Phys. Rev., 50:1131-40.

1937

With John H. Lawrence and Paul C. Aebersold. The comparative effect of neutrons and x-rays on normal and neoplastic tissue. American Association for the Advancement of Science Occasional Publication, No. 4, pp. 215-19.

The biological action of neutron rays. Radiology, 29:313-22.

Science and technology.   Rev. Sci. Instr., 8:311-13; Science, 86:295-98.

With Donald Cooksey.   An improved cyclotron.   Science, 86:411.

Response by Professor Ernest O. Lawrence.   (Acceptance speech upon presentation of the Comstock Prize.)   Science, 86:406-7.

1938

The cyclotron and the elementary course in electricity.   American Physics Teacher, 6:280-81.

With P. F. Hahn, W. F. Bale, and G. H. Whipple.   Radioactive iron and its metabolism in anemia.   Journal of the American Medical Association, 111:2285-86.

1939

Atoms, new and old.   In: *Science in Progress,* 1st Ser., ed. by G. A. Baitsell, pp. 1-34. New Haven, Yale University Press.

With P. F. Hahn, W. F. Bale, and G. H. Whipple.   Radioactive iron and its metabolism in anemia—its absorption, transportation, and utilization.   Journal of Experimental Medicine, 69:739-53.

With Luis W. Alvarez, Wm. M. Brobeck, Donald Cooksey, Dale R. Corson, Edwin M. McMillan, W. W. Salisbury, and Robert L. Thorton.   Initial performance of the 60-inch cyclotron of the William H. Crocker Radiation Laboratory, University of California.   Phys. Rev., 56:124.

The medical cyclotron of the William H. Crocker Radiation Laboratory.   Science, 90:407-8.

1940

Acceptance of the Nobel Prize Award.   In: *The 1939 Nobel Prize Award in Physics to Ernest Orlando Lawrence,* pp. 33-36. Berkeley, University of California Press.

Response.   (Acceptance speech upon presentation of the Nobel Prize.)   Science, 91:329-30.

1941

The new frontiers in the atom.   Smithsonian Institution, Annual Report, 1941, pp. 163-73; Science, 94:221-25.

1942

Nuclear physics and biology. In: *Molecular Films, the Cyclotron and the New Biology*, pp. 63-86. New Brunswick, Rutgers University Press.

1946

High energy physics. In: *The United States and the United Nations*, Rept. Ser. 5, *The International Control of Atomic Energy; Scientific Information Transmitted to the United Nations Atomic Energy Commission, June 14, 1946—October 14, 1946*, Vol. 2, pp. 87-90. Washington, D.C., United States Government Printing Office.

1947

With W. M. Brobeck, K. R. MacKenzie, E. M. McMillan, R. Serber, D. C. Sewell, K. M. Simpson, and R. L. Thornton. Initial performance of the 184-inch cyclotron of the University of California. Phys. Rev., 61:449-50.

1948

High energy physics. (Silliman Lecture, 1947.) American Scientist, 36:41-49. (See 1949.)
A progress report on the cyclotron. Science, 108:677.

1949

High energy physics. In: *Science in Progress*, 6th Ser., ed. by G. A. Baitsell, pp. 55-79. New Haven, Yale University Press.
High energy physics. In: *Centennial of the Scheffield Scientific School*, ed. by G. A. Baitsell, pp. 1-26. New Haven, Yale University Press.

1951

The evolution of the cyclotron. In: *Nobel Lectures: Physics*, pp. 430-43. Amsterdam, Elsevier Publishing Company.

1953

With John S. Foster and E. J. Lofgren. A high vacuum high speed ion pump. Rev. Sci. Instr., 24:388-90.

1955

High-current accelerators. Science, 122:1127-32.
Men and atoms. California Monthly, 66(4):24-27.

1958

Science and the national welfare. In: *Proceedings of The Robert A. Welch Foundation Conferences on Chemical Research.* I. *The Structure of the Nucleus,* ed. by W. O. Milligan, pp. 163-68. Houston, The Robert A. Welch Foundation.

The growth of the Physics Department. In: *Symposium on the Physical and Earth Sciences—Honoring the Twenty-fifth Presidential Year of Robert Gordon Sproul,* pp. 12-27. Berkeley, University of California Printing Department.

DUNCAN ARTHUR MacINNES

March 31, 1885–September 23, 1965

BY LEWIS G. LONGSWORTH AND THEODORE SHEDLOVSKY

I N THE DEATH of Duncan Arthur MacInnes on September 23, 1965, America lost one of its outstanding electrochemists. He was a dedicated scientist and experimentalist, with a passion for precision, whose main interest and whose most important contributions were concerned with solutions of electrolytes. The authors were closely associated with him throughout nearly the entire period of his distinguished career at the Rockefeller Institute and University, and the preparation of this memoir affords us a most welcome opportunity to acknowledge our indebtedness to him for the guidance and encouragement that he so generously accorded us, first as his research assistants and later as his associates. Two years before his death, Dr. MacInnes prepared for the National Academy of Sciences an autobiographical sketch which we shall follow rather closely, except for his too modest appraisal of the significance of his own work.

Duncan Arthur MacInnes was born in Salt Lake City, Utah, on March 31, 1885. His father was a merchant whose prosperity depended upon the violently fluctuating economy of the far West of the time. When Duncan was ten the family moved to

Bingham, Utah, then a small mining town, where his father was engaged in business with his uncle. This was the first of many moves necessitated by such conditions as the varying prices of metals, the exhaustion of mines, and the accompanying economic instability. The depression of 1893 was particularly hard on the West since this area was not self-supporting and depended largely upon the flow of investments from the East. Such a flow naturally dried up during a recession and brought on a protracted period of straitened circumstances for the family. Duncan's father succeeded in finding employment in Evanston, Wyoming, then in Park City, Utah, and finally in Mercur, Utah. There, between his twelfth and sixteenth year, Duncan became aware of the subject of electricity and, with the aid of local electricians, carried out such simple experiments as were possible with the crude materials at hand. Galvanic cell batteries particularly aroused his interest and continued to do so throughout his life. The Daniel cell, then widely used in railway signal systems, had many features, such as its liquid junction, that later provided areas of research in which he made probably his most significant contributions.

An event that greatly influenced Duncan's life was a nearly fatal streetcar accident at the age of thirteen. In addition to the loss of two fingers of his left hand, one leg was seriously injured, incapacitating him for athletic activities for a number of years. Thus, restricted in his contacts with fellow students and dissatisfied because the public schools of the towns in which the family lived absorbed little of his energy, he spent much time on books of popular science. His mother, although having little formal education, was widely read in English and American literature and her intellectual interests were naturally communicated to her two children, Duncan and his younger sister, Jean. Mrs. MacInnes did not oppose her son's early attempts at experiments in science, but there is good reason to believe that she would have been better pleased if he had chosen something other than a scientific career.

At the age of sixteen, Duncan entered the preparatory school of the University of Utah with the idea, prevalent among many youths of the time, of becoming an electrical engineer. He had the good fortune to board at the same house with S. F. Acree, who later became head of the pH Standards Division of the National Bureau of Standards, and this intimate contact with a man actively engaged in research had a most significant influence on him. With Dr. Acree's aid he was allowed to enter the college freshman course in chemistry during the second year of his preparatory work, and despite some disapproval by his parents, who had little knowledge or understanding of chemistry as a career, he decided to become a chemist. On entering the freshman class at the University of Utah in 1903, he found his excellent chemistry teacher, Dr. W. C. Ebaugh, helpful in many ways that aided in confirming his growing desire to prepare himself for scientific chemical investigations.

Just before Duncan was to enter college, the town of Mercur was almost completely destroyed by fire, and with Mr. MacInnes' business gone, the family moved to Salt Lake City. By serving as a student assistant in the chemical laboratories of the University in his junior and senior years, Duncan was able to contribute to the support of the family while paying for his tuition. Although this work, in addition to his regular studies, proved arduous, it gave him familiarity with the details of elementary chemistry. It was Dr. Acree, however, who aroused his interest in physical chemistry.

After his graduation from the University of Utah in 1907 with the degree of B.S. in chemical engineering, Duncan found it difficult to obtain employment because the country was in the midst of another depression, but he finally secured a position with the Phelps-Stokes Company at Berlin, Nevada. Here he encountered what was probably the last of the frontier in the United States and his subsequent development as an effective and ardent supporter of the conservation of the beauties of nature was doubtless kindled by this experience. Although the work was not uninteresting, there was little in the life associated with mining operations that attracted him. In any case the mine was soon closed and he returned to Salt Lake City in search of further employment. This he found at a mine located on the border of Utah and Nevada, but again the job was of short duration and the summer of 1908 found him with his family in American Falls, where his father had once more become established in business.

During the year that he was out of college young MacInnes applied for fellowships at a number of eastern schools and considered himself most fortunate in obtaining one at the University of Illinois, where the Department of Chemistry had been recently reorganized under the leadership of Professor W. A. Noyes. He arrived in Urbana in the autumn of 1908 and, having chosen physical chemistry as his major interest, he started study and research under Dr. E. W. Washburn, who had just come to Illinois from the Research Laboratory of Physical Chemistry at the Massachusetts Institute of Technology in Boston. After a brief, but difficult, period of adjustment, MacInnes found the atmosphere of the Chemistry Department most stimulating, from the point of view of both study and research.

The renaissance in physics had not yet begun, however, and the graduate courses in that area were less stimulating to him than those in chemistry. In later years he regretted his failure as a graduate student at Illinois to take advantage of the excellent facilities that were available in mathematics, an oversight that may account, in part at least, for his subsequent main concentration on experimental research. His graduate work, a study of moderately concentrated aqueous salt solutions, was conducted under the direction of Professor Washburn and led to the Ph.D. degree in 1911. Although this work failed to answer a question that it raised, namely, the magnitude of ion hydration, it did provide a background for the recognition of the complete dissociation of strong electrolytes in aqueous solution that came a few years later.

On completion of his doctoral work in 1911 MacInnes was appointed instructor in physical chemistry and three years later was advanced to associate. On obtaining, with some struggle, permission to do research on a problem of his own choosing, he started work on the application of simple galvanic cells to the determination of the properties of salt solutions. Although the title of his first independent publication, "The Mechanism of the Catalysis of the Decomposition of Hydrogen Peroxide by Colloidal Platinum," does not suggest an interest in galvanic cells, this excursion into surface and interface chemistry provided the necessary background for his subsequent work on hydrogen overvoltage. It was followed, however, by a paper with Karr Parker entitled "Potassium Chloride Concentration Cell" in which the experimental results were theoretically interpreted in terms of ion activities, rather than simple concentrations, a view that held his interest in later years, as it continues to do for electrochemists to this day. Of the nine papers that he published during his six years on the staff of the University of Illinois, five were in collaboration with others, and the same number were concerned directly with galvanic cells.

In 1917 he left Illinois, presumably for a year of study at the Research Laboratory of Physical Chemistry at the Massachusetts Institute of Technology, now no longer in Boston but in Cambridge. There he was appointed assistant professor and in 1921 was promoted to associate professor. Although the founder and director of the Laboratory, Professor Arthur A. Noyes, was dividing his time between M.I.T. in Cambridge and Throop College (now the California Institute of Technology) in Pasadena when MacInnes arrived, Duncan found the research atmosphere stimulating indeed since he had many interests in common with the director. An early research project at M.I.T. was concerned with X-rays and crystal structure but the results of this work did not appear until 1924-1926. X-ray crystallography was then in its early phases and MacInnes was inclined to ascribe his failure to grasp the opportunity that this work afforded to his insufficient background in physics and mathematics. It should be noted, however, that his bibliography for the interval from 1919 to 1924 lists fourteen publications originating at M.I.T., all of which are in the area of electrochemistry, suggesting, as later work confirmed, that his X-ray investigations were a digression. They did, however, result in the initial association of one of us with him, a relationship that remained close throughout the rest of his life.

The work with X-rays brought MacInnes into contact with W. R. Whitney of the General Electric Company and he accepted, somewhat reluctantly, an offer, made through Dr. Whitney, to supplement his academic income by organizing research work for the F. C. Huyck Company in Rensselaer, New York. The main business of the company was the manufacture of papermakers' woolen felts. Accordingly, in conjunction with a control laboratory at the factory, he conducted pertinent experimental work with a few assistants at M.I.T. on a part-time basis. At this time textile manufacturers in the United States had employed few chemists or physicists, for whom a proper approach to a number of practically useful problems was relatively simple. Although some useful and profitable results were obtained, MacInnes had little heart or interest in industrial research and resented the time and energy that it required.

He found his close contact with the top management of the rather small company to be rewarding in other ways, however, such as providing some insight into the modern business world and disclosing that liberal views which he held, but perhaps not as strongly as did his mother, were not necessarily inconsistent with sound business. F. C. Huyck was one of the early companies to adopt profit sharing, medical and dental care of employees, and, in general, a liberal labor policy. But, on the whole, this experience in industrial research had little, if any, effect on his scientific work, except possibly to retard it somewhat.

In 1925 MacInnes obtained a sabbatical leave from M.I.T. for study and travel in Europe. He would have preferred to work with Peter Debye, whose theory of interionic attraction had been published with Hückel two years previously. But Debye was in America in 1925. Consequently much of the year was spent in Paris, where concern with mathematics and thermodynamics was pleasantly supplemented by visits to museums, churches, and galleries and, of course, in learning French. With Paris as a center he visited Holland, Switzerland, and Italy. His longest visit, of about two months, was to England where he met many of the workers in physical chemistry and where he particularly enjoyed the friendship and hospitality of F. G. Donnan. Although he was entertained more in England than in the other countries he visited, he was least happy there. It was a period in which the war debts were under discussion and, although he found the English to be kind as individuals, he left with the impression that Americans were not too popular and that the general atmosphere was somewhat hostile, an impression that was to be dispelled on subsequent visits.

Back at the Massachusetts Institute of Technology in the autumn of 1925 he continued his research on electrolytes. His experimental work dealt with the development of the moving boundary method for determining transference numbers and the measurement of the potentials of galvanic cells containing liquid junctions. It was also during this period that he started to write a treatise on electrochemistry that appeared some twelve years later.

During his absence abroad he had been assigned to the teaching of a course in colloid chemistry. At that time this was a subject in which reproducible and precise measurements were difficult to realize, and his lack of enthusiasm for the assignment may have been a consideration in his acceptance of a position at the Rockefeller Institute for Medical Research in New York in 1926. During his years in Cambridge he had become acquainted with W. J. V. Osterhout, a professor at Harvard who had transferred to the Rockefeller Institute in 1925. Dr. Osterhout was a physiologist who was convinced that his science could benefit from advances in fundamental electrochemistry, and it was through his influence that MacInnes was offered a position as Associate Member at the Rockefeller Institute, where he worked for the remainder of his life, becoming a Member in 1940 and Member Emeritus in 1950. The arrangement was not that he should do biological work but that he should continue his researches on the electrochemistry of solutions and be available for consultation on physico-chemical problems. On the positive side the change offered him freedom from formal teaching, a generous budget, technical assistance, as well as the welcome abandonment of his industrial consultative work. On the negative side there was relative isolation from workers in related fields. This was relieved somewhat by contacts with chemists at Columbia and New York universities, and associations with colleagues who were soon added to the staff of the Rockefeller Institute and who formed a small group of researchers in physical chemistry. This group included his present biographers, one of whom came in 1927 to work on electrolytic conductivities and the other in 1928 as a Fellow of the National Research Council to work on the moving boundary method. Both have remained at Rockefeller to the present and have continued work, for the most part, in areas pioneered by MacInnes.

The work at Rockefeller involved transference numbers by the method of moving boundaries, concentration cells with transference, and electrometric titrations. It was in the course of studies in the last field that he hit upon a method for making small and sensitive glass electrodes for measuring the pH values of solutions. Later, with Malcolm Dole, a successful search was made for a suitable glass that soon became commercially available. These results, based on the earlier researches of Haber and Hughes, attracted attention quite out of proportion to their scientific importance, but they did have the virtue of being decidedly useful for biological and medical purposes. One such application was the adaptation of automatic pH control in bacterial cultures with the aid of a Compton electrometer as a potentiometric detector. The present widespread use of the glass electrode for pH control, however, had to await the development of electronic technology.

MacInnes considered perhaps his most important scientific contribution to be the experimental confirmation of the Debye-Hückel theory of ionic interaction afforded by the work of his group. As an early exponent of the conjecture that strong electrolytes are completely dissociated in aqueous solutions, he recognized the significance of this theory for electrochemistry and of its extension to transport processes by Onsager and Fuoss. The confirmation involved both strong and weak electrolytes. For strong electrolytes the potentials of concentration cells were combined with transference numbers, measured by the method of moving boundaries, to obtain the salt activity. Since these cells required but one type of electrode, it was possible to make measurements on solutions so dilute that the finite sizes of the ions could be neglected and the theory thus confirmed in the limit of small concentrations. In the case of weak electrolytes, conductivity measurements were made at still lower ion concentrations, and these afforded an even more convincing test of the Debye-Hückel limiting law.

With the appearance, in 1937, of Tiselius' work on the electrophoresis of proteins, the activity of the laboratory shifted to that field. The change was made relatively easily since much of the experience gained in the development of the moving boundary method for strong electrolytes could be adapted to materials of high molecular weight. Following improvement of the optical procedure for observing the boundaries, studies were made of naturally occurring protein mixtures such as egg white and normal and pathological human sera and plasmas. Many cooperative researches were carried out with workers both in and outside the Rockefeller Institute, a summary of which formed the core of a Sigma Xi lecture that was given in 1940.

A field of research in which MacInnes maintained an interest for many years was the EMF centrifuge, the earlier work with which was done by des Coudres and Tolman. Aside from its theoretical interest he considered the instrument to have decided possibilities as a tool for investigating solutions of electrolytes in nonaqueous solvents. The work on sedimentation potentials was undoubtedly triggered by the conviction that transport data could thereby be obtained for nonaqueous systems approaching the complexity of those encountered at the membranes and phase boundaries of biological material. The research in this area was done in collaboration with Drs.

Roger Ray, Margaret Dayhoff, and Robert Kay. Simultaneously he initiated an experimental study of the iodine coulometer with the objective of obtaining a more accurate value of one of the fundamental constants, the Faraday equivalent. This was a natural outgrowth of his other interests since it involved precision current control, already used in the determination of transference numbers, and accurate electrometric titrations. The closing years of his life were spent in active work on this research, which was unfortunately interrupted by his death.

For a number of years he worked with the New York Academy of Sciences, helping to arrange a series of small conferences designed to promote active discussion of different scientific topics; in 1944 he became president of that organization. For the conferences to achieve their objective, he considered it essential that the topics be in areas in which actual work was in progress and that participation be restricted to currently active investigators in the designated fields. Although the early conferences sponsored by the New York Academy achieved this objective, he felt that the effectiveness of later ones was impaired by their success in attracting too large a crowd. Profiting by this experience he suggested to Dr. Jewett, then president of the National Academy of Sciences, that conferences on topics of active research interest be arranged under the auspices of that Academy, limiting the maximum number of participants to twenty-five, and providing as much time as possible for informal discussion. With the enthusiastic support of Presidents Richards and Bronk, thirteen conferences following this plan took place in the years 1945 to 1953. Of these, eight were for periods of three days at Rams Head Inn, Shelter Island, Long Island, where distraction from scientific matters was minimal. In MacInnes' view, these conferences filled several needs for the following reasons: (a) meetings of scientific societies have become so huge that workers in specific fields have difficulty in getting in touch with one another; (*b*) the time for discussion is never sufficient; (*c*) the United States is so large that it is better to organize the key men in a field rather than to leave the matter to chance; and (*d*) adequate discussion of any topic invariably cuts across the artificial divisions of science as represented by the many societies. He derived much satisfaction from the vital role that he played in the development of these conferences and justifiably considered his achievement a major contribution to American science. The stimulus provided by these conferences, and by the published reports resulting therefrom, has invariably served to catalyze advances in the given area. A glance at the current calendar of scientific meetings reveals that many of them are modeled after the conferences initiated by MacInnes and thus indicates the continuing value of his plan.

Although published nearly thirty years ago, his book *Principles of Electrochemistry* is still widely used and references to it are to be found in scientific journals published throughout the world. In common with classics from other branches of science it is available in paperback edition.

As its President, 1935-1937, and as the recipient of its Acheson Medal, 1948, MacInnes was recognized by the Electrochemical Society for his outstanding contributions to the science to which he devoted much of his life. The award of the Nichols Medal by the American Chemical Society in 1942 indicates that his interests included areas of physical chemistry other than electrochemistry. During World War II he was active in the field of chemical warfare as director of a group of investigators at the Rockefeller Institute. For this work he was granted the Presidential Certificate of Merit in 1948. On another OSRD contract he also participated in an early study directed toward isolation of uranium 235. The honors that he cherished most highly were his election to the National Academy of Sciences (1937) and the American Philosophical Society (1942).

Born in mountainous country, he returned to such surroundings for recreation whenever possible. His outdoor activities included hiking, canoeing, skiing, and mountain climbing. In the practice of this last avocation he developed considerable technical skill and on at least one occasion his judgment and mountaineering experience saved his party from a potentially serious mishap. It was doubtless inevitable that his love of the wilderness should make him an ardent and effective conservationist. He was a member of the American Alpine Club and the Appalachian Mountain Club, and in working with the latter organization he took part in active propaganda for the preservation of the natural beauty of our environment, especially for the national park system.

BIBLIOGRAPHY

KEY TO ABBREVIATIONS

Ann. N.Y. Acad. Sci. = Annals of the New York Academy of Sciences
Chem. Rev. = Chemical Reviews
Cold Spring Harbor Symp. Quant. Biol. = Cold Spring Harbor Symposia on Quantitative Biology
Ind. Eng. Chem. Anal. Ed. = Journal of Industrial and Engineering Chemistry, Analytical Edition
J. Am. Chem. Soc. = Journal of the American Chemical Society
J. Bacteriol. = Journal of Bacteriology
J. Chem. Phys. = Journal of Chemical Physics
J. Exp. Med. = Journal of Experimental Medicine
J. Gen. Physiol. = Journal of General Physiology
J. Phys. Chem. = Journal of Physical Chemistry
Phys. Rev. = Physical Review
Proc. Nat. Acad. Sci. = Proceedings of the National Academy of Sciences
Rev. Sci. Instr. = Review of Scientific Instruments
Trans. Am. Electrochem. Soc. = Transactions of the American Electrochemical Society (later, Trans. Electrochem. Soc.)
Trans. Electrochem. Soc. = Transactions of the Electrochemical Society (formerly, Trans. Am. Electrochem. Soc.; later, Journal of the Electrochemical Society)

1911

With Edward W. Washburn. The laws of "concentrated" solutions. III. The ionization and hydration relations of electrolytes in aqueous solution at zero degrees: A. Cesium nitrate, potassium chloride and lithium chloride. J. Am. Chem. Soc., 33:1686-1713.

1914

The mechanism of the catalysis of the decomposition of hydrogen peroxide by colloidal platinum. J. Am. Chem. Soc., 36:878-81.

1915

With Karr Parker. Potassium chloride concentration cell. J. Am. Chem. Soc., 37:1445-61.
Liquid junction potentials. J. Am. Chem. Soc., 37:2301-7.

The potentials at the junctions of salt solutions. Proc. Nat. Acad. Sci., 1:526-30.

1916

Polarization in LeClanche cells. Trans. Am. Electrochem. Soc., 29:315-21.

1917

With J. M. Braham. Heats of dilution. I. A calorimeter for measuring heats of dilution. II. The heat of dilution of three normal ethyl alcohol. J. Am. Chem. Soc., 39:2110-26.

With R. G. Kreiling. An improved Victor Meyer vapor-density apparatus. J. Am. Chem. Soc., 39:2350-54.

1919

With Leon Adler. Hydrogen overvoltage. J. Am. Chem. Soc., 41:194-207; Proc. Nat. Acad. Sci., 5:160-63.

The activities of the ions of strong electrolytes. J. Am. Chem. Soc., 41:1086-92.

With A. W. Contieri. Hydrogen overvolatge. II. Applications of its variation with pressure to reduction, metal solution and deposition. J. Am. Chem. Soc., 41:2013-19.

With A. W. Contieri. Some applications of the variation of hydrogen overvoltage with the pressure. Proc. Nat. Acad. Sci., 5:321-23.

1920

With Arthur A. Noyes. The ionization and activity of largely ionized substances. J. Am. Chem. Soc., 42:239-45.

With L. Adler and D. E. Joubert. The reactions of the lead accumulator. Trans. Am. Electrochem. Soc., 37:641-51.

With James A. Beattie. The free energy of dilution and the transference numbers of lithium chloride solutions. J. Am. Chem. Soc., 42:1117-28.

1921

The ion mobilities, ion conductances, and the effect of viscosity on the conductances, of certain salts. J. Am. Chem. Soc., 43:1217-26.

With Yu Liang Yeh. The potentials at the junctions of mono-valent chloride solutions. J. Am. Chem. Soc., 43:2563-73.

1922

With Eric B. Townsend. An electro-volumetric method for lead. Journal of Industrial and Engineering Chemistry, 14:420.

With William R. Hainsworth. The effect of hydrogen pressure on the electromotive force of a hydrogen-calomel cell. I. J. Am. Chem. Soc., 44:1021-32.

1923

With Edgar Reynolds Smith. A study of the moving boundary method for determining transference numbers. J. Am. Chem. Soc., 45:2246-55.

1924

With Edgar R. Smith. The moving boundary method of deter-mining transference numbers. II. J. Am. Chem. Soc., 46:1398-1403.

With W. R. Hainsworth and H. J. Rowley. The effect of hydrogen pressure on the electromotive force of a hydrogen-calomel cell. II. The fugacity of hydrogen and hydrogen ion at pressures to 1000 atmospheres. J. Am. Chem. Soc., 46:1437-43.

With T. Shedlovsky. The intensities of reflection of the char-acteristic rays of palladium from fluorite. Phys. Rev., 23:290.

1925

With T. B. Brighton. The moving boundary method for deter-mining transference numbers. III. A novel form of apparatus. J. Am. Chem. Soc., 47:994-99.

With E. R. Smith. The moving boundary method for determining transference numbers. IV. The transference numbers of some chloride solutions. J. Am. Chem. Soc., 47:1009-15.

The transference numbers of solutions of mixed chlorides. Dis-cussion of papers by Schneider and Braley and by Braley and Hall. J. Am. Chem. Soc., 47:1922-27.

1926

With Theodore Shedlovsky. The relative intensities of reflection of x-rays from the principal atomic planes of fluorite. Phys. Rev., 27:130-37.

With Irving A. Cowperthwaite and Kenneth C. Blanchard. The moving boundary method for determining transference numbers. V. A constant current apparatus. J. Am. Chem. Soc., 48:1909-12.

The ionization of weak electrolytes. J. Am. Chem. Soc., 48:2068-72.

With L. Harris and S. J. Bates. The relative intensities of reflection of x-rays from the principal atomic planes of powdered sodium chloride. Phys. Rev., 28:235-39.

With Paul T. Jones. A method for differential potentiometric titration. J. Am. Chem. Soc., 48:2831-36.

1927

With Irving A. Cowperthwaite and T. C. Huang. The moving boundary method for determining transference numbers. VI. Further developments in experimental technique. J. Am. Chem. Soc., 49:1710-17.

With Irving A. Cowperthwaite. The ionization of some typical strong electrolytes. Transactions of the Faraday Society, 23:400-4.

Differential electrometric titration as a precision method. Zeitschrift fuer Physikalische Chemie, 130:217-21.

1928

The effect of the position of substitution on the ionization constants of some organic acids. J. Am. Chem. Soc., 50:2587-95.

1929

With Irving A. Cowperthwaite. The effect of diffusion at a moving boundary between two solutions of electrolytes. Proc. Nat. Acad. Sci., 15:18-21.

With Malcolm Dole. Differential potentiometric titration. III. An improved apparatus and its application to precision measurements. J. Am. Chem. Soc., 51:1119-27.

With Malcolm Dole. Tests of a new type of glass electrode. Ind. Eng. Chem. Anal. Ed., 1:57-59.

With Lewis G. Longsworth. An improved constant current regulator. Journal of the Optical Society of America, 19:50-56.

With Malcolm Dole. A glass electrode apparatus for measuring the pH values of very small volumes of solution. J. Gen. Physiol., 12:805-11.

With Irving A. Cowperthwaite and Theodore Shedlovsky. The conductance and transference number of the chloride ion in mixtures of sodium and potassium chloride. J. Am. Chem. Soc., 51:2671-76.

1930

With Malcolm Dole. The behavior of glass electrodes of different compositions. J. Am. Chem. Soc., 52:29-36.

1931

With I. A. Cowperthwaite. Differential potentiometric titration. IV. (a) An adaptation of the method to the use of hydrogen electrodes. (b) A test of standards for precise acidimetry. J. Am. Chem. Soc., 53:555-62.

With Malcolm Dole. The transference numbers of potassium chloride. New determinations by the Hittorf method and a comparison with results obtained by the moving boundary method. J. Am. Chem. Soc., 53:1357-64.

With Theodore Shedlovsky. The ionization constant of acetic acid. J. Am. Chem. Soc., 53:2419-20.

1932

With Donald Belcher. Further studies on the glass electrode. J. Am. Chem Soc., 53:3315-31.

With Theodore Shedlovsky. The determination of the ionization constant of acetic acid, at 25°, from conductance measurements. J. Am. Chem. Soc., 54:1429-38.

With Theodore Shedlovsky and Lewis G. Longsworth. The limiting equivalent conductances of several univalent ions in water at 25°. J. Am. Chem. Soc., 54:2758-62.

With L. G. Longsworth. Transference numbers by the method of moving boundaries. Theory, practice and results. Chem. Rev., 11:171-230.

With Theodore Shedlovsky and Lewis G. Longsworth. Limiting

mobilities of some monovalent ions and the dissociation constant of acetic acid at 25°. Nature, 130:774-75.

1933

With D. Belcher. A durable glass electrode. Ind. Eng. Chem. Anal. Ed., 5:199-200.

With Donald Belcher. The thermodynamic ionization constants of carbonic acid. J. Am. Chem. Soc., 55:2630-46.

With Theodore Shedlovsky and Lewis G. Longsworth. The conductance of aqueous solutions of electrolytes and the interionic attraction theory. Chem. Rev., 13:29-46.

The meaning and calibration of the pH scale. Cold Spring Harbor Symp. Quant. Biol., 1:190-94; The Collecting Net, 8(7):219-23.

1934

With Theodore Shedlovsky and Alfred S. Brown. The conductance of aqueous electrolytes. Trans. Electrochem. Soc., 66:165-78.

1935

With A. S. Brown. The determination of the solubility of silver chloride by an electrometric titration method. J. Am. Chem. Soc., 57:459-65.

With Lewis G. Longsworth. Bacterial growth with automatic pH control. (A) An apparatus. (B) Some tests on the acid production of *Lactobacillus acidophilus*. J. Bacteriol., 29:595-607.

With Alfred S. Brown. The determination of activity coefficients from the potentials of concentration cells with transference. I. Sodium chloride at 25°. J. Am. Chem. Soc., 57:1356-62.

With Donald Belcher. The thermodynamic ionization constants of carbonic acid at 38° from electromotive force measurements. J. Am. Chem. Soc., 57:1683-85.

With Theodore Shedlovsky. The first ionization constant of carbonic acid, 0° to 38°, from conductance measurements. J. Am. Chem. Soc., 57:1705-10.

1936

With Lewis G. Longsworth. Bacterial growth at constant pH. Quantitative studies on the physiology of *Lactobacillus acidophilus.* J. Bacteriol., 31:287-300.

With A. S. Brown. The determination of activity coefficients from the potentials of concentration cells with transference. Chem. Rev., 18:335-48.

With Lewis G. Longsworth. Bacterial growth at constant pH. Apparent oxidation-reduction potential, acid production, and population studies of *Lactobacillus acidophilus* under anaerobic conditions. J. Bacteriol., 32:567-85.

With Theodore Shedlovsky. The determination of activity coefficients from the potentials of concentration cells with transference. II. Hydrochloric acid at 25°. J. Am. Chem. Soc., 58:1970-72.

With L. G. Longsworth. The potentials of galvanic cells with liquid junction. Cold Spring Harbor Symp. Quant. Biol., 4:18-26.

1937

With Theodore Shedlovsky. The determination of activity coefficients from the potentials of concentration cells with transference. III. Potassium chloride. IV. Calcium chloride. J. Am. Chem. Soc., 59:503-6.

The contribution of Josiah Willard Gibbs to electrochemistry. Trans. Electrochem. Soc., 71:65-72.

With L. G. Longsworth. The measurement and regulation of pH with the glass electrode. Trans. Electrochem. Soc., 71:73-88.

The interionic attraction theory of electrolytes. Science, 86:23-29.

With L. G. Longsworth. Transference numbers and ion mobilities of some electrolytes in deuterium oxide and its mixtures with water. J. Am. Chem. Soc., 59:1666-70.

1938

With Donald Belcher and Theodore Shedlovsky. The meaning and standardization of the pH scale. J. Am. Chem. Soc., 60:1094-99.

The conductance of aqueous solutions of electrolytes. Journal of the Franklin Institute, 225:661-86.

With L. G. Longsworth. Transference numbers of lanthanum chloride at 25° by the moving boundary method. J. Am. Chem. Soc., 60:3070-74.

1939

With Theodore Shedlovsky. The determination of activity coefficients from the potentials of concentration cells with transference. V. Lanthanum chloride at 25°. J. Am. Chem. Soc., 61:200-3.

With L. G. Longsworth. Ion conductances in water-methanol mixtures. J. Phys. Chem., 43:239-46.

With L. G. Longsworth. Electrophoresis of proteins by the Tiselius method. Chem. Rev., 24:271-87.

With L. G. Longsworth and Theodore Shedlovsky. Electrophoretic patterns of normal and pathological human blood serum and plasma. J. Exp. Med., 70:399-413.

Introduction to the conference on electrophoresis. Ann. N.Y. Acad. Sci., 39:107-9.

1940

With L. G. Longsworth. An electrophoretic study of nephrotic sera and urine. J. Exp. Med., 71:77-82.

With L. G. Longsworth. The interpretation of simple electrophoretic patterns. J. Am. Chem. Soc., 62:705-11.

With L. G. Longsworth and R. Keith Cannan. An electrophoretic study of the proteins of egg white. J. Am. Chem. Soc., 62:2580-90.

The motion of ions and proteins in electric field. In: *Science in Progress*, 2d Ser., ed. by G. A. Baitsell, pp. 197-231. New Haven, Yale University Press.

1942

With Lewis G. Longsworth. An electrophoretic study of mixtures of ovalbumin and yeast nucleic acid. J. Gen. Physiol., 25:507-16.

Symposium on physiochemical methods in protein chemistry. Introduction to the symposium. Chem. Rev., 30:321-22.

Introduction to the conference on the ultracentrifuge. Ann. N.Y. Acad. Sci., 43:175-76.

The effect of centrifugal fields on the electromotive force of galvanic cells. Ann. N.Y. Acad. Sci., 43:243-51.

1943

The use of stroboscopic patterns in the determination of speeds of rotation. Rev. Sci. Instr., 14:14-16.

1944

With Lewis G. Longsworth. The electrophoretic study of proteins and related substances. In: *Colloid Chemistry*, Vol. 5, ed. by Jerome Alexander, pp. 387-411. New York, Reinhold Publishing Corporation.

1948

Criticism of a definition of pH. Science, 108:693.

Pure science research. Journal of the Electrochemical Society, 94:61N-63N.

1949

With Roger B. Ray. An apparatus for determining the effect of centrifugal force on the potentials of galvanic cells. Rev. Sci. Instr., 20:52.

With Roger B. Ray. The effect of centrifugal force on galvanic potentials: (a) The transference numbers of potassium iodide; (b) The iodide-iodine ion. J. Am. Chem. Soc., 71:2987-92.

1950

With T. Shedlovsky and L. G. Longsworth. Macroscopic space charge in electrolytes during electrolysis. J. Chem. Phys., 18:233.

1951

pH. Scientific American, 84:40.

With Margaret O. Dayhoff. A study of iodide-iodine solutions with the electro-motive-force centrifuge. National Bureau of Standards, Circular, No. 524, pp. 41-50.

With Margaret O. Dayhoff and Roger B. Ray. A magnetic float

method for determining the densities of solutions. Rev. Sci. Instr., 22:642-46.

1952

With Margaret O. Dayhoff. The partial molal volumes of potassium chloride, potassium and sodium iodides and of iodine in aqueous solution at 25°. J. Am. Chem. Soc., 74:1017-20.

With M. O. Dayhoff and G. E. Perlmann. The partial specific volumes, in aqueous solution, of three proteins. J. Am. Chem. Soc., 74:2515.

With Margaret O. Dayhoff. A study of iodide-iodine solutions with the emf centrifuge. J. Chem. Phys., 20:1034.

1953

The electromotive-force centrifuge, the development of a tool for research. Proceedings of the American Philosophical Society, 97:51.

With Margaret O. Dayhoff. The apparent and partial molal volumes of potassium iodide and of iodine in methanol at 25° from density measurements. J. Am. Chem. Soc., 75:5219.

1957

With Robert L. Kay. The electromotive-force centrifuge, factors affecting precision. J. Phys. Chem., 61:657.

With Chia-chih Yang and Alfred R. Pray. A redetermination of the value of the Faraday with the iodine coulometer. I. A precision constant current apparatus. J. Phys. Chem., 61:662.

With A. R. Pray. A redetermination of the value of the Faraday with the iodine coulometer. (Progress Report.) Nuovo Cimento, 6 (Supplemento 1):232-41.

1958

With S. Granick. Leonor Michaelis, 1875-1949. National Academy of Sciences, Biographical Memoirs, 31:282-321.

William F. Meggers

WILLIAM FREDERICK MEGGERS

July 13, 1888–November 19, 1966

BY PAUL D. FOOTE

WILLIAM FREDERICK MEGGERS was born in Clintonville, Wisconsin, on July 13, 1888, of German parents who came to Wisconsin from Pomerania before 1872. Most of his youth was spent on a farm two miles west of Clintonville. He attended the public schools in Clintonville and was graduated as valedictorian by the high school in 1906. In 1907 he entered Ripon College on a scholarship and earned most of his expenses by organizing a dance orchestra in which he played the slide trombone. He was awarded a B.A. degree in 1910 and remained another year as graduate assistant to Professor William H. Barber, head of the Physics Department. During the academic year 1911-1912 he served the University of Wisconsin as laboratory assistant and was a graduate student under the physicists Max Mason, C. E. Mendenhall, and L. R. Ingersoll.

In September 1912 Meggers moved to Pittsburgh where he became an instructor in physics at the Carnegie Institute of Technology. In March 1914, after reading the classical paper on "Constitution of Atoms and Molecules" by Niels Bohr, he decided to become a spectroscopist. He passed a two-day civil service examination and was appointed on June 12, 1914, at considerable financial sacrifice, a laboratory assistant with the National Bureau of Standards.

Here he served continuously for more than half a century in spectroscopy, photography, and atomic physics. He was officially retired in 1958 as Chief of the Spectroscopy Section but continued working until a few days before his death in 1966. By working a seven-day week and utilizing vacations and accumulated leave for academic studies, he earned the master's degree from the University of Wisconsin in 1916 and his doctorate from Johns Hopkins in 1917.

His lifework can be summarized under four general headings: (a) precision measurement of standard wavelengths, (b) detailed descriptions of photographed spectra, (c) quantum interpretation of these spectra, and (d) practical applications of spectroscopy.

Most atomic and ionic spectra embrace thousands of different wavelengths that for correlation and standardization purposes must be measured with a precision of one part in one to twenty million. Meggers holds the world's record for contributions to this program over the past fifty years. The first international standards of wavelength were taken in 1910 from an iron arc by measuring with interferometers selected spectral lines relative to the red cadmium line then adopted as the primary standard of wavelength. Since 1919 the work has been under the supervision of the International Astronomical Union, to which Meggers was the chief contributor. His iron lines from 2100 to 10,216 Angstroms are unique. In 1925 he initiated a program of interferometric measurement of absorption lines in the solar spectrum, the first modern spectroscopic standards in astrophysics.

In 1947 he developed a lamp utilizing mercury 198 transmuted from gold, demonstrated its superiority, and proposed its adoption as a primary standard of length, but so far it has not received international acceptance. He later suggested that better secondary standards could be derived from a mercury

198 electrodeless microwave-excited lamp containing thorium iodide. Using this source, in 1958 he published 222 wavelengths to eight significant figures, and in 1965 extended the range to 510 wavelengths. These thorium standards are ten times as accurate as the iron standards.

Spectra are usually measured at atmospheric pressure but must be corrected for the refractive index of air if employed for atomic interpretation. In 1960 Meggers provided a two-volume *Table of Wavenumbers* for converting wavelengths from 2000 to 10,000,000 Angstroms to wave numbers per centimeter *in vacuo* with an accuracy of one part in one hundred million.

In 1914 the characteristic spectra of atoms and ions were only partially and poorly described, partly because photographic emulsions were insensitive to long wavelengths, and also because satisfactory standards throughout the spectrum were still lacking. Consequently Meggers' second contribution to spectroscopy was to exploit photosensitizing dyes to record spectra in the long wave visible and near infrared. Thus with dicyanin-stained photographic plates he extended records of laboratory arc spectra and the sun's spectrum to 9600A in 1918. By 1934, using new infrared-sensitized emulsions prepared by the Eastman Kodak Company, he succeeded in observing laboratory spectra beyond 13,000A. Later he produced infrared spectral data for more than 70 elements and undertook the improvement of spectral descriptions throughout the entire photographic range (2000 to 13,000A) for all the recently discovered or refined elements such as hafnium, rhenium, technitium, promethium, actinium, niobium, vanadium, scandium, yttrium, lanthanum, thulium, and others. These descriptions are adequate and definitive for spectrochemical analysis and for structural analysis, but there is plenty of work remaining for the future, a single example being his 1966 paper with Corliss

on the spectra of YbI, II, III, IV. Possibly the thousands of lines
he evaluated quantitatively for intensity relations may prove
to be one of his most important achievements.

Meggers' third major activity involved the quantum theory
interpretation of complicated spectra. Multiplets were discovered in 1922 and the vector model of the atom was proposed
in 1924-1925 to explain multiplet structure and the anomalous
Zeeman effect. During the next forty or more years he disen-
tangled the spectra of some eighty heavy elements and ions, and
determined their various quantized energy states and the binding forces on their electrons.

His fourth major activity was the laboratory application
of spectra for the identification and quantitative analysis of
chemical compositions. In this field he was a pioneer; in 1914
his was probably the only laboratory in the country that regarded spectrochemical analysis as practical and useful. Now
there are over 3000 spectrochemical laboratories active in the
United States and similar conditions exist in all the other
technologically advanced countries of the world. Wavelengths,
of course, uniquely identify chemical elements for qualitative
analysis, but for quantitative analysis the relative intensities
of the lines are required. Until recently the intrinsic intensities
of relatively few spectral lines had been measured. In 1961,
after twenty-eight years of intermittent investigation, Meggers
published *Tables of Spectral-Line Intensities* containing relative energies of 39,000 spectral lines in the range 900 to 9000A
characteristic of 70 metallic elements observed under standardized conditions. Such data are not only necessary for the chemical laboratory but are of great interest in interpreting the quantum probability theory of collision and reactions. In the early
days, working jointly with Keiven Burns, Meggers constructed
the first practical stigmatic grating mounting of the so-called

Wadsworth type, in a form that is now widely manufactured commercially.

Every scientist is familiar with the Welch charts of the periodic table of the elements that hang on the walls of every college and high school laboratory. These were first pictorially developed by Henry D. Hubbard and after his death were continually revised and extended by Meggers together with a descriptive booklet or explanatory key summarizing the physical properties of the elements.

Meggers was president of the Optical Society of America from 1949 to 1951, and its representative on the governing board of the American Institute of Physics from 1952 to 1958. Later he was made honorary member of the Optical Society. He received the Frederick Ives medal in 1947 and the C. E. K. Mees medal in 1964. He was awarded the Department of Commerce gold medal in 1949; the medal of the Society of Applied Spectroscopy in 1952; the Cresson medal of the Franklin Institute in 1953; and the Pittsburgh Spectroscopy award in 1963. He was elected to the National Academy of Sciences in 1954. At various times he was chairman of the National Research Council Committee on line spectra; president of the International Joint Committee for Spectroscopy; and president of the Wavelength Commission of the International Astronomical Union. He was a member of Phi Beta Kappa and Sigma Xi and was active in many of the technical societies and organizations.

William Frederick Meggers died November 19, 1966, after a brief illness, at the age of seventy-eight. He is survived by his wife, Edith Marie Raddant; a daughter, Betty Jane Evans, an archaeologist; a son, William Frederick Meggers, Jr., a physicist and electronic engineer; and three grandchildren. A second son, John Charles Meggers, an engineer, preceded him in death by only a few weeks.

BIBLIOGRAPHY

KEY TO ABBREVIATIONS

Anal. Chem. = Analytical Chemistry
Astrophys. J. = Astrophysical Journal
Internat. Critical Tables = International Critical Tables
J. Opt. Soc. Am. = Journal of the Optical Society of America
J. Opt. Soc. Am. Rev. Sci. Instr. = Journal of the Optical Society of America and Review of Scientific Instruments
J. Res. Nat. Bur. Std. = Journal of Research of the National Bureau of Standards
J. Wash. Acad. Sci. = Journal of the Washington Academy of Sciences
Nat. Bur. Std. Sci. Pap. = National Bureau of Standards, Scientific Papers
Nat. Bur. Std. Tech. News Bull. = National Bureau of Standards, Technical News Bulletin
Phil. Mag. = Philosophical Magazine
Phys. Rev. = Physical Review
Proc. ——— Summer Conf. Spectry. Applications = Proceedings of the ——— Summer Conference on Spectroscopy and Its Applications
Publ. Allegheny Obs. Univ. Pittsburgh = Publications of the Allegheny Observatory of the University of Pittsburgh
Publ. Astron. Soc. Pacific = Publications of the Astronomical Society of the Pacific
Rev. Mod. Phys. = Reviews of Modern Physics
Sci. Monthly = Scientific Monthly
Spectrochim. Acta = Spectrochimica Acta
Trans. Internat. Astron. Union = Transactions of the International Astronomical Union
Z. Physik = Zeitschrift fuer Physik

1915

Notes on comparisons of light waves by interference methods, and some wave lengths in the spectrum of neon gas. Nat. Bur. Std. Sci. Pap., 12:198-205.

1916

With K. Burns and P. W. Merrill. Interference measurements of wave lengths in the iron spectrum (3233—6570 A). Nat. Bur. Std. Sci. Pap., 13:245-72.

1917

Wave length measurements in spectra from 5600 A to 9600 A. Nat. Bur. Std. Sci. Pap., 14:371-95.

1918

The properties and testing of optical instruments. National Bureau of Standards, Circular No. 27, pp. 1-41.

Photography of the solar spectrum from 6800 A to 9600 A. Astrophys. J., 47:1-6.

With C. C. Kiess. Wavelengths in the red and infrared spectra of iron, cobalt and nickel arcs. Nat. Bur. Std. Sci. Pap., 14:637-51.

With C. G. Peters. Measurements on the index of refraction of air for wave lengths from 2218 A to 9000 A. Nat. Bur. Std. Sci. Pap., 14:697-740.

With K. Burns and P. W. Merrill. Measurements of wave lengths in the spectrum of neon. Nat. Bur. Std. Sci. Pap., 14:765-75.

1919

Solar and terrestrial absorption in the sun's spectrum from 6500 A to 9000 A. Publ. Allegheny Obs. Univ. Pittsburgh, 6:13-44.

With C. G. Peters. Measurements on the index of refraction of air for wave lengths from 2218 A to 9000 A. Astrophys. J., 50:56-71.

With C. C. Kiess. Wave lengths longer than 5500 A in the arc spectra of seven elements. Nat. Bur. Std. Sci. Pap., 16:51-73.

1920

With I. G. Priest, K. S. Gibson, E. P. T. Tyndall, and H. J. McNicholas. Color and spectral composition of certain high-intensity search light arcs. Technological Papers of the National Bureau of Standards, No. 168, pp. 1-14.

With P. D. Foote. A new microphotometer for photographic densities. Nat. Bur. Std. Sci. Pap., 16:299-308; J. Opt. Soc. Am., 4:24-34.

With P. D. Foote. Atomic theory and low-voltage arcs in caesium vapor. Nat. Bur. Std. Sci. Pap., 16:309-26; Phil. Mag., 40:80-97.

With F. J. Stimson. Dyes for photographic sensitizing. J. Opt. Soc. Am., 4:91-104.

With F. L. Mohler and P. D. Foote. Resonance potentials and low-voltage arcs for metals of the second group of the periodic tables. Nat. Bur. Std. Sci. Pap., 16:725-39; J. Opt. Soc. Am., 4:364-70.

1921

Standard wavelengths. J. Opt. Soc. Am., 5:308-22.

With P. D. Foote and F. L. Mohler. The excitation of the enhanced spectrum of magnesium in a low-voltage arc. Phil. Mag., 42:1002-15.

Interference measurements in the spectra of argon, krypton and xenon. Nat. Bur. Std. Sci. Pap., 17:193-202.

Standard wavelengths and constant frequency differences in the spectra of inert gases. Phys. Rev., 18:160-161. (A)

1922

1921 Report of Committee on Standard Wave Lengths. J. Opt. Soc. Am. Rev. Sci. Instr., 6:135-39.

With P. D. Foote and F. L. Mohler. A significant exception to the principle of selection. Phil. Mag., 43:659-61.

With P. D. Foote and F. L. Mohler. The excitation of the enhanced spectra of sodium and potassium in a low-voltage arc. Astrophys. J., 55:145-61.

With C. C. Kiess. False spectra from diffraction gratings. I. Secondary spectra. J. Opt. Soc. Am. Rev. Sci. Instr., 6:417-29.

With K. Burns. Notes on standard wavelengths, spectrographs, and spectrum tubes. Nat. Bur. Std. Sci. Pap., 18:185-99.

With C. C. Kiess and F. J. Stimson. Practical spectrographic analysis. Nat. Bur. Std. Sci. Pap., 18:235-55.

1923

The measurement of wave lengths. In: *The Dictionary of Applied Physics,* Vol. 4, ed. by R. T. Glazebrook, pp. 882-95. New York, The Macmillan Company.

Regularities in the arc spectrum of vanadium. J. Wash. Acad. Sci., 13:317-25.

1924

Vanadium multiples and Zeeman effect. J. Wash. Acad. Sci., 14:151-59.

Standard wave lengths and regularities in the spectrum of the iron arc. Astrophys. J., 60:60-75.

Spectrum regularities for scandium and ytrrium. J. Wash. Acad. Sci., 14:419-30.

Regularities in the arc spectrum of columbium. J. Wash. Acad. Sci., 14:442-46.

With C. C. Kiess and F. M. Walters, Jr. The displacement law of arc and spark spectra. J. Opt. Soc. Am., 9:335-74.

With P. D. Foote and R. L. Chenault. Visible radiation from solid targets. J. Opt. Soc. Am., 9:541-43.

With C. C. Kiess and K. Burns. Redetermination of secondary standards of wave length from the new international iron arc. Nat. Bur. Std. Sci. Pap., 19:263-72.

With C. C. Kiess. Interferometer measurements of the longer waves in the iron-arc spectrum. Nat. Bur. Std. Sci. Pap., 19:273-80.

1925

The periodical structural regularities of spectra as related to the periodic law of the chemical elements. Proceedings of the National Academy of Sciences, 11:43-47.

With B. E. Moore. Quartet-system multiplets in the arc spectrum of yttrium. J. Wash. Acad. Sci., 15:207-10.

Arc spectra of the platinum metals (4500 A to 9000 A). Nat. Bur. Std. Sci. Pap., 20:19-45.

With O. Laporte. Arc spectrum regularities for ruthenium. Science, 61:635-36.

With Otto Laporte. Some rules of spectral structure. J. Opt. Soc. Am. Rev. Sci. Instr., 11:459-63.

Multipletts im Spektrum des Ionisierten Vanadiums. Z. Physik, 33:509-28.

With K. Burns. Standard solar wave lengths 4073-4754 A. Publ. Allegheny Obs. Univ. Pittsburgh, 6:105-24.

1926

With C. C. Kiess.   Spectral structures for elements of the second long period. J. Opt. Soc. Am. Rev. Sci. Instr., 12:417-47.

Multipletts im Spektrum des Ionisierten Vanadiums. II. Z. Physik, 39:114-22.

With O. Laporte.   Absorption spectra of the palladium and platinum triads. Phys. Rev., 28:624-64.

Investigations on the platinum metals. VII. Arc spectra of the platinum metals. Chemical News, 132(3429):6-10.

1927

Regularities in the arc spectrum of lanthanum. J. Wash. Acad. Sci., 17:25-35.

The structure of the La II spectrum. J. Opt. Soc. Am. Rev. Sci. Instr., 14:191-204.

With K. Burns.   Hyperfine structure of lanthanum lines. J. Opt. Soc. Am. Rev. Sci. Instr., 14:449-54.

Wave length measurements in the arc spectrum of scandium. Nat. Bur. Std. Sci. Pap., 22:61-71.

With F. M. Walters, Jr.   Absorption spectra of iron, cobalt, and nickel. Nat. Bur. Std. Sci. Pap., 22:205-26; Phys. Rev., 29:358. (A)

With H. N. Russell.   An analysis of the arc and spark spectra of scandium (Sc I and Sc II). Nat. Bur. Std. Sci. Pap., 22:329-73; Phys. Rev., 29:606. (A)

1928

Multiplets in the Co II spectrum. J. Wash. Acad. Sci., 18:325-30.

With B. F. Scribner.   Regularities in the spark spectrum of hafnium (Hf II). J. Opt. Soc. Am. Rev. Sci. Instr., 17:83-90.

Wave length measurements in the arc and spark spectra of hafnium. J. Res. Nat. Bur. Std., 1:151-87; Phys. Rev., 31:1133-34. (A)

With K. Burns and C. C. Kiess.   Standard solar wave lengths (3592-7148 A). J. Res. Nat. Bur. Std., 1:297-317.

Wave lengths and Zeeman effects in yttrium spectra. J. Res. Nat. Bur. Std., 1:319-41.

With C. C. Kiess.   Tables of theoretical Zeeman-effects. J. Res. Nat. Bur. Std., 1:641-84.

1929

With R. M. Langer. Regularity in frequency shifts of scattered light. Phys. Rev., 33:287. (A)

Persistent lines and raies ultimes of the chemical elements. Internat. Critical Tables, 5:322-25.

Structures of the optical spectra of atoms. Internat. Critical Tables, 5:408-9.

Report of Commission 14 (Longueur d'Onde). Trans. Internat. Astron. Union, 3:236-39.

Proceedings of the Assay Commission, 1929. Treasury Department, Document No. 3006, pp. 7-10.

With H. N. Russell. An analysis of the arc and spark spectra of ytrrium (Yt I and Yt II). J. Res. Nat. Bur. Std., 2:733-69; Phys. Rev., 31:1124. (A)

With T. L. deBruin and C. J. Humphreys. The first spectrum of krypton. J. Res. Nat. Bur. Std., 3:129-52; Phys. Rev., 33:1097-98. (A)

With T. L. deBruin and C. J. Humphreys. The first spectrum of xenon. J. Res. Nat. Bur. Std., 3:731-63.

With T. L. deBruin. The arc spectrum of arsenic. J. Res. Nat. Bur. Std., 3:765-81.

1930

With A. G. Shenstone. The spark spectrum of ruthenium. Phys. Rev., 35:868. (L)

With B. F. Scribner. Regularities in the arc spectrum of hafnium (Hf I). J. Res. Nat. Bur. Std., 4:169-75.

With R. M. Langer. Light scattering in liquids. J. Res. Nat. Bur. Std., 4:711-35.

With B. F. Scribner. Regularities in the spectra of lutecium. J. Res. Nat. Bur. Std., 5:73-81; Phys. Rev., 35:1420. (A)

1931

The optical spectrum of rhenium. Phys. Rev., 37:219-20.

With A. S. King. Preliminary report of an investigation of the spectrum of columbium. Phys. Rev., 37:226-27.

The rhenium atom. Sci. Monthly, 32:475-77.

Rhenium. Sci. Monthly, 33:413-18.

With C. E. Moore.   The absence of rhenium from the solar spectrum. Publ. Astron. Soc. Pacific, 43:345-46.

With J. A. Wheeler.   The band spectra of scandium-, ytrrium-, and lanthanum monoxides.   J. Res. Nat. Bur. Std., 6:239-75; Phys. Rev., 37:106. (A)

With C. J. Humphreys and T. L. deBruin.   Regularities in the second spectrum of xenon.   J. Res. Nat. Bur. Std., 6:287-93; Phys. Rev., 37:106-7. (A)

The arc spectrum of rhenium.   J. Res. Nat. Bur. Std., 6:1027-50; Phys. Rev., 37:1702. (A)

With A. S. King and R. F. Bacher.   Hyperfine structure and nuclear moment of rhenium. Phys. Rev., 38:1258-59. (L)

1932

With T. L. deBruin and C. J. Humphreys.   Further description and analysis of the first spectrum of krypton.   J. Res. Nat. Bur. Std., 7:643-57.

With C. C. Kiess and C. J. Humphreys.   Infrared spectrum photography.   J. Opt. Soc. Am., 22:428. (A)

With C. E. Moore.   The presence of ytterbium in the sun. Publ. Astron. Soc. Pacific, 44:175-77.

With G. H. Dieke.   Infrared spectra of helium.   J. Res. Nat. Bur. Std., 9:121-29.

With C. J. Humphreys.   Infrared spectra of the noble gases. Phys. Rev., 40:1040. (A)

Wave lengths and Zeeman effects in lanthanum spectra.   J. Res. Nat. Bur. Std., 9:239-68.

With C. C. Kiess.   Infrared arc spectra photographed with xeno- cyanine.   J. Res. Nat. Bur. Std., 9:309-26.

With H. N. Russell.   An analysis of lanthanum spectra.   J. Res. Nat. Bur. Std., 9:625-68.

1933

Report of Commission 14 (Wave-Lengths).   Trans. Internat. As- tron. Union, 4:233-36.

With B. F. Scribner.   The Zeeman effect on hafnium lines.   J. Opt. Soc. Am., 23:121. (A)

With C. C. Kiess and C. J. Humphreys.   Further description

and analysis of the first spectrum of krypton. J. Res. Nat. Bur. Std., 7:643-47.

With C. J. Humphreys. Infrared spectra of neon, argon and krypton. J. Res. Nat. Bur. Std., 10:427-48.

Long-wave arc spectra of alkalis and alkaline earths. J. Res. Nat. Bur. Std., 10:669-84.

The infrared arc spectra of manganese and rhenium. J. Res. Nat. Bur. Std., 10:757-69.

With T. L. deBruin and C. J. Humphreys. The second spectrum of krypton. J. Res. Nat. Bur. Std., 11:409-40.

1934

With C. J. Humphreys. Interference measurements in the spectra of noble gases. J. Res. Nat. Bur. Std., 13:293-309.

With B. F. Scribner. Second spectrum of hafnium (Hf II). J. Res. Nat. Bur. Std., 13:625-57.

1935

The seventieth anniversary of Professor P. Zeeman. Sci. Monthly, 41:85-87.

Interference measurements in the infrared arc spectrum of iron. J. Res. Nat. Bur. Std., 14:33-40.

Infrared spectra of noble gases (10,500 A to 13,000 A). J. Res. Nat. Bur. Std., 14:487-97.

With B. F. Scribner. Multiplets and terms in the first two spectra of columbium. J. Res. Nat. Bur. Std., 14:629-47.

1936

Report of Commission 14 (Wave-Lengths). Trans. Internat. Astron. Union, 5:299-303.

With A. S. King. Arc and spark spectra of columbium. J. Res. Nat. Bur. Std., 16:385-419.

With H. N. Russell. Term analysis of the first spectrum of vanadium (V I). J. Res. Nat. Bur. Std., 17:125-92.

1937

Available tables of wave lengths for spectrochemical analysis. Proc. 5th Summer Conf. Spectry. Applications, pp. 57-59.

With C. J. Humphreys. Interference measurements of wave

lengths in the ultraviolet spectrum of iron. J. Res. Nat. Bur. Std., 18:543-57.

With B. F. Scribner. Arc and spark spectra of lutecium. J. Res. Nat. Bur. Std., 19:31-39.

With B. F. Scribner. Arc and spark spectra of ytterbium. J. Res. Nat. Bur. Std., 19:651-64.

1938

With Charlotte E. Moore. The second spectrum of vanadium. J. Opt. Soc. Am., 28:176. (A)

With W. W. Watson. Spectrum of lutecium monoxide. J. Res. Nat. Bur. Std., 20:125-28.

With B. F. Scribner. A bibliography of spectrochemical analysis, 1920-1937. Proc. 6th Summer Conf. Spectry. Applications, pp. 112-13.

Standard wave lengths. Proc. 6th Summer Conf. Spectry. Applications, pp. 114-17.

1939

With C. J. Humphreys and T. L. deBruin. Zeeman effect in the second and third spectra of xenon. J. Res. Nat. Bur. Std., 23:683-99.

Report of Commission des Étalons de Longuer d'Onde et des Tables de Spectres Solaires. Trans. Internat. Astron. Union, 6:79-102.

Spectroscopic apparatus. Journal of Applied Physics, 10:734-40.

A quarter century of spectrochemical analysis at the National Bureau of Standards. Proc. 7th Summer Conf. Spectry. Applications, pp. 1-6.

Some spectroscopic suggestions. Proc. 7th Summer Conf. Spectry. Applications, pp. 73-76.

With B. F. Scribner. *Index to the Literature on Spectrochemical Analysis, 1920-1937.* Philadelphia, American Society for Testing Materials. 59 pp.

1940

First spectrum of tin. J. Res. Nat. Bur. Std., 24:153-73; J. Opt. Soc. Am., 29:258. (A)

With C. E. Moore. Description and analysis of the second spectrum of vanadium (V II). J. Res. Nat. Bur. Std., 25:83-132.
With H. D. Hubbard. *Periodic Chart of the Atoms (1940 edition)*. Chicago, W. M. Welch Scientific Company.
With H. D. Hubbard. *Key to Periodic Chart of the Atoms*. Chicago, W. M. Welch Scientific Company. 16 pp.

1941

Sir C. V. Raman (a brief biography). J. Opt. Soc. Am., 31:510-11.
With B. F. Scribner. *Index to the Literature on Spectrochemical Analysis, 1920-1939*. 2d ed. Philadelphia, American Society for Testing Materials. 94 pp.
Notes on the physical basis for spectrographic analysis. J. Opt. Soc. Am., 31:39-46.
Emission spectra of the rare earth elements. J. Opt. Soc. Am., 31:157-59.
The strongest lines of singly ionized atoms. J. Opt. Soc. Am., 31:605-11.

1942

The primary standard of wavelength. Rev. Mod. Phys., 14:59-63.
Atomic spectra of rare earth elements. Rev. Mod. Phys., 14:96-103.
With C. J. Humphreys. The first spectrum of antimony. J. Res. Nat. Bur. Std., 28:463-78.

1943

Harry John McNicholas. (Obituary.) J. Wash. Acad. Sci., 33:192.

1944

With H. Kayser. *Tabelle der Schwingungszahlen*. Rev. ed. Ann Arbor, Michigan, Edwards Brothers, Inc. 106 pp.

1945

With C. J. Humphreys. Term analysis of the first two spectra of columbium. J. Res. Nat. Bur. Std., 34:477-585.

1946

Spectroscopy, past, present and future. J. Opt. Soc. Am., 36:431-48.

1947

With B. F. Scribner. *Index to the Literature on Spectrochemical Analysis, Pt. 2, 1940-1945.* Philadelphia, American Society for Testing Materials. 180 pp.

Periodic Chart of the Atoms (1947 edition). Chicago, W. M. Welch Scientific Company.

With H. D. Hubbard. *Key to Periodic Chart of the Atoms (1947 edition).* Chicago, W. M. Welch Scientific Company. 48 pp.

Electron configurations of "rare-earth" elements. Science, 105:514-16.

Principals and principles of spectrochemical analysis. Spectrochim. Acta, 3:5-17.

The second spectrum of ytterbium. J. Opt. Soc. Am., 37:988-89. (A)

Light wave of mercury 198 as ultimate standard of length. Nat. Bur. Std. Tech. News Bull., 31:133-37.

1948

Principals and principles of spectrochemical analysis. Society for Applied Spectroscopy Bulletin, 3(2):1-12.

Ives medalist for 1947. J. Opt. Soc. Am., 38:1-6.

A wave length of artificial mercury as the ultimate standard of length. J. Opt. Soc. Am., 38:7-14.

Wavelengths emitted by mercury-198. J. Opt. Soc. Am., 38:665. (A)

Spectroscopy. In: *Encyclopaedia Britannica,* Vol. 21, pp. 180-95. Chicago, Encyclopaedia Britannica, Inc.

Light wave of mercury 198 as ultimate standard of length. Science Counselor, 11(2):50-51, 70-71.

Measurement by mercury. Scientific American, 179:48-53.

1949

The ultimate standard of length. Sci. Monthly, 68:311.

Emission spectroscopy. Anal. Chem., 21:29-31.

With Bourdon F. Scribner. Emission spectra of technetium. J. Opt. Soc. Am., 39:1059. (A)

1950

Emission spectroscopy. Anal. Chem., 22:18-23.

With B. F. Scribner and W. R. Bozman. Absorption and emission spectra of promethium. J. Opt. Soc. Am., 40:262. (A)

Periodic Chart of the Atoms (1950 edition). Chicago, W. M. Welch Scientific Company.

With H. D. Hubbard. *Key to Periodic Chart of the Atoms (1950 edition).* Chicago, W. M. Welch Scientific Company. 48 pp.

With F. Oliver Westfall. Lamps and wave lengths of mercury 198. J. Res. Nat. Bur. Std., 44:447-55.

With A. G. Shenstone and Charlotte E. Moore. The first spectrum of arsenic. J. Res. Nat. Bur. Std., 45:346-56.

With Karl G. Kessler. Wave lengths of mercury 198. J. Opt. Soc. Am., 40:737-41.

With Bourdon F. Scribner. The arc and spark spectra of technetium. J. Res. Nat. Bur. Std., 45:476-89.

With Karl G. Kessler. Nuclear spin of 43Tc^{99}. Phys. Rev., 80: 905-6.

Report of Commission des Étalons de Longueur d'Onde et des Tables de Spectres Solaires. Trans. Internat. Astron. Union, 7:146-54.

1951

Atomic standards of length now available. Nat. Bur. Std. Tech. News Bull., 35:29-31.

With B. F. Scribner and W. R. Bozman. Two new elements confirmed. Nat. Bur. Std. Tech. News Bull., 35:31-33.

With Bourdon F. Scribner and William R. Bozman. Absorption and emission spectra of prometheium. J. Res. Nat. Bur. Std., 46:85-98.

With Karl G. Kessler. The magnetic moment of 43Tc^{99}. Phys. Rev., 82:341-42.

Multiplets and terms in technetium spectra. J. Res. Nat. Bur. Std., 47:7-14.

Fundamental research in atomic spectra. J. Opt. Soc. Am., 41:143-48.

The fundamental standard of wave length. The Astronomical Journal, 56:116-18.

The spectrochemistry of technetium and promethium. Spectrochim. Acta, 4:317-26.

With Mark Fred and Frank S. Tomkins. Some spectra of actinium. J. Opt. Soc. Am., 41:867. (A)

With Frank S. Tomkins and Mark Fred. Nuclear spin of actinium 227. Phys. Rev., 84:168. (L)

1952

With M. A. Catalán and R. Velasco. Zeeman effect in rhenium. J. Opt. Soc. Am., 42:288. (A)

Emission spectroscopy. Anal. Chem., 24:23-27.

Report of Commission des Étalons Longueur d'Onde et Tables des Spectres Solaires. Trans. Internat. Astron. Union, 8:188-98.

With Robert J. Murphy. The arc spectra of gallium, indium, and thallium. J. Res. Nat. Bur. Std., 48:334-44.

A description of the arc and spark spectra of rhenium. J. Res. Nat. Bur. Std., 49:187-216.

What use is spectroscopy? Applied Spectroscopy, 6(4):6-10.

1953

With George R. Harrison. Zeeman effect in spark lines of ruthenium. J. Opt. Soc. Am., 43:816. (A)

Periodic Chart of the Atoms (1953 edition). Chicago, W. M. Welch Scientific Company.

Key to Periodic Chart of the Atoms (1953 edition). Chicago, W. M. Welch Scientific Company. 48 pp.

With W. R. Bozman, C. H. Corliss, and R. E. Trees. An intersystem transition in the first spectrum of beryllium. J. Res. Nat. Bur. Std., 50:131-32.

With C. E. Moore. Collecting of data concerning atomic spectra. Report of Subcommittee *b*. Transactions of the Joint Commission for Spectroscopy. J. Opt. Soc. Am., 43:415-16.

With C. E. Moore. Notation for atomic spectra. Report of Subcommittee *e*. Transactions of the Joint Commission for Spectroscopy. J. Opt. Soc. Am., 43:422-25.

Stark effect. In: *Encyclopaedia Britannica,* Vol. 21, pp. 334-35. Chicago, Encyclopaedia Britannica, Inc.

Zeeman effect. In: *Encyclopaedia Britannica,* Vol. 23, pp. 940-41. Chicago, Encyclopaedia Britannica, Inc.

1954

Emission spectroscopy. Anal. Chem., 26:54-58.

Standard wave lengths. In: *Smithsonian Physical Tables,* 9th rev. ed., pp. 568-78. Washington, D.C., Smithsonian Institution.

Zeeman effect in the first spectrum of hafnium. J. Opt. Soc. Am., 44:348-49. (A)

Periodic Chart of the Atoms (1954 edition). Chicago, W. M. Welch Scientific Company.

Key to Periodic Chart of the Atoms (1954 edition). Chicago, W. M. Welch Scientific Company. 48 pp.

Series relations in atomic spectra. In: *Smithsonian Physical Tables,* 9th rev. ed., pp. 578-85. Washington, D.C., Smithsonian Institution.

With B. F. Scribner. *Index to the Literature on Spectrochemical Analysis, Pt. 3, 1946-1950.* Philadelphia, American Society for Testing Materials. 226 pp.

With Karl G. Kessler and Charlotte E. Moore. Extension of the arc spectra of palladium and platinum (6500 to 12,000 A). J. Res. Nat. Bur. Std., 53:225-28.

1955

With K. G. Kessler. New vacuum wavelengths for Hg^{198}. J. Opt. Soc. Am., 45:902. (A)

With Charles H. Corliss and Bourdon F. Scribner. Intensities of 30,000 spectral lines. Science, 121:624. (A)

With Mark Fred and Frank S. Tomkins. Nuclear moments of Ac^{227}. Phys. Rev. 98:1514. (L)

With K. G. Kessler. Arc and spark spectra of ruthenium. J. Res. Nat. Bur. Std., 55:97-126.

Opening address by President William F. Meggers at the Rydberg Centennial Conference on Atomic Spectroscopy. Lund Universitets Arsskrift. N. F. Avd. 2, Bd. 50, Nr. 21.

Report of Commission des Étalons de Longueur d'Onde et des

Tables de Spectres Solaires. Trans. Internat. Astron. Union, 9:201-27.

1956

Emission spectroscopy. Anal. Chem., 28:616-21.

With Charlotte E. Moore. Collecting of data concerning atomic spectra. Report of Subcommittee *b*. Transactions of the Joint Commission for Spectroscopy. J. Opt. Soc. Am., 46:145-52.

1957

With R. W. Stanley. Wave lengths from iron-halide lamps. J. Res. Nat. Bur. Std., 58:41-49; J. Opt. Soc. Am., 47:1057. (A)

With C. E. Moore. Collecting data of atomic spectra. Report of Subcommittee *e*. Transactions of the Joint Commission for Spectroscopy. J. Opt. Soc. Am., 47:1035-41.

Emission spectra of actinium. Nat. Bur. Std. Tech. News Bull., 41:49-51.

With Mark Fred and Frank Tomkins. Emission spectra of actinium. J. Res. Nat. Bur. Std., 58:297-315.

With P. F. Klinkenberg, R. Velasco, and M. A. Catalán. Term analysis of the first spectrum of rhenium (Re I). J. Res. Nat. Bur. Std., 59:319-48.

The spectrochemistry of actinium. Spectrochim. Acta, 10:195-200.

1958

With Robert W. Stanley. Wavelengths from thorium-halide lamps. J. Res. Nat. Bur. Std., 61:95-103.

With Charles H. Corliss. Improved description of hafnium spectra. J. Res. Nat. Bur. Std., 61:269-324.

With A. G. Shenstone. The second spectrum of ruthenium (Ru II). J. Res. Nat. Bur. Std., 61:373-411.

With M. A. Catalán and M. Sales. Term analysis of the second spectrum of rhenium (Re II). J. Res. Nat. Bur. Std., 61:441-61.

1959

Periodic Chart of the Atoms (1959 edition). Chicago, W. M. Welch Scientific Company.

Key to the Periodic Chart of the Atoms (1959 edition). Chicago, W. M. Welch Scientific Company. 48 pp.

With C. H. Corliss and C. J. Humphreys. Improved description of ytterbium spectra. J. Opt. Soc. Am., 49:1130. (A)

With C. H. Corliss and B. F. Scribner. Residual arc spectra of seventy elements diluted in copper. Colloquium Spectroscopium Internationale, 8:119-21.

With B. F. Scribner. *Index to the Literature on Spectrochemical Analysis, Pt. 4, 1951-1955*. Philadelphia, American Society for Testing Materials. 314 pp.

Present status of the question of the spectra of rare earths from the experimental point of view. Journal of Optics and Spectroscopy, 6:430-33.

The present state and future prospects in emission spectroscopy. Proceedings of the 7th International Colloquium on Spectroscopy. Revue Universelle des Mines, 15(9):230-37.

1960

With C. H. Corliss. First spectrum of ytterbium (Yb I). J. Opt. Soc. Am., 50:1136. (A)

Present experimental status of rare-earth spectra. Transactions of Joint Commission for Spectroscopy. J. Opt. Soc. Am., 50:405-6.

With C. D. Coleman and W. R. Bozman. *Table of Wavenumbers*. Nat. Bur. Std. Monograph 3, Vol. 1, 2000 to 7000 A, 500 pp.; Vol. 2, 7000 A to 1000 μ, 34 pp. Washington, D.C., United States Government Printing Office.

With Jack L. Tech. The centennial of spectrochemistry. J. Opt. Soc. Am., 50:1035-38.

1961

With Charles H. Corliss and Bourdon F. Scribner. Relative intensities for the arc spectra of seventy elements. Spectrochim. Acta, 17:1137-72.

With C. H. Corliss and B. F. Scribner. Spectral-line intensity tables. Nat. Bur. Std. Tech. News Bull., 45:201-2.

With Charles H. Corliss and Bourdon F. Scribner. *Tables of Spectral-Line Intensities*. Nat. Bur. Std. Monograph 32, Pt. 1, 476 pp., Pt. 2, 277 pp. Washington, D.C., United States Government Printing Office.

1963

Periodic Chart of the Atoms (1963 edition). Chicago, W. M. Welch Scientific Company.

Key to the Periodic Chart of the Atoms (1963 edition). Chicago, W. M. Welch Scientific Company. 48 pp.

Review of reviews of atomic spectroscopy. Applied Optics, 2(7):657-63.

1964

Henry Crew, 1859-1953. National Academy of Sciences, *Biographical Memoirs*, 37:33-54.

With Miguel A. Catalán and Olga Garcia-Riquelme. The first spectrum of manganese (Mn I). J. Res. Nat. Bur. Std., 68A:9-59.

Spectra inform us about atoms. Physics Teacher, 2:303-11.

1965

With Robert W. Stanley. More wavelengths from thorium lamps. J. Res. Nat. Bur. Std., 69A:109-18.

Periodic Chart of the Atoms (1965 edition). Chicago, W. M. Welch Scientific Company.

Key to the Periodic Chart of the Atoms (1965 edition). Chicago, W. M. Welch Scientific Company. 48 pp.

1966

With Charles H. Corliss. Wavelengths, intensities and Zeeman patterns in ytterbium spectra (Yb I, II, III, IV). J. Res. Nat. Bur. Std., 70A:63-106.

1967

The second spectrum of ytterbium (Yb II). J. Res. Nat. Bur. Std., 71A:396-544. (Edited by Charlotte E. Moore.)

With W. R. Bozman and C. H. Corliss. An improved description of technetium spectra (Tc I and Tc II), 2000 to 9000 A. J. Res. Nat. Bur. Std., 71A:547-65.

ARMoulton

FOREST RAY MOULTON

April 29, 1872–December 7, 1952

BY CHARLES E. GASTEYER*

FOREST RAY MOULTON was born April 29, 1872, in a log cabin near LeRoy, Michigan. His parents, Belah G. and Mary C. Moulton, and his grandparents were long-lived and of pioneer stock. They were, for the most part, farmers and teachers. Forest Ray's parents were active in church affairs and in establishing a local school. His mother wrote a charming book[1] about the lives of her ancestors, including stories of Indian attacks and a chase by a pack of wolves. The book also describes her early married life and some episodes in the boyhood of Forest Ray and her other children.

When he was born, his grandfathers disputed about a name for him, so his mother decided "that his name should be Forest Ray, for he was a perfect ray of light and happiness in that dense forest." He was the oldest of seven brothers and a sister. Five of the brothers were later listed in *Who's Who in America*.

F. R. Moulton became the first boy in his town to get a college education, at nearby Albion College. According to his mother's book, his example was an inspiration to many others. When he was a college sophomore, he solved by an original method

---

* Transmitted by G. M. Clemence.

[1] Mary C. Moulton, *True Stories of Pioneer Life* (Chicago: Press of James Watson and Co., 1924). A copy of this rare book is in the files of the National Academy of Sciences, Washington, D.C.

a mathematical problem which his professor had attempted un-successfully, whereupon the professor appointed him as an assist-ant in teaching astronomy. Although Moulton had a three-year preparatory deficiency to make up when he started college, he graduated in 1894 after only the usual four years of residency. Many years later Albion College awarded him an honorary Sc.D. degree in mathematics and astronomy.

In 1895 Moulton enrolled as a graduate student at the University of Chicago. He received a Ph.D. degree in mathe-matics and astronomy *summa cum laude* in 1899. For the next twenty-seven years he remained at that university in successive academic positions from instructor to full professor. During this time he carried out most of his scientific researches.

Moulton is probably best known as co-author of the plane-tesimal hypothesis with the geologist T. C. Chamberlin. This hypothesis was developed, during the years 1897 to 1900, to explain why the planets revolve around the sun in nearly circu-lar, coplanar orbits and why nearly all of them revolve around the sun and rotate on their axes in the same direction. The earlier nebular hypothesis failed to explain the present form of the sun and the planets for reasons given by Moulton in an article written in 1900 (see the bibliography). The planetesimal hypothesis, described by Moulton in 1905, states that the planets owe their existence to another star which passed close to the sun. The passing star's gravitational force drew out of the sun matter which then began to revolve around it as a swarm of little planets or planetesimals. Later, the planetesimals coalesced into the large planets which now exist. A modified form of this hypothesis, called the tidal theory, was developed by Sir James Jeans and Harold Jeffreys in 1918;[2] a dispute about the author-ship of the basic ideas of the theory arose between Jeffreys and

[2] Sir James Jeans, *Problems of Cosmogony and Stellar Dynamics* (Cambridge: Cambridge University Press, 1919), pp. 275-85.

Moulton in 1928 (see the bibliography). In 1930 F. Nölke showed that matter drawn out of the sun—a necessary part of both the planetesimal hypothesis and the tidal theory—will dissipate into space before it can condense into planets, because of solar gravitation.[3] These theories were later superseded by the hydrodynamical vortex theory of C. F. von Weizsäcker and G. P. Kuiper.[4]

Moulton was also interested in mathematics. He investigated periodic coefficients and the convergence of series expressions used in the solution of differential equations. Some of this work was published in his text *Differential Equations* (1930).

Moulton studied some special cases of the restricted three-body problem. With the help of his graduate students at the University of Chicago, he investigated the series of orbits for a particle without mass which revolves, first, around one of the two bodies having finite mass at a very small distance from it and, next, in successively larger orbits which finally embrace both bodies at a great distance from them. His classification of different kinds of orbits in the restricted three-body problem has been criticized. His researches are summarized in the book *Periodic Orbits* (1920).

During World War I Moulton was a major in the United States Army and was in charge of the Ballistics Branch of the Ordnance Department. He carried out an original theoretical and experimental study of projectile motion, for use in aiming the newly developed long-range guns. His work included the problem of projectile rotation during flight, about which very little was then known. His results are described in the book *Exterior Ballistics* (1926).

After 1930, Moulton made a study of the size of the meteor-

---

[3] *Der Entwicklungsgang unseres Planetensystems,* pp. 187-91.
[4] G. P. Kuiper, "On the Origin of the Solar System," in J. A. Hynek, ed., *Astrophysics: A Topical Symposium* (New York: McGraw-Hill, 1951), ch. 8.

ite which produced Meteor Crater in Arizona. Assuming that the crater had once been a level plain, mining engineers estimated the amount of work necessary to transport enough material from the crater's center to make its surrounding walls. Moulton calculated the mass of a falling meteorite which could do this work, assuming reasonable values for the object's space velocity and angle of incidence and for the atmospheric retarding effect. For a nearly spherical meteorite composed mostly of iron and nickel and having the required mass, Moulton found that the diameter must be several hundred feet. He also suggested that the crater might be due to a swarm of meteorites, in which case the diameter of the whole swarm must have been considerably larger. His estimates of mass and size agree well with modern experimental studies.[5] Moulton's investigations of Meteor Crater were never published because he wished to avoid arguments with people who had published different opinions about the meteorite's size. His manuscripts are now kept by Dr. Lincoln LaPaz, Director of the Institute of Meteoritics at the University of New Mexico.[6]

Moulton had considerable influence on his contemporaries as a teacher and counselor. Students who worked on advanced degrees under his supervision included the astronomers E. P. Hubble and Walter Bartky and the mathematician T. H. Hildebrandt. It was Moulton who encouraged G. D. Birkhoff to start a study of Poincaré's works.[7] His qualities as a teacher are shown by the lucid style of his books *Introduction to Astronomy, Celestial Mechanics,* and *Differential Equations,* and by his many semitechnical articles published in the magazine *Popular Astronomy.*

[5] Norman Rostoker, "The Formation of Craters by High-Speed Particles," *Meteoritics,* 1 (1953):no. 1.

[6] Letter from Dr. LaPaz, March 11, 1956.

[7] Obituary of Birkhoff by Marston Morse, *Bulletin of the American Mathematical Society,* 52:357.

During his lifetime Moulton received wide recognition from scientific colleagues. While still a young man, he was a research associate of the Carnegie Institution of Washington. He became a member of many scientific societies: American Astronomical Society (1899), Royal Astronomical Society (1900), American Mathematical Society (1900), Circolo Matematico di Palermo (1905), National Academy of Sciences (1910), American Philosophical Society (1916), section on mathematics and astronomy of the American Academy of Arts and Sciences (1919), executive board of the National Research Council (1927). He was a member of the commission on dynamical astronomy and astronomical tables of the International Astronomical Union in 1922 and 1925. He held the offices of president and executive councilor in the Society of the Sigma Xi. He was an honorary member of the British Association for the Advancement of Science. Honorary degrees were awarded to him by Drake University (1939) and the Case Institute of Technology (1940). He assisted in the editing of the *Journal of Geography* in the early 1900s, the *Transactions of the American Mathematical Society* (1908-1925), and the *Astronomical Journal* (1914-1949). He was also a director of the Gould Fund of the National Academy of Sciences.

Almost as important as Moulton's purely scientific work was his deep interest in general education and in the organization of American science. He founded the first Parent-Teacher Association in Chicago. About 1920 he started a Society for the Promotion of Visual Education, the journal of which he edited for several years. He was active in the American Association for the Advancement of Science as secretary of its sections on mathematics and astronomy (1913-1924), member of the executive committee (1925-1929), permanent secretary (1937-1946), and administrative secretary (1946-1948). While he was permanent and administrative secretary, the A.A.A.S. acquired ownership of the magazines *Science* and *Scientific Monthly,* purchased its own office building on a valuable site, and increased its membership from 18,000 to 43,000. According to an associate of Moulton at the University of Chicago and in the A.A.A.S., he deserves much credit for these achievements.[8] As permanent secretary, Moulton edited more than twenty A.A.A.S. symposia, mostly on medical subjects. He considered them suitable for publication both as scientific studies and as means for raising funds for the association. He edited the A.A.A.S. Bulletin (1942-1946), a vehicle for his personal essays about the philosophy of science and the application of science to human affairs. He helped organize support among A.A.A.S. members for establishment of the National Science Foundation.

Several business ventures occupied Moulton's interest and illustrate his versatility and industry. In 1906 he bought a farm in Michigan and managed it for a few years. In 1912 he was architect and contractor for a Chicago apartment building. He resigned his professorship at the University of Chicago to become a director of the Utilities Power and Light Company in that city (1926-1937). He was a personal counselor to the president of the company, advising him on business and financial policies and on the scientific problems of the power industry. Moulton became director of concessions and a trustee of the Chicago "Century of Progress" World's Fair (1933-1934). Although the Great Depression was then at its height, the concessions brought in much revenue, and the fair itself was a financial success.

The career of F. R. Moulton bears some similarity to that of the eighteenth-century French scientist, Jean-Sylvain Bailly.[9] Both men started their careers as astronomers and ended them in public service. Both were interested in medicine and in

---

[8] Obituary of Moulton by A. J. Carlson, *Science,* 117 (1953):545-46.

[9] Edwin B. Smith, "Jean-Sylvain Bailly—Astronomer, Mystic, Revolutionary—1736-1793," *Transactions of the American Philosophical Society,* 44 (1954):pt. 4.

philosophy. Both were prolific writers but not always critical thinkers.

Moulton married Estella L. Gillette in 1896; they were divorced in 1936. There were five children from this marriage. He married Alicia Pratt in 1939; they were divorced in 1951.

Moulton was a man of frugal habits. He did not smoke or drink. He enjoyed sports, playing football while in college and tennis afterward, until he suffered a coronary thrombosis at the age of sixty. He recovered from this attack after three or four years and then kept in physical trim by working at his son's farm on weekends. For many years he played billiards. He liked poetry, often quoting from Milton and Byron. He did not like card games, spectator sports, or the theater.

Moulton spent his last two years in Evanston, Illinois. He died December 7, 1952.

According to his close associates, he was outwardly a friendly man but inwardly quite reserved. He very seldom discussed his private life. "Dr. Moulton was apparently gentle, never showed annoyance even under extreme provocation, never raised his voice in anger or used profanity, but underneath he was the toughest, strongest character I have ever known."[10]

Moulton occasionally engaged in scientific and personal controversies with other astronomers, and he did not hesitate to use blunt language. This fact is borne out by his published scientific disputes with Percival Lowell (1909), his accusation of plagiarism against T. J. J. See (1912), and his dispute with Harold Jeffreys about the priority of formulation of the planetesimal hypothesis (1928).

Especially during his association with the A.A.A.S. Moulton wrote at length on social questions and the philosophy of science. From his writings his basic viewpoint seems to have been mainly optimistic and socially oriented. Before World War II he ex-

[10] Manuscript obituary of Moulton by F. L. Campbell.

pressed great faith in the probability of human progress through science.[11] During the war, this optimism was tempered by some moralizing about the social obligations which must accompany the pleasures and privileges of mankind.[12] Moulton never wrote much about formal religion. In his book *Consider the Heavens* (1935) he has a passionate account of the trial and persecution of Galileo by the Inquisition and warns against the careless use of scientific evidence to buttress theological beliefs.

Throughout his life, Moulton believed deeply in the humanistic value of scientific studies. A quotation about astronomy from his book *The Nature of the World and Man* (1926) illustrates his attitude: "To an astronomer the most remarkable and interesting thing about that part of the physical universe with which he has become acquainted is not its vast extent in space, nor the number and great masses of its stars, nor the violent forces that operate in the stars, nor the long periods of astronomical time, but that which holds him awestruck is the perfect orderliness of the universe and the majestic succession of the celestial phenomena."

The author gratefully acknowledges the help of several persons, mentioned in the footnotes, who supplied valuable details of Moulton's life and work. Especial thanks are due to the subject's brothers, Elton J. Moulton and Harold G. Moulton, for sending information which the author, who was not personally well acquainted with F. R. Moulton, could not have obtained otherwise.

[11] Century of Progress Exposition, *Bulletin*, No. 2, 1933, and *Science*, 88 (1938):324-26.

[12] *Social Science*, 16 (1941):356-64, and 17 (1942):5-19.

BIBLIOGRAPHY

KEY TO ABBREVIATIONS

Am. J. Math. = American Journal of Mathematics
Am. Math. Monthly = American Mathematical Monthly
Ann. Math. = Annals of Mathematics
Astron. J. = Astronomical Journal
Astrophys. J. = Astrophysical Journal
Bull. Am. Math. Soc. = Bulletin of the American Mathematical Society
Carnegie Inst. Wash. Publ. = Carnegie Institution of Washington Publication
Popular Astron. = Popular Astronomy
Soc. Sci. = Social Science
Trans. Am. Math. Soc. = Transactions of the American Mathematical Society

1895

An important method of solving Kepler's equation. Popular Astron., 3:136-41.

1896

A method of measuring the distances, dimensions, and masses of binary systems by the use of the spectroscope. Popular Astron., 3:337-43.

1897

Some points which need to be emphasized in teaching general astronomy. Popular Astron., 4:400-7.
Note on Mr. Miller's article, "Where did Mars get its Moons?" Popular Astron., 4:573-74.
The problem of three bodies. Popular Astron., 5:407-11.

1898

Professor Chamberlin on the nebular hypothesis. Popular Astron., 5:508.
Perturbations of the heavenly bodies. Popular Astron., 6:88-101.
On the best method of solving the markings of judges of contests. Am. Math. Monthly, 5:68-72.
Theory of the influence of a resisting medium upon bodies moving in parabolic orbits. Astron. J., 19:33-39.

1899

A graphical method of finding the elements of a parabolic orbit. Popular Astron., 7:193-201.

The limits of temporary stability of satellite motion, with an application to the question of the existence of an unseen body in the binary system F. 70 Ophiuchi. Astron. J., 20:33-36.

The spheres of activity of the planets. Popular Astron., 7:281-85.

Theory of the determination of the elements of a parabolic orbit from two observations of apparent position and one of motion in the line of sight. Astrophys. J., 10:14-21.

1900

An attempt to test the nebular hypothesis by an appeal to the laws of dynamics. Astrophys. J., 11:103-30.

A meteoric theory of the gegenschein. Astron. J., 21:17-22.

On a class of particular solutions of the problem of four bodies. Trans. Am. Math. Soc., 1:17-29.

With T. C. Chamberlin. Certain recent attempts to test the nebular hypothesis. Science, 12:201-8.

1901

A general method of determining the elements of orbits of all eccentricities from three observations. Astron. J., 22:43-52; Science, 14:399 (abbreviated version).

1902

A representation of the co-ordinates of the moon in power series which are proved to converge for a finite interval of time. Science, 16:132.

A simple non-Desarguesian plane geometry. Trans. Am. Math. Soc., 3:192-95.

An Introduction to Celestial Mechanics. New York, The Macmillan Company; rev. ed., 1914. (Translated into German and Russian.)

1903

On the motions of the planets. Popular Astron., 11:284-94.

The true radii of convergence of the expressions for the ratios of the triangles when developed as power series in the time intervals. Astron. J., 23:93-102.

1904

Time. Popular Astron., 12:391-401.

On certain rigorous methods of treating problems in celestial mechanics. Yerkes Observatory Publications, 2:117-42.

1905

On the evolution of the Solar System. Astrophys. J., 22:165-81; *ibid.*, 355-57 (reply to objection by W. H. Pickering).

1906

A class of periodic solutions of the problem of three bodies with application to the lunar theory. Trans. Am. Math. Soc., 7:537-77.

An Introduction to Astronomy. New York, The Macmillan Company. Rev. ed., 1916, 1921. xviii + 557 pp. (Chap. on the evolution of the Solar System translated into Russian.)

1907

Direct computation of the expressions for the co-ordinates in elliptic motion. Astron. J., 25:145-49; in: *Periodic Orbits,* pp. 55-66, 1920.

1909

Remarks on recent contributions to cosmogony. Science, 30:113-17.

A reply to Dr. Percival Lowell. Science, 30:639-41.

With T. C. Chamberlin. The development of the planetesimal hypothesis. Science, 30:642-45.

On certain implications of possible changes in the form and dimensions of the sun, and some suggestions toward explaining certain phenomena of variable stars. Astrophys. J., 29:257-80.

The tidal and other problems. On certain relations among the possible changes in the motions of mutually attracting spheres when disturbed by tidal interactions. Carnegie Inst. Wash. Publ., 1:77-134.

Notes on the possibility of fission of a contracting rotating fluid mass. Carnegie Inst. Wash. Publ., 1:135-60; Astrophys. J., 29:1-13 (abbreviated version).

1910

The singularities of the solution of the two body problem for real initial conditions. Bull. Am. Math. Soc., 16:304.

The straight-line solutions of the problem of n bodies. Ann. Math., 12:1-17.

1911

The influence of astronomy on mathematics. Science, 33:357-64.

On the solutions of certain types of linear differential equations with periodic coefficients. Am. J. Math., 33:62-96.

The spherical pendulum. Rendiconti del Circolo Matematico di Palermo, 32:338-64.

1912

Capture theory and capture practice. Popular Astron., 20:67-82. (A dispute with T. J. J. See.)

Obituary of Henri Poincaré. Popular Astron., 20:621-34.

Closed orbits of ejection and related periodic orbits. Painlévé's theorem. Proceedings of the London Mathematical Society, 11:367-97; in: *Periodic Orbits,* pp. 456-84, 1920.

A class of periodic orbits of superior planets. Trans. Am. Math. Soc., 13:96-108.

Descriptive Astronomy: An Elementary Exposition of the Facts, Principles, and Theories of Astronomical Science. Chicago, American Technical Society. 259 pp.

1913

On orbits of ejection and collision in the problem of three bodies. Bull. Am. Math. Soc., 19:450.

On the solutions of linear equations having small determinants. Am. Math. Monthly, 20:242-49; Astron. J., 28:103-24, 1914 (incorporated into an article on orbit determination); Science, 84:574-75, 1936 (brief form).

Relations among families of orbits in the restricted problem of three bodies. Proceedings of the 5th International Mathematical Congress, 2:182-87; Bull. Am. Math. Soc., 18:273-74 (brief account).

Oscillating satellites when the finite masses describe elliptical orbits. Mathematische Annalen, 73:441-79.

1914

Obituary of G. W. Hill. Popular Astron., 22:391-400.

The problem of three bodies. Popular Astron., 22:197-207.

Deviations of falling bodies. Ann. Math., 15:184-94.

On the stability of direct and retrograde satellite orbits. Monthly Notices of the Royal Astronomical Society, 75:40-57.

Memoir on the theory of determining orbits. Astron. J., 28:103-24.

1915

The importance of observing meteors. Publications of the Astronomical Society of the Pacific, 27:123-25.

Solution of an infinite system of differential equations of the analytic type. Proceedings of the National Academy of Sciences, 1:350-54.

1916

The progress of mathematical astronomy. Popular Astron., 24:547-50.

1917

An extended solution of differential equations. Bull. Am. Math. Soc., 23:256.

1918

The principle of conservation of moment of momentum. Popular Astron., 26:117-20.

1919

Theory of tides in pipes on a rigid earth. Astrophys. J., 50:346-55.

1920

With D. Buchanan, T. Buck, F. L. Griffin, W. R. Longley, and

W. D. MacMillan. *Periodic Orbits*. Washington, D.C., Carnegie Institution of Washington. Publication No. 161. xiii + 524 pp.

1921

On the age of stars. Popular Astron., 29:23.

1922

Larger worlds. Popular Astron., 30:65-70.

1923

Solutions of ordinary differential equations. Bull. Am. Math. Soc., 29:201.

1926

New Methods in Exterior Ballistics. Chicago, University of Chicago Press. vi + 257 pp. (Reply to a reviewer's comments about the book in Am. Math. Monthly, 35:248-50, 1928.)

Astronomy. In: *The Nature of the World and Man*, pp. 1-30. Chicago, University of Chicago Press. (Reissued in 1937 as *The World and Man as Science Sees Them*.)

1928

The planetesimal hypothesis. Science, 68:549-59; Science, 69:246-48, 1929 (reply to criticisms by Harold Jeffreys).

1930

Método gráfico para resolver la ecuación de Kepler. Revista Astronómica, 2:409-13.

Differential Equations. New York, The Macmillan Company. 395 pp.

1931

Astronomy. New York, The Macmillan Company. 549 pp.

Some quantitative aspects of the fall of meteors. Popular Astron., 39:17-18.

Obituary of A. A. Michelson. Popular Astron., 39:307-10.

1933

Chicago. Century of Progress International Exposition. World's Fair Series Bulletin No. 2. *A Century of Progress in Science.* 11 pp.

1935

Consider the Heavens. New York, Doubleday, Doran & Company, Inc. 332 pp.

1936

Significant figures in statistical constants. Science, 84:574-75.

1937

Science. Science, 85:571-75.

Editor. *The World and Man as Science Sees Them.* New York, Doubleday, Doran & Company, Inc. xix + 533 pp.; 2d ed., 1939.

Astronomy. In: *The World and Man as Science Sees Them,* pp. 1-47.

1938

War and science. Science, 88:324-26.

1941

Biography of G. W. Hill. Popular Astron., 49:305-11.

The natural sciences and social crises. Soc. Sci., 16:356-64.

1942

Our social order. Soc. Sci., 17:5-19.

1945

The editing of science. (Biographies of the Cattell family as editors of AAAS journals.) Science, 101:8-10.

Editor with J. J. Schifferes. *The Autobiography of Science.* New York, Doubleday, Doran & Company, Inc. xxxi + 666 pp. (Reissued in 1951.)

George B. Pegram

GEORGE BRAXTON PEGRAM

October 24, 1876–August 12, 1958

BY LEE ANNA EMBREY

O N January 9, 1912, George B. Pegram, associate professor of physics at Columbia University, wrote to Albert Einstein inviting him to visit the University as a special lecturer in physics. The choice of subject he left to Professor Einstein, noting, nevertheless, that "of course, we would want to hear something from you on the Relativity Principle and perhaps also on the theory of 'Energiequanten.' " Then he added: "Personally I have been very much interested in the Relativity Theory since my attention was first directed to it by Professor Lorentz, and I should be glad to see greater appreciation of it in America, where I confess our physicists have been rather slow to take it up."

Twenty-seven years later, on March 16, 1939, Pegram wrote Admiral S. C. Hooper, Chairman of the Naval Research Committee, as follows:

Experiments in the physics laboratories at Columbia University reveal that conditions may be found under which the chemical element uranium may be able to liberate its large excess of atomic energy, and that this might mean the possibility that uranium might be used as an explosive that would liberate a million times as much energy per pound as any known explosive. My own feeling is that the probabilities are against this, but my colleagues and I think that the bare possibility should not be disregarded, and

I therefore telephoned . . . this morning chiefly to arrange a channel through which the results of our experiments might, if the occasion should arise, be transmitted to the proper authorities in the United States Navy.[1]

The years separating these two letters represent approximately one half of Pegram's extraordinary career at Columbia University and mark the transition to the new age of atomic power that he had almost subconsciously anticipated from his youth onwards.

Pegram came to Columbia in 1900 as a young assistant in physics and retired in 1956 as chairman of the Committee on Government-Aided Research two years before his death. It is awesome to contemplate that his tenure at Columbia spanned more than a quarter of the history of the 200-year-old institution. During these years as teacher, research investigator, and administrator he witnessed and played a key role in bringing about America's rise to greatness in the field of physics. At the outset of his career, like many another aspiring American student of science, he had gone to Europe to round out his education, and by the close of his long career, students from all over the world were beating new paths to the great centers of physics in the United States.

BACKGROUND AND EARLY LIFE

From Pegram's background one might easily have predicted the academic career that he was to pursue. He falls into the now familiar pattern, characteristic of so many scientists of his generation, in coming from a scholarly family in which higher education and a professional career were taken for granted as objectives for the children.

According to the genealogy handed down by his grandfather, George Washington Pegram, the Pegrams had come to Virginia

[1] Laura Fermi, *Atoms in the Family* (Chicago: University of Chicago Press, 1954), p. 162.

from England around the middle of the eighteenth century, and one branch of the family had moved south to North Carolina. George's father was William Howell Pegram, professor at Trinity College, now an integral part of Duke University. His mother was Emma Craven, daughter of Braxton Craven, founder and first president of Trinity College. Both his father and grandfather are honored on the Duke University campus by buildings named for them, and the elder Pegram is also honored in the William Howell Pegram Chair of Chemistry. George was honored in his own lifetime in the naming of the George B. Pegram Laboratory adjacent to the Pupin Physics Laboratory on the Columbia campus, a structure that houses the six-million-electron-volt Van de Graaf generator dedicated in November 1955. George and his two sisters and two brothers were all graduated from Trinity College; his sister Annie went on to teach mathematics for many years at Greensboro College. This remarkable family is a brilliant case in point for those who find a strong influence of heredity in families of noted achievers.

After receiving his A.B. degree from Trinity in 1895, young George Pegram taught secondary school in North Carolina for a few years before going to Columbia in 1900, where he pursued graduate studies. He received his Ph.D. in 1903; his dissertation, with its prophetic overtones for the events that dominated the latter part of his life, was on "Secondary Radioactivity in the Electrolysis of Thorium Solutions."

His files for that period contain a letter of December 12, 1906, from Ernest Rutherford, who was then at McGill University, evidently in response to a request from Pegram for confirmation of research results: "Send your radium along in a closed vessel (to allow emanations to collect) and we shall be glad to test it. Eve has everything in shape for an immediate comparison with our standard."

Professor Hermon W. Farwell, who retired from the Physics

Department of Columbia in 1949, recalls the early days of a fifty-three-year friendship with Pegram that began in the summer of 1905 when Pegram was employed by the Coast and Geodetic Survey in a periodic redetermination of the earth's magnetic elements at established stations. During the summer in question, his duties took him to Hanover, New Hampshire, where Farwell, then a young instructor, was teaching physics at Dartmouth. It was in the course of that summer work, Farwell recalls, that Pegram showed clearly some of the traits that characterized his actions in the years to come. The local "station" was on a knoll near the old observatory. Pegram was not satisfied with results of his measurements because they were not in agreement with earlier ones and seemed to be in disagreement with those that his observations on neighboring stations had led him to expect. Consequently, he spent additional time in determining the values of dip and declination at various points on all sides of this modest elevation. The results obtained showed definitely that the station had been built over a considerable amount of magnetic rock and was therefore unrepresentative of the surrounding area. He then directed his efforts to the establishment of a new station on the golf links, well away from that unusual feature. As Professor Farwell observes: "This was doing the job properly, not just following a routine."

THE TYNDALL YEAR

Pegram's abilities received early recognition at Columbia and in 1907-1908 he was awarded the Tyndall Fellowship for study abroad.

The Tyndall Fellowship, constituting, as it does, a milestone in the history of physics in the United States, deserves comment in passing. It honors the memory of John Tyndall, noted British physicist, colleague and contemporary of Faraday. In 1872, Joseph Henry, representing the National Academy of Sciences, and other distinguished American scientists including President Frederick A. P. Barnard of Columbia, invited Professor Tyndall to deliver a course of lectures in several American cities. The purpose of the lectures was "to show the uses of experiment in the cultivation of natural knowledge," in the hope that this "would materially promote scientific education in this country."

Tyndall gave six nontechnical lectures on light in the winter of 1872-1873, speaking in Boston, New York, Philadelphia, Baltimore, and Washington. The success of the lectures surpassed the most sanguine expectations. The crowds were large, the interest and discussion intense.

At a farewell dinner for Professor Tyndall, he and others spoke eloquently on the benefits of pure research, and Tyndall announced that he expected to give all the proceeds of his lecture tour (after deducting his expenses) to the education of young American philosophers in Germany. There was every reason why Tyndall's proposal should be both appropriate and welcome, for as Flexner was later to observe:

> The German university has for almost a century and a half fruitfully engaged in teaching and research. As long as those two tasks combine in fertile union, the German university, whatever its defects of detail, will retain its importance. It has stimulated university development in Great Britain; from it has sprung the graduate school of the new world; to it industry and health and every conceivable practical activity are infinitely indebted.[2]

By 1885 a fund was set up, the income of which was to be used for the Tyndall Fellowship to be available to one or more American pupils with demonstrated talent in physics who preferably intended "to devote their lives to the advancement of the theoretic sciences and original investigations in the department of learning." It was to be awarded to a Columbia student and the value was then $648.

[2] Abraham Flexner, *Universities* (New York-London-Toronto: Oxford University Press, 1930), p. 315.

Michael Pupin, then in Cambridge studying theoretical physics and mathematics, was chosen to be the first recipient. He went to see Tyndall and was most sympathetically received and wisely counseled in his desire to choose the best place for experimental work. Tyndall considered Helmholtz's Laboratory in Berlin to be the best possible place and gave Pupin a letter to Helmholtz.

The importance of Professor Tyndall's visit to this country and the subsequent development can scarcely be overestimated. His visit sparked an upsurge in interest and scholarly effort long overdue in a culture devoted up to that time almost entirely to commerce and industry.

Pegram was clearly one to appreciate fully the potentialities of the opportunity offered by the Tyndall Fellowship. Interestingly enough, the state of physics at about the time he was finishing his own graduate study was summarized many years later by Pegram himself in a chapter on "Physics" that he contributed to *A Quarter Century of Learning*.[3] In that chapter he noted:

> . . . we may briefly depict conditions at the boundaries of knowledge of physics in 1904 by stating seven questions that were uppermost in the minds of physicists in 1904. . . .
>
> 1. Why is it not possible to detect some effect of the motion of the planet earth through the ether?
>
> 2. Is all matter composed solely of electricity?
>
> 3. How can the photo-electric effect be explained?
>
> 4. What is the nature of X-rays?
>
> 5. What is the meaning and scope of the quantum hypothesis?
>
> 6. What gives rise to the peculiar sequence of frequencies in the lines of a spectrum?
>
> 7. What is the relation of gravitation to the rest of physics?

[3] *A Quarter Century of Learning, 1904-1929* (New York: Columbia University Press, 1931), pp. 297-98.

One may be sure that these and other questions that pre-occupied the scholars of his day were uppermost in his own mind as he set off for centers of learning in Europe.

Pegram's plan of study, described in his own words, survives in a handwritten letter to President Nicholas Murray Butler, dated December 31, 1907.

Courbierestrasse 15, Berlin, Germany

. . . I have been matriculated as a student in the Berlin University, hearing lectures by Professors Planck, Nernst, and Slabry; the lectures by Professor Planck on electromagnetic theory being by far the most important ones. I have also attended the meetings of the Physikalisches Colloquium weekly.

Much of my time has been spent in reading and study, especially of the journals of physics, in the libraries here, in connection with subjects which seem at present to be most open to investigation.

I have written a paper entitled "Heat developed by Thorium Oxide due to its Radioactivity," which gives the results of experiments made by Mr. Harold W. Webb and myself in the Phoenix Physical Laboratories at Columbia. We were able to measure the rate at which energy is continuously and spontaneously liberated in the form of heat in any mass of thorium oxide, as a result of its radioactivity.

A theoretical problem, in the mechanics of sound waves in air, referred to in my first report, occupied much of my attention for a few weeks. I regret to say that I have been unable to arrive at a solution.

It is my intention to go in March from Berlin to Cambridge, England.

In a much less formal letter, written to his colleague and department head, Professor William Hallock, he comments (in part):

Berlin, Courbierestrasse 15
(Ber Burkhart) Nov. 20, 1907

My *pension* is out in the western part of the city, over two miles from the University, in a section that suits me much better as a place to live than any section near the University, and not far from what is called the American Section. As to lectures, I am not hearing any very serious course except Prof. Planck's. I had hoped to find a good course on partial differential equations, etc., given here, but there is none. I talked with Prof. Planck about mathematical courses, and about all he could say was that the courses are all too *rein*. After hearing some of the lectures I agreed with him and haven't been to any more. Prof. Planck's own lectures are very fine. He speaks remarkably fast, but with great clearness, so that it is very easy to understand him. His subject is electromagnetic theory, treated in a deductive manner from the starting point of only four notions: proportionality of electric energy density to field strength squared, the same for magnetic energy, Poynting's law, and the "relaxation time." I have been reading Lorentz, and Cohn, and others along with the lectures.

Nernst, I hear in a short course on chemical thermodynamics, which goes along very nicely. Then I have been going to hear a number of other men just to try them. Van't Hoff is lecturing on the influence of the knowledge of radioactivity on chemical conceptions. His knowledge of chemical conceptions appears to be much more exact than his knowledge of radioactivity. But the amusing lectures are those of Prof. Slabry on wireless telegraphy. He started out by setting forth the result, deducible from Neumann's statement of the law of induction, for instance, that as a current is varied in a straight infinite conductor, the E.M.F. per unit length of a parallel conductor depends on the inverse *first* power of the distance between the conductors. Then he applied this at once to the case of induction between || conductors of *finite* length, saying that the coefficient of mutual induction depends on the inverse *first* power of the distance between them. So, he said, with pity for the poor physicist who has to cumber his brain with the complex notion of Maxwell's theory, and with pride in his own ability to see things clearly, anybody who had been clever enough to think of making a simple calculation according to Neumann's law, could have invented wireless telegraphy forty years ago! Then he paid his respect to Maxwell's theory, which he said had been of no use whatever to the technical man, though doubltless all right for the physicist. In fact he considers it a pity that wireless telegraphy was developed in such a roundabout way through Maxwell and Hertz.

Of course everybody went next time to hear what was to come next. He spent an hour and a half getting a solution for the charge and current in an oscillatory condenser discharge, and because the results did not all by themselves come out in the form in which his technical mind had been accustomed to seeing them, said there was a big mistake in his work somewhere. —All of which goes to show that the ignorant, not to say stupid, self-sufficiency of the technical man, who thinks he can get along without any exact theory, is quite as prevalent as the proud abstraction of the theorist, who will not have anything to do with practical applications.

I go to the colloquium every Wednesday evening, to find it subject to the same faults and virtues as ours. For the most part the reviews are shorter than ours, which strikes me as a virtue, perhaps, but one man attempted to review a mathematical paper with just the usual effect—some went to sleep, and nobody paid any attention finally. Rubens held out bravely until near the end, after Planck had given up, but finally quit pretending to understand.

I have seen very little of the laboratory as yet, preferring to wait until I become better acquainted with the various men working there, so that I can see it thoroughly, though several have offered to guide me through it. Dr. Hahn took me over the chemical laboratory. He has a room over there in which he is continuing his investigation of mezzo-thorium, and is also working some with Boltwood's ionium.

I spend considerable time in the library in the Phys. Inst., which is pretty well supplied with periodicals and books and is a quiet place to work. There is also a library of theoretical physics in Prof. Planck's office, from which we can borrow books without restriction as to number or how long we keep them.

Americans are plentiful here, and are a constant temptation to me. I already have met forty or fifty on various occasions, and at the Thanksgiving Day dinner next week I expect to meet a good many more. Still, I talk a good deal of German during the day, and think I would make rapid progress learning it if I would take a little more time to study it, which I am almost certain not to do.

I spend an evening or two a week at the theater, opera, or concert. Amusements of that sort are certainly much cheaper here than at home, but the necessaries of life are not really a great deal cheaper here than at home—not as much cheaper as I had expected to find them.

In closing this letter, he comments:

You will probably turn this over to Mrs. Hallock to rtad also, and she will probably say—"Oh, what does he write so much about old lectures and laboratories for, why doesn't he say how he likes Berlin and what he thinks of it and the Germans?" Well, this time I just didn't get started in that direction. However, I like Berlin and the Germans pretty well and am likely to write more as to that later.

An aura of those far-off student days comes through an elegantly engraved little card, tucked away in Pegram's files of the Tyndall year, which translates as follows:

> Grunewald, Wangenheimstr. 21
> January 1908
>
> Professor Dr. M. Planck and Mrs. Planck would be happy to see their young acquaintances and friends at a simple supper on Wednesday evenings, January 14, January 29, February 12, and February 26, from 8:30 to 11:00.

Of the second half of his Tyndall year, Pegram wrote formally to President Butler:

> 70 Regent St.
> Cambridge, England
> June 30, 1908
>
> During the first quarter I have been in Cambridge, England, where I have heard lectures by Professor J. Larmor and have been engaged in the study of subjects of theoretical physics, namely, thermodynamics, kinetic theory of gases, and fundamental electromagnetic theory. So far my work here has not resulted in a completed research, as I had hoped it would, but at least I have gained a much better acquaintance with methods of

approach of some questions, and I shall naturally continue working on them.

It may not be amiss for me to remark that so far as immediate output of results of investigation is concerned, I might well have been more productive as Tyndall fellow, had I spent the whole year in one laboratory and worked all the time on experimental investigation. In any case it seemed wiser to try to get from the best sources in Europe the acquaintance with European laboratories, schools of ideas, and physicists, which cannot be obtained in America and not to give my time to experimental labor, which could be better undertaken in our own laboratories at Columbia.

To that end I have visited twenty of the university and government physical laboratories of Europe; have made the acquaintance of and talked with many physicists in the universities, at the German Scientific Association meeting in Dresden, the Congress of Mathematicians in Rome, and elsewhere; have studied under Planck and Nernst in Berlin; and have studied under Larmor and come in touch with the Cambridge school of physicists. As a completed research I may mention the one (with Mr. Webb, my successor as Tyndall Fellow) on the heat generated by the radioactivity of thorium, published in the *Physical Review,* though most of the experimental labor was done before my incumbency of the Tyndall Fellowship began.

Again, on the lighter side, he wrote Professor Hallock in the closing days of his Tyndall Fellowship:

> 70 Regent St.
> Cambridge
> July 4, 1908

Fizz—bang!! There! that's my only firecracker to celebrate this glorious Fourth. I'm sure you'll allow me that.

I enclose my final report as Tyndall fellow, and relinquish that honorable title to my very worthy successor, to whom I wish all success. He may be able to show up more research completed at the end of his year, probably he will, but I am not greatly saddened when I think of what I have got out of this year, and I hope to still be in the research business for some time to come.

Toward the close of this largely personal letter, he notes:

> I am in no hurry to leave Cambridge, but as the time comes
> near I find myself getting fairly eager to get home, and I hope
> Fayerweather will not be too thinly populated when I arrive,
> for meeting men at other universities doesn't lessen one's ap-
> preciation of those at Columbia a bit, I can tell you.

MARRIAGE AND ADVANCEMENT

The Tyndall year proved to be a turning point in his life
in more ways than one. On his way to Europe on the *Rheindam,*
he met, on almost the last day out, a young Wellesley graduate,
Miss Florence Bement of Philadelphia and Boston. Undoubtedly
regretting the opportunity he had missed of getting to know her
better on shipboard, he succeeded in coaxing from her aunt
the itinerary of their trip. When they arrived at Lucerne, Pegram
turned up there shortly thereafter, and the two young people
climbed the Rigi together. Later he put in an appearance in
Munich, where Miss Bement, her aunt, and a cousin were attending the performance of Wagner's Ring cycle. There they
went hiking in the Bavarian woods. In her recollections Mrs.
Pegram notes ruefully, "I should have recognized his propensity
for catching trains by the least possible margin, or even missing
them, which he did at the Munich depot, while we 'tooted'
off to Herrenchiemsee."

Despite this mischance, Pegram managed to keep in touch
with Miss Bement, and when the illness of her aunt made it
necessary to cut short their trip and sail for home, he sent her
a novel steamer letter consisting of a postcard for each day out.
From that auspicious beginning sprang up a correspondence
that lasted through the Tyndall year.

From the outset they were drawn together by a common
interest in art and music. Florence, the daughter of Frank
Bement and Grace Furbush, was born in "a huge house in

Philadelphia where there was one of the first of the privately owned art galleries in that city," a circumstance that undoubtedly contributed to her own interest in art. She attended private schools in the Philadelphia area and developed a fondness for such games as baseball, soccer, and relay events—games that she later passed on to her own sons.

Both her father and grandfather were in the business of machine tool manufacture. Her parents were divorced around 1900, and she notes with regret that the divorce separated her almost completely from the Bement side of the family. Her mother moved to Boston to live, and Florence entered Wellesley in September 1901. Carrying on a tradition of travel, she interrupted her studies at Wellesley in 1903-1904 for a year abroad.

It was during this trip, on which she was accompanied by her mother, that the two American ladies became acquainted in Rome with an English gentleman, William Cleverly Alexander, and two of his daughters. This was the beginning of a friendship during which Miss Bement and her mother were the guests of the Alexanders, in different years, both in their London home and in their country estate, Heathfield Park, near Tunbridge Wells. Mrs. Pegram recalls being met upon their arrival in London by a brougham, with coachman and footman, driven out to Kensington, and shown into a lovely Queen Anne house, next door to Holland House. Their hostess at afternoon tea was "Miss Alexander," now grown up, whose charm as a child had been captured by James McNeill Whistler in the portrait that hangs in the National Gallery, Millbank, London. Thus, when Miss Bement met Pegram in 1906, she was already a seasoned European traveler and able to share with him many of the things she had enjoyed earlier.

Pegram lost no time, after returning from the Tyndall year, in traveling to Boston to renew his friendship with Miss Bement, and in 1909 they became engaged. They were married on June 3,

1909, at her aunt's home in West Newton, Massachusetts. Eager to show his bride to family and colleagues in North Carolina, Pegram took her south on their honeymoon, and she recalls standing in line during the Commencement exercises at Trinity College! Later there was a trip through the mountains and visits to friends and relatives.

Returning to New York from their wedding trip, the young couple set up housekeeping in an apartment, loaned for the summer, at the corner of Morningside Drive and West 118th Street. During that summer, Florence Pegram met many of her husband's scientific colleagues at the small, old-fashioned house that was the Faculty Club.

The young physics instructor had an 18-foot sponson canoe, in which he used to sail and paddle with his friend Tufts, also of the Physics Department, around Manhattan Island. Mrs. Pegram relates that on moonlit nights she and her husband sometimes put comforters over the slats in the canoe, which was kept in the Columbia boathouse at 116th Street, and went for a moonlight ride up the Hudson. It was occasionally a struggle to pass the ferry at 125th Street, but after that they would cross the Hudson and paddle until sleepy. Then they would put a lantern in the bow and anchor just offshore. In the morning they would land at some beautiful estate by the river bank, where they would get water and prepare a breakfast of bread and butter, eggs, and coffee from provisions transported in a fireless cooker serving as an improvised refrigerator.

Mrs. Pegram recalls that another favorite jaunt of her husband's was over to Sheepshead Bay, where he liked to look at the early airplanes strung together of bamboo and wires and resembling Bleriot's. Her comment, "Only lack of money saved him then," implies that it was this one circumstance that prevented him from trying to fly one of the monsters.

Following two years in apartments near Columbia, the Pegrams moved to Fieldston (Riverdale-on-Hudson) and rented a house while they built their own large stone house. There they were both able to indulge their love of tennis. A colleague, commenting on Pegram's tall, well-built athletic figure, observes that he was good at tennis until well into his sixties, when he won a "cup," soldered together out of laboratory junk, for besting all other tennis players at a summer meeting of the American Physical Society. Mrs. Pegram recalls that for many years they followed the Davis Cup and other matches, first at West 238th Street, and later at Forest Hills. A fellow tennis enthusiast of the early days was Dr. H. H. Janeway, of Memorial Hospital, who frequently sought Pegram's help in developing early methods of radium therapy.

Settled in their new home in Fieldston, Mrs. Pegram began to entertain for her husband, inviting graduate students, visiting scientists, and others to tea. Later there were parties for the various departments housed in the new Physics Building. On other occasions, young married couples from the faculty were invited to dinner and then on to the Tennis Club for dancing afterwards.

A special interest of Pegram's in those days was the Riverdale Choral Society, under the direction of Howard Barlow. Barlow, who later became known to millions as conductor of the Columbia Broadcasting System orchestra, was studying at Columbia University in those days and worrying about "how to learn to be a conductor with nothing to conduct." Pegram had sung in the choir back at Trinity but had not kept up his singing when he moved to New York. It was not until the last years of his life that his wife realized how he had longed to sing and had even got around to taking lessons when it was too late.

In 1910 their first son, William, was born to the Pegrams, and six years later, the second son, John. In the meantime, Pegram was moving up the academic ladder rapidly, particularly for a period when academic advancement was not so frequent as it is in these competitive times. An assistant professor of physics in 1909, he was made an associate in 1912, and in 1918 full professor.

He was made acting dean of Columbia School of Mines, Engineering, and Chemistry in 1917, and dean in 1918, holding that post until 1930. The esteem in which he was held by his colleagues is evident in the letter that he received in March of 1917 from F. J. E. Woodbridge, who was then dean of the graduate faculties, on leave to the University of California at Berkeley. After expressing his pleasure in Pegram's appointment as acting dean, Woodbridge observed:

I should think everybody would have complete confidence in you. We need just such men in administrative positions, men who have the keenest appreciation of scientific scholarship and who are approachable and democratic. It would be a joy to work with you. You have seen, just as I have, that the success of Columbia does not depend on bringing in outsiders to help us out but on bringing about hearty cooperation among ourselves and a clear idea of what we ought to be doing. We have got to break down distrust and fault-finding and stimulate mutual confidence and enthusiasm. You are so clear-headed, so sane, so sincere—but I need not express compliments. Yet I want to express my happiness and my confidence. You will let me do that.

The details of Pegram's activities during World War I are interesting, not only intrinsically, but also because they forecast to some degree his great involvement in World War II, particularly in antisubmarine warfare devices. The use of scientists in World War I was on a much smaller scale than occurred during World War II; nevertheless, they were pressed into service in a variety of tasks. In a very brief curriculum vitae, drafted apparently many years later, Pegram noted that during World War I he was a "member of the Administrative Board, Student Army Training Corps, at Columbia University; dean, U.S. Army

Radio School, also at Columbia University; U.S. Army School of Photography; Ordnance Department, School of Explosives; director of research for Signal Corps, U.S. Army."

The armed forces were concerned, as always, with sight and photography under difficult conditions, principally in the dark. In the School of Photography research was carried on and instruction given in photography. Professor Pegram had a hand in acquiring workers for the research, was consulted on projected research, and received regular progress reports from the research people.

He played a very large part in the establishment of the Student Army Training Corps. Early in September 1918 the War Department called for mobilization of all the resources of the nation's universities and colleges. With so many members of the Columbia staff already engaged in urgent war work, further involvement seemed impossible. Under the leadership of President Nicholas Murray Butler, however, arrangements were made in a remarkably short time to house, educate, and drill officers for the United States Army. On October 1, 1918, the school was opened with 2,500 in the student body and 60 officers. The schedule of studies was prepared by Dean Hawkes (Columbia College) and Professor Pegram. A report on Columbia's war work states that the organization of the S.A.T.C. and this schedule of studies were adopted practically without change by the War Department for use in all the colleges of the country having S.A.T.C. units.

The work of the New York Committee of the National Research Council on submarine detection was carried on as might be expected without public notice. The committee had its origin in a group of New Yorkers who, anxious to serve the government in the matter of defense against enemy submarines, held several meetings to discuss how such assistance might be rendered. Dr. George E. Hale and Dr. Robert Millikan, chairman and vice chairman respectively of the NRC, and Commander Bridge of the British Navy attended one of the meetings at which it was arranged for the New York group to operate as a subcommittee of the NRC. The formal organization of the committee took place on May 25, 1917, with nine members, including President Butler, Professor Pegram, and Professor Michael I. Pupin. President Butler was elected chairman, and Professor Pegram executive secretary.

An interesting summary of many projected methods of coping with enemy submarines is contained in the records of the subcommittee. After the formation of the subcommittee further study of the more important of these types of detection or control was assigned to its various members. In the end, mainly because the Navy and other agencies had become engaged in many of the fields considered, the subcommittee decided to concentrate upon the topic assigned to Professor Pupin, namely, the use of sound waves for detecting and locating submarines. On May 30 and 31, Professors Pupin and Pegram attended an NRC conference of about forty physicists and engineers to hear reports on the state of the art of submarine detection by the British and French. As a result of this meeting, it seemed best for the New York subcommittee to undertake the problem of submarine detection by *echoes,* under the direction of Professor Pupin.

Experimental work was begun at once in the physics laboratories at Columbia with Professor A. P. Wills of the Physics Department added to the research group to work with Professor Pupin on designing apparatus for producing very high frequency sound waves. In a short time it was decided to confine the research to development of a quartz piezo-electric sound detector. Professor John H. Morecroft of the Columbia Department of Electrical Engineering joined the group to work on the circuits needed, and a little later Professor H. W. Farwell of the Physics Department took over the responsibility for search-ing out and acquiring suitable quartz.

The work was pursued with great vigor. Professor Pegram, of course, was acquainted with all the problems of the research and was constantly in the counsel of the workers. His functions were to provide working space and people to assist the work, to locate and purchase materials, to manage the finances, and to keep the records as secretary.

By early February 1918 the apparatus was tried out at Key West with sufficient success that further work at Columbia was pursued with the close cooperation of the Navy Experimental Station at New London. By September 1918 research results seemed sufficiently promising for the Naval Experimental Sta-tion to take over the work and to finance it. With this step mention of the work ceased in the Columbia papers.

Until the spring of 1918 the work had been financed by two members of the New York subcommittee, one a member of the three-man finance committee of the subcommittee who made cash contributions, the other a Columbia professor who, be-ginning in October 1917, turned back his salary to Columbia. In the spring of 1918 a manufacturer of machinery established a credit to cover the cost of apparatus if furnished by his com-pany to the committee. A most important equivalent source of funds was the research facilities of the Columbia Physics De-partment put without stint at the disposal of the submarine re-search. All the persons and amounts concerned in this financing appear in Professor Pegram's reports.

In 1917 and 1918 the subcommittee financed also a small research project to test the concealment of ships by clouds of fine spray sent out from high-pressure nozzles suitably distrib-uted over the vessel. This was suggested by H. P. Quick, an engineer not connected with Columbia. The Navy advanced several cogent objections to his scheme, but it was decided to go ahead with a test, which was performed in the summer of 1918. Professor Pegram's part here seems to have been the procurement of materials and the payment of bills. The test showed that this method of spray camouflage was not very promising and the project was abandoned.

Following the "flu" epidemic of 1918, the Pegrams' older son William kept having recurrences; so after consulting doctors and his school, Mrs. Pegram took the two boys to Europe. Hoping that the climate along the Riviera would be conducive to William's full recovery, she enrolled them in a boys' school at Théoule, across the bay from Cannes, where the two youngsters learned French very naturally from hearing it constantly spoken.

ADMINISTRATIVE RESPONSIBILITIES

Shortly after the death of Professor Hallock in 1913, Pegram had become executive officer of the Physics Department and served continuously until 1945, carrying the responsibilities of that post along with other heavy administrative duties. Despite his obvious talents for administration and the effectiveness with which he performed as dean, he had little taste for the duties of the deanship, however, and longed to devote full time to his work in physics, which he so much enjoyed. His correspondence indicates that from 1925 on he had sought to persuade President Butler to relieve him of the deanship; finally, in January of 1930, he was permitted to resign. In his letter of resignation as dean, he noted that his term of office had not only exceeded his own expectations but had lasted longer than that of any of his five predecessors except one.

"As you know," he wrote President Butler, "my professorship of physics, in a department that has large responsibilities, can well absorb all my effort. It is my hope that I may thus serve the University more, rather than less, effectively by now resigning the deanship."

President Butler not only wrote him a warm personal letter on that occasion, but five months later, on June 4, 1930, in a memorandum addressed to the members of the Faculty of Engineering, commented:

Absence from the University at the time of the last meeting of the Faculty of Engineering for the present academic year deprived me of the pleasure of recording formally at that time, in the presence of the Faculty, my appreciation of the work which has been done for us by Professor George B. Pegram during his thirteen years of service as Dean, and my admiration for his mind, his character, and his unselfish devotion to the University's highest interests. At a time of change and development, with many perplexing problems to face and with new adjustments of teaching and research work to be made, Professor Pegram has guided us with large intelligence, with an open mind, and with unceasing diligence. At his own request he lays aside administrative duties in order that he may concentrate his efforts for years to come upon his own special field of advanced teaching and research in the Department of Physics. He carried with him to that work our grateful thanks for his years of service to the Faculty of Engineering and our confident prediction that new success and new distinction await him.

Karl K. Darrow, who has so ably summarized Pegram's life and work in a Biographical Memoir for the American Philosophical Society, has the following comment on the six-year intermission between Pegram's resignation of the deanship of the Faculty of Engineering and his assumption of the duties as dean of the Graduate Faculties:

During that period Pegram went back to the laboratory and associated himself with several brilliant young students. The neutron had just been discovered, and to use a colloquialism, Pegram and his group were "in on the ground floor." Their experiments were the first to reveal some of the major properties of neutrons and their interactions with matter, and Columbia University became one of the world centers of neutron research, a rank which it has never lost though it has many rivals now. By no means did he put his name always first in the by-lines of the papers which originated from his work. Those who shared it with him remember him as a partner who normally came in very late in the evening, after more than a normal day's work in executive and other tasks, and continued sometimes into the small hours. After Pegram re-entered deanship [1936] there were no longer hours enough in the day and the night.[4]

INTEREST IN RADIOACTIVITY

Pegram maintained an interest in the field of radioactivity throughout his life, but efforts to reconstruct what led him into this field originally have been unsuccessful. Perhaps he was influenced to some extent by the intellectual interests of his father. In 1911 the elder Pegram's presidential address to the North Carolina Academy of Science was entitled "The Problem of the Constitution of Matter." In closing paragraphs of that address, Professor Pegram observed:

The spontaneous disintegration of matter in the field of radioactivity reveals the atom as a reservoir of energy. The measurements of Curie and Labord show that the disintegration of one gram of radium produces 300,000 times as much energy as is produced by combustion of one gram of coal. Thompson estimates that enough energy is stored within the atoms of one gram of hydrogen to raise a million tons through a hundred yards. This enormous supply of energy found within the atom has been used to account for the sun's heat, and to greatly modify our opinion as to the age of the earth. Probably the most important problem before the physicist today is that of making this enormous energy available in the world's work.[5]

Professor Lucy J. Hayner of the Department of Physics at Columbia, and a long-time colleague of Dean Pegram's, notes:

[4] *Year Book of the American Philosophical Society,* 1961, pp. 154-55.

[5] William Baskerville Hamilton, *Fifty Years of the South Atlantic Quarterly* (Durham, N.C.: Duke University Press, 1952), pp. 146-47.

During all his life from his days doing radioactive research at Columbia, Professor Pegram had a keen and active interest in the use of radium and other radioactive substances for medical purposes, principally, of course, in the treatment of cancer. He became acquainted with men who were prospecting for radioactive minerals—mainly in the west, in those who were refining the products, and, of course, was very closely associated with doctors who were trying to develop radiation treatment for their patients.

He was in constant touch with the staff of the Memorial Hospital—where there was one of the early large supplies of radium—and had an unofficial influence on their methods of treatment and research. He was a close associate of Dr. Francis Carter Wood, who was engaged in cancer research for many years at St. Luke's Hospital and who later headed the Crocker Institute for Cancer Research at Columbia where X-rays were being used in the treatment of cancer. I think that his interest in these topics never abated, but his activity was greatest in the very early years.

As far as I can discover there was the most intense interest among medical men in radioactive materials, but very little information as to scientific methods of measurement. Dean Pegram and several other members of the Columbia Physics Department carried on a brisk business in measuring the strengths of radioactive samples submitted by doctors who had purchased radium, and in testing all sorts of materials sent in to him from far and wide in the hope that they might prove radioactive. Mineral water of various types was one of the most common types of substances on which tests were desired. The whole subject of radioactivity and its biological effects was of course a great mystery to the general public which was inclined to be hopeful for a panacea for all sorts of ills. Professor Pegram established standards and methods of measurement. In this Professor Ernest Rutherford of McGill University was cordial and helpful.

On several occasions Professor Pegram received some prominence in the newspapers when he was able to find radium that had been mislaid or thrown away inadvertently. He enjoyed all this activity very much, since it had scientific meaning and at the same time involved people. This was the pattern of his interests, always.

Professor Farwell recalls one incident from the early period:

There must have been some solution containing a relatively small amount of radium (perhaps large for those days) which was accidentally spilled somewhere on the carpet in a large room. No one could find where it was until Pegram laid down photographic plates all around and soon located the exact area. I don't know what happened next, but I do know that it was big news, and not many years later I heard directly from one of the reporters who "covered the story" how fortunate he was to have the assignment, and what a gold mine it was for him.

Mrs. Pegram remembers that during the height of public interest in radium she was awakened at odd hours of the night by telephone calls from reporters and she felt she had to be "careful not to say the wrong thing."

In view of Pegram's prominence on the faculty and his deep personal interest in the phenomenon of radioactivity, it is not surprising that he should have been named to serve as Mme Curie's personal escort when she received the degree of Doctor of Science Honoris Causa at the Columbia Commencement, June 1, 1921. In Eve Curie's book about her mother, *Madame Curie*, Pegram is pictured walking beside her, his tall figure in academic gown towering above her tiny one.

Farwell's comment (in relation to the status of the Physics Department in the decade following the University's move uptown to 116th Street in 1897) that "Pegram continued his work in radioactivity, but to graduate students it did not seem to be a promising field," is an interesting footnote to history.

TALENTS AS AN ADMINISTRATOR

One thread running through Farwell's reminiscences is his strong admiration of Pegram's ability for planning and administration. On one occasion he suggested to Dr. Pegram, as executive officer of the department, that his budget request to the Trustees include provision for two instructors in addition to the usual number of teaching assistants. He recalls his own surprise when authorization was granted. Pegram's response was that the need was plain and that Farwell had been fully justified in his request. "However," he added, "don't imagine that the authorities are unaware of a common practice of asking for much more than is needed."

The conscientious and scrupulous care with which Pegram carried out his administrative duties is undoubtedly one of the traits that earned for him the lasting respect and confidence of President Butler at a time when faculties of science were still something of a novelty in the American university. Professor Hayner saw him as "the one who managed things, the one who fought for money—very tight in those early days—and the one who was truly interested in the frontiers of research."

Professor Farwell notes that, as an administrator, Pegram sometimes found himself in difficult situations in relation to older men on the staff who were resistant to change. In response to a query as to why he did not exercise the authority of his office and remove some of these reactionaries, Pegram replied, "As long as men with such violent opposition to change remain on the campus, I can know what they are doing."

In another situation the department was strongly in need of a top-ranking man in theoretical physics, at a time when a number of well-trained men seemed to be available. Some of his colleagues could not understand Pegram's hesitation in recruiting one of them. His response was that there were numerous directions in their activities, some of which naturally would ultimately be shown by experience to be quite unacceptable. "The trouble is," he said, "that some men have gotten so far out on a limb that they will find it difficult or impossible to get back to the main trunk."

When a new building (Pupin) was being considered for the Physics Department, he concerned himself intimately with its structural details. Long before there was definite assurance of such a building, in fact, Pegram had appointed a committee to lay out plans based on what the men of the department considered essential for the needs of a growing research group and an active teaching staff. His basic idea was for a structure with features borrowed from warehouse design, that is, regular framing throughout, no special internal features, rooms adjustable to whatever size was needed, because inside walls were not to be load-bearing walls.

The decision to have the largest lecture room occupy two floors, in order to have the seats arranged in ascending rows, shocked the architects, who pointed out that, in order to support the columns for the floors above the lecture room, an 8-foot plate girder would have to be placed squarely across the middle of the space in front of the demonstration table. Pegram's response was to draw a rough sketch for them to show that, by building a truss on each side of the corridor of the floor immediately above the lecture room, the necessary columns could be amply supported, and by suitable design of the trusses the available space on the next floor would not be seriously reduced. Years later, an architect for a midwestern university called at Columbia University to say that he had been directed to visit the Pupin Physics Laboratory, although he frankly could not see why he should study a building built in 1926 when so many more modern buildings were available as models. After he had studied Pupin he understood. He saw the two-floor lecture room that had been called an architectural impossibility by the original planners until Dean Pegram showed them how to do it. He departed with the comment that Pupin was better adapted for physics than most buildings he had seen.

If Pegram could be faulted at all as an administrator, it

was probably in his reluctance to delegate authority and in his tendency to absorb himself in details when the load might well have been shared by someone else. During one period of particular involvement, his friend Farwell was prompted to inquire whether he remembered the 18th chapter of Exodus. "He probably did," observed Farwell, "but it was part of his nature to deal directly with his problems."

The lasting impact of the Tyndall year is evident in the care that he took to expose his students at Columbia to as many as possible of the great minds to which he himself had been exposed in his year in Germany and England. Although Einstein had been unable to accept the invitation tendered by the young associate professor, those who did arrive over the years included such great names as Lorentz, Larmor, Planck, and Born.

Pegram retained his own interest in Einstein and his theory through the years. Mrs. Pegram recalls that once in the early days of their marriage, when he was to lecture about the Einstein theory at the New York Museum of Natural History, he awoke her at midnight, read his paper to her, and asked if it meant anything to her. When she replied that she had noted two or three ideas, he appeared satisfied, saying, "That is all I can expect from the public."

THE YEARS OF WORLD WAR II

The period during which he was free of the burdens of the deanship was short lived. In 1936, shortly before the June commencement, Howard Lee McBain, dean of the Graduate Faculties, died very suddenly. This unexpected loss at a crucial time in the academic year created a near panic among the staff. It was obvious that something would have to be done immediately and equally apparent that Pegram was the only man who could step into the job and assume its burdens. It was in this manner, then, that he took over administration of Columbia's great and influential graduate school on the eve of World War II.

If it is true, as Pasteur is quoted as saying, that "Fortune favors the prepared mind," there is every reason why the science faculties of Columbia, under Pegram's leadership, should have been off to a head start in the application of science to the defense of the nation. In 1929 he had brought into the Physics Department as assistant a young graduate student from Nebraska Wesleyan University, John R. Dunning. Dunning was interested in the application of electronics to nuclear physics. He built the linear amplifier, so that Columbia was ready when Chadwick discovered the neutron in 1932.

When Pegram had learned, in the late thirties, of Enrico Fermi's desire to bring his family to the United States in order to remove them from the political climate of wartime Italy, he invited Fermi to join the staff at Columbia. The significance of this move is graphically described by Samuel K. Allison in his Biographical Memoir of Fermi:

Two weeks after Fermi's arrival at Columbia University in January, 1939, Professor Niels Bohr landed from Copenhagen, bringing the news of the discovery of the fission of uranium under neutron bombardment. If it could be demonstrated that, in turn, neutrons were a fission product, the possibility for release of energy in macroscopic amounts was open. Many physicists at once attempted to detect neutrons from fission, and Fermi, with the group forming around him at Columbia, soon demonstrated their presence, which was also announced, practically simultaneously, from many other laboratories.

Fermi's new group, at first consisting of Herbert L. Anderson, Leo Szilard, and Walter H. Zinn, soon demonstrated, with the help of a trace of separated U^{235}, prepared by A. O. Nier of the University of Minnesota, that as Bohr had predicted, the rare isotope U^{235} was the thermally fissionable isotope of natural uranium.[6]

[6] National Academy of Sciences, *Biographical Memoirs*, XXX (New York: Columbia University Press, 1957), 130-31.

It was the success of their early experiments that had prompted Dean Pegram's letter to Admiral Hooper, a copy of which Mrs. Fermi found among the family papers more than ten years after it was written. Mrs. Fermi comments:

Professor Pegram's attitude was due to his cautious judgment that warned him against jumping to premature conclusions. His skepticism about the outcome of the work in his own laboratories was shared by many other scientists and was probably caused by a hope that nuclear weapons should prove unfeasible. And Enrico himself, when talking to Admiral Hooper, doubted the relevance of his predictions.[7]

The device used by the Columbia group consisted of a lattice structure or "pile" described by Smyth as follows:

About July 1941 the first lattice structure of graphite and uranium was set up at Columbia. It was a graphite cube about 8 feet on an edge, and contained about 7 tons of uranium oxide in iron containers distributed at equal intervals throughout the graphite.[8]

In a speech at the University in January 1954, Fermi recalled some of the problems associated with the construction of the pile:

This graphite "pile" was expanded, he disclosed, until it grew too large for space it occupied in Columbia's Pupin Physics Laboratories. "We went to Dean Pegram," said Dr. Fermi, "who was then the man who could carry out magic around the University, and we explained to him that we needed a big room. He scouted around the campus and we went with him to dark corridors and under various heating pipes and so on, to visit possible sites for this experiment and eventually a big room was discovered in Schermerhorn Hall." By July 1941, he said, this pile had grown to eight feet square by eight feet high and weighed about seven tons. The physicists handling the graphite material, a black substance, "started looking like coal miners and the wives to whom

---

[7] Fermi, *Atoms in the Family*, pp. 164-65.

[8] Henry D. Smyth, *Atomic Energy for Military Purposes* (Princeton: Princeton University Press, 1946), pp. 59-60.

these physicists came back tired at night were wondering what was happening," Dr. Fermi revealed. He added that to handle the heavy graphite bricks made "people very black and required strong people" to accomplish the task. He said that Dr. Pegram suggested that the scientists use a dozen husky members of the Columbia football squad to work on the graphite. "It was a marvelous idea," Dr. Fermi continued, "and it was really a pleasure for once to direct the work of these husky boys, canning uranium —just shoving it in—handling packs of 50 or 100 pounds with the same ease as another person would have handled three or four pounds."[9]

Pegram's connection with the atomic project was twofold in nature. First, as the person at Columbia University who had assembled and coordinated the team of physicists performing those early crucial experiments in nuclear fission, he had operating responsibility for Columbia's role as a major center of atomic research. As has been noted, he was the very first person to make contact, through his letter to Admiral Hooper, with the United States government on the possibilities of atomic power. Secondly, Pegram was an active participating member in the series of advisory groups that were established beginning in 1939 and the early 1940s and that continued until the project was a going operation and was turned over to the Manhattan District of the Army Corps of Engineers.

The administrative history of the atomic project is admirably set forth in the Smyth report. Pegram's role may be summarized somewhat as follows: In the spring of 1939, following the announcement of the hypothesis of fission, a small group of foreign-born scientists in the United States undertook to impose voluntary self-censorship of papers in the field, for fear the idea might be exploited for military purposes. According to Smyth, American-born scientists were so unaccustomed to the idea of their science being used for such purposes that they hardly

9 Columbia University Files.

realized what needed to be done. But the idea gained momentum, and in the spring of 1940 the Division of Physical Sciences of the National Research Council took action that led to the appointment of the "Reference Committee" to control publication policy in *all* fields of potential military interest. The chairman of the committee was L. P. Eisenhart, and Pegram was a member both of the main committee and of the subcommittee on uranium fission. Editors of journals submitted prospective manuscripts to the committee, which advised them as to whether or not publication of the paper in question was in the national interest. Smyth found that this voluntary nongovernmental arrangement worked very well; it continued throughout the war, obviously with modification in the light of government security regulations.

The first *official* advisory body was the Advisory Committee on Uranium, appointed by President Roosevelt in July 1939. The only members of this group were L. J. Briggs, director of the National Bureau of Standards; Colonel K. F. Adamson, of Army Ordnance; and Commander G. C. Hoover, of the Navy Bureau of Ordnance. A number of scientists, including Dean Pegram, met with the Advisory Committee on Uranium from time to time. A special advisory group, called together by Briggs at the National Bureau of Standards on June 15, 1940, recommended to the Uranium Committee

"that funds should be sought to support research on the uranium-carbon experiment along two lines:
"(A) further measurements of the nuclear constants involved in the proposed type of reaction;
"(B) experiments with amounts of uranium and carbon equal to about one fifth to one quarter of the amount that could be estimated as the minimum in which a chain reaction would sustain itself.
"It was estimated that about $40,000 would be necessary for further measurements of the fundamental constants and that ap-

proximately $100,000 worth of metallic uranium and pure graphite would be needed for the intermediate experiment." (Quotations from memorandum of Pegram to Briggs, dated August 14, 1940)[10]

The next major organizational step was the establishment of the National Defense Research Committee in June 1940 and an order from the President placing the Uranium Committee under Vannevar Bush as chairman of the NDRC. When the committee was reconstituted by Bush, Dean Pegram was among the scientists who were added to its membership. The very first contract recommended by this group went to Columbia University for work along the lines recommended in the Pegram memorandum cited above.

In the summer of 1941, the NDRC itself was absorbed into a new and larger governmental organization for wartime research, the Office of Scientific Research and Development, with Vannevar Bush as director. The Advisory Committee on Uranium now became the Uranium Section (Section S-1 of the NDRC) and Pegram became vice chairman of the committee as a whole and chairman of the subsection on power production.

Meanwhile, cautious and unofficial interchange of information on atomic developments had been going on between the Americans and the British, and the first official British report of July 15, 1941, was transmitted to James B. Conant as chairman of NDRC on October 3, 1941. On the strength of the earlier reports, Pegram and Harold Urey were sent to England in the fall of 1941 to get firsthand information on what the British were doing. Smyth notes that this was the first time that any Americans had been to England specifically in connection with the uranium problem. Their report, strengthened by a series of reports by a special committee of the National Academy of Sciences appointed to review the uranium problem, rein-

[10] Smyth, *Atomic Energy,* pp. 48-49.

forced Bush's determination to pursue the uranium work even more vigorously.

MISSION TO ENGLAND

It might be noted parenthetically that, at the time he undertook this special mission to England, Pegram was sixty-five years old, the age conventionally associated with retirement, or at the very least, a slacking off of activity. Yet his important and vigorous leadership of Columbia's wartime research program lay still largely before him.

The decision to launch an all-out effort in the atomic field, accompanied by further reorganization of the S-1 group, was announced by Conant at an S-1 Section meeting on December 6, 1941, the day before Pearl Harbor. Pegram was again made vice chairman of the reconstituted group and served in that capacity until May 1942, when Bush terminated the S-1 Section and replaced it with an executive committee. This action preceded by only a few months the establishment by the Army of the Manhattan District to take over and administer the engineering aspects of the atomic project. A year later, in May 1943, all the OSRD S-1 contracts were formally transferred to the Manhattan District.

Dean Pegram's wartime activities at Columbia were by no means limited to the atomic project. Throughout the war he headed Columbia's Committee on War Research, which directed a variety of projects, of which those connected with undersea warfare were second in importance only to the atomic project. The contract with the United States Navy Underwater Sound Laboratory at New London, Connecticut, was the largest of Columbia's contracts not concerned with atomic energy. In 1941 a group of scientists, organized by Columbia, began its part of the secret project that led to the invention and development of the magnetic airborne detector (MAD), which played a tremendous role in clearing the Atlantic of Nazi submarines. The Airborne Instruments Laboratory, established by Columbia at Mineola, Long Island, was a focal point for much of the work on MAD.

When the war ended and Columbia contracts with the government were no longer limited to military problems, Dean Pegram was made chairman of Columbia University's Committee on Government-Aided Research, serving in that capacity from 1945 to 1950 and again in 1951 through 1956. He served from 1949 to 1950 as vice president of the University, becoming vice president emeritus and special adviser to the President in 1950.

SERVICE TO SCIENCE

In much that has been written and said of him, Pegram is described as "the physicists' physicist,"[11] a description that undoubtedly stems not only from his activities as teacher, mentor, and advocate, but also from his tireless services to the cause of organized physics. It is clear from the record that, despite his arduous labors at Columbia, he devoted much of what should have been his free time to the American Physical Society and later to the American Institute of Physics.

With respect to the Physical Society, Darrow has the following comment:

He never quite got over his regret at having missed, through some absurd mischance or quite uncharacteristic negligence, the convening of some forty-five (the exact number is unknown) American physicists from which sprang the American Physical Society. This occurred in a small room of Fayerweather Hall of Columbia University in May of 1899. Pegram did attend the first of the meetings of the new Society in October of that year, and

11 In his informal recollections, *At Ease* (New York: Doubleday, 1967, p. 346) Dwight Eisenhower notes, "George Pegram, a scientists' scientist, occupied an office immediately above mine and was always ready to drop in to chat about anything from common fractions to nuclear fission and fusion."

fifty-six years later he was still attending them. He was Treasurer of the Society for thirty-nine years (1918-1957), the longest term of service ever given to the Society by any individual. On the other hand his term as President of the Society was the shortest on record, and this was for a reason that was characteristic of him. In the middle of what should have been Pegram's year of presidency, the Vice-President who in the normal course of events should have succeeded him announced that he would not accept the nomination for the year to come, because of serious illness in his family. Pegram instantly resigned the presidency, and the Vice-President was forthwith appointed to that rank to fill out the year, so that his name follows that of Pegram in the roster of the Presidents. Pegram always said that he had resigned because he was so busy, but we all knew the truth.

It would be impossible to overstate the influence of George Pegram on the evolution of the American Physical Society. Already in the middle thirties when I first sat upon its Council, he was the elder statesman whose opinion was always sought, who was a reservoir of knowledge on the history and practices of the Society, and whose judgment was always held in great respect.[12]

John Van Vleck recalls that once during the early fifties, when scientists were frequently traveling between New York and Boston on the New Haven's night sleeper, the Owl, Pegram missed the Owl on a trip to Boston. In order not to be late for the meeting of the Physical Society the next morning, he caught the next train (all coaches) and sat up all night. When one recalls that he was in his seventies at that time, the depth of his devotion to the Physical Society becomes apparent.

Together with the late Karl T. Compton, then president of M.I.T., Pegram played a leading role in the development of the American Institute of Physics in the thirties. Henry A. Barton, first director of the Institute (now retired), who was closely associated with the two men, has related to the author of this

[12] Karl K. Darrow, *Year Book of the American Philosophical Society*, 1961, p. 157.

memoir the circumstances under which the concept of the AIP developed.

A number of independent societies had been or were about to be formed, specializing in certain subfields or aspects—the teaching of physics, for example—so that the organizational unity of the profession, theretofore provided by the American Physical Society, was in danger of being lost. It became obvious that some sort of all-inclusive federation was needed to unite the strength of all these groups for the aim that they had in common, namely, the advancement of physics.

The *Physical Review* was alarmingly short of funds for the publication of the results of all good research, and the situation in the post-depression years offered no hope of improvement short of drastic measures. Money for physics could come from the economy only if industry, government, and the public could be made aware of the importance of the subject; and physics at that time was generally regarded as a rather academic field of endeavor. Therefore some different mechanism was needed to assure continuing financial support for the journal.

Compton and Pegram presented the proposed American Institute of Physics to the five original societies: the American Physical Society, the Optical Society of America, the Acoustical Society of America, the Society of Rheology, and the fledgling American Association of Physics Teachers. From the Chemical Foundation they had received a promise to underwrite the initial expense of the new Institute, and Dr. Barton opened his office as director on October 1, 1931, in a room provided by that Foundation. The AIP had formally existed since May 3, 1931, as a joint board of representatives of the founder societies.

At first, the AIP had legal status as a "voluntary association," but a few months or so later it sought status as a membership corporation under the statutes of the State of New York. Dr. Barton recalls:

I will not forget a memorable hour in which Pegram *dictated* to me without notes a "Constitution and By-Laws" which with few changes was subsequently adopted by the Governing Board and by the Councils of the Societies. This was done slowly so I could get it down longhand and with pauses for comment and discussion to which I had little to contribute. It was a kind of master-student session! He was able to perform this remarkable feat because he had a lawyer's ability to read and grasp the legal language of the pertinent statutes and he had an intimate knowledge of the constitutions of various other organizations. That of the Engineering Foundation was the model most nearly appropriate to our purpose. Years later the AIP Constitution was used liberally as a model for federations of societies in other major scientific areas. A far-reaching precedent was thus established.

Pegram was one of the six signers of the Articles of Incorporation, adopted May 20, 1932; and from the actual founding of the Institute in May 1931 until 1955 he served in a series of offices including the key posts of secretary and later that of treasurer. Dr. Barton observes:

Of the several original protagonists of the AIP, Pegram was the one who, first as secretary and later also as treasurer, contributed the most time and thought to its operation and policies. His levelheadedness was essential in compromising the sometimes divergent views which inevitably arise in a federation of autonomous groups.

I think I must have phoned, written, or visited him at least a thousand times. I remember not one instance of impatience nor ever a difficulty of access except under conditions obviously beyond his control. It gave me a great feeling of confidence when he supported my course of action and when, on the other hand, he talked me out of proposals, he did it without any discouraging effect. In those years I sometimes thought his approach to things was conservative but certainly he had no lack of independent enterprise in the face of unprecedented situations.

We all learned much from him. I recall an APS Council meeting when a particularly puzzling problem was under discussion. Finally, Professor G. W. Stewart of the University of Iowa said, "Pegram, you know everything. What shall we do?" There and elsewhere it often came to that.

For his long-time service he was twice honored by the AIP— in 1956 by special resolution, and in 1957, as hereinafter noted, by the award of the first Karl Taylor Compton Medal.

ORGANIZATIONAL ACTIVITIES

In addition to his work with the American Physical Society and the American Institute of Physics, Pegram was a member of many other organizations—in a number of instances over long periods of time—including the Academy of Political Sciences; Acoustical Society of America; American Association for the Advancement of Science (Fellow; Vice President, 1938); American Association for Physics Teachers; American Institute of Radio Engineers; American Philosophical Society; American Society of Mechanical Engineers; Association of University Professors (President, 1930); Federation of American Scientists; Institute of Aeronautical Sciences; National Education Association; New York Academy of Sciences (Recording Secretary and Vice President, 1948-1950; President, 1952); Sigma Xi (Treasurer from 1917 to 1949; President, 1925). He was a member of the Board of Trustees of both Associated Universities, Inc., and the Oak Ridge Institute of Nuclear Studies. He was chairman of the Anglo-American-Hellenic Bureau of Education.

There is nothing in the recollections of friends and associates or in the written record to suggest that George Pegram had more than an ordinary interest in politics, but—as illustrated by several incidents in his life—on issues that mattered to him he was there to be counted.

IDENTIFICATION WITH CAUSES

Both Pegrams, father and son, were closely identified with a celebrated case involving academic freedom at Trinity College shortly after the turn of the century—the elder Pegram as senior member of the faculty, and George as a promising young alumnus engaged in graduate work at Columbia University. The issue involved the *South Atlantic Quarterly,* a new and broadly liberal journal set to grapple with the multitudinous social and economic problems that beset the South. As recounted by William Baskerville Hamilton, "The young men of Trinity College who launched the *South Atlantic Quarterly* represented almost the first generation of postgraduate scholars trained in the United States. . . . Everything was possible to them. They were filled with the anticipatory excitement of Poggio about to enter some great unexplored monastic library or of a physicist opening his laboratory in the middle of the twentieth century."[13]

The moving spirit and first editor of the *Quarterly* was John Spencer Bassett, an alumnus of Trinity College and The Johns Hopkins University, who leaped into print with provocative editorials that quickly brought a storm down on his head. An editorial article entitled "Stirring Up the Fires of Race Antipathy" in the issue of October 1903 precipitated a controversy that threatened the College itself, and Bassett offered to resign in order to protect Trinity. Both alumni and faculty quickly rallied to his support and challenged the Board of Trustees to defend his rights and those of the College. In a memorial from the faculty presented to the Board of Trustees, December 1, 1903, the faculty made it clear that they neither supported nor endorsed Bassett's views but that a far greater principle was at stake. Their statement declared in part:

If American colleges are to be the home of seekers after truth, their atmosphere must be favorable to the free expression of opinion. It is the duty of a college professor, as of every other citizen, to consider well all his opinions and the form of their expression. If he err, he is subject to criticism, to rebuke, to

[13] Hamilton, *Fifty Years of the South Atlantic Quarterly,* p. 31.

refutation, equally with all others. The principle of academic freedom, as we understand it, merely requires that while the public hold him to his duty as it holds other men, it shall not invade his rights, which are not less than other men's.[14]

William Howell Pegram led the list of signatories, which included every member of the faculty except one who happened to be out of town; the faculty members had already decided among themselves to resign in a body if the Board rejected their position. George was one of a group of alumni, including Walter Hines Page, later United States Ambassador to Great Britain, and Bruce R. Payne, later President of Peabody, that urged the Board of Trustees to stand firm.

The Board debated the issue through the night of December 1 and into the early hours of the following day. Finally, between two and three o'clock in the morning of December 3, the college bell rang out summoning the students to a victory celebration.

Following World War II and the demonstration by the United States of the power of the atomic bomb as an ultimate weapon, the technical problems that had preoccupied the nation's physicists for so long gave way to moral questions of overriding concern. One of the phenomena of the immediate postwar period was the tremendous political activity on the part of the scientific community to ensure civilian control of atomic energy and the bomb. The movement was spearheaded by the Federation of Atomic Scientists—groups of scientists who had worked on the Manhattan Project in various parts of the country and who had organized themselves into political units to lobby for wise legislation in the field of atomic energy. When victory had been secured in this country, they turned their attention to the problem of international controls.

Alice Kimball Smith, wife of Cyril Smith, director of metal-

14 *Ibid.*, p. 65.

lurgy at Los Alamos, and herself assistant editor of the *Bulletin of the Atomic Scientists* from 1946 to 1948, has fully documented these efforts in her book, *A Peril and a Hope*.

Pegram was a member of the Federation, and although he was not active in the movement, Mrs. Smith points out that when the struggle moved into the international area and the question of banning the bomb was seriously raised, "it was not by the younger element in the federation but by senior faculty members at Columbia University, representing science, law, history, sociology, and economics, who recommended that the President declare a bomb holiday so that discussion in the newly established UNAEC might proceed in 'an atmosphere of full good faith and of confidence in their successful outcome for international peace.' Of the five scientists who framed this proposal in a letter to the New York *Times*—Selig Hecht, Edgar Miller, George B. Pegram, I. I. Rabi, and Jan Schilt—only Hecht was an active supporter of the FAS."[15]

RECOGNITION AND HONORS

George B. Pegram's work, his selfless leadership, his qualities of mind and spirit were well appreciated in his lifetime. He was the recipient of many honors. On one such occasion he was the New York *Times* "Man of the News" and was described in its headlines as "Much Honored Physicist." He was honored by both a king and a prince—King Paul of Greece and Prince Philip, Duke of Edinburgh.

From King Paul he received the Gold Cross of the Commander, Royal Greek Order of the Phoenix, for his work on behalf of the Anglo-American-Hellenic Bureau of Education. This is an organization with headquarters in New York, whose purpose is to enable Greek students of ability and character

---

[15] Alice Kimball Smith, *A Peril and a Hope: The Scientists' Movement in America, 1945-47* (Chicago and London: University of Chicago Press, 1965), p. 448.

to be educated in American colleges and universities and to return to Greece to pursue their careers. More than 200 American colleges and universities and a number of preparatory schools and hospitals participate in this effort. Dean Pegram was associated with it soon after its inception in 1941 and served as Chairman of the Board from 1944 to 1954, when he stepped down from the active chairmanship and assumed honorary status because of failing health.

At a special convocation of the Permanent Greek Delegation to the United Nations on October 26, 1956, His Excellency, Christian X. Palamas, Greek Ambassador to the UN, bestowed the Gold Cross on Dean Pegram in the name of the King.

The following year, Prince Philip, who was in New York at the time, conferred upon him the first Karl Taylor Compton Gold Medal for Distinguished Service in the Advancement of Physics, awarded by the American Institute of Physics. On that occasion, too, he received a congratulatory message from President Eisenhower, which read in part:

As the first recipient of the Karl Taylor Compton Gold Medal, Dr. Pegram personifies the highest standards of scholarship, character and service. His distinguished career has brought strength to your society and his confident plans will forever be an inspiration to those who use this new building. Moreover, I have a personal gratification because of the deep friendship I have felt toward Dr. Pegram ever since I first met him at Columbia.[16]

It is quite possible, however, that even more than these formal words of the President, he cherished the comments of General Eisenhower when in 1948, as president-designate of Columbia, he addressed the annual commencement luncheon of the Columbia Alumni Federation. Dean Pegram was the guest of honor, and General Eisenhower, speaking on that occasion, remarked "that no freshman ever had been more in terror than

16 New York *Times,* Oct. 22, 1957.

he was as a 'freshman college president' and that no freshman ever had been more grateful for a 'friendly face than he had been for Dean Pegram's kindness to him in his first days at Columbia.' "[17]

The National Academy of Sciences elected Pegram to membership at its annual meeting in the spring of 1949. When his friend Jesse Beams, professor of physics at the University of Virginia, wrote to welcome him to the Section of Physics of the Academy, Pegram responded with typical modesty:

10 May 1949

Dear Beams:

Your kind note of May 4 is very much appreciated, both because it comes from you as a friend and from you as Chairman of the Physics Section of the National Academy of Sciences. Since so large a part of my active life has been spent in University administration and only a smaller part in direct scientific accomplishment, I really had never entertained any aspirations to membership in the National Academy. Election to it is probably all the more gratifying because it was so unexpected.

In 1953 he was honored with a special citation by the Consular Law Society, an organization whose objective in its own words is "to promote a knowledge of international law and diplomacy, thereby contributing to international understanding." The citation read:

First, as Dean of Columbia's School of Mines, Engineering, and Chemistry; then, as Dean of the Graduate Faculties; and later, as Vice-President of the University, he has striven to strengthen the University as a national and international force for the promotion of intellectual emancipation and cooperation. Through numerous societies, including the American Physical Society and the New York Academy of Sciences (whose hospitality we accept today), he has exerted a constructive influence wherever men of science collaborate in search of truth.[18]

[17] News Office, Columbia University, November 1955.
[18] 10th Anniversary Report, 1943-1953.

Pegram was one of five incorporating trustees of Associated Universities, Inc., the consortium of nine eastern universities that operates the Brookhaven National Laboratory on behalf of the U.S. Atomic Energy Commission. His role in the establishment of AUI, and the subsequent creation of Brookhaven, have been described by Norman F. Ramsey,[19] who himself was one of the prime movers in this project.

Ramsey relates how in the fall of 1945 he and I. I. Rabi discussed ways and means of making a nuclear reactor available to Columbia. They were also concerned with similar problems pertaining to high-energy accelerators. When it became clear that this objective could not be achieved within the resources of the Physics Department, they discussed with members of the department and Dean Pegram the possibility of interesting other educational institutions in the New York area in cooperating in the construction of such a facility. Dean Pegram called a meeting of twenty-one major research institutions, which was held on January 16, 1946.

As a result of this meeting a committee, headed by Dean Pegram, was instructed to prepare a proposal for transmittal to General Leslie R. Groves, head of the Manhattan District Corps of Engineers. The proposal stressed the need for a regional laboratory in the nuclear sciences in the New York area. The Manhattan District was definitely interested, but since a Massachusetts group with similar interests was also making a bid for a regional laboratory at that time, the two groups were told by the Manhattan District that they would have to cooperate in order to achieve a single facility.

The two groups, in a series of discussions, managed to achieve a remarkable degree of unanimity, and out of these discussions and negotiations nine universities—Columbia, Cornell, Har-

[19] "Early History of Associated Universities and Brookhaven National Laboratory," Brookhaven Lecture Series No. 55, March 31, 1966. BNL 992 (TO421).

vard, Johns Hopkins, Massachusetts Institute of Technology, University of Pennsylvania, Princeton, University of Rochester, and Yale—came together to form the consortium that ultimately became AUI. Pegram served as a member of the Board of Trustees from July 1946 to October 1956, and was briefly Chairman of the Board in 1951.

At the time of his death, the Board of Trustees adopted a Memorial Resolution setting forth his intimate relationship with the organization and administration of AUI. It reads in part:

To the governing body of Associated Universities, Inc., Dr. Pegram brought not only his broad experience as a scientist, a teacher, and a university administrator, but also unfailing common sense in the consideration of the wide variety of problems on which the Board of Trustees acts, or, more often, gives advice. All who were associated with him will vividly recall the clear reasoning and succinct expression of his opinions and recommendations, whether given formally, sometimes in the report of an ad hoc committee, or informally in the course of general discussion. . . .

In the words of Dr. Leland J. Haworth, Director of Brookhaven National Laboratory, "he will always remain the inspiring leader and devoted friend who more than any other individual brought to fruition the original organizing activities and who in the succeeding years has unceasingly and unstintingly contributed his wisdom and his counsel to our affairs."

Just prior to his death in August 1958, the Board of Trustees initiated in his honor the annual George B. Pegram Lectureship at Brookhaven National Laboratory. The lectureship is supported by the corporation through an annual appropriation and is expected to be continued indefinitely. Among the distinguished lecturers who have participated in the series are Lee Alvin DuBridge, René J. Dubos, Barbara Ward, and Louis S. B. Leakey.

Seven universities conferred honorary degrees upon him, including Columbia University, which awarded him the degree of Doctor of Science in 1929 on the occasion of the 175th anniversary of the issuance of the original charter of King's College. The extent to which he was moved by this particular honor is evident in the handwritten draft of his reply to President Butler, obviously worked and reworked with great care and emotion and scratched through many times. Finally, with characteristic dignity and simplicity, he appears to have satisfied himself with the following:

Your letter of June 4 advising me that the Trustees have placed my name on the list of faculty members upon whom the degree of Doctor *honoris causa* is to be conferred on October 31, next, has so overwhelmed me that I have not yet discovered how to make appropriate reply. Simply to say as I really feel that my efforts are not deserving of such high honor, would not compliment those who have the responsibility for doing this. My feeling is one of grateful wonder at the most kindly and generous judgment of yourself, of my other colleagues, and of the Trustees who placed my name on the list of those to be honored at the celebration of the 175th anniversary of the chartering of the University. I think no one could receive this honor with more sense of modesty of feeling than mine.

With deepest appreciation and with cordial regard, I remain

RETIREMENT AND DEATH

In 1950 Pegram retired as professor of physics and as vice president of the University. (He had resigned as executive secretary of the Physics Department in 1945.) He then became vice president emeritus and special adviser to the president of the University. In the meantime he had been continuously associated since 1939 with Columbia's research on behalf of the war effort, serving as chairman of the Columbia Committee on War Research from its inception. After the war, the Committee was renamed (1946) the Committee on Government-Aided Research. Pegram remained chairman until June 1950, and after a brief hiatus of a year resumed the chairmanship in 1951 and continued until June 1956.

Earlier, when he had begun to face the fact of impending retirement, he had cast about for some means of escaping the heavy burden of New York state taxes. A close friend of Pegram's and a trustee of Columbia, Marcellus Hartley Dodge, who was living in Madison, New Jersey, suggested that the Pegrams look around for a place there. They found a small house that pleased them, and since the location seemed to offer a number of advantages for retirement, they purchased it in 1950 intending to live there temporarily. In the meantime, however, Pegram had committed himself to continue on as chairman of the Committee on Government-Aided Research, without remembering to tell Mrs. Pegram until after arrangements for the New Jersey home had been consummated.

By then it was too late to reverse the contemplated move; and since it was out of the question for Pegram to commute daily between Madison and Columbia, he arranged for accommodations at Butler Hall, an apartment-hotel, traveling to Madison on weekends. His health, which was failing, deteriorated steadily through the early 1950s. Early in 1958, he developed a mild case of pneumonia and was hospitalized in St. Luke's Hospital until January 26, 1958, when his elder son William took him out of the hospital and back home with him to Swarthmore. In the meantime, Mrs. Pegram rented an apartment in Swarthmore so that her husband could be near William and his family and also to gratify his own desire to be near the Franklin Institute in Philadelphia. The younger Pegrams found nurses for him, and his last days were spent in the apartment that in effect constituted his own little private sanitarium. He died August 12, 1958. His body was cremated and his ashes were taken back to his native North Carolina for burial.

ACKNOWLEDGMENTS

The biographical memoir of George B. Pegram represents the combined contributions of a number of his colleagues and long-time friends. Lucy J. Hayner, Professor Emeritus of Physics and Special Lecturer in Physics, Columbia University, researched Dean Pegram's voluminous files, selecting the correspondence that is so basic to the memoir, and in addition made valuable contributions to the text. Hermon Farwell, Professor Emeritus of Physics, Columbia University, who had known Dean Pegram from the beginning of his career at Columbia, was most gracious in setting down the reminiscences of a lifelong friendship.

Helpful leads to the background of the Pegram family in Durham, North Carolina, and its associations with Trinity College and Duke University were furnished by Paul Gross, William Howell Pegram Professor Emeritus of Chemistry, Duke University.

Henry Barton, retired president, American Institute of Physics, was kind enough to supply perceptive insights regarding Dean Pegram as a "physicists' physicist" and particularly of his association with the beginnings of the Institute.

Among those who read the manuscript and contributed helpful comments were John Van Vleck, Professor of Physics, Harvard University; Norman F. Ramsey, Professor of Physics, Harvard University; Joseph C. Boyce and the late Alan T. Waterman of the Academy staff.

The willingness of Mrs. George B. Pegram* to recall the circumstances of her meeting with her future husband, her marriage, and her life with him has helped to round out the memoir of Dean Pegram as husband and father, as well as scientist and administrator.

---

* Deceased June 21, 1969.

BIBLIOGRAPHY

KEY TO ABBREVIATIONS

Atti Accad. Naz. Lincei Rend. Classe Sci. Fis. Mat. Natr. = Atti della Accademia Nazionale dei Lincei, Rendiconti, Classe di Scienze Fisiche, Matematiche e Naturali

Phys. Rev. = Physical Review

1901

Radio-active minerals. Science, 13:274.

Radioactive substances and their radiations. Science, 14:53-59.

1903

Secondary radioactivity in the electrolysis of thorium solutions. Phys. Rev., 17:424-40.

1904

With H. W. Webb. Energy liberated by thorium. Science, 19:826.

Detection and measurement of radioactivity. Archives of Electrology and Radiology, 4:313.

1908

With H. W. Webb. Heat developed in a mass of thorium oxide due to its radioactivity. Phys. Rev., 26:410. (A)

With H. W. Webb. Heat developed in a mass of thorium oxide due to its radioactivity. Phys. Rev., 27:18-26.

1917

Unipolar induction and electron theory. Phys. Rev., 10:591-600.

1931

Physics. In: *A Quarter Century of Learning, 1904-1929,* pp. 290-318. New York, Columbia University Press.

1933

With J. R. Dunning. Scattering and absorption of neutrons. Phys. Rev., 43:497-98. (L)

With J. R. Dunning. Absorption and scattering of neutrons. Phys. Rev., 43:775. (A)

With J. R. Dunning. On neutrons from a beryllium-radon source. Phys. Rev., 44:317. (A)

With J. R. Dunning. Neutron emission. Phys. Rev., 45:295. (A)

1934

With J. R. Dunning. The scattering of neutrons by H^1_2O, H^2_2O, paraffin, Li, B, and C, and the production of radioactive nuclei by neutrons found by Fermi. Phys. Rev., 45:768. (A)

1935

With J. R. Dunning. Electrolytic separation of polonium and Ra D. Phys. Rev., 47:325. (A)

With J. R. Dunning and G. A. Fink. Capture, stability and radioactive emission of neutrons. Phys. Rev., 47:325. (A)

With J. R. Dunning, G. A. Fink, and D. P. Mitchell. Interaction of low energy neutrons with atomic nuclei. Phys. Rev., 47:416-17. (L)

With J. R. Dunning. Absorption and scattering of slow neutrons. Phys. Rev., 47:640. (A)

With J. R. Dunning, G. A. Fink, and D. P. Mitchell. Absorption and velocity of slow neutrons. Phys. Rev., 47:796. (A)

With J. R. Dunning, G. A. Fink, and D. P. Mitchell. Thermal equilibrium of slow neutrons. Phys. Rev., 47:888-89. (L)

With J. R. Dunning, G. A. Fink, and D. P. Mitchell. Slow neutrons. Phys. Rev., 47:970. (L)

With J. R. Dunning, G. A. Fink, and D. P. Mitchell. Interaction of neutrons with matter. Phys. Rev., 48:265-80.

With J. R. Dunning, G. A. Fink, D. P. Mitchell, and E. Segrè. The velocity of slow neutrons by mechanical velocity selector. Phys. Rev., 48:704. (L)

With D. P. Mitchell, J. R. Dunning, and E. Segrè. Absorption and detection of slow neutrons. Phys. Rev., 48:774-75. (L)

1936

With J. R. Dunning, G. A. Fink, and D. P. Mitchell. The velocities of slow neutrons. Phys. Rev., 49:103. (L)

With F. Rasetti, E. Segrè, G. A. Fink, and J. R. Dunning. On the absorption law for slow neutrons. Phys. Rev., 49:104. (L)

With J. R. Dunning, G. A. Fink, and E. Segrè. Experiments on slow neutrons with velocity selector. Phys. Rev., 49:198. (A)

With J. R. Dunning, D. P. Mitchell, G. A. Fink, and E. Segrè. Sulla velocità dei neutroni lenti. Atti Accad. Naz. Lincei Rend. Classe Sci. Fis. Mat. Natr., 23:340-42.

With F. Rasetti, E. Segrè, G. A. Fink, and J. R. Dunning. Sulla legge di assorbimento dei neutroni lenti. Atti Accad. Naz. Lincei Rend. Classe Sci. Fis. Mat. Natr., 23:343-45.

With J. R. Dunning and D. P. Mitchell. Absorption of slow neutrons with lithium and boron as detectors. Phys. Rev., 49:199. (A)

With G. A. Fink, J. R. Dunning, and E. Segrè. Production and absorption of slow neutrons in hydrogenic material. Phys. Rev., 49:199. (A)

With G. A. Fink and J. R. Dunning. The absorption of slow neutrons in carbon. Phys. Rev., 49:340. (L)

With G. A. Fink and J. R. Dunning. Slow neutron production and absorption. Phys. Rev., 49:642. (A)

With P. N. Powers and G. A. Fink. On the absorption of neutrons slowed down by paraffin at different temperatures. Phys. Rev., 49:650. (A)

With F. Rasetti, D. P. Mitchell, and G. A. Fink. On the absorption of slow neutrons in boron. Phys. Rev., 49:777. (L)

With H. C. Urey and J. Huffman. Distilling apparatus for separation of isotopes. Phys. Rev., 49:883. (A)

With D. P. Mitchell, F. Rasetti, and G. A. Fink. Some experiments with photoneutrons. Phys. Rev., 50:189. (L)

With D. P. Mitchell, F. Rasetti, and G. A. Fink. Experiments with photo-neutrons. Phys. Rev., 50:401. (A)

With H. C. Urey and J. R. Huffman. The concentration of the oxygen isotopes. Journal of Chemical Physics, 4:623.

ACKNOWLEDGMENTS FOR THE PHOTOGRAPHS

Photograph of Dirk Brouwer
by Yale University News Bureau

Photograph of Rollin Thomas Chamberlin
by Bachrach

Photograph of Joseph Erlanger
by Duane Coe Studio

Photograph of Albert Wallace Hull
by General Electric Research Laboratory

Photograph of Adolph Knopf
by Stanford University Photographic Department

Photograph of Ernest Orlando Lawrence
by University of California
Lawrence Radiation Laboratory

Photograph of Duncan Arthur MacInnes
by Carter

Photograph of William Frederick Meggers
by National Bureau of Standards

Photograph of Forest Ray Moulton
by Fabian Bachrach

Photograph of George Braxton Pegram
courtesy of Columbia University Archives